Teaching Terror

Teaching Terror

Strategic and Tactical Learning in the Terrorist World

Edited by
James JF Forest

ROWMAN & LITTLEFIELD PUBLISHERS, INC.
Lanham • Boulder • New York • Toronto • Oxford

ROWMAN & LITTLEFIELD PUBLISHERS, INC.

Published in the United States of America
by Rowman & Littlefield Publishers, Inc.
A wholly owned subsidary of The Rowman & Littlefield Publishing Group, Inc.
4501 Forbes Boulevard, Suite 200, Lanham, Maryland 20706
www.rowmanlittlefield.com

P.O. Box 317, Oxford OX2 9RU, UK

British Library Cataloguing in Publication Information Available

Library of Congress Cataloging-in-Publication Data

Teaching terror: strategic and tactical learning in the terrorist world / edited by
James J.F. Forest.
    p. cm.
  Includes bibliographical references (p. 273) and index.
  ISBN-13: 978-0-7425-4077-4 (cloth : alk. paper)
  ISBN-10: 0-7425-4077-4 (cloth : alk. paper)
  ISBN-13: 978-0-7425-4078-1 (pbk. : alk. paper)
  ISBN-10: 0-7425-4078-2 (pbk. : alk. paper)
  1. Terrorists—Training of. 2. Organizational learning. 3. Terrorists—Training
of—Case studies. 4. Organizational learning—Case studies. I. Forest, James J. F.
  HV6431.T427 2006
  363.325071'5—dc22   2005035012

Printed in the United States of America

∞ ™ The paper used in this publication meets the minimum requirements of
American National Standard for Information Sciences—Permanence of Paper
for Printed Library Materials, ANSI/NISO Z39.48-1992.

Contents

Part II   Case Studies

Acronyms

AAIA	(Aden-Abyan Islamic Army) [Yemen]
ANO	(Abu Nidal Organization)
AMAL	(Afwaj al-Muqawama al Lubnnania) ["Lebanese Resistance Detachment."]
ASG	(Abu Sayyaf Group)
CBI	(Central Bureau of Investigation) [India]
CBRN	(chemical, biological, radiological, and nuclear)
CISAC	(Center for International Security and Cooperation)
CPRS	(Center for Palestine Research and Studies)
CTC	(Combating Terrorism Center) [U.S.]
DHS	(Department of Homeland Security) [U.S.]
DI	(Darul Islam) [Indonesia]
DIA	(Defense Intelligence Agency) [U.S.]
DFLP	(Democratic Front for the Liberation of Palestine)
DOT	(Department of Transportation) [U.S.]
DDII	(Dewan Dakwah Islamiyah Indonesia)
EIG	(Egyptian Islamic Group)
EIJ	(Egyptian Islamic Jihad)
ELN	(National Liberation Army) [Colombia]
EPL	(People's Liberation Army) [Colombia]
ETA	(Euskadi Ta Askatasuna) ["Basque Homeland and Liberty"] [Spain]
EZLN	(National Liberation Zapatista Army) [Mexico]
FAA	(Federal Aviation Administration) [U.S.]
FARC	(Revolutionary Armed Forces of Colombia)

FBI	(Federal Bureau of Investigation) [U.S.]
FFI	(Defense Research Establishment) [Norway]
FMLN	(National Liberation Farabundo Martí Front) [El Salvador]
FPMR	(Patriotic Front Manuel Rodríguez) [Chile]
FSLN	(National Liberation Sandinista Front) [Nicaragua]
GAO	(General Accounting Office) [U.S.]
GIA	(Armed Islamic Group) [Algeria]
GICM	(Moroccan Islamic Combatant Group)
GPII	(Gerakan Pemuda Islam Indonesia)
GPS	(global positioning system)
GSISS	(Graduate School of Islamic and Social Sciences)
GSPC	(Groupe Salafiste pour la Predication et le Combat)/(Salafist Group for Preaching and Combat) [Algeria]
HEU	(highly enriched uranium)
HIG	(Hizb-I Islami Gulbuddin) [Afghanistan]
HUJI	(Harkat-ul-Jihad-al-Islam) [Bangladesh]
IAEA	(International Atomic Energy Agency)
ICG	(International Crisis Group)
IDF	(Israeli Defense Forces)
IED	(improvised explosive device)
IIB	(International Islamic Battalion)
IIPB	(Islamic International Peacekeeping Brigade) [Chechnya]
IMU	(Islamic Movement of Uzbekistan)
IRA	(Irish Republican Army)
ISNA	(Islamic Society of North America)
JEM	(Jaish-e-Mohammed) [India/Pakistan]
JI	(Jemaah Islamiyah) [Indonesia]
JMA	(Jemaah Mujahidin Anshorullah) [Indonesia]
JMCC	(Jerusalem Media and Communications Center)
JRA	(Japanese Red Army)
KMM	(Kumpulan Militan Malaysia)
KMM	(Kumpulan Mujahideen Malaysia)
KSM	(Khalid Sheikh Mohammed)
LET	(Lashkar-e-Taiba) [Afghanistan/Pakistan]
LTTE	(Liberation Tigers of Tamil Eelam) [Sri Lanka]
MEMRI	(Middle East Media Research Institute)
MILF	(Moro Islamic Liberation Front) [Phillipines]
MMI	(Muslim Mujahidin Council) [Indonesia]
NATO	(North Atlantic Treaty Organization)
NCS	(National Communications System)
NII	(Islamic State in Indonesia)
NIOSH	(National Institute for Occupational Safety and Health) [U.S.]
NIPC	(National Infrastructure Protection Center) [U.S.]

NMO   (New Method of Operations)
NPA   (New People's Army) [Philippines]
OIF   (Operation Iraqi Freedom) [U.S.]
PA   (Palestinian Authority)
PCC   (Colombian Communist Party)
PCCC   (Clandestine Communist Party of Colombia)
PFLP   (Popular Front for the Liberation of Palestine)
PIJ   (Palestinian Islamic Jihad)
PIRA   (Provisional Irish Republican Army)
PKI   (Indonesian Communist Party)
PKK   (Partiya Karkeren Kurdistan)/(Kurdish Workers Party) [Turkey]
PLO   (Palestinian Liberation Organization)
PNCIS   (Pacific Northwest Colloquia in International Security)
PRIF   (Peace Research Institute Frankfurt) [Germany]
RPGs   (rocket propelled grenades)
TATP   (triacetone triperoxide)
UNITA   (Unity for Total Independence of Angola)
UTM   (Universiti Teknologi Malaysia)
VCDs   (video CD-ROM discs)
WAR   (White Aryan Resistance)
WBGS   (West Bank and Gaza Strip)
WMDs   (weapons of mass destruction)
ZOG   (Zionist Occupation Government)

Preface

Throughout the last four decades, a growing body of research has emerged to analyze (and find ways to thwart) terrorist organizations. A common framework within the study of terrorism suggests that terrorist attacks are the product of two primary elements: motivation and capabilities. A large portion of the scholarly literature in this area has focused on terrorist motivations—particularly the religious ideological motivations of the Islamic Jihadist movement; the ethnonationalist motivations of groups like the Chechens in Russia, the ETA (Euskadi Ta Askatasuna—"Basque Homeland and Liberty") in Spain, the Tamil Tigers in Sri Lanka, and the Partiya Karkeren Kurdistan (Kurdish Workers Party, or PKK) in Turkey; and the political motivations of early anarchists in Western Europe, the United States, and Latin America. A number of authors have also studied various aspects of terrorist capabilities, addressing such topics as training, financial networks, state sponsorship, and weapons acquisition. This volume furthers our understanding in both dimensions by exploring how terrorist groups apply the principles of organizational learning to improve their ability to motivate new members, equip them with new skills, and become smarter and more lethal terrorists.

Exploring the transfer of knowledge between individuals and organizations adds an important dimension to our study of the terrorist world. International terrorists have developed a global knowledge network through which tactics and strategies are increasingly shared. Within a particular group, new recruits learn from veteran fighters, while on the global level, organizations learn from each other. For example, there is increasing evidence that al Qaeda has learned new strategies and tactics from Hizballah, and vice versa. Recent studies suggest various forms of collaboration between terrorist organizations and criminal organizations, including—for example—in the Tri-Border region of South America. Experts from the Central Intelligence Agency (CIA), Defense Intelligence Agency (DIA), and the Federal Bureau of Investigation (FBI) have discovered that Islamic and non-Islamic terrorists have used the same designs for car bombs in Africa, Asia, Europe, Latin America, and the Middle East. And the increasingly widespread availability of information technology has enabled terrorist organizations to share knowledge in new and more effective ways (including websites, user groups, chat rooms, and e-mail). The chapters of this volume thus explore the centrality of learning in the terrorist world, with an overall goal of informing our understanding of—and responses to—the global threat of terrorism.

The volume begins with an introduction to the topic of knowledge transfer, addressing both individual and organizational learning dimensions. Following this introductory chapter, the volume is organized into two sections. Six chapters in the first section provide conceptual overviews and analyses that help us understand the complex nature of knowledge transfer in the terrorist world. Michael Kenney begins this discussion by illustrating how terrorists acquire their skills through training and experience and adapt their practices in response to counterterrorism, in the process becoming more difficult for governments to destroy. He notes that terrorism is a specialized pursuit, requiring knowledge of light weapons, demolitions, clandestine operations, and a host of related activities. Terrorists learn their violent tradecraft through informal apprenticeships and formal training programs that convey the abstract ideals of extremist ideologies and the concrete techniques of asymmetric warfare, while strengthening their identities as devoted militants and enhancing their capacity to attack enemy soldiers and civilians. Chapter 3, by Horacio Trujilio and Brian Jackson, furthers this discussion by providing an overall definition of organizational learning for the study of terrorism, as well as a model describing stages of learning within terrorist organizations. This approach enables them to develop a typology of terrorist group learning and explore factors that can influence such groups' ability to learn effectively. Their chapter concludes with a discussion of how organizational learning can shed light on terrorist groups' strategic and tactical activities.

The next chapter explores the past, present, and future centers of learning in the terrorist world—places in the physical and digital world where professional training materials and activities enable an individual to become a *bona fide* terrorist. Our understanding of the terrorist world must incorporate the means by which individuals learn the terrorist trade, from professional training manuals and other documented sources of knowledge (both in print and on the Internet) to physical locations such as training camps. Gabriel Weimann's chapter examines the terrorists' use of the Internet to provide virtual training camps that provide an online forum for indoctrination as well as the distribution of terrorist manuals, instructions, and data. Drawing from an extensive research project (funded by the U.S. Institute of Peace), Weimann discusses how terrorist organizations and their supporters maintain hundreds of websites, exploiting the unregulated, anonymous, and easily accessible nature of the Internet for various purposes. Clearly, it is important for us to become better informed about how terrorists use the Internet, and from this knowledge find better ways to monitor and counter their activities.

The next chapter, by Cindy Combs, explores the important role of the media as a forum for knowledge transfer in the terrorist world. The media have, to varying extents in different cultures, become a tool of modern terrorists, offering a "showcase" through which those carrying out terrorist acts can impress and threaten an audience, recruit and train new members, and support and coordinate an emerging network of followers. In order to better understand the use of the media as a "teaching tool" for terrorism today, Combs examines the symbiotic relationship that exists between terrorists (who seek attention from an audience) and news organizations (which seek dramatic stories to increase their readership and ratings). She concludes that because violent behavior can be "learned," and since "copycat" behavior among individuals and groups is common, the media do play a significant role in modern terrorism, suggesting implications for better media self-regulation.

The first section of the volume concludes with a chapter by Annette Schaper, addressing one of the critical challenges presented by the proliferation of weapons of mass destruction—the role of knowledge transfer in weaponizing nuclear and radiological technology. The possession, threatened use, or outright use of a nuclear or radiological weapon is desired by some terrorist organizations for two primary purposes: inflicting mass casualties and drawing attention to itself and its goals. This chapter addresses the unique attributes of these weapons and their potential impact, including physical destruction and psychological, social, and economic impact. As the worldwide proliferation of knowledge about these weapons continues to be dynamic and poses increasingly greater risks, this analysis calls for continued and heightened vigilance, particularly regarding the trade in radiological materials on regional and global black markets, and the increasing availability of scientific literature on the Internet.

The second section of the volume offers four case studies on how learning takes place within the context of a terrorist organization. Rohan Gunaratna begins with an analysis of al Qaeda's lose and learn doctrine. In this case, we see a terrorist network that clearly demonstrates the attributes of a learning organization: a willingness to experiment with new approaches, analyze the results, and develop new strategy and tactics based on those lessons learned. The implications for countering the threat from al Qaeda, as well as for our understanding of other terrorist organizations, are striking. In the next chapter, Kim Cragin explores how the Islamic Resistance Movement (commonly known as Hamas) has learned to adapt to a changing operational environment and Israeli tactics in the Middle East, while maintaining its support networks among Palestinian communities. Her analysis illustrates an often overlooked dimension of knowledge transfer: while terrorism experts often look at organizational learning in the context of technology or tactics, few have explored the role of strategic learning and community involvement in building and sustaining a terrorist group's long-term operational capabilities.

Román Ortiz provides another important study of terrorist learning by exploring the strategic innovations and evolution of FARC (a Colombian guerrilla movement) over the last several decades. His research highlights how clandestine networks for exchanging technology and military information between terrorist groups and criminal organizations have offered FARC critical channels through which they could expand their fighting capability. And Kumar Ramakrishna's case study of Jemaah Islamiyah reviews the historical role of Islam in Indonesia; the influence of training and ideas gathered by JI members participating in the jihad in Afghanistan; the ideological influences from Egypt and elsewhere; and the importance of social developments in Indonesia and the region. His analysis reveals an array of sociocultural and individual psychological dimensions that form the identity of the JI terrorist, and that frame our understanding of how JI rejuvenates its membership. What JI members and leaders "know" (and how this knowledge is produced and transferred among members of the organization) plays a vital role in how JI members see themselves, their groups, the world, and their role in changing the world.

The final chapter of the volume reviews the key themes and conceptual patterns identified throughout the volume and draws connections to the central theme of knowledge transfer in the terrorist world, before offering a handful of suggestions for policymaking and further research. In prosecuting its Global War on Terrorism, the U.S. and its allies face a thinking, adapting enemy. Thus, the more we can learn about knowledge transfer in the terrorist world, the better we can devise effective counterterrorism initiatives.

In sum, this volume approaches the problem of global terrorism from a central lens of knowledge—specifically, what do we know about knowledge in the terrorist world, and how is it used to maintain a terrorist organization's capacity to carry out its deadly operations? The chapters of this volume support the notion that terrorist groups are learning organizations: they capture, store, and analyze knowledge—both from their own history as well as from the experiences of other groups—and by doing so are able to develop the means of achieving their goals with increasing sophistication. Our ability to combat the terrorist threat requires a better understanding of how and where these knowledge-based activities take place, before devising ways to disrupt or degrade the terrorists' organizational capabilities.

James JF Forest
September 1, 2005

Acknowledgments

Many colleagues and friends have supported this effort. To begin with, I extend my sincere thanks to the faculty and staff of the Combating Terrorism Center (CTC) at West Point (Jarret, Kip, Brian, Lianne, Bill, Clint, Thalia, Rick, and Joe), from whom I continue to learn much every day. General (retired) Wayne Downing, distinguished chair of the CTC, and two of our senior fellows—Dr. Rohan Gunaratna and Dr. Bruce Hoffman— have been enormously positive influences and advocates of my research, and I thank them for their continued support. Also, my faculty colleagues in the Department of Social Sciences at West Point—particularly Colonel Mike Meese, Head of the Department, and Colonel Cindy Jebb, Deputy Head—have provided continual of encouragement and guidance, which I sincerely appreciate.

I have learned a great deal about terrorism and counterterrorism from the authors represented in this volume, and I am extremely grateful for the opportunity to showcase their work here. Each of these chapters is the product of thoughtful research and analysis, and I offer my heartfelt thanks to the authors for their hard work and commitment to excellence. It is my sincere hope that their words will inspire a new generation of scholars to address complex research questions in the field of terrorism and counterterrorism studies. Finally, and of course most importantly, I owe a great debt of gratitude to my wife Alicia, whose patience, under-standing, and encouragement have meant the world to me.

1

✛

Introduction

James JF Forest

Knowledge is a vital resource for anyone or any organization. It can make the difference between success and failure, right and wrong, or even life and death. Thus, from the imperial Chinese mandarins who studied administration in Confucian schools and the Tokugawa samurai who studied in Hanko schools of Bushido and Han service, to the modern-day Humboldtian research university and online/distance education, the transfer of knowledge has played a central role throughout the history of mankind.[1] Today, how a society or an organization views knowledge and learning is seen as critical to its success. As a result, in virtually all public and private sectors, efforts to promote the lifelong education of employees and citizens have become commonplace. In the business world, models of strategic planning, performance assessment, and continual learning reinforce the centrality of knowledge to the long-term success of the company.

Knowledge and learning are also important in the world of terrorism. Indeed, successful terrorist attacks are rarely accomplished by idiots; rather, in order to carry out their lethal agenda, terrorists require a broad range of knowledge that incorporates skills, competency, creative thinking, some understanding of engineering, coded communications, and so forth. Without such knowledge, terrorists are more easily thwarted, apprehended, or otherwise likely to fail. Of course, this is not to say that all terrorists are smart—indeed, interrogation of several religiously indoctrinated, heavily drugged would-be suicide bombers in Iraq and elsewhere suggests that (as with most any organization) the foot soldiers are typically not the brains of the outfit. Within a terrorist organization, there

1

must be different levels of knowledge attained and used by different members for different purposes. How these levels of knowledge are acquired by individuals and shared throughout the organization is the primary subject of this volume.

From a global perspective, there are basically two distinct types of knowledge that matter most in the world of terrorism: individual and organizational. The chapters of this volume explore both of these, some using a general level of analysis and others presenting individual terrorist group case studies. This introductory chapter seeks to define and distinguish the various forms of learning in the terrorist world and provide context for the remaining chapters.

INDIVIDUAL LEARNING IN THE TERRORIST WORLD

On the morning of July 7, 2005, the city of London was attacked by a coordinated team of suicide bombers as the morning rush hour drew to a close. Three bombs were detonated on underground trains, and a fourth explosion ripped through a double-decker bus, killing fifty-two people and injuring over seven hundred. The subsequent investigation revealed that the suicide bombers had been four young British citizens, motivated by al Qaeda's extremist ideology (but not formally connected to this or any other organization).

When detectives searched the apartment of an individual suspected of involvement in this attack—Magdi Mahmoud al-Nashar, an Egyptian who taught chemistry at Leeds University—they found signs that quantities of a compound called triacetone triperoxide (or TATP) had been converted into a powerful explosive. TATP can be made from easily obtainable household ingredients, like drain cleaner, hair bleach, and acetone, and has been frequently used by Hamas and other Islamist extremist groups responsible for suicide bomb attacks in Israel. The chemical composition of TATP is fairly easy, although authorities believe the explosives used in the London attack were developed by a trained chemist. This is the same explosive that another British citizen—Richard Reid—had used a few years earlier in an improvised shoe bomb, when he attempted to blow up an American Airlines flight from Paris to Miami. Reid was a follower of Sheikh Abu Hamza al-Masri, the leader of the Finsbury Park mosque in North London who was arrested in 2004 and charged with a variety   of terror-related offenses.[2] Ironically, the July 2005 bombings in London occurred the same week that the trial of Sheikh Abu Hamza al-Masri was beginning. Two weeks later, on July 21, another bombing attack on the London transportation system was carried out by a group of Islamist extremists. Once again, they were spread out around the capital and once again there were three on underground trains and one on a bus. However, this time the bombs failed to detonate properly, and no lives were lost. Failed devices were found on trains at several underground stations, a bus, and a park, providing police with a wealth of forensic material, and the would-be bombers were apprehended a short while later.

Meanwhile, during the summer of 2005, Turkey was also suffering from a wave of terrorist attacks, some blamed on Kurdish militants, others on Islamist extremists. On July 2, a bomb attack on a passenger train in eastern Turkey killed six people and injured at least twelve, and on July 16, an explosion on a minibus in the Turkish resort of Kusadasi killed five people. Weeks later, on August 8, two men were killed in Istanbul when the bomb they were assembling in their apartment building blew up prematurely.[3] In this instance, police are certain that the would-be bombers made a critical error, suggesting they may not have had the bomb-making sophistication required. However, the bombers who carried out the attacks two days later (August 10) on two small hotels and a gas plant in Istanbul, killing two people and injuring nine others, obviously did know what they were doing.

And on August 17, 2005, officials in Bangladesh reported that more than three hundred explosions had taken place almost simultaneously in fifty cities and towns across the country. Although they were placed in many crowded areas, including government buildings and courts, relatively few people were killed or injured by the blasts, which involved small, homemade bombs with timing devices wrapped in tape or paper. An outlawed Islamist group, Jamatul Mujahideen Bangladesh, took responsibility through a series of leaflets found at the site of several attacks, calling for the establishment of Islamic law in the country.[4] These attacks (and attempted attacks) in England, Turkey, and Bangladesh are but a few recent examples of how important knowledge is in the terrorist world. As terrorism analyst Brian Jackson recently observed, "the well-trained terrorist sets a bomb that achieves his tactical and operational goals; the poorly trained terrorist sets a bomb that kills himself, rather than the intended victims of the attack."[5]

There are four main categories of terrorism which pose a threat to the civilized world: terrorism carried out by organizations (like al Qaeda) that possess an international infrastructure and global agenda; domestic terrorist groups (like the Abu Sayyaf Group or the FARC) with a national agenda; acts of terrorism carried out by individuals motivated by extremist ideology (like Timothy McVeigh, the Oklahoma City bomber, or Buford Furrow, who attacked a Jewish day care center in the Los Angeles area in 1999); and terrorism carried out via state sponsorship (e.g., Iran's support for the Lebanese terrorist group Hizballah).[6] Within each of these categories, various kinds of terrorist knowledge play important roles.

Individual perpetrators of terrorist attacks typically acquire two distinct kinds of knowledge: *motivational* (most often of an ideological nature), and *operational* (that which provides strategic and tactical capabilities).[7] Put another way, motivational knowledge transfer usually addresses the central question of *why* an individual or group seeks to use violent means to achieve political, social, and/or religious goals, while operational knowledge transfer addresses the question of *how* to most effectively use violent means for achieving these goals. Beyond the individual level, organizations require both operational/tactical and strategic knowledge in order to achieve their objectives. While the former typically addresses how the organization can carry out its attacks more successfully, the latter focuses on a broad range of organizational learning dimensions, including environmental scanning, long-range planning, and continual self-improvement.

Motivational knowledge is typically disseminated in oral, print, and online formats, and largely deals in the realms of psychological, social, cultural, intellectual, and emotional development. The acquisition of such knowledge is seen as vital to developing an individual's *will to kill*. Centers of learning where this type of knowledge can be found include colleges and universities, mosques, churches, temples, and prisons. These are places where significant indoctrination (and, by extension, terrorist recruitment) can take place. However, these types of institutions rarely support the transfer of operational knowledge, a much more action-oriented realm of learning that arguably presents the greatest present danger to the civilized world. Motivational knowledge without operational capability is far less harmful than operational knowledge (with or without motivation).

In contrast, operational knowledge—*the skill to kill*—is the primary key to any terrorist organization's capability to achieve its objectives. As described in chapter 4 of this volume, centers of learning in this realm are far fewer and typically require a combination of resources, geographic isolation, and individuals with specific abilities. However, the globalization of access to information technology has had a dramatic impact on the dissemination of this type of knowledge. As Bruce Hoffman aptly observed, "using commercially published or otherwise readily accessible bomb-making manuals and operational guides to poisons, assassinations and chemical and biological weapons fabrication, . . . the 'amateur' terrorist can be just as deadly and destructive as his more 'professional' counterpart."[8] In essence, operational knowledge can be seen as the most vital tool in the terrorist's toolkit.

As a result, the codification and transfer of operational knowledge in the terrorist world has been an important part of any group's operations. Much of this knowledge transfer has taken place most commonly at training camps, and encompasses a wide breadth of skills and abilities. For example, terrorists need to learn how to move from one location to another without detection; how to mount rocket launchers in the beds of pickup trucks; how and where to launder money; how to successfully conduct a kidnapping; how to conduct target identification, surveillance, and reconnaissance; how and where to build camouflage-covered trenches; and how to covertly communicate with other members of a group or network—for example, the use of personal messengers (particularly on horseback, motorcycle, or bicycle) rather than electronic communications, or changing frequencies when using electronic communications in battle. Operational knowledge transfer in the terrorist world includes developing a recruit's ability to decide what types of weapons will be most effective (and how they must be assembled, transported, and used), and in many cases (but not necessarily, such as in suicide attacks) securing escape routes once the attack has been carried out. They must learn the nuances of securing organizational assets; planning the roles and responsibilities of members involved in the attack; identifying risks to the operation; and examining the advantages of using certain kinds of vehicles over others—for example, al Qaeda's use of Toyota Corollas for transporting militants and weapons on winding mountainous roads. This seemingly exhaustive list of operational knowledge is obviously not all-inclusive, but is meant to illustrate the types of skills and capabilities that are needed in the terrorist world, and that have been part of the curriculum at various training camps around the world.[9]

In addition to training camps, throughout most of the nineteenth and twentieth centuries the distribution of literature complemented face-to-face contact as primary vehicles for both recruitment and training of new supporters of terrorist organizations. Books and magazines have always played a particularly important role in disseminating both motivational knowledge and operational knowledge to new and potential terrorists worldwide. One of the earliest prominent examples was Carlos Marighella's book *The Liberation of Brazil*, portions of which were widely translated and employed by Latin American and European terrorists.[10] In one chapter of his book, entitled "Handbook of Urban Guerilla Warfare," Marighella encouraged physical training and manual skills, as well as the mastery of small arms and explosives, and stated that only a guerilla who had passed initial tests should be selected for additional training or tasking.[11]

In the world of the jihadists, prominent books include Sayyid Qutb's *Under the Umbrella of the Koran*, which underscored the importance of monotheism in Islam,[12] and his *Signposts along the Road*, in which he damned Western and Christian civilization and urged jihad against the enemies of Islam.[13] Qutb's teachings have had considerable influence over Osama bin Laden, and informed the writings of his deputy, Ayman al-Zawahiri, as reflected in his book *Knights Under the Banner of the Prophet*.[14] Another influential Islamic scholar was Sheikh Abdallah Azzam, whose books on jihad include *Join the*

Caravan, Signs of Ar-Rahman in the Jihad of the Afghan, Defense of the Muslim Lands, and *Lovers of the Paradise Maidens.* Azzam's combat experiences in the Palestinian territories and Afghanistan contributed to the unique reverence given to his writings by Islamist radicals.

In terms of U.S.-based domestic terrorist groups, one of the most oft-cited sources of motivational knowledge is *The Turner Diaries.* Written by William Pierce—a former physics professor and, at the time, the founding leader of the white supremacist group The National Alliance—and published under the pseudonym Andrew MacDonald, the book describes a fictional civil war in the United States in which white Aryans fight what the author and other right-wing extremists call the Zionist Occupation Government (ZOG), killing Blacks and Jews indiscriminately. The dramatic highlights are the ruthless destruction of American cities to pave the way for the dream of a white America and a white world.[15] Since its publication in 1980, the book has influenced a whole generation of right-wing extremists, from Christian Identity adherents to Neo-Nazis, Klansmen, militia, and survivalist activists. *The Turner Diaries* was a favorite book of Oklahoma City bomber Timothy McVeigh, who used its description of the FBI headquarters' destruction as a blueprint for his real-life terror attack.[16]

While a significant majority of the publications in the terrorist world deal with the motivational realm of knowledge (most often of a religious and/or political flavor), the proliferation of operationally focused magazines and training manuals is cause for some concern. Al Qaeda's occasionally published magazine, *Mu'askar al-Battar* ("The Al Battar Training Camp"), features essays on military training amid a plethora of appeals for Muslims to join the fight. For example, Issue 19 (released October 2004) includes advice on survival techniques in the wild, the care and use of a revolver, and instruction in map reading and orientation. One monograph on tactical training, *Al-Baqaa fi al-Zuruf al-Sa'ba* (Survival in Difficult Circumstances), is actually a translation of a U.S. army manual.[17]

Other jihadi periodicals—many of which are linked to al Qaeda—include *Sawt al-Jihad* ("Voice of Jihad"), which has appeared in print and online circulation since 2000, and *Tora Bora,* the May 2004 issue of which included an analysis of Pakistan's campaign in the Waziristan province and an extended article on "The Secret of Success in Battle." The April 2005 issue of *Sawt al-Jihad* is focused largely on describing the clashes between Saudi security forces and Islamist extremists in that country, following a rash of terrorist attacks, and carries an appeal for young new recruits to the global jihad.[18] On August 20, 2004, the "Women's Information Office in the Arab Peninsula" released the first issue of a journal called *Al Khansa,* which carried articles such as "Biography of the Mujahidat" (female mujahideen) and "Raising Children on Jihad's Teachings." In Algeria, a new magazine appeared in May 2004 (Al-Jama'a, or "The Group") which noticeably imitates al Qaeda publications. Posted on the website of the *Groupe Salafiste pour la Predication et le Combat* (GSPC), the first issue of this publication was large on motivational knowledge, but short on operational knowledge.[19] In Syria, a new online magazine—the *Risalat al-Mujahideen* ("Message of the Mujahideen"), produced by the online publishers Minbar Suriya al-Islami (Islamic Pulpit of Syria)[20]—focuses much of its attention on encouraging Sunni Islamist extremists to target members of the Alawi community (from which much of the country's regime and elite are drawn, even though Alawites represent no more than 12 percent of the overall population).[21]

Another periodic jihadist publication, the *In the Shadow of the Lances* series, first appeared after 9/11. The majority of the issues of this magazine were written by al Qaeda spokesman Sulaiman Abu Gaith and were largely focused on motivational knowledge transfer. For example, in the June 2002 issue, Abu Gaith writes that "America knows only the language of force. This is the only way to stop it and make it take its hands off the Muslims and their affairs . . . America is kept at bay by blood alone." As Michael Kenney describes (in his chapter of this volume), the fifth and sixth installments of *In the Shadow of the Lances* were written by Sayf al Adl (believed to be a high-ranking member of al Qaeda's military operations) and provided tactical lessons learned from the battle against U.S. forces in Afghanistan.[22] And in April 2005, a new magazine appeared on the Internet: *Sawt al-Qoqaz* ("The Voice of the Caucasus"). In the first issue, guerilla leader Shamil Basayev offers his views on the Chechen struggle, and describes the level of military cooperation between the various jihadi groups operating in the arena. The issue includes a discussion of lessons and experiences from the Chechen jihad, and a plea is made to Muslims across the world to come to the aid of the mujahideen fighting in the region.[23]

Other prominent sources of operational knowledge transfer include *The Anarchist Cookbook* and *The Mujahideen Poisons Handbook*. The *Terrorist's Handbook*, published by "Chaos Industries and Gunzenbombz Pyro Technologies," offers 98 pages of step-by-step operational knowledge.[24] But the multivolume *Encyclopedia of the Afghan Jihad*, written in Arabic and distributed on paper and on CD-ROM, is perhaps one of the most oft-cited terrorist training manuals in existence today. It contains a wealth of operational knowledge for new terrorists, covering topics such as recruitment of new members, discharging weapons, constructing bombs, and conducting attacks. Specific examples are included, such as how to put small explosive charges in a cigarette, a pipe, or a lighter in order to maim a person; drawings of simple land mines that could be used to blow up a car (not unlike the improvised explosive devices [IEDs] seen most recently in Iraq); and radio-controlled devices that could be used to set off a whole truckload of explosives, like those used to destroy the U.S. embassies in Kenya and Tanzania in August 1998.

In the U.S., Tom Metzger—the guru of the "lone wolf" or "leaderless resistance" model of activism—has provided right-wing extremist groups
with strategic guidance for several decades. Through his *White Aryan Resistance* (WAR) monthly newspaper, books, a telephone hotline, a website,
and a weekly e-mail newsletter (*Aryan Update*), Metzger's work can be
seen as the operational knowledge counterpart to the motivational knowledge contribution of *The Turner Diaries*. His primary contribution to the
field of terrorist knowledge has been in advocating individual or small-cell
underground activity, as opposed to aboveground membership organizations. He argues that individual and cellular resistance leaves behind the
fewest clues for law enforcement authorities, decreasing the chances that
activists will end up getting caught. Specific guidelines for this strategy include: act alone and leave no evidence; do not commit robbery to obtain
operating funds; act silently and anonymously; do not deface your body
with identifiable tattoos; understand that you are expendable; and whatever happens, do not grovel.[25] While Metzger intended his operational
knowledge to improve the capabilities of like-minded racists, some observers have noted its salience for (and adoption by) other terrorist-
minded groups as well. Indeed, similar guidelines for avoiding detection
and capture are provided in al Qaeda's training manual, *Military Studies in
the Jihad Against the Tyrants,* among other prominent online resources for
terrorist learning.

These and other forms of operational knowledge transfer are complemented by the terrorists' actions, which showcase successes and failures
that other groups can learn from, and provide an important vehicle for in-
spiring other individuals (like the London and Madrid bombers) to commit their own murderous acts of terrorism. One al Qaeda training manual
describes the importance of conducting terrorist attacks for:[26]

- boosting Islamic morale and lowering that of the enemy
- preparing and training new members for future tasks
- a form of necessary punishment
- mocking the regime's admiration among the population
- removing the personalities that stand in the way of the [Islamic]
  Da'wa [Call]
- agitating [the population] regarding publicized matters
- rejecting compliance with and submission to the regime's practices
- giving legitimacy to the Jama'a [Islamic Group]
- spreading fear and terror through the regime's ranks
- bringing new members to the organization's ranks

Overall, in conducting attacks of terrorism, terrorist groups carry out a
form of strategic communication that addresses multiple audiences, in-

cluding their enemies, their supporters, and potential new recruits. Further, successful attacks can provide useful operational knowledge to other terrorist groups, who can learn from the tactics demonstrated. As Cindy Combs observes in her chapter in this volume, the global news media help facilitate this transfer of motivational and operational knowledge each time they broadcast details of how a successful attack was carried out.[27] Extensive news coverage of innovative tactics used by one terrorist group provides particularly helpful information for other groups.

Satellite television has also proven to be a useful means for terrorist groups to reach new audiences, in essence facilitating the spread of a group's ideology and other forms of motivational knowledge. The Lebanese Hizballah is currently the only terrorist organization that operates its own television station. Al-Manar, the Arabic word for beacon, grew from a small local station that serviced part of Beirut to a regional broadcaster and, after switching to satellite broadcasting in 2000, to a global television channel that offers its own programs around-the-clock.[28] Millions of Muslims watch Al-Manar's one-sided programs regularly, consume the station's traditional anti-Israel propaganda, and, more recently, watch an equally aggressive anti-American information campaign. Other satellite television networks, such as Al Jazeera and Al Arabiya, are to some degree less one-sided in their coverage, but are global in their appeal throughout the Islamic world.[29]

As described later in this volume, the global presence on the Internet of al Qaeda and its affiliate groups has already become a well-studied phenomenon. Thousands of websites and bulletin boards now offer videos, images, statements, and speeches that demonstrate the Internet's centrality to the global jihadist movement. According to Reuven Paz, who heads the Project for the Research of Islamist Movements in Israel, the Web has become "an open university for jihad," a place where terrorist organizations can connect with younger generations.[30] Some Islamist extremist groups, such as Hizb ut-Tahrir and Hizballah, offer music and computer games via the Internet in order to introduce their ideology and engender anger and hatred against old enemies among a new generation.[31]

Today, a new generation of terrorists is acquiring both motivational and operational knowledge in the comfort of their own home, through videos, discussion forums, training manuals, and websites. In many cases, these online resources are even subtitled in English so Western Muslims who don't speak Arabic can understand them.[32] According to a report by the National Academy of Sciences, a casual Internet surfer can easily find instructions for making explosives such as nitroglycerine, ANFO (ammonium nitrate/fuel oil mixture), dynamite, and even the military explosive RDX (research department explosive; hexahydro-1,3,5-trinitro-1,3,5 triazine, which is also known as cyclonite). "The instructions typically list useful chemicals and sources where they may be purchased or stolen. In many cases, the chemicals can be easily obtained at local lawn and garden stores, hardware stores, or drugstores, or purchased by mail order from chemical supply houses. Furthermore, a chemical process facility is not needed to produce large quantities of improvised explosives; most can be made by someone working at home."[33] In addition to manuals and diagrams, training videos have become increasingly common among terrorist websites. For example, in early June 2005, a contributor to the militant Arabic language web forum *Tajdid Al-Islami* posted a series of training videos for beginner mujahideen that included the topics of basic fitness, *ninja* arts, proper uniform, and communication techniques.[34] Making good on a promise to follow these initial lessons with more advanced ones, the contributor posted a new message to *Tajdid Al-Islami* in August 2005 featuring a seven-part lesson on how to use a handheld, portable global positioning system (GPS) receiver.[35]

In addition to indoctrination, tactical and strategic training, and a location in which these activities can take place, researchers point to another, more personal level of the transformation that takes place in becoming a true terrorist.[36] It is one thing to learn how to pull a trigger or create and detonate a bomb, or to simulate the killing of others through video games and role playing, but in real life, killing is not as easy as it might seem. As several psychologists have observed, most human beings develop a certain set of moral guidelines that generally work to restrict their willingness to murder someone or blow up that café full of innocent bystanders.[37] The terrorist organization therefore faces the challenge of ensuring that a new recruit will be able to follow a lethal mission through to its completion.

Developing the will and ability to kill involves a range of psychological conditioning activities. Few—if any—individuals are born to be terrorists or become lethal terrorists overnight. Indeed, recent studies have revealed that the isolation of attributes or traits shared by terrorists is fraught with difficulty, and efforts to create a profile or "typical" terrorist have yielded mixed results.[38] Instead, terrorist experts like Ehud Sprinzak and Ariel Merari have shown that new recruits evolve gradually into terrorists through a process of radicalization that involves a disengagement of moral self-sanctions from violent conduct.[39] In exploring this "moral disengagement," renowned psychologist Albert Bandura identified several developmental processes that can disengage morality from an individual's conduct, such as reconstruing conduct as serving moral purposes; obscuring personal agency in bad activities; disregarding consequences of actions; and blaming or dehumanizing victims.[40]

According to this body of research, in order for individuals to become lethal terrorists, they must acquire an ability to sanctify harmful conduct as honorable and righteous, which explains why terrorists often see themselves as patriots doing the bidding of the group's leaders (in religious groups, the bidding of God; or, in state terrorism, the state), thus absolving themselves of responsibility for their actions.[41] For example, Masami Tsuchiya, a brilliant chemist, used his skills to help Aum Shinrikyo—the terrorist cult responsible for the lethal attack on the Tokyo subway in 1995—develop poison gas and the hallucinogen PCP. Throughout his trial—at which he was sentenced to death for his role in the production of sarin that was used in two deadly nerve gas attacks—Tsuchiya consistently described himself as a "direct disciple of the guru" (in reference to Aum's leader, Shoko Asahara) and refused to accept responsibility for doing anything wrong in serving his "sonshi" (or honorable master).[42] Moral disengagement also involves the ability to minimize the consequences of murderous acts for which the individual is responsible. This disregard for consequences makes it easier for a new terrorist recruit to hurt or kill others, particularly when decisions are made by superiors who are removed from those in the group who follow orders. And finally, Bandura notes, people find violence easier if they don't consider their victims as human beings.[43]

Psychologist Jerrold Post agrees with Sprinzak, Bandura, and other scholars that powerful psychological forces are involved in transforming an individual into a terrorist.[44] His research led him to coin the term "psychologic" to describe how the terrorist constructs a personal rationalization for acts they are psychologically compelled to commit. In essence, the polarizing and absolutist "us versus them" rhetoric of terrorists reflects their underlying views of "the establishment" as the source of all evil, and provides a psychologically satisfying explanation for what has gone wrong in their lives. According to Post, the fixed logical conclusion of the terrorist—that the establishment must be destroyed—is driven by the terrorist's search for identity, and as he strikes out against the establishment, he is attempting to destroy the enemy within.[45] Acquiring this destructive capability is thus a key goal of many terrorist group recruits, while equipping them with this capability—through knowledge transfer—is a key goal and function of terrorist organizations.

Several studies of terrorism have indicated that of all terrorist organizations, religiously motivated ones offer the highest potential for mass casualties, in part because for them, violence is perceived to be part of an all-encompassing struggle between good and evil.[46] Characterizing the victims of a terrorist attack as a dehumanized form of evil enables perhaps the most potent type of "moral disengagement" suggested by Sprinzak, Bandura, and others. Some groups, however—even religiously oriented ones—may incorporate additional methods to ensure the lethality of their members. For example, Aum Shinrikyo is known to have used hypnosis, drugs, and a strenuous physical regimen to increase the "suggestibility" of new recruits to the messages of its leader, Shoko Asahara.[47]

Often, terrorist training also involves certain forms of coercive psychological persuasion. According to Margaret Singer, a leading authority on mind control and cults, "Coercive psychological systems are behavioral change programs which use psychological force in a coercive way to cause the learning and adoption of an ideology or designated set of beliefs, ideas, attitudes or behaviors."[48] Along with cults, terrorist organizations need to establish control over the new recruit's personal social environment, time, and sources of social support. Cults will often use a system of rewards and punishments; social isolation is promoted; and in many cases, new recruits are brought to a geographically remote location to ensure they have contact only with other members of the group during this formative period.[49] This aspect of terrorist training camps, while often overlooked, plays an important role in promoting the long-term development of terrorist organizations.

SUMMARY

In sum, individual knowledge transfer in the terrorist world involves mostly two forms—motivational and operational. Motivational knowledge transfer (developing the will to kill) often takes place simultaneously with operational knowledge transfer (developing the skill to kill). However, terrorist organizations use ideological/motivational knowledge more for recruitment; it plays a secondary/supporting role in training. There are many types of places (or "centers of learning," as described in chapter 4 of this volume) where both types of knowledge transfer take place. Centers of motivational knowledge transfer are virtually ubiquitous—including churches, schools, mosques, prisons, community centers, and so forth—while centers of operational knowledge are not as common (largely because, in most countries, terrorist training camps are illegal). As a result, there are more students, teachers, and activities in the realm of motivational knowledge than in operational knowledge. Further, a potential terrorist typically acquires motivational knowledge before seeking and acquiring operational knowledge—indeed, rarely does a nonmotivated individual seek and gain operational knowledge. Also, it is important to note that not all motivated individuals take those next crucial steps to acquire operational knowledge.

An appreciation for individual knowledge transfer informs our understanding of organizational learning in the terrorist world. The terrorist groups of greatest concern to the counterterrorism community are those which analyze the activities of their members, learn from the mistakes and successes of their members, and incorporate these lessons into the doctrine and training programs used for new members. From building a better improvised explosive device to ensuring the security of their covert communications, terrorist organizations—at least, the more sophisticated and lethal ones—constantly look for ways to improve what they do. In many cases, this search leads them to scrutinize the operational successes and failures of other terrorist organizations as well, even those with different political or ideological agendas. Through their commitment to learning, these terrorist groups grow smarter and more capable of achieving their deadly objectives.

THE PROLIFERATION OF KNOWLEDGE

Terrorist organizations learn from each other by sharing knowledge via training manuals, websites, and other media. For example, Indonesian radical groups with links to the Jemaah Islamiyah terrorist network have been found with videos documenting how Chechen separatists make and use land mines.[50] However, perhaps the most important form of organizational knowledge transfer takes place through the migration of fighters from one operational theater to another (e.g., from Afghanistan to Bosnia or Iraq), where face-to-face interaction allows for the more robust kinds of teacher-learner knowledge transfer typical of more traditional educational settings.[51] In this arena, few organizations have contributed more to the global spread of operational knowledge than al Qaeda. During the war to oust the Soviets from Afghanistan, as well as throughout much of the 1990s, thousands of individuals received instruction in al Qaeda–affiliated training camps, and have carried this knowledge with them to new organizations. Many of the combatants came to Afghanistan from South Asia and Central Asia, and many went on to campaigns in the 1990s in Chechnya, Uzbekistan, Pakistan, and other locations.[52]

Today, according to Ivo Daalder, a senior fellow at the Brookings Institution, "Al Qaeda is no longer a hierarchical organization, but rather an enabler for myriad terrorist groups and sympathizers to fight the jihadist holy war."[53] Indeed, according to the U.S. Department of State's annual review of global terrorism and other sources, the relationship between al Qaeda and a variety of regional and global groups is well-known, including:[54]

Abu Sayyaf Group (ASG): Several members of this small, violent Muslim separatist group operating in the southern Philippines—including former leader Abdurajak Abubakar Janjalani—fought in Afghanistan. The group has committed a variety of terrorist attacks, including bombings, beheadings, assassinations, and kidnappings for ransom.

Aden-Abyan Islamic Army (AAIA): This organization was founded by Yemeni and other Arab fighters who helped the Afghans oust the Soviets, and in mid-1998 it released a series of communiqués that expressed support for Osama bin Laden, appealed for the overthrow of the Yemeni government, and called for operations against U.S. and other Western interests in Yemen. AAIA is responsible for the bombing of the British Embassy in Sanaa in October 2000, and an attack in June 2003 against a medical assistance convoy in the Abyan Governorate.

Ansar al-Islam: Ansar al-Islam is a radical Islamist group of Iraqi Kurds and Arabs who have vowed to establish an independent Islamic state in Iraq. Leaders of this group visited al Qaeda leaders in Afghanistan, with the intention of creating a base for terrorist operations in northern Iraq. According to the U.S. State Department, the group is closely allied with al Qaeda—some of its members trained in al Qaeda camps in Afghanistan, and the group provided safe haven to al Qaeda fighters before Operation Iraqi Freedom (OIF). Recently, the group has been held responsible for the bombing of the United Nations compound and the Jordanian Embassy in Iraq.

Armed Islamic Group (GIA): Members of this extremist group, which is based in Algeria, are known to have received training in al Qaeda camps in Sudan and Afghanistan. The organization aims to overthrow the secular Algerian regime and replace it with an Islamic state. Since 1992, the GIA has conducted a terrorist campaign of civilian massacres, sometimes wiping out entire villages in its area of operation.

Assirat Al-Moustaquim: A splinter group of another radical Islamist movement, Salafia Jihadia, this Moroccan group includes members who are suspected of the 2003 terrorist attacks in Casablanca. One of the spiritual leaders, a twenty-eight-year-old cleric named Abdel-Wahab Raqiqi, alias Abu Hafs, was among the Arab mujahideen in Afghanistan during the early 1990s.

Egyptian Islamic Jihad (EIJ): Active since the 1970s, the EIJ's primary goals traditionally have been to overthrow the Egyptian Government and replace it with an Islamic state, and to attack U.S. and Israeli interests in Egypt and abroad. EIJ was responsible for the assassination in 1981 of Egyptian President Anwar Sadat, and for the Egyptian Embassy bombing in Islamabad, Pakistan, in 1995. Members of the group fought in Afghanistan, and under the leadership of Ayman al-Zawahiri, the relationship between EIJ and al Qaeda was formalized in February 1998, when they merged into a single group.

Harkat-ul-Jihad-al-Islam (HUJI): By one account, Osama bin Laden sent his private secretary to attend a meeting of HUJI in Bangladesh to draft a strategy for the region. HUJI is also believed to have received funding from al Qaeda, and a twenty-five-member team of al Qaeda/Taliban fighters were in Bangladesh in June 2001 to give arms training to HUJI.*Hizb-I Islami Gulbuddin (HIG)*: Founded in 1977 by the Islamist militant Gulbuddin Hekmatyar, HIG became one of the major mujahideen groups fighting in the war against the Soviets. In the early 1990s, Hekmatyar ran several terrorist training camps in Afghanistan and was a pioneer in sending mercenary fighters to other Islamic conflicts. HIG has long-established ties with Osama bin Laden, and offered him shelter after he fled Sudan in 1996. The group has remained allied with Taliban and al Qaeda fugitives, and is currently assisting al Qaeda in targeting international forces and peacekeepers in Afghanistan.

Islamic International Peacekeeping Brigade (IIPB): Chechen extremist leader Shamil Basayev established the IIPB in 1998, which he led with Saudi-born Ibn al-Khattab until the latter's death in March 2002. According to some reports, Khattab fought alongside Osama bin Laden in Afghanistan. Arab mujahideen leader Abu al-Walid has since taken over Khattab's leadership role in the IIPB, which consists of Chechens, Arabs, and other foreign fighters seeking to establish an independent, Islamic state in Chechnya.

Islamic Movement of Uzbekistan (IMU): This coalition of Islamist militants from Uzbekistan and other Central Asian states is closely affiliated with al Qaeda and, under the leadership of Tohir Yoldashev, has embraced Osama bin Laden's anti-U.S., anti-Western agenda. The IMU in recent years has participated in attacks on U.S. and Coalition soldiers in Afghanistan and plotted attacks on U.S. diplomatic facilities in Central Asia, including an attempted attack on the U.S. Embassy and a nearby hotel in Bishkek, Kyrgyzstan.

Jaish-e-Mohammed (JEM): With a presence throughout India and Pakistan (but primarily in the Kashmir region), this Islamist extremist group has hundreds of members who were trained by al Qaeda during the 1990s. Masood Azhar, the leader of JEM, also received training in Yemen with al Qaeda members, and has been linked to the murder of American reporter Daniel Pearl as well as to a suicide attack on the Jammu and Kashmir legislative assembly building in Srinagar.

Jemaah Islamiyah (JI): JI is led by radical cleric Abu Bakar Bashir, who is now under the detention of the Indonesian police for alleged involvement in the Bali and Jakarta bombings. Several members of JI, particularly those responsible for establishing the group's training facilities in Mindanao (in the southern Philippines), received training in al Qaeda's Afghanistan camps during the 1990s. (More on JI and its relationship to al Qaeda is provided in chapter 11 of this volume.)

Kumpulan Mujahideen Malaysia (KMM): This group seeks the overthrow of the Malaysian government and the creation of an Islamic state comprising Malaysia, Indonesia, and the southern Philippines. Several KMM militants received military training in Afghanistan, and some fought with the Afghan mujahideen during the war against the former Soviet Union. Al-Qaeda is believed to be a source of financial and military support for the group.

Lashkar-e-Taiba (LET): This organization used training facilities in Afghanistan and received funding from al Qaeda. Abu Zubaydah, a senior operational leader of al Qaeda in 2001, was arrested while hiding out in the house of an LET leader in the Pakistani town of Faisalabad, suggesting that some LET members are facilitating the movement of al Qaeda members in the region.

Moro Islamic Liberation Front (MILF): MILF is the largest Islamist separatist group in the Philippines, with an estimated fifteen thousand members, and is closely linked with the al Qaeda affiliate group Jemaah Islamiyah. The group has carried out a campaign of attacks against civilian and military targets throughout the southern region of the country, as well as a series of bombings in the capital city of Manila.

Moroccan Islamic Combatant Group (GICM): GICM was formed in the late 1990s by Moroccans who had trained in al Qaeda's camps in Afghanistan, and seeks to establish an Islamic state in Morocco while supporting al Qaeda's jihad against the West. One founding leader, Mohamed el Garbouzi, was involved in a meeting with some al Qaeda leaders which was held in Istanbul in January 2003.

Salafist Group for Preaching and Combat (GSPC): This group of Islamist militants, an outgrowth of the GIA (whose members are known to have received training in al Qaeda camps in Sudan and Afghanistan), is considered the most effective armed group inside Algeria today. In 2003, the new leader of GSPC expressed the group's support for a number of jihadist causes and movements, including al Qaeda.

Tawhid wal Jihad (Unity and Holy War): Headed by the notorious Abu Musab al Zarqawi, the group is the most feared militant group in Iraq and has been responsible for numerous beheadings of foreigners, roadside bombings, and other attacks. In October 2004, Zarqawi pledged allegiance to al Qaeda, saying it agreed with al Qaeda over strategy and the need for unity against "the enemies of Islam." He also announced a new name for the group—it would now be called the Al Qaeda Committee for Jihad in the Land of the Two Rivers. In response, messages from Osama bin Laden, Ayman al-Zawahiri, and other leaders of al Qaeda have expressed support for Zarqawi's group. For example, in a May 2005 statement, al Qaeda military commander Sayf Al Adl offered advice for Zarqawi and other affiliates that includes a detailed strategic framework for the jihadist movement.[55]

Each of these groups (among others) has been involved in some form of knowledge transfer relationship with al Qaeda. However, al Qaeda is certainly not the only terrorist organization to have provided motivation, training, and material support for other like-minded terrorists. For example, the IRA is long known to have nurtured international links with paramilitary organizations, including ETA in Spain and Palestinian terrorist groups, and in 2001 three alleged IRA members were arrested in Bogotá, Colombia, and charged with training members of the Revolutionary Armed Forces of Colombia (FARC)—a group of Marxist rebels waging an ongoing war against the government—in urban terrorist techniques.[56] While organizational knowledge transfer has often taken place through these kinds of individual contacts, the Internet also provides an increasingly useful means by which terrorists can teach and learn. Today, the growing number of terrorist training manuals, videos, and other resources available online provide an important and common form of knowledge sharing among terrorist groups.

As a result of Internet-based sharing of knowledge, loosely organized groups of al Qaeda–motivated (but not necessarily affiliated) individuals have been responsible for recent terrorist attacks in Madrid, London, Istanbul, Riyadh, and elsewhere. Indeed, according to some Western intelligence agencies and terrorism specialists, the "global jihad movement" has become a "Web-directed" phenomenon.[57] In recent years, some jihadist cells have even formed among like-minded strangers who met online. For example, on March 29, 2004, Canadian police arrested Mohammed Momin Khawaja, a twenty-four-year-old computer programmer, and charged him with involvement in what Canadian and British authorities described as a transatlantic plot to bomb targets in London and Canada. British prosecutors alleged in court that Khawaja met his acquaintances online, where he showed them images of explosive devices found on the Web and told them how to detonate bombs using cell phones.[58]

The potent mixture of ideological motivation and technical knowledge sharing seen among the new generation of Islamist extremists—particularly those willing to serve as suicide bombers—is clearly cause for alarm. If knowledge is seen as a key asset used by organizations to promote the spread of global terrorism, we should be quite concerned indeed about the widely available reservoir of manuals, guides, and videos on everything from creating chemical weapons to assembling and firing a surface-to-air missile against an airline, a tactic seen recently in Kenya and Iraq.[59] The greatest concern of all, however, is the amount of evidence that has surfaced which indicates that groups like al Qaeda are trying to get their hands on biological, chemical, or radiological materials that can be weaponized. The death toll from the London attack (for example) would have been far worse had the bombs been filled with anthrax or sarin. And unfortunately, instructions for designing and building weapons of mass destruction are becoming increasingly common on the Internet.

For example, a fifteen-page Arabic language document titled "Biological Weapons" was posted during the summer of 2005 on the website of al

Qaeda fugitive leader Mustafa Setmariam Nasar, one of the jihadist movement's most important propagandists, often referred to by the *nom de guerre* Abu Musab al-Suri. This document described "how the pneumonic plague could be made into a biological weapon," if a small supply of the virus could be acquired. Nasar's guide drew on U.S. and Japanese biological weapons programs from the World War II era and showed "how to inject carrier animals, like rats, with the virus and how to extract microbes from infected blood . . . and how to dry them so that they can be used with an aerosol delivery system."[60] According to Jarret Brachman, a professor at the Combating Terrorism Center at West Point, al-Suri also authored "one of the most expansive investigations of contemporary jihadist thought produced . . . a single ideological reference for past, present and future information about how and why Muslims must wage violent jihad." Further, al-Suri's links with Osama bin Laden are clear—according to court testimony and other sources, he worked closely with Abu Khabab al-Masri to train extremists in poisons and chemicals during his time in Afghanistan, and was also involved in training at the infamous al-Ghuraba terrorist camp. Given his extremist views, his importance to the global jihadi movement, and his interest in (and experience with) chemical weapons, it is no wonder that the U.S. Government has offered a $5 million reward for his capture.

In essence, individuals like al-Suri can be seen as key organizational assets, serving as both repositories and conduits of valuable knowledge in the realms of both ideology and operations. Thus, organizations tend to encourage the strategic thinking of such individuals and provide means for which their ideas can be disseminated. The benefits to the organization of doing this are fairly obvious. If—as suggested earlier in this discussion—knowledge is truly seen as a vital resource, it becomes imperative for the organization to identify, capture, analyze, and incorporate the kinds of knowledge that will ensure its long-term success. As a review of the business and education literature reveals, this is precisely what learning organizations do.

ORGANIZATIONAL LEARNING IN THE TERRORIST WORLD

The term "learning organization" describes an organization that, through purposefully applying its resources toward the acquisition of knowledge about itself and its environment, is continually expanding its capacity to meet present and future challenges with increasing sophistication and success.[61] Attributes of a learning organization include the ability to identify knowledge useful to its long-term success and incorporate that knowledge into the operations and future plans of the organization. In doing so, they create for themselves a competitive advantage, in that learning allows it to adapt to an increasingly fluid environment faster and more effectively than other organizations.[62]

The first major publication to advance these concepts came from Peter Senge in 1990, in which he described learning organizations as "organizations where people continually expand their capacity to create the results they truly desire, where new and expansive patterns of thinking are nurtured, where collective aspiration is set free, and where people are continually learning to see the whole together."[63] Other authors have stressed the importance of team learning, capturing knowledge, and connecting learning to the goals of the organization.[64] In some cases, organizations have even taken the extra step of identifying individuals or units who are responsible for facilitating organizational learning, sometimes reflected in an organizational learning plan with measurable objectives. An overarching question which all learning organizations ask themselves is, "what do we need to learn in the process of achieving our goals?" Questions such as this reflect a philosophy of ingrained flexibility and encourage an organization to think about the strategic environment and their future within it, and thus anticipate and respond to change more effectively.

Some of the best examples of organizational learning in the world of terrorism come from studies of the Irish Republican Army (IRA) and a splinter group, the Provisional Irish Republican Army (PIRA). According to RAND terrorism analyst Brian Jackson, both organizations adapted their capabilities and techniques in response to an evolving operational environment. "Applying tactics ranging from selective assassination to large-scale bombing operations, the group had to build expertise in a wide range of subject areas to maintain its desired level of military capability. Faced with the constant threat of penetration and compromise by technologically adept and sophisticated security forces, PIRA also had to build the capabilities required to persist under on-going counterterrorist pressures."[65] Thus, PIRA ensured that cross-training among cells within a group would provide a mechanism for knowledge diffusion throughout the organization.[66]

In addition to increasing their security through cellular networked structures and covert communications, terrorist organizations have also been forced to adapt the ways in which they recruit and train new members. As Brian Jackson recently observed, "training processes that bring together specialists within the organization for group training and knowledge exchange have obvious security risks. Such mechanisms also spread information about who is in the group broadly and increase the potential damage if the group is penetrated or a member persuaded to inform on group activities to the security forces or police."[67] As a result, many terrorist groups have moved their training efforts away from physical training camps and onto the Internet.

Further, as terrorist groups increasingly make use of the Internet, they are incorporating the newest forms of technology, like Macromedia Shockwave animation. Jihadist software developers have even created a Web browser that restricts online navigation to preapproved websites, filtering out all nonjihadist websites and keeping those interested in the movement sheltered from alternative viewpoints. Members of the online extremist community are also monitoring each others' websites, and posting messages to bulletin boards to help their comrades avoid Western counterterrorism efforts. For example, a recent message alerted the forum's participants that the European Union had changed its policy about monitoring Internet activity at cybercafes, and encouraged everyone to be extra careful at those locations in the future. Guidance offered for terrorist communications via the Internet has included using only public computers, masking the computer's IP addresses while navigating, never using identifying information in online forum registration, and actually stopping communication by e-mail wholesale and instead relying on Web bulletin boards for communication purposes. In essence, the Internet is providing a new vehicle for organizational learning and adaptation, and improving the terrorists' ability to achieve their strategic objectives. More on this is provided in later chapters of this volume. Overall, by evolving the means through which they transfer knowledge—and particularly, in taking advantage of modern Western technology—terrorist organizations are demonstrating the adaptive capabilities of learning organizations.

Knowledge transfer in the terrorist world takes many forms. Some studies have noted that when members of the IRA were captured and sent to British or Irish prisons, they were immediately debriefed by other inmates, who then smuggled the information (and lessons learned) to IRA members outside the prison walls. Particularly useful information passed on by the imprisoned terrorists could include how they were caught, what information the captors were looking for, what (if anything) might have gone awry with a planned attack being carried out, and who (if anyone) might have played a role in their capture.[68] This process of debriefing and knowledge transfer reflects the fact that learning organizations require the ability and willingness to examine both success and failure. For example, between 1981 and 1991 the PIRA learned to use rocket propelled grenades (RPGs)—and even developed their own improvised versions of commercial systems—with increasing lethality.[69] When the group began using RPGs, the result did not always achieve the intended objective. In some cases, the rocket malfunctioned, hit the wrong target, and/or killed innocent civilians. However, over time the PIRA developed new weapons of this type as well as an improved capacity to use them, resulting in greater organizational effectiveness.

Similar examples of terrorist organizations learning to use new weapons come from the realm of maritime security. In October 2001, Tamil Tiger separatists carried out a coordinated suicide attack on the *MV Silk Pride*, an oil tanker which was carrying more than 650 tons of diesel and kerosene to the port of Jaffna, in northern Sri Lanka. The attackers used five boats in the attack. One rammed the tanker, triggering an explosion on board, and three sailors died in the attack.[70] A year later, in October 2002, an explosive-laden boat slammed into the French oil tanker *Limburg* in the port of Ash Shihr, off the coast of Yemen, splitting the vessel's hull. At the time of the blast, which killed one crew member and sent more than ninety thousand barrels of Iranian crude oil pouring into the Gulf of Aden, the *Limburg* was picking up a pilot to guide it into the terminal.[71]

Terrorists are not only attacking commercial vessels on the open seas; there is also evidence that suggests they are looking for ways to use these ships as weapons. For example, in March 2003, ten armed hijackers commandeered the chemical tanker *Dewi Madrim* off the coast of Sumatra, Indonesia. Armed with machine guns and machetes, they disabled the ship's radio, took the helm, and steered the vessel, altering speed, for about an hour. Then they left in their speedboats, taking with them some cash, equipment, technical documents, and the captain and first officer, who are still missing.[72] For anyone familiar with the *9/11 Commission Report*, this event seems eerily reminiscent of how terrorists took flight lessons in the United States in order to learn how to fly—but not necessarily land—passenger airliners.[73] Other maritime-related learning involves the development of an underwater terrorist threat. For example, the naval wing of the Tamil Tigers in Sri Lanka—the so called "Black Sea Tiger suicide squad"—has developed underwater bombs, usually based on RDX and a timer detonator, which are used in suicide attacks by members who have received SCUBA training. Knowing this, the FBI has been investigating reports of Middle Eastern suspects approaching scuba diving clubs in America and inquiring about training, and a diving school in the Netherlands was recently investigated after a diving instructor and three of the students were suspected of al Qaeda links.[74]

Another recent example of organizational learning in the terrorist world is seen in how Islamist extremists in Iraq have continually adapted their use of improvised explosive devices to achieve greater effectiveness in their attacks on U.S. and Iraqi security forces. In a June 2005 *New York Times* article, Lt. Gen. John Vines, a senior American ground commander in Iraq, reported that the Iraqi insurgents' tactics "have become more sophisticated in some cases," and that they were probably drawing on bomb-making experts from outside Iraq and from the old Iraqi Army.[75] Another senior military officer described how the insurgents have begun detonating their explosives by using infrared lasers, an innovation aimed at bypassing electronic jammers used to block radio-wave detonators. According to one account, "Counterinsurgency experts are alarmed by how fast the other side's tactics can evolve. A particularly worrisome case is the ongoing arms race over improvised explosive devices. The first IEDs were triggered by wires and batteries; insurgents waited on the roadside and detonated the primitive devices when Americans drove past. After a while, U.S. troops got good at spotting and killing the triggermen when bombs went off. That led the insurgents to replace their wires with radio signals. The Pentagon, at frantic speed and high cost, equipped its forces with jammers to block those signals, accomplishing the task this spring. The insurgents adapted swiftly by sending a continuous radio signal to the IED; when the signal stops or is jammed, the bomb explodes. The solution? Track the signal and make sure it continues. Problem: the signal is encrypted. Now the Americans are grappling with the task of cracking the encryption on the fly and mimicking it—so far, without success. Still, IED casualties have dropped, since U.S. troops can break the signal and trigger the device before a convoy passes. That's the good news. The bad news is what the new triggering system says about the insurgents' technical abilities."[76] Capturing knowledge so that it remains accessible as part of the organizational memory also characterizes a learning organization. Knowledge created by an individual or small group is held for public view (in today's world, frequently via the Internet), where it contributes to discussion and new understanding. This sharing of new knowledge allows the learning to take root within that group, members of which then bring it to other areas of the organization or movement.

Organizational learning also involves scanning the operating environment, looking for anything that may offer a tactical advantage in pursuit of the organization's objectives. One reflection of this form of learning can be found in the changes of targets chosen by terrorists for their attacks. Jihadists have recently moved away from attacking hard targets like planes and government buildings, instead opting for softer targets like nightclubs (Bali), banks (Istanbul), hotels (Jakarta), commuter railways (Madrid and London), and oil tankers (Sri Lanka and Yemen). In chapter 11 of Ayman al-Zawahiri's book *Knights Under the Prophet's Banner,* he describes how "the mujahid Islamic movement must escalate its methods of strikes" and states that "the target as well as the type and method of weapons used must be chosen to have an impact on the structure of the enemy and deter it."[77] Today, it is widely recognized in the counterterrorism community that terrorist organizations like al Qaeda are seeking to strike targets which will not only yield casualties, dramatic news footage, and widespread fear, but will also have a political and economic impact.

A similar reflection of organizational learning in the terrorist world is seen in al Qaeda's adoption of fourth generation warfare tactics.[78] The concepts of fourth generation warfare were first presented in a 1989 *Marine Corps Gazette* article titled "The Changing Face of War: Into the Fourth Generation," which argued that such warfare was "likely to be widely dispersed and largely undefined; the distinction between war and peace will be blurred to the vanishing point."[79] The authors of this article also provide what became an ominous prediction of the terrorist threat we now face: The "political infrastructure and civilian society [will] become battlefield targets." Adherents of fourth generation warfare call for the use of psychological operations (including propaganda) and terrorism to erode an enemy's moral, mental, and physical ability to wage war over many years until they eventually lose their willingness to stay in the fight. According to one well-received definition, fourth generation warfare is an "evolved form of insurgency [that] uses all available networks—political, economic, social, military—to convince the enemy's decision makers that their strategic goals are either unachievable or too costly for the perceived benefit."[80]

The advantages of this approach for any subnational or transnational group are fairly obvious: decentralized, networked terrorist organizations are less vulnerable to the traditional counterterrorism measures used by the hierarchically organized security forces of a national government. In February 2002, the Middle East Media Research Institute (MEMRI) reported that an al Qaeda document posted to the Internet embraced fourth generation warfare. "This new type of war presents significant difficulties for the Western war machine," the publication said. "Fourth generation wars have already occurred and . . . the superiority of the theoretically weaker party has already been proven; in many instances, nation-states have been defeated by stateless nations."[81] Al Qaeda's adoption of fourth generation warfare tactics offer a useful case study for understanding organizational learning in the world of terrorism.

According to most counterterrorism analysts today, al Qaeda has evolved from a centrally directed organization into a worldwide franchiser of terrorist attacks.[82] Indeed, since the war in Afghanistan, which destroyed bin Laden's command and control, al Qaeda has become increasingly decentralized, and is seen by some as more of a "movement" than any other form of organization. According to Roger Cressey, the National Security Council's deputy director of counterterrorism in the Clinton and Bush administrations, "we've seen a growth in this global Sunni extremist movement, partly driven by Iraq, but also by other events, which is much more difficult to track, follow and ultimately disrupt. So as we're doing really well against what was al Qaeda, we've got a new threat—this movement, which is much more of a challenge."[83]

As inspirational leaders of this movement, bin Laden and al-Zawahiri have provided ideological guidance, while leaving planning and financing of operations to the local commanders of allied but autonomous organizations. The 2004 attack in Madrid, which killed 191 people, is often cited as the key turning point in the evolution of this global Islamist extremist movement.[84] Initially, Spanish and U.S. counterterrorism officials sought links with al Qaeda, but quickly they realized there weren't any. The attack was put together in eight weeks, using stolen explosives and cell phone detonators assembled by one of the conspirators. It required no central direction from the mountains of Pakistan, simply a charismatic leader with links to men trained in the war in Afghanistan against the Soviet Union. For motivation, though, they had Spanish help for the U.S. war in Iraq, and for inspiration they had bin Laden and the 9/11 attacks.

Other groups have followed this model. For example, there is no evidence to suggest that attacks that killed dozens of Westerners in Casablanca, Morocco were carried out with the knowledge of al Qaeda leadership. Further, investigators do not believe al Qaeda played any role in the July 7 mass transit attack in London, although a videotape produced afterward by al-Zawahiri applauded the suicide bombers. In essence, al Qaeda is becoming what its earliest architects had hoped it would be: a support "base" for Islamist radicals around the world. Even "al Qaeda in Iraq," the new name for Abu Musab al Zarqawi's group, does not take orders from bin Laden or his No. 2, Ayman al-Zawahiri, rather just inspiration, technical support, and military guidance.[85]

From a strategic perspective, it makes sense that Osama bin Laden and his colleagues would seek to nurture this sort of evolution in the terrorist world. Indeed, al Qaeda's leaders have recognized that the achievement of their ultimate goals and objectives requires a more decentralized, networked approach—a reflection of the fact that learning organizations consciously assess their own vulnerabilities, and are capable of adapting their operations to preserve the longevity of the organization. For example, as a result of damage caused to the group by security force penetration, the PIRA reorganized into a more compartmented cellular structure in the late 1970s.[86] In 2001, following the ouster of the Taliban from Afghanistan, a number of al Qaeda leaders suddenly found themselves bundled onto a CIA Gulfstream V or Boeing 737 jet and headed for long months of interrogation. Abu Zubaydah, al Qaeda's "dean of students," who directed training and placement for the group, was captured in Faisalabad, Pakistan, in February 2002. Ramzi Bin al-Shibh, the organizer of the Hamburg, Germany, cell that formed the core of the 9/11 hijackers, was captured in Karachi, Pakistan, on the first anniversary of the attacks. These and other counterterrorism successes ultimately led to the capture of Khalid Sheikh Mohammed, the mastermind of 9/11 and the financier of the first World Trade Center attack, in Rawalpindi, Pakistan, in March 2003, as well as Tawfiq Attash Kallad, the mastermind of the *USS Cole* attack, a month later in Karachi. In response to the loss of key leaders, according to Spanish counterterrorism judge Baltasar Garzon, al Qaeda convened a strategic summit in northern Iran in November 2002, at which the group's consultative council came to recognize that it could no longer exist as a hierarchy, but instead would have to become a decentralized network and move its operations out over the entire world.[87] By evolving in this way over the past few years, al Qaeda is demonstrating the type of adaptive flexibility that has become a hallmark of learning organizations—the subject of the next two chapters of this volume.

CONCLUSION

After reviewing these dimensions of individual learning, knowledge proliferation, and organizational learning, it becomes clear that the remaining chapters in this volume offer useful contributions to the field of terrorist studies. Knowledge and intellectual capital are vital resources for any organization. From doctrinal learning to tactical training, issues of knowledge acquisition and sharing among terrorists are an important topic of analysis—a mode of inquiry which should help us develop insights and creative ideas for countering global terrorism. As the world confronts the modern-day rise in terrorism, it is important that we apply the concepts of the learning organization to develop a better understanding of the terrorist organization and its members. Just like the business, education, and other sectors in our society, terrorists have found ways to take advantage of the tools and free-flowing networks of the information age. Further, while some terrorist groups are hierarchical and traditional (like the FARC in Colombia), others have adapted a more dynamic, networked approach that provides for a faster, more successful sharing of important knowledge. Appreciating how this occurs is a critical part of understanding the threat of terrorism we face today. As part of this, we need to better understand where the fertile ground is for motivational knowledge transfer. In today's loosely networked global terrorist movement, ideology plays a critical role. We must understand and fight both operational and motivational kinds of knowledge transfer in the terrorism world.

The remaining chapters of this volume offer important examples of research on knowledge development, legitimization, and transmission among terror networks as well as within certain terrorism cell structures. Some chapters will address these issues in a multiorganizational context, while other chapters provide case studies which demonstrate how terrorist networks can be viewed as learning organizations, able to draw on situational awareness to adapt their behavior in ways that (for example) render technology—such as unmanned aerial vehicles and satellite phones—ineffective. Overall, this volume provides a collection of insights on the transfer of knowledge in the world of terrorism, offering policy implications for counterterrorism professionals, scholars, and policymakers. As the old adage confirms, the value of knowledge can never be overestimated, and the price of ignorance can never be underestimated. The global struggle for survival against terrorism exemplifies this in unprecedented ways.

NOTES

I would like to thank Brigadier General (retired) Russell Howard and Major George Stewart III for their thoughtful guidance in revising this chapter. The views expressed are those of the author and not of the Department of the Army, the U.S. Military Academy, or any other agency of the U.S. Government.

1. James J. F. Forest, "Teaching and Learning in Higher Education," in *The International Handbook of Higher Education,* ed. James J. F. Forest and Philip G. Altbach (Dordrecht, Netherlands: Springer, 2006).

2. For the ongoing news reports on this story, see www.arabnews.com, www.bbc.com, and abu-hamza-news.newslib.com.

3. "Two Killed in Istanbul Flat Blast," *BBC News,* August 8, 2005.

4. "Bombs Explode Across Bangladesh," *BBC News,* August 17, 2005.

5. Brian A. Jackson, "Training for Urban Resistance: The Case of the Provisional Irish Republican Army," in *The Making of a Terrorist: Recruitment, Training and Root Causes,* vol. 2, ed. James JF Forest (Westport, CT: Praeger, 2005).

6. Testimony of David A. Harris to the National Commission on Terrorism (chaired by L. Paul Bremer) on March 2, 2000.

7. Portions of this chapter were presented as a paper at the 2004 Joint Conference of the International Security and Arms Control Section of the American Political Science Association, and the International Security Studies Section of the International Studies Association (Washington, DC, October 29–30, 2004), and have appeared in volume 2 of *The Making of a Terrorist: Recruitment, Training and Root Causes,* ed. James JF Forest (Westport, CT: Praeger Publishers, 2005).

8. Bruce Hoffman, *Inside Terrorism* (New York: Columbia University Press, 1998), 203.

9. For more on terrorist training camps, please see chapter 4 of this book as well as volume 2 of *The Making of a Terrorist: Recruitment, Training and Root Causes,* ed. James JF Forest (Westport, CT: Praeger Publishers, 2005).

10. Christopher Dobson and Ronald Payne, *The Terrorists, Their Weapons, Leaders and Tactics* (New York: Facts on File Publications, 1982), 12–13.

11. David E. Smith, "The Training of Terrorist Organizations" (CSC Report, 1995), 6. Available online at www.globalsecurity.org/military/report/1995/SDE.htm [accessed 24 July 2003].

12. See Ibrahim M. Abu-Rabi, *Intellectual Origins of Islamic Resurgence in the Modern Arab World* (Albany: State University of New York Press, 1996).

13. Anonymous, *Through Our Enemy's Eyes* (Dulles, Virginia: Brasseys, Inc., 2003), 274.

14. Paul Berman, "Al Qaeda's Philosopher: How an Egyptian Islamist Invented the Terrorist Jihad from his Jail Cell," *New York Times Magazine* (23 March 2003). Available online at www.nytimes.com.

15. See Brigitte Nacos, "The Role of the Media," in *The Making of a Terrorist: Recruitment, Training and Root Causes,* vol. 1, ed. James JF Forest (Westport, CT: Praeger, 2005).

16. Nacos, "Role of the Media."

17. Stephen Ulph, "A Guide to Jihad on the Web," *Terrorism Focus* 2, no. 7 (March 31, 2005).

18. Stephen Ulph, "The Voice of Jihad Is Back," *Terrorism Focus* 2, no. 8 (April 28, 2005).

19. For an analysis of this publication, see Stephen Ulph, "A New Journal for Algerian Jihad," *Terrorism Monitor* 2, no. 15 (July 29, 2004).

20. Online at www.nnuu.org.

21. Stephen Ulph, "New Online Magazine Indicates Growing Jihadi Movement in Syria," *Terrorism Focus* 2, no. 7 (March 31, 2005).

22. Ben Venzke and Aimee Ibrahim, "Al Qaeda's Advice for Mujahideen in Iraq: Lessons Learned in Afghanistan," *IntelCenter Report V1.0* (April 14, 2003). Available online at www.intelcenter.com.

23. Stephen Ulph, "The Voice of the Caucasus—A New Jihadi Magazine," *Terrorism Focus* 2, no. 8 (April 28, 2005).

24. Hoffman, *Inside Terrorism*, 203.

25. See "Leaderless Resistance Strategy Gains Momentum Among Militant White Supremacists," and "Aryan National Congress Focuses on Revolutionary Tactics," *Klanwatch Intelligence Report* no. 74, August 1994, 6–9. Also see "Tom Metzger/White Aryan Resistance," on the "Extremism in America" Anti-Defamation League website at www.adl.org.

26. Ben Venzke and Aimee Ibrahim, "Al Qaeda Tactic/Target Brief, v. 1.5" *IntelCenter* (June 14, 2002), 6.

27. See the chapter by Cindy Combs in this volume.

28. See Nacos, "Role of the Media."

29. Nacos, "Role of the Media."

30. Steve Coll and Susan B. Glasser, "Terrorists Turn to the Web as Base of Operations," *Washington Post* (August 7, 2005), A01.

31. Madeleine Gruen, "Innovative Recruitment and Indoctrination Tactics by Extremists: Video Games, Hip Hop, and the World Wide Web," in *The Making of a Terrorist: Recruitment, Training and Root Causes*, vol. 1, ed. James JF Forest (Westport, CT: Praeger, 2005): 11–22.

32. In addition to this volume, more on terrorists' use of the Internet is provided in *The Making of a Terrorist: Recruitment, Training and Root Causes*, ed. James JF Forest (Westport, CT: Praeger, 2005).

33. National Academy of Sciences, Commission on Physical Sciences, Mathematics, and Applications, *Containing the Threat from Illegal Bombings: An Integrated National Strategy for Marking, Tagging, Rendering Inert, and Licensing Explosives and Their Precursors* (Washington, DC: National Academies Press, 1998), available online at http://books.nap.edu/books/0309061261/html.

34. See "Hostile Website Provides Series of Videos for Beginner Mujahideen," *Global Issues Report*, 6 June 2005: 2.

35. " الان / دورة سلاح الملاحة للمجاهد الم " (Navigation Weapons [Training] Session for the Mujahideen of the Forum)." *Tajdid Al-Islami*, August 3, 2005, August 11, 2005, at www.tajdeed.org.uk/forums/showthread.php?s=657f1e552c93b00d81aab4b7507d8275&threadid=37147.

36. The following discussion of psychological conditioning is excerpted from the introductory chapter (by this author) of *The Making of a Terrorist: Recruitment, Training and Root Causes* vol. 2, ed. James JF Forest (Westport, CT: Praeger, 2005).

37. For example, see Albert Bandura, "Mechanisms of Moral Disengagement," in *Origins of Terrorism: Psychologies, Ideologies, Theologies, States of Mind*, ed. Walter Reich (Baltimore: Woodrow Wilson Center Press, 1998), 161–191; and Albert Bandura, "Training for Terrorism through Selective Moral Disengagement," in *The Making of a Terrorist: Recruitment, Training and Root Causes*, vol. 2, ed. James JF Forest (Westport, CT: Praeger, 2005).

38. For example, see Rex A. Hudson, *Who Becomes a Terrorist and Why: The 1999 Government Report on Profiling Terrorists* (Guilford, CT: The Lyons Press, 2001); and Robert A. Pape, "The Strategic Logic of Suicide Terrorism," *American Political Science Review* 97, no. 3 (August 2003): 343–361.

39. See Ehud Sprinzak, "Fundamentalism, Terrorism, and Democracy: The Case of the Gush Emunim Underground" (paper presented at the Woodrow Wilson Center, Washington, D.C., September 1986); Ehud Sprinzak, "The Psychopolitical Formation of Extreme Left Terrorism in a Democracy: The Case of the Weathermen," in *Origins of Terrorism: Psychologies, Ideologies, Theologies, States of Mind*, ed. Walter Reich (Baltimore: Woodrow Wilson Center Press, 1998), 65–85; and Ariel Merrari, "The Readiness to Kill and Die: Suicidal Terrorism in the Middle East," in *Origins of Terrorism: Psychologies, Ideologies, Theologies, State of Mind*, ed. Walter Reich (Baltimore: Woodrow Wilson International Center Press, 1998).

40. Bandura, "Mechanisms of Moral Disengagement" and "Training for Terrorism."

41. Bandura, "Mechanisms of Moral Disengagement" and "Training for Terrorism."

42. Yumi Wijers-Hasegawa, "Aum Chemist Sentenced to Hang," *Japan Times*, January 31, 2004.

43. Bandura, "Mechanisms of Moral Disengagement," and "Training for Terrorism."

44. Jerrold M. Post, "Terrorist Psycho-logic: Terrorist Behavior as a Product of Psychological Forces," in *Origins of Terrorism: Psychologies, Ideologies, Theologies, States of Mind*, ed. Walter Reich (Baltimore: Woodrow Wilson Center Press, 1998), 25–40.

45. Post, "Terrorist Psycho-logic."

46. For example, see Gavin Cameron, *Nuclear Terrorism: A Threat Assessment for the 21st Century* (New York: St. Martin's, 1999); and Adam Dolnik, "Die and Let Die: Exploring the Links between Suicide Terrorism and Terrorist Use of Chemical, Biological, Radiological, and Nuclear Weapons," *Studies in Conflict and Terrorism* 26, no. 1 (Jan–Feb 2003): 17–35.

47. See Marc Galanter, *Cults: Faith, Healing and Coercion*, 2nd ed. (New York: Oxford University Press, 1999), 18–33. Also see Marc Galanter and James JF Forest, "Cults, Charismatic Groups and Social Systems: Understanding the Transformation of Terrorist Recruits," in *The Making of a Terrorist: Recruitment, Training and Root Causes*, vol. 2, ed. James JF Forest (Westport, CT: Praeger, 2005).

48. Dr. Margaret Singer, before she passed away, was a professor emeritus at UC Berkeley and a leading authority on mind control and cults. Some of her work is available online at www.factnet.org/coercivemindcontrol.html.

49. See www.factnet.org/coercivemindcontrol.html.

50. Wong Chun Wai and Lourdes Charles, "Indonesian Radical Groups Learning Chechen Terrorist Tactics," *Star* (Singapore), September 27, 2004. Available online at http://thestar.com.my/news/list.asp?file=/2004/9/27/nation/8943512&sec=nation.

51. For more on this topic, please see chapter 4 of this volume.

52. Douglas Jehl, "Iraq May Be Prime Place for Training of Militants, CIA Report Concludes," *Washington Post*, June 21, 2005.

53. Peter Grier, "The New Al Qaeda: Local Franchiser," *Christian Science Monitor*, July 11, 2005. Online at www.csmonitor.com/2005/0711/p01s01-woeu.html.

54. The following terrorist group descriptions are provided by the 2003 and 2004 issues of the U.S. Department of State, *Patterns of Global Terrorism Report* (available online at www.state.gov/s/ct) as well as a variety of other open source materials. Also, Rohaiza Ahmad Asi from the International Center for Political Violence and Terrorism Research in Singapore provided a profile of Al Qaeda (dated May 9, 2005), which details the relationships between these and other terrorist groups, and from which some of these group descriptions are drawn.

55. "Detained Al Qaeda Leader Sayf al-Adl Chronicles Al-Zarqawi's Rise in Organization," *FBIS Report*, May 21, 2005. Cited in Chris M. Blanchard, "Al Qaeda: Statements and Evolving Ideology," Congressional Research Service report, June 20, 2005, 9.

56. "Colombians Search for Irish Trio," *BBC News*, December 20, 2004; and "Q&A: the Colombia Connection," *BBC News*, December 16, 2004. Online at http://news.bbc.co.uk.

57. Coll and Glasser, "Terrorists Turn to the Web," A01.

58. Coll and Glasser, "Terrorists Turn to the Web," A01.

59. For example, see Lisa Myers, "Al Qaeda Web Message Offers Missile Tutorial," *MSNBC.com,* March 30, 2005. Online at www.msnbc.msn.com/id/7339768/.

60. Coll and Glasser, "Terrorists Turn to the Web," A01.

61. Case Willoughby, "Learning Organizations," in *Higher Education in the United States: An Encyclopedia,* ed. James J.F. Forest and Kevin Kinser (Santa Barbara, CA: ABC-CLIO, 2002), 391.

62. Willoughby, "Learning Organizations," 391–393.

63. Peter Senge, *The Fifth Discipline: The Art and Practice of the Learning Organization* (New York: Doubleday, 1990), 3.

64. Willoughby, "Learning Organizations," 391–393.

65. Jackson, "Training for Urban Resistance."

66. Jackson, "Training for Urban Resistance."

67. Brian A. Jackson, "Training for Urban Resistance: The Case of the Provisional Irish Republican Army," in *The Making of a Terrorist: Recruitment, Training, and Root Causes,* vol. 2, edited by James J.F. Forest (Westport, CT: Praeger Security International, 2005), 127.

68. See J. Bowyer Bell, *The IRA, 1968–2000: Analysis of a Secret Army* (London: Frank Cass, 2000). See also David E. Smith, *Training of Terrorist Organizations.*

69. Brian A. Jackson, "Provisional Irish Republican Army," in *Aptitude for Destruction,* vol. 2, *Case Studies of Organizational Learning in Five Terrorist Groups,* ed. Brian Jackson, John C. Baker et al. (Santa Monica: Rand Corporation, 2005), 107–109.

70. "Tamil Tigers Claim Tanker Attack," *BBC News,* 31 October 2001. Online at http://news.bbc.co.uk/1/hi/world/south_asia/1628218.stm.

71. "Yemen Says Tanker Blast was Terrorism," *BBC News,* 16 October 2002. Online at http://news.bbc.co.uk/1/hi/world/middle_east/2334865.stm; and "Craft 'Rammed' Yemen Oil Tanker," *BBC News,* 6 October 2002. Online at http://news.bbc.co.uk/2/hi/middle_east/2303363.stm.

72. "Pirates Board Indonesian Tanker," *CBS News,* 29 March 2003. Online at www.cbsnews.com/stories/2003/03/29/world/main546695.shtml; also, Michael Richardson, "Terror at Sea: The World's Lifelines are at Risk," *Straits Times* (Singapore), November 17, 2003, www.stevequayle.com/News.alert/03_Terror/031117.terror.at.sea.html.

73. National Commission on Terrorist Attacks Upon the United States. *Report of the National Commission on Terrorist Attacks Upon the United States* (the 9/11 Commission Report). Washington, DC: U.S. Government Printing Office, 2004. Available online at www.gpoaccess.gov/911.

74. Michael Smith, "Al-Qaeda Threat to Trafalgar Fleet," *Sunday Times* (Britain), April 24, 2005, www.timesonline.co.uk/article/0,,2087-1582733,00.html); and "Divers at Eindhoven dive school suspected of Al-Qaeda connection," *Divernet News,* August 22, 2003.

75. David S. Cloud, "Iraqi Rebels Refine Bomb Skills, Pushing Toll of GI's Higher," *New York Times,* June 22, 2005.

76. Scott Johnson and Melinda Liu, "The Enemy Spies," *Newsweek,* June 27, 2005, www.msnbc.msn.com/id/8272786/site/newsweek.

77. Ben Venzke and Aimee Ibrahim, "Al Qaeda Tactic/Target Brief, v. 1.5," *IntelCenter* (14 June 2002), 6.

78. For further definition and examples of "fourth generation warfare," see John Arquilla and David F. Ronfeldt, eds., *Networks and Netwars: The Future of Terror, Crime, and Militancy* (Santa Monica: RAND Corporation, 2002); Robert Bunker, ed., *Non-State Threats and Future Wars* (London: Frank Cass Publishers, 2002); Bard E. O'Neill, *Insurgency and Terrorism: Inside Modern Revolutionary Warfare* (Dulles, VA: Potomac Books, 2001); and Sun Tzu, *The Art of War* (Mineola, NY: Dover Publications, 2002).

79. William S. Lind, Keith Nightengale, John F. Schmitt, Joseph W. Sutton, and Gary I. Wilson, "The Changing Face of War: Into the Fourth Generation," *Marine Corps Gazette,* October 1989, 22–26.

80. See *Armed Forces Journal*, November 2004, as cited in Myke Cole, "From the Military: Applying 4GW Theory to the Intelligence Community," *Defense and the National Interest* (August 10, 2005). Available online at www.d-n-i.net/fcs/cole_lessons_from_the_military.htm.

81. Scott Wheeler, "Expert Links Probing Attacks to 'Fourth-Generation Warfare,'" *CNS News*, August 16, 2004. Online at www.cnsnews.com/ViewSpecialReports.asp?Page=/SpecialReports/archive/200408/SPE20040816a.html.

82. Peter Grier, "The New Al Qaeda: Local Franchiser," *Christian Science Monitor*, July 11, 2005. Online at www.csmonitor.com/2005/0711/p01s01-woeu.html.

83. Robert Windrem, "The Frightening Evolution of al-Qaida," *MSNBC.com*, June 24, 2005. Online at http://msnbc.msn.com/id/8307333.

84. Windrem, "Frightening Evolution of al-Qaida."

85. Windrem, "Frightening Evolution of al-Qaida."

86. Jackson, "Training for Urban Resistance."

87. Windrem, "Frightening Evolution of al-Qaida."

I

UNDERSTANDING KNOWLEDGE TRANSFER IN THE TERRORIST WORLD

2

✛

How Terrorists Learn

Michael Kenney

Terrorism is a form of political violence that requires knowledge of demolitions, weaponry, and clandestine operations, among other areas. "No one is born with the knowledge of how to build bombs, use a pistol, conduct surveillance, or hijack airplanes," explains Larry C. Johnson, former deputy director of the State Department's Office of Counterterrorism. "These are skills that must be taught and practiced."[1] Like other skilled practitioners, including law enforcement and intelligence agents that confront them, political extremists learn their craft through training programs, apprenticeships, and actual practice (in this case, combat). In recent years, al Qaeda and other extremist networks have developed training courses and instructional materials to teach aspiring jihadists their brand of terrorism and guerilla warfare. These instructional programs serve the dual purpose of spreading the network's knowledge among thousands of militants, while allowing leaders to observe, select, and recruit the most promising trainees. Terrorists also rely on local knowledge and the cunning intelligence gained from experience, including planning and executing violent attacks. They learn by doing, adapting their know-how to the opportunities and constraints provided by each operation.

Deepening our understanding of how terrorists learn is critical to crafting effective counterterrorism strategies. Learning lies at the heart of terrorists' ability to spread their knowledge among like-minded extremists and to adapt their tactics in the face of intensive government efforts to destroy them. Indeed, terrorists' ability to learn—from study and experience—helps account for the resilience of al Qaeda and other networks

since the war on terror began four years ago. Today, despite the elimina-
tion or capture of hundreds of "high-value" al Qaeda targets, state officials from Washington to Jakarta confront a decentralized Islamist movement that includes surviving elements of al Qaeda and home-grown
extremists from the Middle East, North Africa, and Central and Southeast
Asia. These militants continue to adapt their activities in response to
counterterrorism operations in the post-9/11 era. This chapter illustrates
how terrorists acquire their skills through training and experience and
adapt their practices in response to counterterrorism, in the process becoming more difficult for governments to identify and eliminate.

TRAINING IN TERRORISM

Terrorists often learn through military-style training programs, sometimes with the support of obliging state sponsors. During the Cold War,
the United States and the Soviet Union, either directly or indirectly
through proxies, offered military training to extremist groups later identified as terrorist organizations and government security agencies subsequently involved in terrorist acts. Recipients of Soviet largesse included
the Palestine Liberation Organization and the Popular Front for the Liberation of Palestine, both of which established training camps modeled after Soviet facilities. Palestinian militants, in turn, provided training in
armed assaults, kidnappings, and demolitions to Western European and
Latin American extremists, some of whom later carried out attacks in support of their benefactors' cause.[2] During the war against Soviet occupation forces in Afghanistan, the U.S. Central Intelligence Agency provided
funding and weapons to the Pakistani Inter-Services Intelligence Direc-
torate, which distributed them among various resistance groups fighting
in Afghanistan. These national resistance fighters, in turn, trained foreign
Islamic militants who were helping them overthrow the Soviets. Tragically, some of these foreign mujahideen later expanded their holy war
against the United States and other Western countries. Also during the
Cold War, Washington provided substantial military aid and training to
several Latin American intelligence agencies and armies, elements of
which were later implicated in state terror against their own citizens.

The U.S. and the Soviet Union have not been the only direct or indirect
state sponsors of military instruction for violent extremists. Terrorist
training facilities have been reported in a number of countries, including
Afghanistan, Iran, Lebanon, Libya, Northern Ireland, Pakistan, the Sudan,
Tunisia, and Yemen. For years the Irish Republican Army trained its recruits in weapons handling, explosives, and surveillance in Northern Ireland.[3] The Abu Nidal Organization (ANO), which splintered from the

Palestine Liberation Organization in the early 1970s, provided training to terrorists from several countries in Libya under the protection of Colonel Muammar Qaddafi. The ANO also maintained training and administrative facilities in Iraq, Syria, and Lebanon's Bekaa Valley. In Syrian-controlled areas of the Bekaa Valley, trainers from the Iranian Revolutionary Guards—many of whom were trained by the Palestinians—provided Hizballah with instruction in automatic weapons, explosives, rocket launchers, clandestine infiltration, and close quarter combat. As the *9/11 Commission* report documents, Iranian operatives and Hizballah militants later instructed al Qaeda members in munitions, intelligence, and security at training camps in Iran and the Bekaa Valley.[4]

Al Qaeda Training

During the 1990s, al Qaeda provided training to thousands of supporters at camps located in Afghanistan, Bosnia, Chechnya, Indonesia, the Philippines, Somalia, the Sudan, and Yemen. In Afghanistan alone, at least six camps (and perhaps a dozen or more) provided detailed instruction in different aspects of guerrilla warfare and terrorism. According to Rohan Gunaratna, the Afghan camps provided three standard courses of instruction to recruits: basic, advanced, and specialized. "Basic training is for recruits. Advanced training is for people who are going to participate in active combat, to prepare them mentally and physically. Specialized training is for those mostly who are going on terrorist missions."[5] Many participants in the al Qaeda camps received only basic training, which included instruction in Islamic law and history and training in guerrilla warfare, small arms (handguns and rifles), and explosive devices. Following basic instruction, some militants were selected to fight in Islamic jihads then raging in Kashmir, Chechnya, and Bosnia. Other extremists returned home to their respective countries, sometimes with instructions to form "sleeper" cells and await further directives from al Qaeda leaders.[6]

Some recruits that performed exceptionally well in al Qaeda's basic training—as well as others with highly prized linguistic talents or citizenship in countries where the network hoped to develop cells—were invited to continue their extremist education in advanced courses at smaller camps in Afghanistan covering heavy weapons, explosives, kidnapping, assassination, surveillance and countersurveillance, and cell management. One promising student, Mohamed Rashed al-'Owhali, received an audience with Osama bin Laden, who encouraged him to continue his military training, which he apparently did, receiving advanced instruction in information security, intelligence, hijackings, and related activities. Later on, when al-'Owhali agreed to participate in the Kenya embassy bombing attack of 1998 (a crime for which he was subsequently convicted in a Manhattan courtroom), he underwent, as one Federal Bureau of Investigation (FBI) agent recalls, "very specialized training" in the management and operation of clandestine cells.[7]

Al-'Owhali's experience, and testimony from other al Qaeda militants turned government informants—including L'Houssaine Kherchtou and Ahmed Ressam—suggests that these training programs were designed not only to spread the network's formal knowledge among thousands of committed extremists, but also to evaluate and recruit the most promising candidates for full membership in al Qaeda.[8] These select few were invited to pledge their fealty to bin Laden and his vision of *jihad*. Whether or not they became card carrying members of al Qaeda, participation in the network's basic and advanced training courses solidified militants' devotion to the *jihadi* movement, extended their connections among fellow extremists, deepened their identities as Islamic warriors, and improved their ability—and confidence—to carry out terrorist attacks.[9]

TERRORIST KNOWLEDGE

As described in the previous chapter of this volume, the knowledge of terrorism is codified in handbooks, manuals, novels, videos, CD-ROMs, and other artifacts that, in an age of expanding information technology, are widely disseminated among political and religious extremists. Militiamen, white supremacists, Marxist revolutionaries, and Islamic radicals have all "published" handbooks and manuals of variable quality and authenticity. The widely circulated *Militia of Montana Field Manual* contains instructions on urban guerrilla warfare, as well as plans for paralyzing the U.S. economy, eliminating "traitorous" government officials, and assassinating prominent public personalities. The *Anarchist's Cookbook* includes detailed information on various household poisons and explosive devices, while the *Terrorist's Handbook* instructs readers how to make a variety of low and high impact explosives.[10]

While these and other murder manuals are available to "amateur" terrorists through mail-order publishers and the Internet, many professional terrorist groups produce their own handbooks describing organizational goals and practices. Members learn the recipes of terrorism, as practiced by their respective groups, through these materials. Recruits to the Irish Republican Army (IRA) absorb an entire curriculum of training materials, including the (in)famous *Green Book* and the *Handbook for Volunteers of the Irish Republican Army*. The *Green Book* covers the "the duties and responsibilities of volunteers," explains one former IRA militant, along with "the history of the movement, the rules of military engagement, and anti-interrogation techniques."[11] Both manuals are written by senior members who draw heavily on their paramilitary experience confronting "imperialist" British troops.

The IRA and other extremist groups also use British and American military manuals to train for guerrilla warfare and terrorism. In some cases, these manuals are obtained by militants who served in the armed services of their respective countries, including the United States. Members of a small aspiring extremist clique labeled the "Virginia jihad network" allegedly received combat training from a former U.S. Marine Corps clerk who subsequently pled guilty to criminal charges for his participation in the conspiracy. In his courtroom testimony, the informant acknowledged that he instructed his fellow conspirators in combat tactics using one of his basic training manuals.[12]

Al Qaeda has produced several training and operations manuals for its members, including the *Encyclopedia of Afghan Jihad* and the *Declaration of Jihad Against the Country's Tyrants*. The *Encyclopedia* was compiled to document the experience of Islamic resistance fighters in Afghanistan's war against the Soviet Union during the 1980s and share this knowledge with their fellow mujahideen in Bosnia, Chechnya, and Kashmir. The multivolume document contains diagrams copied from the U.S. Army's field manual series, allegedly acquired by Ali Mohamed, a former al Qaeda member turned U.S. government informant. Mohamed obtained copies of the manuals when he was a supply sergeant assigned to Fort Bragg, North Carolina, home of the John F. Kennedy Special Warfare Center. According to one of his former government handlers, Ali Mohamed translated the manuals and had sent them to al Qaeda leaders, who included the material in the *Encyclopedia*, which contains instruction on guerrilla warfare, intelligence, weapons, explosives, topography, and training.[13]

The *Declaration* contains eighteen "lessons" for successful terrorist operations, including sections on "Counterfeit Currency and Forged Documents," "Member Safety," "Prisons and Detention Centers," "Training," and two separate chapters on "Espionage." Both manuals outline religious and ideological justifications for various acts of violence and describe rules and routines in detail. For example, the *Declaration*'s fifth lesson, "Means of Communication and Transportation," reminds readers that communication in clandestine operations is always a "double-edged sword," and stipulates numerous security precautions, including the use of code words in telephone conversations and secret signals in face-to-face meetings.[14]

Al Qaeda training manuals are updated over time to accommodate and record the network's growing body of terrorist experience. Associates have enhanced the *Encyclopedia of Afghan Jihad* by adding supplementary volumes to the document, including one on chemical and biological warfare (available on CD-ROM).[15] In January 2004, al Qaeda issued a new online publication, *The Base of the Vanguard*, aimed at new recruits and supporters who operate "below the radar" of state intelligence agencies and therefore may not wish to risk undergoing formal training. The document includes articles on physical training, security procedures for operations cells, and use of small arms, along with testimony from a reputed suicide bomber.[16] Osama bin Laden's network has also recorded a series of videos offering instruction on assassinations, bomb making, chemical weapons, hostage taking, paramilitary raids, surface-to-air weapons, even motorcycle drive-by shootings, similar to the *parrilleros* perfected by Colombian killers in recent decades. As with al Qaeda's training manuals, the videos serve the twin purpose of documenting the network's extensive experience in guerrilla warfare and recruiting and training new generations of Islamic extremists.

ELIMINATING TERRORIST TRAINING CAMPS

Terrorists' reliance on training camps and instructional materials creates potent vulnerabilities that governments can exploit by destroying training facilities and seizing records. Training camps that double as repositories of organizational knowledge often contain a treasure trove of intelligence authorities can use to learn more about their adversaries and disrupt their activities. In Operation Enduring Freedom, American and allied troops significantly weakened al Qaeda and disrupted its ability to plan and execute attacks by destroying dozens of training facilities in Afghanistan and Pakistan. Many counterterrorist operations in Afghanistan included Defense Intelligence Agency document exploitation teams that analyzed records seized during raids to inform additional raids and investigations. On a larger scale, the U.S. counterterrorism offensive has made it more difficult for terrorist networks to establish formal training facilities. This represents an important victory in the campaign against terrorism, and U.S. officials should continue to work closely with their counterparts in Afghanistan, Pakistan, Indonesia, Iraq, and elsewhere to prevent the creation of new camps.

Not surprisingly, Islamist extremists have adapted their training in response to the new security environment—presenting additional challenges to counterterrorism officials. Some aspiring jihadists have begun training in small, closely-knit groups during weekends and vacations. These part-time training sessions are led by local extremists who draw on their own military experience to instruct their fellow militants. As Marc Sageman points out in *Understanding Terror Networks*, the perpetrators of the May 2003 Casablanca bombings underwent weekend training from local mujahideen who received training in Afghanistan. While the quality of the training received by the Moroccan bombers is questionable, it did not prevent them from carrying out coordinated bombings that killed forty-one people and injured more than one hundred others.[17]

According to Sageman, a critical breakthrough in the Moroccan group's preparations came when it discovered a lighter, more reliable munitions recipe on the World Wide Web. This is consistent with the post-9/11 migration of Islamic extremism to the Internet. As governments root out and destroy terrorist training camps in numerous countries, Internet-savvy supporters within the broader extremist movement have created virtual training camps through online publications, chat rooms, and discussion boards. Terrorists use these online resources to raise funds, recruit supporters, share information, and coordinate their activities.

Al-Battar ("the sharp-edged sword"), an online al Qaeda journal that has appeared regularly since 2003, provides readers with instruction in weapons handling, kidnapping, poisoning, guerrilla tactics and targeting, and secure communications. The fifth and sixth installments of *In the Shadow of the Lances*, another al Qaeda publication, details lessons learned in the Afghanistan campaign, including deploying fighters in small, mobile units led by experienced mujahideen, to minimize losses from U.S. precision guided munitions, and using human couriers to communicate, rather than advanced communications technologies that can be intercepted by American forces. In keeping with al Qaeda tradecraft, a senior operative wrote the installments as a sort of after action review to be shared with Islamic insurgents then preparing to fight American forces in Iraq.[18]

While the loss of al Qaeda's training infrastructure in Afghanistan, Pakistan, and other locations has reduced the potential skills of many would-be extremists in the immediate future, the preceding examples suggest that the network's substantial body of terrorist knowledge continues to spread within the broader fundamentalist movement, even as state authorities press on with the campaign against terrorism. Videotapes, CD-ROMs, computer disks, and paper manuals documenting terrorist tactics are copied and shared among like-minded militants by mail, by the Internet, and through human couriers.[19]

The diffusion of al Qaeda's brand of terrorist knowledge "means you don't need Afghanistan anymore to teach people how to make bombs and chemical agents," observes Magnus Ranstorp, director of the Center for the Study of Terrorism and Political Violence at the University of St. Andrews.[20] State authorities have discovered al Qaeda instructional materials in numerous countries, including Pakistan, Indonesia, Northern Ireland, and Iraq. After forcing *Ansar al-Islam*, a local extremist group, from its traditional base of operations in northern Iraq in March 2003, American and Kurdish security forces discovered digital and paper copies of al Qaeda manuals, posters, and lesson plans, which one Special Forces officer identified as "the al Qaeda mobile curriculum." Al Qaeda sent instructors and experienced fighters to the area to train militants in demolitions, poisons, and combat tactics, and assist with the terrorist group's growing administrative needs.[21] While the loss of al Qaeda's training camps in Afghanistan and elsewhere may reduce the skills of Islamic mujahideen in the immediate future, its knowledge is not likely to be lost, even if state authorities eventually dismantle the network.

LEARNING TERRORISM BY DOING

Not all the skills of terrorism can be boiled down to abstract, formally codified principles disseminated to recruits through formal training programs. Intuition and local knowledge can be just as crucial. Terrorists learn by doing: building bombs and detonators, discharging rifles and handguns, engaging in armed combat, infiltrating "enemy" territory, casing potential targets, writing intelligence reports, communicating by code and secret signals, and performing a host of other clandestine activities. In the field, militants assume false identities to mask their intentions from police officials and potential informants. Unlike police officers who go undercover for short periods of time to arrange drug deals, professional terrorists must convincingly play their roles for weeks, even months at a stretch, often while living in foreign countries. Such "deep" undercover assignments require talents not readily imparted through training programs, including quick thinking and flexibility. Some terrorist networks seek recruits who already possess many of the skills required for effective undercover work. Among the "necessary qualifications and characteristics" for membership in al Qaeda, as described in the second lesson of the *Declaration of Jihad Against the Country's Tyrants*, is the "ability to act, change positions and conceal oneself."[22]

Terrorists develop practical experience and local knowledge through informal apprenticeships, on-the-job training, and combat simulations. In some cases, trainees undergo lengthy apprenticeships with knowledgeable associates, allowing them to gain experience under controlled settings. After he received preliminary instruction in weapons handling and undercover operations, one ANO member was assigned to senior operatives, who socialized him to the organization's rules and routines, and provided him with a series of increasingly challenging assignments, such as obtaining false passports and photographing American and Israeli embassies in Europe.[23] Another recruit underwent a similar apprenticeship with the Irish Republican Army. During a two-year period the terrorist-in-training participated in a series of increasingly deadly operations, including reconnaissance, bombings, and assassinations, under the tutelage of more experienced IRA members. "I look back on that time as my apprenticeship," he recalls in his memoirs. "I learned how to be an effective IRA member: how to gather intelligence, how to set up operations, how to avoid mistakes."[24]

However, many militants receive only rudimentary instruction in weaponry and guerrilla warfare before undergoing their "real education" in sustained combat operations against enemy forces. During the 1980s, Arab mujahideen frequently learned their combat skills fighting against Soviet troops.[25] Conflicts in Kashmir, Bosnia, and Chechnya in the 1990s provided additional opportunities for militants—including many who went through the al Qaeda camps—to supplement their training with combat experience. While estimates of the number of foreign jihadists fighting in Iraq vary widely, from several hundred to several thousand, counterterrorism analysts worry that Iraq has become a training ground for Middle Eastern, North African, and European extremists, some of whom could continue their activities once they return to their own countries armed with the practical knowledge and personal intuition essential for conducting spectacular terrorist operations. "[I]t's going to be a big problem with this radicalized new generation," explains Peter Bergen, author of *Holy War, Inc.* "When they go home to wherever they go home to," he continued, "they're not going to go back and open falafel stands, they're going to be part of the next generation of jihadists."[26]

In recent years, al Qaeda and other extremist groups have provided their members with simulations in combat tactics, weapons, and explosives. Al Qaeda reportedly developed a series of urban combat simulations performed in a replica of a "small Western-style city," where trainees used explosives to destroy mock bridges, offices, and houses. "It is more advanced than training," notes Rohan Gunaratna, who analyzed videotapes of the exercises. "It is almost like doing the operation, so that when they go to the real operational theater, they will be a hundred percent confident."[27] Videotapes uncovered by U.S. forces in Afghanistan show various hostage-taking scenarios where al Qaeda trainees learn how to assault large buildings and conduct ambushes on six-lane highways, similar to those found in the United States and Europe. In these role-playing exercises, militants practice issuing commands to "hostages" in English and learn how to identify, separate, and control law enforcers and armed citizens in captive groups.[28]

When preparing for large-scale attacks, al Qaeda militants hone mission-specific skills and rehearse different aspects of the operation. In the weeks leading up to 9/11, several so-called "muscle" hijackers worked out at local gyms, and at least one terrorist brushed up on his kickboxing and knife-fighting skills by taking martial arts classes. Meanwhile, the prospective hijacker-pilots enrolled in flight training courses, made practice flights on small rented planes, took test runs on commercial flights to gather intelligence on cockpit access and airport security, and purchased commercially available flight deck simulation videos and software programs. Meticulous preparation increased the hijackers' ability to perform their assigned tasks effectively, with tragic results for the United States. The *9/11 Commission* reports that "simulator training was critical for the hijacker to familiarize himself with the cockpit controls and proper operation of the Boeing 757 and 767 . . . and to gain the operational proficiency, 'feel,' and confidence necessary to fly the aircraft into an intended target."[29]

INTELLIGENCE COLLECTION AND ADAPTATION

Terrorist groups routinely gather information about their activities and government counterterrorist efforts, seeking to learn from their own and others' successes and failures and identify vulnerabilities in their state adversaries. Sources of inspiration and imitation include media accounts describing successful attacks, trade publications detailing counterterrorism measures, and court documents from judicial proceedings against alleged extremists. Over the years many extremist groups have conducted pre-attack surveillance and monitored law enforcement and military activities. According to the FBI, militants from the Animal Liberation Front and the Earth Liberation Front read trade publications and videotaped potential targets in preparing for property damage attacks against logging companies, ski resorts, government agencies, and other perceived culprits of environmental degradation.[30]

Information gathering is frequently undertaken with an eye toward preventing costly errors and improving existing operations. "Terrorists often analyze the 'lessons' to be drawn from mistakes made by former comrades who have been either killed or apprehended," writes Bruce Hoffman, head of the RAND Corporation's terrorism research unit. "Press accounts, judicial indictments, courtroom testimony, and trial transcripts are meticulously culled for information on security force tactics and methods and then absorbed by surviving group members."[31] During the 1980s, members of the Red Army Faction, a small German terrorist group, studied court testimony provided by police officials to learn antiterrorist techniques and develop appropriate countermeasures, including applying a special ointment to their fingers that prevented them from leaving incriminating prints for criminal investigators.[32] When Irish Republican Army (IRA) militants land in British or Irish prisons "they are immediately approached by other incarcerated members of their cadre and debriefed on their capture," according to another source. "This information is smuggled out of the institution and provided to the command structure for analysis by leaders and promulgation to members at large."[33]

Al Qaeda likewise places considerable emphasis on intelligence collection. Network associates gather information from personal contacts, public officials, newspapers, radio and television broadcasts, courtroom testimony, and other open sources, taking advantage of press freedoms and transparent government reporting enjoyed in many Western democracies. According to an unclassified CIA memorandum, al Qaeda operatives search the media for information about U.S. counterterrorism activities and alter "their practices in response to what they have learned in the press about our capabilities,"[34] including restricting their use of cellular telephones.

Al Qaeda has also been known to send qualified associates to reconnoiter potential targets of attack or to investigate opportunities for fundraising. Jamal al Fadl, a former al Qaeda militant who testified during the East African embassy bombing trial in Manhattan, discussed a research trip he made in the early 1990s at the behest of several al Qaeda leaders, including Osama bin Laden and Abu Fadhl al Makkee. "When I was in Khartoum," he explained, "they told me also we need after you finish Budapest trip [sic], you go to Bosnia, to Zagreb, and we need you to study how the business over there because we learn the government in Croatia has sold some companies and we want to know what kind of companies and how much and how the investments over there and we need you to bring reward about the business over there."

"Did you actually go to Bosnia and bring back a report about the businesses?" the prosecuting attorney asked.

"Yes," replied Al Fadl.

"And who did you bring that report back to?"

"I bring it to Abu Fadhl al Makkee and I give it [sic] to him."[35]

More recently, Iyman Faris, an Ohio truck driver who pleaded guilty to providing material support to al Qaeda on several occasions between 2000 and 2003, was allegedly tasked by network managers to research "ultralight aircraft" and "gas cutters," both of which were intended for conducting terrorist attacks in the United States. In his plea bargain agreement, Faris admitted to researching these technologies using the Internet and an unwitting acquaintance with the appropriate technical background, and reporting his results to al Qaeda through coded e-mail messages.[36]

Over the years, al Qaeda has recorded its substantial base of knowledge on intelligence collection in its how-to terrorism manual, the *Declaration of Jihad Against the Country's Tyrants*. This document contains two chapters on "espionage," which it defines as "the covert search for and examination of the enemy's news and information for the purpose of using them when a plan is devised." The manual identifies two sources of information: public and secret. From the former, "it is possible to gather at least 80% of information about the enemy," the manual claims, "depending on the government's policy on freedom of the press and publication." The manual identifies "newspapers, magazines, books, periodicals, official publications, and enemy broadcasts" as important public sources of intelligence in liberal democratic states. It also describes how to conduct an open source search: "The one gathering public information should be a regular person (trained college graduate) who examines primary sources of information published by the enemy (newspapers, magazines, radio, TV, etc.). He should search for information directly related to the topic in question."[37]

Secret or covert intelligence includes "information about government personnel, officers, important personalities," their families, and "information about strategic buildings, important establishments, and military bases." Such knowledge, the *Declaration* makes clear, is critical to planning and conducting terrorist attacks: "The Organization's command needs detailed information about the enemy's vital establishments, whether civilian or military, in order to make safe plans, reach firm decisions, and avoid surprises." The manual identifies several methods for obtaining secret information, including surveillance, observation, theft, interrogation, and informant recruitment, and describes these methods in detail—including tips and techniques for casing potential targets, avoiding government surveillance, and testing the veracity of informants.[38]

While the *Declaration* distills al Qaeda's extensive information on covert intelligence in the form of simplified recipes and rules of thumb, the manual also emphasizes the need for experiential knowledge when conducting activities such as interrogating "enemy" personnel. To prevent "being deceived by misinformation," the manual counsels that the interrogator "should have knowledge and expertise about people's behavior and morals," and "should possess a sixth sense based on practice and experience."[39]

Al Qaeda and other terrorist networks draw on intelligence to plan and execute successful attacks against their adversaries. Prior to bombing the U.S. embassy in Nairobi, Kenya, in 1998, al Qaeda scouts allegedly entered the embassy by posing as informants with an ominous warning: unidentified terrorists were preparing to bomb the building. The scouts then observed the building during the next few days, gathering information on the security procedures taken by embassy personnel to counter the threat. Then they packaged their raw intelligence with operational plans containing handwritten notes, photographs, and computerized maps, which they sent to al Qaeda leaders for review.[40] In Afghanistan, Osama bin Laden and other *shura majlis* (consultative council) members met to discuss the intelligence, analyze vulnerabilities in the embassy's security precautions, and design an attack plan based on this analysis. The ensuing attack, along with a simultaneous bombing at the U.S. embassy in Dar es Salaam, Tanzania, killed more than three hundred people and injured five thousand others.

Terrorists also use intelligence to change their operations to prevent state security officials from destroying them. After all, success for terrorists who operate in hostile environments depends on their ability to outmaneuver law enforcement and military bureaucracies. To this end they routinely modify their activities to prevent state authorities from identifying patterns and practices that can be used to infiltrate their operations. "You change your tactics to keep them guessing," explains an experienced IRA militant. "If you stick to one tactic, you can become predictable and be tracked down."[41]

These adaptations are often fairly simple, yet maddeningly effective. After learning from news reports that U.S. intelligence agencies were monitoring his satellite telephone calls, Osama bin Laden reportedly changed phones and reduced his use of the technology, making it harder for American authorities to track him down. "Once that information was out," complained Deputy Secretary of Defense Paul Wolfowitz, referring to the unauthorized leaks by government officials to newspaper reporters that allegedly tipped bin Laden off, "we never again heard from his satellite phone."[42] More recently, numerous al Qaeda militants stopped using a particular brand of cell phone to communicate sensitive messages, switching to e-mail, Internet phone calls, and human couriers. Investigating officials believe the suspected terrorists changed their communications because they had determined that their cell phones were vulnerable to government interception.[43]

Al Qaeda operatives have also been known to adapt their activities in response to difficulties that arise when planning and preparing for specific attacks. The 9/11 attacks provide a sobering example. Belying its catastrophic outcome, the "planes operation" encountered numerous problems, forcing Khalid Sheikh Mohammed and Mohammad Atta to repeatedly alter their plans. As detailed in the *9/11 Commission's* preliminary and final reports, tactical problems that threatened to derail the operation included two hijackers who were tasked to pilot airplanes but failed to obtain sufficient pilot training due to their poor English, numerous participants who unexpectedly backed out of the mission or were removed from the operation by al Qaeda leaders, and interpersonal squabbling among at least two conspirators. Khalid Sheikh Mohammed, Ramzi bin al-Shibh, and Mohammad Atta changed their plans in response to each challenge by reassigning participants to different tasks, recruiting and training better-skilled hijackers, and persuading operatives to overcome personal animosities for the greater good of the suicide mission.[44] The ability of these extremists to adapt to a constantly changing environment and their commitment to proceeding with the suicide mission at all costs ensured that the planes operation, imperfect as it was, ultimately achieved devastating results.

Many terrorist adaptations are driven by the need to safeguard organizational integrity in hostile law enforcement systems and to keep pace with developments in counterterrorist tactics and technologies. For example, over the last several decades airlines have instituted a number of security procedures to protect domestic and international flights against terrorist attacks. While these precautions have enhanced aviation security, enterprising terrorists have responded to each innovation, circumventing new technologies and procedures to carry out hijackings and other attacks of devastating effectiveness. After terrorists carried out a number of airline hijackings in the late 1960s, the U.S. and other countries responded by installing metal detectors and X-ray machines in airports to screen passengers and deter potential attacks. While this policy decreased the number of skyjackings worldwide, it led to an increase in terrorist assassinations and hostage-taking incidents, as committed militants switched to other forms of political violence.[45]

Nor did improvements in airport security prevent all skyjackings. In 1985, Hizballah members circumvented screening devices for their successful hijacking of TWA Flight 847 by having airline workers hide weapons in the airplane lavatory, which prompted airlines to conduct background checks on ground crews. A year later, as Gregory Raymond recounts, explosives were found in a woman's luggage in London, apparently hidden there by her erstwhile boyfriend. Airlines responded by requiring workers to ask passengers if they packed their own baggage. Terrorists countered by checking their own bomb-laden baggage and then not boarding the flights. Again, the airlines responded, this time by matching checked luggage with boarded passengers, under the now tragically discredited assumption that terrorists would avoid suicide skyjackings.[46]

Driven by what Bruce Hoffman describes as a "fundamental organizational imperative" to continue their attacks, terrorist groups adapt in response to all manner of counterterrorist operations. "An almost Darwinian principle of natural selection thus seems to affect terrorist organizations," observes Hoffman, "whereby . . . every new terrorist generation learns from its predecessors, becoming smarter, tougher, and more difficult to capture or eliminate."[47] Hoffman describes the case of the Irish Republican Army in detail, where bomb-makers—under considerable pressure from British authorities, and hoping to reduce the risk of accidental explosions to IRA militants—repeatedly improved their explosives and detonation systems over the years. Each time British Ministry of Defense engineers responded to IRA bombing innovations by developing successful countermeasures, IRA technicians returned to their basement "research and development" labs and modified their detonation systems, allowing them to overcome the government's counterterrorism efforts, and enhancing their ability to conduct terrorist attacks within an intensely hostile enforcement environment.[48]

These and other technological innovations have given IRA militants a well-deserved reputation for "innovative expertise, adaptability and cunning," and Hoffman notes the grudging respect displayed by several British army officers toward their terrorist adversaries. "I would rate them very highly for improvisation," explains one officer. "IRA bombs are very well made." "I don't think there is any organization in the world as cunning as the IRA," observes another. "They have had twenty years at it and they have learned from their experience. We have a great deal of respect for their skills . . . not as individuals, but their skills."[49] Of course, not all terrorist networks are as sophisticated as the IRA and al Qaeda. Fortunately for them, and unfortunately for the rest of us, they do not have to be to exploit vulnerabilities in government enforcement efforts by adapting their operations in response to information and experience.

CONCLUSION

Terrorism is a specialized pursuit, requiring knowledge of light weapons, demolitions, clandestine operations, and a host of related activities. Terrorists learn their violent tradecraft through informal apprenticeships and formal training programs that convey the abstract ideals of extremist ideologies and the concrete techniques of asymmetric warfare, while strengthening their identities as devoted militants and enhancing their capacity to attack enemy soldiers and civilians. Many terrorist networks, including al Qaeda, Hizballah, and the IRA, devote considerable resources to the instruction of their militants, as reflected in the near professional quality of their training materials. These extremist networks are similar to the state security agencies that seek to destroy them: they provide basic military training to all recruits; they select promising candidates for advanced and specialized instruction; and they provide their members with specific tasks and responsibilities based on their level of training and expertise.

However, terrorists supplement their formal training with the personal intuition and local knowledge that come from practical experience. Over time, many militants develop the sort of cunning intelligence that is difficult to codify in knowledge-based artifacts. For this reason, the capture of senior terrorists matters, and governments can—at least temporarily—degrade the capabilities of extremist networks by apprehending their most experienced operatives. But even the highest of the "high-value" targets, Osama bin Laden, Ayman al-Zawahiri, are not irreplaceable. Al Qaeda has already adapted to the loss of high-level cadre by promoting midlevel militants and decentralizing its transnational operations. Meanwhile, the continuing spread of al Qaeda's terrorist knowledge to new generations of militants and supporters suggests that its expertise will endure, even if the network itself is ultimately destroyed.

NOTES

Previous versions of this chapter were presented at the Center for International Security and Cooperation (CISAC) at Stanford University, the Pacific Northwest Colloquia in International Security (PNCIS) at the University of Washington, and the forty-fifth annual convention of the International Studies Association in Montreal, Quebec, Canada, March 17–20, 2004. I would like to thank Lynn Eden, Karen Guttieri, Elizabeth Kier, Jonathan Mercer, Manus Midlarsky, Scott Sagan, Todd Sandler, Paul Stockton, and participants in the CISAC and PNCIS seminars for their thoughtful remarks.

1. Senate Subcommittee on International Operations and Terrorism, Committee on Foreign Relations, "Prepared Statement of Larry C. Johnson, former Deputy Director, Office of Counterterrorism, Department of State," *Al Qaeda International*, 107th Cong., 1st sess., 18 December 2001, 17.

2. Charles A. Russell, Leon J. Banker, Jr., and Bowman H. Miller, "Out–Inventing the Terrorist," in *Terrorism: Theory and Practice*, ed. Yonah Alexander, David Carlton, and Paul Wilkinson (Boulder, CO: Westview, 1979), 8–9; Edward Heyman and Edward Mickolus, "Observations on Why Violence Spreads," *International Studies Quarterly* 24, no. 2 (June 1980): 299–305; Edward Heyman and Edward Mickolus, "Imitation by Terrorists: Quantitative Approaches to the Study of Diffusion Patterns in Transnational Terrorism" in *Behavioral and Quantitative Perspectives on Terrorism*, ed. Yonah Alexander and John M. Gleason (New York: Pergamon Press, 1981), 175–228.

3. Bruce Hoffman, "Terrorism Trends and Prospects," in *Countering the New Terrorism*, ed. Ian O. Lesser et al. (Santa Monica, CA: RAND, 1999), 20; David E. Smith, *The Training of Terrorist Organizations*, CSC Report, www.globalsecurity.org/military/library/report/1995/SDE.htm [accessed 24 July 2003]; Patrick Seale, *Abu Nidal: A Gun for Hire* (New York: Random House, 1992), 20; John Swain and Tony Allen-Mills, "Fanatics Move on to Training Camps in Iran," *Sunday Times* (London), 14 April 2002; Jessica Stern, *The Ultimate Terrorists* (Cambridge, MA: Harvard University Press, 1999), 6–7; and David Tucker, *Skirmishes at the Edge of Empire: The United States and International Terrorism* (Westport, CT: Praeger, 1997), 35, 40.

4. National Commission on Terrorist Attacks Upon the United States, *The 9/11 Commission Report: Final Report of the National Commission on Terrorist Attacks Upon the United States* (New York: W.W. Norton, 2004), 61, 68, 240.

5. Rohan Gunaratna, quoted in Mark Baker, "11 September: Does Al-Qaeda Represent a Different Type of Terrorism? (Part 2)," *Radio Free Europe/Radio Liberty*, 2 September 2002. Available at www.rferl.org/features/2002/09/02092002142833.asp [accessed 8 June 2004].

6. Rohan Gunaratna, *Inside Al Qaeda* (New York: Columbia University Press, 2002), 71–73. Also, see Joint Intelligence Committee, "Written Statement for the Record of the Director of

Central Intelligence Before the Joint Inquiry Committee," *Joint Investigation*, 107th Cong., 2nd sess., October 17, 2002, http://intelligence.senate.gov/0210hrg/021017/tenet.pdf [accessed 26 December 2003], 7; and Jessica Stern, *Terror in the Name of God; Why Religious Militants Kill* (New York: Ecco, 2003), 260–261.

7. "Testimony of Stephen Gaudin," *United States of America v. Usama bin Laden et al.*, United States District Court, the Southern District of New York, 7 March 2001. http://news.findlaw.com/hdocs/docs/binladen/binladen030701tt.pdf [accessed June 3, 2004]: 1997–1998, 2003.

8. "Testimony of L'Houssaine Kherchtou," *United States of America v. Usama bin Laden et al.*, United States District Court, the Southern District of New York, 26 February 2001, http://cryptome.org/usa-v-ubl-10.htm [accessed 7 June 2004]; "Testimony of Ahmed Ressam," *United States of America v. Mokhtar Haouari*, United States District Court, the Southern District of New York, 3 July 2001, http://news.findlaw.com/hdocs/docs/haouari/ushaouari70301rassamtt.pdf [Accessed 4 June 2004].

9. Marc Sageman, *Understanding Terror Networks* (Philadelphia: University of Pennsylvania Press, 2004), 121; Stern, *Terror in the Name of God*, 260.

10. Bruce Hoffman, *Inside Terrorism* (New York: Columbia University Press, 1998), 116; Jessica Stern, "The Protean Enemy," *Foreign Affairs* 82, no. 4 (July–August 2003), www.foreignaffairs.org/20030701faessay15403/jessica-stern/the-protean-enemy.html [accessed 25 July 2003].

11. Eamon Collins with Mick McGovern, *Killing Rage* (London: Granta Books, 1997), 66.

12. Jerry Markon, "Jihad Trial Witness Says Paintball Was Training Drill," *Washington Post*, 12 February 2004, http://web.lexis-nexis.com/universe/ [accessed 27 May 2004], A16.

13. Author interview with former U.S. counterterrorism official (10 December 2004). Also see Peter L. Bergen, *Holy War, Inc.: Inside the Secret World of Osama bin Laden* (New York: Free Press, 2001), 127–133; and Gunaratna, *Inside Al Qaeda* 70–71.

14. *Declaration of Jihad Against the Country's Tyrants*, www.usdoj.gov/ag/trainingmanual .htm [accessed 1 October 2002].

15. Gunaratna, *Inside Al Qaeda*, 70.

16. Jason Burke, "Al Qaeda Launches Online Terrorist Manual," *Observer*, 18 January 2004. Available at www.guardian.co.uk/alqaida/story/0,12469,1125879,00.html [accessed 27 May 2004].

17. Sageman, *Understanding Terror Networks*, 53–54, 179.

18. Ben Venzke and Aimee Ibrahim, "Al Qaeda's Advice for Mujahideen in Iraq: Lessons Learned in Afghanistan," *IntelCenter Report V1.0*, 14 April 2003. Online at www.intelcenter.com.

19. For more on terrorists' use of the Internet, please see the chapters by Gabriel Weimann, Cindy Combs, and James Forest in this volume.

20. Judith Miller, "Qaeda Videos Seem to Show Chemical Tests," *New York Times*, 19 August 2002, nytimes.com/2002/08/19/international/asia/19CHEM.html [accessed 19 August 2002]; Nic Robertson, "Tapes Show al Qaeda Trained for Urban Jihad on West," *CNN*, 21 August 2002, cnn.com/2002/US/08/20/terror.tape.main/index.html [accessed 23 August 2002].

21. C. J. Chivers, "Instruction and Methods from Al Qaeda Took Root in North Iraq with Islamic Fighters," *New York Times*, 27 April 2003. Available at http://web.lexis-nexis.com/universe/ [accessed 27 May 2004], 26.

22. *Declaration of Jihad Against the Country's Tyrants*, "Second Lesson: Necessary Qualifications and Characteristics for the Organization's Member," www.usdoj.gov/ag/manualpart1_1.pdf [accessed 30 July 2003].

23. Seale, *Abu Nidal*, 20–25.

24. Collins, *Killing Rage*, 65.

25. Smith, *Training of Terrorist Organizations*.

26. "Three Years after 9/11: An Interview with Peter Bergen," *Jamestown Terrorism Monitor*, 2, no. 10, 13 September 2004.

27. Nic Robertson, "Tapes Show al Qaeda."

28. Bryan Peterson, "Inside Al Qaeda's Training Camps," *National Review*, 1 October 2002, www.nationalreview.com/comment/comment-preston100102.asp [accessed 2 June 2004].

29. National Commission on Terrorist Attacks Upon the United States, *The Four Flights*, Staff Statement No. 4, www.9-11commission.gov/hearings/hearing7/staff_statement_4.pdf [accessed 11 May 2004], 5. Also see National Commission on Terrorist Attacks Upon the United States, *Outline of the 9/11 Plot*, Staff Statement No. 16, www.911commission.gov/hearings/hearing12/staff_statement_16.pdf [accessed 16 June 2004], 9–10; and Gunaratna, *Inside Al Qaeda*, 107–108.

30. U.S. House of Representatives Resources Committee, Subcommittee on Forests and Forest Health, "Statement of James F. Jarboe, Domestic Terrorism Section Chief, Counterterrorism Division, Federal Bureau of Investigation: The Threat of Eco-Terrorism," 12 February 2002, www.fbi.gov/congress/congress02/jarboe021202.htm [accessed 10 May 2004].

31. Hoffman, *Inside Terrorism*, 179.

32. Hoffman, *Inside Terrorism*, 179.

33. Smith, *Training of Terrorist Organizations*.

34. Central Intelligence Agency, unclassified memorandum, 14 June 2002.

35. "Direct Testimony of Jamal Ahmed Al-Fadl," *United States of America v. Usama Bin Laden et al. Defendants*, United States District Court, Southern District of New York, 6 February 2001, http://news.findlaw.com/hdocs/docs/binladen/binladen20601tt.pdf [accessed 2 June 2004], 316.

36. Statement of Facts, *United States of America v. Iyman Faris*, Eastern District of Virginia (no date), http://news.findlaw.com/hdocs/docs/faris/usfaris603sof.pdf [accessed 23 September 2003]. Also see Eric Lichtblau and Monica Davey, "Man in Brooklyn Bridge Plot Spurred Early F.B.I. Interest," *New York Times*, 21 June 2003, www.nytimes.com/2003/06/21/national/21TERR.html [accessed 24 June 2003]; U.S. Department of Justice, Office of the Attorney General, "Prepared Remarks of Attorney General John Ashcroft," 19 June 2003, www.usdoj.gov/ag/speeches/2003/remarks_061903.htm [accessed 24 June 2003]; U.S. Department of Justice, "Ohio Truck Driver Pleads Guilty to Providing Material Support to al Qaeda," 19 June 2003, www.usdoj.gov/opa/pr/2003/June/03_crm_368.htm [accessed 24 June 2003].

37. *Declaration of Jihad Against the Country's Tyrants*, "Eleventh Lesson: Espionage (1) Information-Gathering Using Open Methods," www.usdoj.gov/ag/manualpart1_3.pdf [Accessed 20 August 2003].

38. *Declaration of Jihad Against the Country's Tyrants*, "Twelfth Lesson: Espionage (2) Information-Gathering Using Covert Methods," www.usdoj.gov/ag/manualpart1_4.pdf [accessed 20 August 2003].

39. *Declaration of Jihad Against the Country's Tyrants*, "Twelfth Lesson."

40. Gregory L. Vistica and Daniel Klaidman, "Inside the FBI and CIA's joint battle to roll up Osama bin Laden's international network," *Newsweek*, 19 October 1998, 46. Available at http://web.lexis-nexis.com/universe/document [accessed 12 December 2003]. Also see Senate Subcommittee on International Operations and Terrorism, Committee on Foreign Relations, "Testimony of J. T. Caruso, Acting Assistant Director, CounterTerrorism Division, Federal Bureau of Investigation," *Al Qaeda International*, 107th Cong., 1st sess., 18 December 2001, www.fbi.gov/congress/congress01/caruso121801.htm [accessed 2 June 2004].

41. Bruce Hoffman, "Terrorism Trends and Prospects," in *Countering the New Terrorism*, ed. Ian O. Lesser et al. (Santa Monica: RAND, 1999), 34, fn. 70.

42. Senate Select Committee on Intelligence and the U. S. House Permanent Select Committee on Intelligence, "Prepared Testimony of Paul Wolfowitz," *Joint Investigation*, 107th Cong., 2nd sess., 19 September 2002) www.senate.gov/~intelligence [accessed 3 October 2002]. Also see Judith Miller, interview with Margaret Warner, "Al Qaeda's Web," *NewsHour with Jim Lehrer*, 25 September 2001. Available at www.pbs.org/newshour/bb/terrorism/july-dec01/al_qaeda.html [accessed 22 August 2003].

43. Don Van Natta Jr. and Desmond Butler, "How Tiny Swiss Cellphone Chips Helped Track Global Terror Web," *New York Times*, 4 March 2004, www.nytimes.com/2004/03/04/international/Europe/04PHON.html [accessed 4 March 2004].

44. National Commission on Terrorist Attacks Upon the United States, *Outline of the 9/11 Plot*, Staff Statement No. 16, www.9-11commission.gov/hearings/hearing12/staff_statement_16 .pdf [accessed 16 June 2004]: 12–16; National Commission on Terrorist Attacks, *9/11 Commission Report*, 225, 246.

45. Walter Enders and Todd Sandler, "The Effectiveness of Antiterrorism Policies: A Vector-Autoregression-Intervention Analysis," *American Political Science Review* 87, no. 4 (December 1993): 829–844.

46. Gregory A. Raymond, "The Evolving Strategies of Political Terrorism," in *The New Global Terrorism: Characteristics, Causes, Controls*, ed. Charles W. Kegley (Upper Saddle River: Prentice Hall, 2003), 83.

47. Hoffman, *Inside Terrorism*, 178–179.

48. Hoffman, *Inside Terrorism*, 180–181.

49. Hoffman, *Inside Terrorism*, 182.

3

+

Organizational Learning and Terrorist Groups

Horacio R. Trujillo and Brian A. Jackson

Nearly every day, violent groups in a range of countries engage in acts that can be characterized as terrorism—the systematic and premeditated use or threatened use of violence by nonstate groups or individuals to further political or social objectives. Depending on the motivation and goals of the terrorists, these attacks can be aimed at symbolic sites, key political or economic institutions, government officials, or even civilian populations at large. By definition, acts of terrorism are intended to have a coercive impact on an audience beyond simply those individuals directly affected by the attacks. By shocking and instilling fear in entire populations, terrorist groups seek to influence the policies of states or other entities that they could not otherwise directly impact.[1]

Any use of terror by any person or group is unquestionably a cause for concern. However, the potential destructiveness of various terrorist attacks still varies in accordance with the strategic, operational, and tactical capabilities of their perpetrators. While one terrorist group may only have the capability or desire to carry out an attack at a local level, another may be able to stage operations that shake the psychological foundation and resolve of the international community. Because of this, it has long been a goal of counterterrorism analysis to understand what such groups are capable of doing, whether in terms of the targets that they might threaten, the potential frequency of operations that they might execute, their ability to recruit, or the sources from which they might obtain intelligence, materiel, and financial support.

Similarly, in the face of counterterrorist efforts to disrupt terrorist groups' activities, apprehend their members, and degrade their capabilities, not all groups simply succumb to such measures. Instead, they learn and adapt. In response to whatever efforts might be undertaken to degrade terrorists' capabilities—from heightened law enforcement to target-hardening or preemptive interdiction—terrorist groups act to protect and improve their capabilities. They use new weapons. They adopt new tactics. They change their group and command structures. They select new targets. They even develop new organizational objectives or missions. As a result, counterterrorism efforts face an ever-evolving challenge since, in a rapidly changing world with a dynamic security environment, any terrorist group must make itself a moving target in order to survive.

Simply noting that terrorist groups alter the ways in which they operate, however, does not adequately inform law enforcement and security agencies concerned with countering terrorism. Recognizing change provides only a small part of the insight needed to address and thwart these groups' efforts. To truly prepare ourselves to combat terrorist threats, we must also understand *how* these groups learn and change. When it seeks out a new tactic or operational capability, a terrorist group must work to develop and build it—organizational change does not happen automatically or effortlessly. In planning operations, selecting targets, and applying weapons or other technologies, terrorist groups must gather necessary strategic and tactical information, combine it with their past experience and previous ways of operating, and implement whatever changes are needed to put it to use. Understanding this learning process can both improve our knowledge of terrorist groups' current capabilities and help us to predict how those capabilities may evolve or shift in the future.

Focusing on this question—not on *what* terrorists do, but *how* they learn to do it—could suggest new strategies for degrading the capabilities of extremist groups and reducing the effectiveness of their future attacks. Toward this end, in the following sections we present:

- an overall definition of organizational learning for the study of terrorism,
- a model describing stages of learning within terrorist organizations,
- a typology of terrorist group learning, and
- a discussion of factors that can influence such groups' ability to learn effectively.

We conclude the chapter with a discussion of how organizational learning can shed light on the terrorist groups' strategic and tactical activities, in which we illustrate with examples some of the distinctions we draw in the preceding sections.

DEFINING ORGANIZATIONAL LEARNING
FOR COUNTERTERRORISM

For the concept of organizational learning to be useful in terrorism analysis, it must be clear what is meant by the term. Drawing from the considerable literature on learning in organizations, we define organizational learning as *a process through which the members of an organization develop new knowledge about their actions and outcomes, share this knowledge throughout the organization, incorporate it into the routines of the organization, and store the knowledge in an organizational memory.*[2]

As implied by this definition, an organization's learning is more than simply the sum of the individual learning of each of the group's members.[3] This can give organizations unique advantages in the creation and application of new knowledge over individuals acting alone. As Argyris and Schön (1978)[4] have noted, organizations are not capable of learning independently of all individuals, but they are capable of learning without any one particular individual. This insight allows us to recognize that organizational learning, unlike that of individuals, not only can persist in the absence of any one person but can also grow more rapidly and expansively than that of any single individual alone. This lesson is supported by the work of other theorists who have identified that organizations are much more effective than individuals at continually creating and absorbing new knowledge.[5]

The observation that learning by organizations differs significantly from that of individuals should not be taken too far, however. Researchers have cautioned that it is important not to attribute human characteristics, such as thought, to organizations.[6] Similarly, focusing too greatly on an organization as a single unit can also risk underemphasizing the importance of individuals' contributions to the collective organizations' learning processes. For example, Garratt (1987)[7] points out that in actuality a relatively small number of persons usually have significant influence over the strategic decisions of an organization and, as such, individual leaders' strategic learning may therefore provide a good approximation of how their organizations behave and adapt to their environment. In this respect, the organization plays a critical role as a system that influences, preserves, and distributes the learning of individuals, but is still dependent upon individuals.[8]

Together, such lessons from the organizational learning literature emphasize not only the importance but also the potential complexity of understanding learning within terrorist groups. Group learning is more than individual learning, but the role of specific individuals is still critical. Yet, the learning of individuals cannot be maximally exploited without effective ways to distribute and store such learning so that it is available to the rest of the group. As a result, in the study of terrorist groups and the design of counterterrorist policies, analysts must consider the various stages through which organizational learning progresses, as well as recognize how group characteristics can impact the effectiveness of the learning process.

ORGANIZATIONAL LEARNING AS PROCESSING OF INFORMATION

In our consideration of how terrorist groups learn, we propose a model of organizational learning as an information process. We find this model particularly useful because it identifies four distinct stages through which information must pass—acquisition, distribution, interpretation, and retention—for organizational learning to take place.[9] As such, we believe that the model provides a clear framework for understanding organizational learning within terrorist groups. Furthermore, by decomposing the learning process, the model also suggests a guide for considering what measures might be most effective at degrading terrorist capabilities by specifically targeting certain stages of the learning process.

Acquisition

The acquisition of information occurs in four general ways—through *congenital knowledge, direct experience, vicarious experience,* and *strategic learning actions. Congenital knowledge* is the knowledge that organizations inherit from their original leaders and members. Examples of the use of congenital knowledge by some terrorist groups include the experience brought to many Islamic fundamentalist groups by individuals' experience in the conflict in Afghanistan against the Soviets or the experience possessed by the initial members of the Provisional Irish Republican Army from their earlier experience in the Republican movement. This form of information acquisition will be most relevant to a terrorist group early in its development; as the organization matures and requires new knowledge to survive in a dynamic environment, other forms of knowledge acquisition will become more important. *Direct experience,* or "learning by doing," can occur intentionally, through experiments, but more often occurs unintentionally and unsystematically as groups carry out particular actions or activities.[10] In terms of intentional direct experience, experiments can take various forms, including both regularly executed activities aimed at uncovering new opportunities and more complex and unproven demonstration projects designed to test new ideas. A range of terrorist organizations have carried out such activities in their development and improvement of explosive devices and other weapons systems.

In addition to these internally focused means of acquiring information, organizations also capture information from external sources. The less demanding of these activities is the acquisition of information by monitoring other groups, which we refer to as *vicarious experience*. While this method of acquiring information might appear to be an obvious and even simple technique, it can be both more complex and more challenging than initially perceived. Terrorists can undoubtedly glean insight from other terrorist groups' activities, whether by actively monitoring other groups or passively becoming aware of other groups' activities through public reports. If an organization engages in either of these strategies correctly, it could in fact learn lessons from other examples, such as from drug cartels or counterterrorism agencies themselves. For groups in stable conflict with security forces—such as the Provisional Irish Republican Army, Hizballah in Lebanon, or the Tamil Tigers in Sri Lanka—observation of the activities of counterterrorism organizations has been an important component of the groups' learning activities.

At the same time, however, it is likely that terrorist groups, like other organizations, face considerable challenges in translating the insights they gain from observing others, even other terrorist groups. We suggest that the most important of these challenges stems from the distinction between *tacit knowledge* (generally unrecorded expertise such as internal "know-how" developed by individuals or organizational knowledge about how techniques or technologies are best used for particular purposes) and *explicit knowledge* (information or data that can be readily written down or embodied in physical objects). Simply put, while much terrorist activity can be characterized as explicit knowledge, in that many of the tactics used by various groups are the same as those used by other groups (such as suicide bombing or airline hijacking), the actual execution of these activities depends heavily upon the tacit knowledge of *how* to actually execute such acts effectively. Because it is more difficult for groups to translate and exploit tacit knowledge, with direct experience oftentimes being necessary for groups to develop this tacit knowledge even after their acquisition of information from an external source,[11] terrorist groups cannot as easily replicate other groups' tactics as might be suspected. This challenge can be made even more difficult when groups suffer from what has been termed the "not invented here" syndrome, referring to organizations' inability to meaningfully exploit lessons learned from external sources.[12] Because terrorist organizations, in particular, are often suspicious of ideas that do not originate from within their trusted memberships, this phenomenon cannot be overlooked.

Finally, terrorist groups, like other organizations, can also acquire information by engaging explicitly in *strategic learning actions*, such as internal research and development, technology acquisition, or cooperation with other agents. One recent example of this type of activity is the reported collaboration between the Revolutionary Armed Forces of Colombia (FARC) and the Provisional Irish Republican Army (PIRA), as part of which PIRA members have allegedly provided training to FARC rebels.[13] Aum Shinrikyo, the apocalyptic cult that carried out an attack on the Tokyo subway using the chemical agent sarin, engaged in considerable internal research and development activities. Even this type of information acquisition, however—including the outright acquisition of technology, such as new weaponry—can be difficult to translate into learning that is more than superficial and can actually generate practical improvements in how a group operates.[14]

Distribution

As noted earlier, information acquisition is a necessary but not sufficient condition for organizational learning. Information must also be distributed, interpreted, and stored for organizational learning to occur. Distribution, in particular, plays a critical role in advancing the learning process because the more broadly that information is distributed within an organization the more likely it is to be interpreted and to be interpreted in multiple ways, which can increase the likelihood that it can be applied effectively within the organization. Distribution also plays a central role in facilitating the retention of information and increasing its availability for later use. In this fashion, distribution critically lowers the risk that an organization's learning will deteriorate.[15] Many terrorist organizations utilize a variety of distribution modes to disseminate information among their members. Training activities, such as Islamic groups' use of camps in Afghanistan for many years, are a key mode of passing on military skills to group members who may later disperse to join cells across a group's entire operations area.

Interpretation

Interpretation is the most important step in the organizational learning process. Without interpretation, information alone has no meaning.[16] Factors that influence a group's ability to effectively interpret information include the breadth of distribution of the information within the group, as mentioned above; the extent to which different members of groups share uniform frames of reference;[17] and the richness and feedback speed of the media through which the information is communicated to the group and within the group.[18] As the capacity of groups to interpret information within a certain time interval is a critical variable in the learning process, the manner in which terrorist groups seek to safeguard their knowledge from law enforcement officials is an important constraint on the groups' abilities. If they cannot maintain security without bottlenecking critical information within the group, their ability to interpret information will be degraded, which can lead to discordant or ineffective learning efforts.[19]

Beyond judging and adopting new behaviors, a key part of a group's interpretive efforts must include consideration of when old behaviors must be discarded as ineffective or outmoded. We consider this process, which some parts of the academic literature term *unlearning*, as a part of the learning process.[20] Such unlearning can be particularly relevant to a terrorist organization as the design of counterterrorist and law enforcement activities is frequently based on patterns that can be drawn from groups' past actions and experience.

Retention

Finally, in order to complete the organizational learning process, groups must store the information that they have acquired and interpreted in order to access it in the future. Most often, especially among newer organizations, learning is stored almost exclusively in the individual memories of members of groups and is, as a result, simply a product of information distribution. This is, as can be expected, a rather shallow manner of maintaining information that is highly susceptible to deterioration.[21] Significant amounts of information are stored by terrorist groups in this manner by distributing information through training (discussed above). Beyond this method, however, there are a number of ways in which organizations can store their learning. In particular, language, rituals, symbols, and other forms of culture can store organizational knowledge. Organizational structure, as well as written or unwritten operating guidelines, can also help organizations to institutionalize learning. And, lastly, some groups can also exploit physical storage options as well, such as storing information in computer information systems or other repositories. As the range of terrorist manuals that have been captured by counterterrorist organizations or publicly circulated on the Internet demonstrates, these groups have often chosen combinations of these approaches to store information in written (and readily transferable) resources.

INCREMENTAL AND TRANSFORMATIONAL LEARNING

While the previous discussion introduced a general model for analyzing the stages of learning of terrorist groups, it is also important to recognize the two distinct types of organizational learning through which such groups can evolve—*incremental learning* and *transformational learning*—

with very different consequences.[22] Incremental learning is the changing of repetitive routines, such as the tracking and correction of errors in specific activities, within the existing boundaries, rules, and norms of an organization. In other words, incremental learning takes place as terrorist groups learn how to do activities they already carry out more effectively. While transformational learning can result from adaptations to remedy errors in specific activities, transformational learning entails a philosophical and/or strategic reevaluation of the mission or overall objectives of the organization rather than simple adaptations to routine tactical or operational activities. In other words, the transformational learning of a terrorist group occurs when the group not only evaluates how to do a previously identified activity more effectively, but also reconsiders what activities to engage in and why, with a focus on the long-term effects of the change on the whole of the organization. This reevaluation can be caused by significant shifts in a group's environment that render its current practices ineffective—it must change to survive—or because it recognizes a potential opportunity that requires significant changes to pursue.

Incremental learning is characterized by functional rationality and process improvement, and can be seen in the classic example of the Irish Republican Army's improvement of its explosive devices in response to British countermeasures or, in a more recent example, in the Iraqi insurgents' improvisation of new explosive devices and roadblock strategies.[23] Transformational learning, in comparison, is the innovation of entirely new processes, objectives, or organizational structures. For example, we can identify both al Qaeda's exploitation of a multinational network of semiautonomous cells and its use of airplanes as bombs as outcomes of more transformational rather than simply incremental learning.[24]

Of course, the division between incremental and transformational learning is not always clear, especially when one considers that the end result of incremental change over time can actually be transformational change. Nevertheless, the distinction is a valuable one, as it allows us to focus our attentions more closely on identifying and analyzing those cases that seem likely to have the greatest impact on an organization.[25]

DETERMINANTS OF ORGANIZATIONAL LEARNING

Though all terrorist groups learn to some extent, there are significant differences in that ability from group to group. Based on insights drawn from others' research on a wide range of organizations, we have identified four groups of factors that are key determinants of these differences. While we have mentioned some of these determinants in passing in the previous discussion, the following sections discuss each group in detail and suggest factors affecting their importance to different types of terrorist organizations.

Structure

The structure of authority and communication within an organization is a critical driver of its capacity to acquire, interpret, distribute, and store information. We focus on two aspects of structure in particular: the extent of *hierarchy or centralization within group command and control processes* and the *robustness of communications systems* within organizations. First, a range of studies have suggested that more hierarchical organizations frequently learn less effectively, due in part to the loss of information as it is transmitted through and screened by the different organizational levels.[26] This implies that, in contrast, less structured terrorist operations, such as the radical environmentalist movement, might be more capable of adapting quickly to internal pressures or changes in the environment. On the other hand, the multilevel redundancy of knowledge within hierarchical organizations, such as the Tamil Tigers, can make them more resilient to deterioration of accumulated knowledge, and, because of their formally defined communications paths, they can be less susceptible to some types of information distribution failures.

Importantly, it should be noted that it is not necessary that organizations be either centralized or decentralized or that groups cannot benefit from or suffer from characteristics of both structural configurations. As Podolny and Page (1998)[27] note, both more structured hierarchies and more loosely organized groups can be appropriately described as forms of networks, and, as such, groups can blend strengths and weaknesses of these different structures depending on where they position themselves along the spectrum of network organizational types.[28] Today, the most well-known example is al Qaeda, which has seemingly been able to reap the benefits of both centralization and hierarchy in accumulating and diffusing knowledge while also promoting rapid experimentation by local cells. Such hybrid organizations, however, can also be more difficult to control and can demand more time dedicated to organizational management.

The communications mechanisms within an organization can also facilitate (or impede) organizational learning. In this context, communications should be understood as an expansive concept, which includes explicit training imparted to members, manuals that codify organizational values and practices, implicitly shared operating routines, formal and informal meetings of members, as well as technical infrastructure for communications (i.e., fixed and mobile telephony, radios, Internet systems).

The more robust a group's communications mechanisms, the more capable the organization can be in acquiring, interpreting, distributing, and storing information.

Culture

As organizational culture is oftentimes difficult to define in concrete terms, previous studies have identified various traits and disturbances rooted in an organization's culture that can facilitate or impede learning. We identify two interrelated and mutually reinforcing cultural traits that are conducive to organizational learning—*organizational interest in learning* and *organizational tolerance for risk-taking*. The first of these, organizational interest in learning, is driven primarily by the priority that an organization's leadership places on seeking out new opportunities and options, including undertaking intentional efforts to acquire and distribute new knowledge. The second, tolerance for risk, characterizes the prevailing attitude of leaders and members of an organization toward experimenting with new and even unproven practices. The more an organization is interested in learning and willing to take risks, the more capable the organization is of adapting to exploit new opportunities and avoid emergent threats. For example, in the face of particular types of terrorist attacks, security planners will introduce hardening measures designed to thwart them. A terrorist organization that is unwilling to try new things—transition from placed bombs to mortars, for example— would find its capability significantly eroded over time and its ability to strike desirable targets reduced. In contrast, a group that was willing to experiment, even though transitioning to a new weapon might result in failed operations in the beginning, might eventually circumvent the effect of the new hardening measures.

On the other hand, some elements of an organization's culture can be viewed as "learning disturbances"—traits that impede learning, such as *role constraints, situational and fragmented learning,* and *opportunistic learning*. Role constraints arise from rigid task assignments that limit the ability of individuals within organizations to process information appropriately and, as a result, they inhibit the organization's capacity to transform new information to actionable knowledge and capabilities. In cases of situational and fragmented learning, group culture does not lead to new knowledge gained by individual members being disseminated or stored in such a way that it can be shared meaningfully with and enhance the capabilities of other members. Finally, even when there are appropriate mechanisms in place for storing and distributing organizational knowledge, group culture may result in members not using them. In that case, opportunistic learning occurs in which individuals consciously bypass the prevailing organizational processes they perceive as inadequate or not in their interests and, as a result, although individuals may still learn, the organization does not.[29]

Knowledge Resources

Third, the learning potential of organizations is also highly dependent upon what we refer to as their knowledge resources. This includes the *availability of individuals and other sources of learning*, and the *absorptive capacity* of these resources. As mentioned earlier, a significant determinant of an organization's ability to learn is the degree to which it is appropriately connected to its environment and to similar organizations. The greater the degree of connectivity, the higher the learning potential of the group. Absorptive capacity, or the degree to which an organization is capable of acquiring and interpreting new information, is a product of the skills, and especially the subject-area or technology-specific expertise, of its members. Without sufficient absorptive capacity, terrorist groups will be limited in their capacity to learn regardless of the rate of information acquisition or capacity for storing knowledge.

Environment

Finally, the environments in which terrorist groups operate also affect their capacity for organizational learning. Several observers have linked *environmental uncertainty*, such as significant shifts in the rate of change of an organization's environment or intensity of the competition it faces, with the extent and pace of organizational learning.[30] Al Qaeda's increased willingness to experiment with different configurations of its attack teams in the face of increasing pressure from security forces provides a simple illustration of how greater environmental uncertainty can spur organizational experimentation. For example, in its attempt to explode trucks filled with chemical agents at three sites in Jordan, al Qaeda planned to employ separate drivers for the first time for transporting the chemical-laden trucks into the country and for the actual delivery of the truck bombs to their targets.[31]

Others have identified how organizations can also respond to operational errors and *crises in the environment* as opportunities for sometimes-dramatic learning.[32] These types of environmental factors, which are not under the control of terrorist groups, can significantly influence their strategic and tactical adaptation. This idea has found considerable development in Bruce Barcott's suggestion that James C. Davies' J-curve theory of revolution can help to explain terrorist groups' increased activities and particularly their willingness to experiment with new tactics.[33] For example, Bron Taylor links the founding of the radical environmentalist group Earth First! with the Reagan Administration's dramatic reversal of environmental protection policies adopted under the Carter Administration and the initiation of major firebombings by the related Earth Liberation Front to shifts in federal logging policy.[34] Building an understanding of how terrorist organizations react to environmental change could therefore represent an important component of understanding how these groups learn and the threat that they represent.

APPLYING ORGANIZATIONAL LEARNING THEORY TO TERRORIST GROUPS: LEVELS OF GROUP LEARNING

Finally, in actual application, these broad concepts of organizational learning can be used to assess the adaptation of terrorist groups at several levels, from overall group strategy to the most detailed tactical level. At the highest level, the foundation of a terrorist group's activities is its contextualization of reality in a particular religious, cultural, and/or philosophical worldview. The group combines this contextualization with pragmatic expectations of how international and domestic sociopolitical systems operate and how they might react to various acts of terror in order to identify objectives and actions for the group. In the case of the Provisional Irish Republican Army, for example, the particular religious-nationalist interpretation of the history of British involvement in Ireland and other regions fueled certain assumptions about the potential effectiveness and desirability of armed resistance. More recently, particular interpretations of Islam and assessments of history were critical to framing al Qaeda's expectations of how the United States and its allies would react to the September 11 attacks.

Learning at this strategic level can even lead groups to redefine or add to the types of activities in which they engage, some of which can encompass nonviolent and even beneficent efforts. For example, strategic learning has led some terrorist groups to complement their violent activities with "legitimate" political wings or even programs to provide educational, health care, and other social services to the communities in which they are based or from which they draw support.[35] In this way, the interpretation stage of the learning process plays a particularly critical role in the development of terrorist groups' strategies and in thus directing the actions that they will ultimately choose to carry out.[36]

At the other end of the spectrum is tactical learning, or the efforts that terrorist groups take to collect detailed, factual information necessary for carrying out specific activities.[37] This learning is the basic development of specific knowledge needed for such routines as identifying targets, planning attacks, or identifying risks to the operation. Depending on a group's culture and leadership, the organization will emphasize certain learning requirements and processes, including what type of knowledge is needed, how it is to be collected (and potentially distributed and stored), how much information and what type of information is required before executing an attack, and how the knowledge is expected to influence group planning and decision making.[38]

Finally, operational learning is the development of organizational knowledge and capabilities that bridge strategy and tactics. As such, operational learning largely defines the broad range of terrorist groups' routines or bodies of practice. These routines can include how targets are prioritized, tactics are decided upon, and activities are evaluated. One particularly important body of practice for terrorist groups is the collection of routines that are followed to prepare attacks—covering such questions as how far in advance are attackers trained, to what extent are they trained, and what types of weapons a group will use and how it will use them.[39]

CONCLUSION

To provide a context for considering organizational learning in terrorist organizations, this chapter set out to provide an overall definition of that process and identify some of the variables and distinctions that can describe and explain individual terrorist organization's efforts to learn and change. Analysts of terrorism and terrorist group behavior face a complex world: terrorist groups have adopted a broad variety of structures, operated in a wide range of environments, and chosen to pursue their unique goals through a diverse mix of tactics and operational approaches. To protect the public from the threat of these adaptive terrorist organizations, our policies must take into account and, even more so, anticipate this adaptive behavior.

With this in mind, we have sought to identify how terrorist organizations generally learn, in the hopes of facilitating a common dialogue about terrorist group learning and adaptation and appropriate policy responses. It is our hope that the framework presented here can offer this opportunity for analyzing generally the learning behavior of terrorist groups while at the same time allowing for consideration of the critical differences that distinguish terrorist groups and their unique adaptations. The four stages of learning described—information acquisition, distribution, interpretation, and retention—are general enough to apply to all terrorist organizations across the ideological spectrum. The various classes of determinants of learning, however, provide a way to lay out the differences among groups that impact their ability to carry out any learning process.

Beyond simply understanding group behavior, approaches focused on terrorist groups' organizational learning activities could also suggest novel counterterrorism strategies. From the strategic to the tactical level, the nature of a group's organizational routines defines its actions. As a result, learning processes that alter those routines could provide new opportunities to influence a group's behavior and undermine its activities. Strategies aimed at particular learning processes, such as interfering with or influencing terrorist surveillance and intelligence gathering, have been appreciated and pursued for some time. At other points on a terrorist group's "spectrum of learning" different opportunities may exist to counter or skew the progress or outcome of its activities. Determining whether such actions can offer only incremental improvements to counterterrorism efforts or enable a more transformational change in the way we approach defending society against terrorism remains to be seen. But overall, as described in the subsequent chapters of this volume, how knowledge is captured and transferred within and between terrorist organizations is an important focus of continued research.

NOTES

This project was supported in part by Grant No. 2003-IJ-CX-1022, awarded by the National Institute of Justice, Office of Justice Programs, U.S. Department of Justice. Points of view in this document are those of the authors and do not necessarily represent the official position or policies of the U.S. Department of Justice.

1. The words "terrorism" and "terrorist" are inherently charged and have particular connotations in political discourse. Different sides of a political conflict typically use such terms differently depending on whether they agree or disagree with the goals and objectives of the nonstate group carrying out violent acts. For our purposes, we focus on the *tactic* of terrorism—as defined in the text. As a result, our use of terms such as "terrorists" or "terrorist group" should be read as shorthand for persons or groups choosing to utilize the tactic of terrorism, regardless of the objectives of these actors.

2. This definition is a composite of others that can be found in the organizational learning literature. Ours draws in particular from that of Barnett (no date) cited in Lipshitz et al. (2002) which defines organizational learning as "an experience-based process through which knowledge about action-outcome relationships develops, is encoded in routines, is embedded in organizational memory and changes collective behavior." See Raanan Lipshitz, Micha Popper, and Victor J. Friedman, "A Multifacet Model of Organizational Learning," *Journal of Applied Behavioral Science* 38, no. 1 (2002).

3. Two brief citations from the literature on organizational learning distill the argument of recognizing organizational learning as distinct from individual learning. The first, from Romme and Dillen (1997), emphasizes the nature of organizational learning as focusing on the change of shared beliefs and collective behaviors of members of a group: "Organizations do not have brains but do have cognitive systems and memories at their disposal, through which certain modes of behavior, mental models, norms and values are retained." The second, from Easterby-Smith et al. (2000), emphasizes the supra-individual character of organizational learning: "Members [of an organization] come and go, and leadership changes,

but organizations' memories preserve certain behaviors, mental maps, norms and values over time." See Georges Romme and R. Dillen, "Mapping the Landscape of Organizational Learning," *European Management Journal* 15, no. 1 (1997): 68–78; and Mark Easterby-Smith, Mary Crossan and Davide Nicolini, "Organizational Learning: Debates Past, Present and Future," *Journal of Management Studies* 37, no. 6 (2000): 783–796.

4. Chris Argyris and Donald Schön, *Organizational Learning: A Theory of Action Perspective* (Reading, MA: Addison-Wesley, 1978).

5. Romme and Dillen, "Mapping the Landscape," 68–78.

6. James G. March and Johan P. Olsen, "The Uncertainty of the Past: Organizational Learning Under Ambiguity," *European Journal of Policy Review* 3, no. 2 (1975): 147–171.

7. Robert Garratt, *The Learning Organization* (London: Collins, 1987).

8. Brian Hedberg, "How Organizations Learn and Unlearn," in *Handbook of Organizational Design,* edited by Paul C. Nyström and William H. Starbuck (Oxford: Oxford University Press, 1981), 3–27; Paul Shrivastava, "A Typology of Organizational Learning Systems," *Journal of Management Studies* 20 (1983), 7–28; and C. Marlene Fiol and Marjorie A. Lyles, "Organizational Learning," *Academy of Management Review* 10 (1985): 803–813.

9. Romme and Dillen, "Mapping the Landscape of Organizational Learning," present a brief but detailed treatment of organizational learning as an information process, from which some of this material has been adapted.

10. Richard M. Cyert and James G. March, *A Behavioral Theory of the Firm* (Englewood Cliffs, NJ: Prentice Hall, 1963).

11. Kevin K. Jones, "Competing to Learn in Japan," *McKinsey Quarterly* 1 (1992): 45–57.

12. David A. Garvin, "Building a Learning Organization," *Harvard Business Review* 71 (July–August 1993): 78–91.

13. Adam Ward, "The IRA's Foreign Links: Externalising its Expertise?" *IISS Strategic Comments* 9, no. 5 (2003).

14. Jones, "Competing to Learn."

15. George P. Huber, "Organizational Learning: The Contributing Process and the Literatures," *Organizational Science* 2 (1991): 88–115.

16. Huber, "Organizational Learning."

17. Daniel H. Kim, "The Link Between Individual and Organizational Learning," *Sloan Management Review* 35, no. 1 (1993): 37–50.

18. Huber, "Organizational Learning."

19. Richard L. Daft and Robert H. Lengal, "Organizational Information Requirements: Media richness and structural design," *Management Science* 32 (1986): 554–571.

20. Brian Hedberg, "How Organizations Learn and Unlearn"; and Michael E. McGill and John W. Slocum, Jr., "Unlearning the Organization," *Organization Dynamics* 22 (1993): 67–79. It should be noted that some researchers use the term unlearning to refer to the maladaptation of organizations that results in unwanted or less effective outcomes (see Crossan et al., 1995). We have chosen not to adopt this convention since it is our belief that defining learning as a positive process, and unlearning as simply a mode of learning, simplifies the analysis. From the perspective adopted in this paper, maladaptive learning, rather than unlearning, would be the result of a group attempting to learn but doing it very poorly.

21. Kathleen Carley, "Organizational Learning and Personnel Turnover," *Organization Science* 3 (1992): 20–46; and Daniel H. Kim, "Link between individual and organizational learning."

22. We utilize incremental and transformational learning as roughly equivalent to "single-loop" and "double-loop" learning as discussed in the academic literature on organizational learning. We believe that the distinction originally drawn by Argyris and Schön (1978) is a valuable one, which we borrow from. See Argyris and Schön, *Organizational Learning.*

23. Bruce Hoffman, "Terrorism Trends and Prospects," in *Countering the New Terrorism,* edited by Ian O. Lesser et al. (Santa Monica: RAND, 1999), 7–38; and Rowan Scarborough, "Iraqi guerrillas devise new tactics as Americans fine tune techniques," *Washington Times,* 31 July 2003.

24. John Arquilla and David Ronfeldt, *Networks and Netwars* (Santa Monica: RAND, 2001).

25. Argyris and Schön, *Organizational Learning,* 1978; and Peter Senge, *The Fifth Discipline: The Art and Practice of the Learning Organization* (New York: Doubleday, 1990). In both of these publications, the authors note that most organizations do reasonably well with incremental learning but not with transformational learning.

26. David M. Schweiger, Tugrul Atamer and Roland Calori, "Transnational project teams and networks: making the multinational organization more effective," *Journal of World Business* 38 (2003): 127–140.

27. Joel Podolny and Karen Page, "Network Forms of Organization," *Annual Review of Sociology* 24 (1998): 57–76.

28. For a review of network forms of organization, see Podolny and Page, "Network Forms of Organization."

29. Romme and Dillen, "Mapping the Landscape."

30. Mark Dodgson, "Organizational Learning: A review of some literature," *Organizational Studies* 14 (1993): 375–394; and Garvin, "Building a Learning Organization."

31. DEBKAfile, "Al Qaeda goes regional: Basra, Riyadh bomb blasts coordinated with thwarted chemical strike in Amman," 2004, www.debka.com [accessed April 21, 2004].

32. Christophe Roux-Dufort and Emmanuel Metais, "Building Core Competencies in Crisis Management through Organizational Learning: The Case of the French Nuclear Power Producer," *Technological Forecasting and Social Change* (1999), 113–127. We utilize the definition of crisis as presented by Roux-Dufort and Metais (1999): a crisis is an event that falls outside the normal routines of the organization and necessitates a reexamination of the status quo, by disturbing the elements that represent the very foundation of the firm and the raison d'être of its members.

33. Bruce Barcott, "From Tree-Hugger to Terrorist," *New York Times,* 7 April 2002. This theory suggests that revolution is most likely to occur within a particular social order when a prolonged period of social progress is followed by a short period of sharp reversal. From this foundation it is but a small step to translate this theory to the realm of terrorism, as explained by Christopher Hewitt: "When your hopes have been raised and you feel there's a chance for victory through legitimate political means, you'd be foolish to resort to terrorism. Terrorism is a high-cost option, a weapon of the weak, a tool of last resort. But if your movement suddenly collapses or suffers political reversals, then some activists will be tempted to go for terrorism" (Barcott, "From Tree-Hugger to Terrorist").

34. Bron Taylor, "Religion, Violence and Radical Environmentalism: From Earth First! to the Unabomber to the Earth Liberation Front," *Terrorism and Political Violence* 10, no. 4 (1998): 1–42.

35. For examples of terrorist groups' engagement in "legitimate" activities, see Hanna Rosin, "School May Be Out in West Bank; Crackdown Threatens Respected Hamas-Run Institution," *Washington Post* (31 December 2001), A14; and Roman D. Ortiz, "Insurgent Strategies in the Post-Cold War: The Case of the Revolutionary Armed Forces of Columbia," *Studies in Conflict and Terrorism* 25 (2002): 131.

36. Barbara Levitt and James G. March, "Organizational Learning," *Annual Review of Sociology* 14, no. 324 (1988): 319–340.

37. This process has also been distinguished from other learning by labeling it "learning about" as opposed to "learning how." [For example, George Breslauer quoted in J.S. Levy, "Learning and Foreign Policy: Sweeping a Conceptual Minefield," *International Organization* 48, no. 2 (Spring 1994): 292] Although such a distinction is clearly important, it is also often difficult to clearly distinguish activities in each category. A group "learns

about" reality (a particular target, for example) through a learning process (intelligence gathering). That process could itself be improved in the process, however, at which point the group would be "learning how" to better "learn about" potential future targets.

38. J. Bowyer Bell, "The Armed Struggle and Underground Intelligence: An Overview," *Studies in Conflict and Terrorism* 17 (1994): 115–150.

39. For a more lengthy treatment of this topic, see Brian A. Jackson, "Technology Acquisition by Terrorist Groups: Threat Assessment Informed by Lessons from Private Sector Technology Adoption," *Studies in Conflict and Terrorism* 24 (2001): 183–213.

4

✢

Training Camps and Other Centers of Learning

James JF Forest

While the previous chapters of this volume have explored questions of how terrorist organizations and their members learn to do what they do, this chapter addresses the questions of where the centers of learning are (or have been) in the terrorist world, and what sort of learning occurs within them.[1] Centers of learning are described as places in the physical and digital world where social and psychological conditioning, combined with professional training materials and activities, enable an individual to become an effective terrorist. Two main types of "centers of learning" are covered in this discussion: physical and virtual. While the former have existed for decades, recent years have seen an increasing use of the Internet for the transfer of knowledge, although there are serious limitations to developing a motivated terrorist's skills through distance learning.

In the introductory chapter of this volume, a distinction was made between motivational and operational forms of knowledge transfer in the terrorist world. Centers of learning that provide for the development of motivational learning are quite common, and include madrasas, colleges and universities, mosques, churches, temples, and prisons. However, these types of institutions rarely support the transfer of operational knowledge. Rather, a review of the literature in terrorism studies indicates that training camps are the most common type of institutions that support the transfer of operational knowledge, though they clearly support motivational knowledge transfer as well. Following a brief review of common centers of motivational learning, the bulk of this discussion addresses training camps from an historical perspective, and then explores some modern-day centers of operational learning. The chapter then concludes with a few implications for counterterrorism policy as well as questions for further research.

CENTERS OF MOTIVATIONAL LEARNING

The development of an individual's interest in taking up terrorist activities can involve any number of ideological, social, psychological, and other related factors. Throughout history, a variety of ideologies have furnished small terrorist bands and their members with an exaggerated sense of their own importance, which led them to commit dramatic acts of violence in order to make their objectives known to wide audiences.[2] Of these variants, religious ideology is considered by many to be among the more powerful motivating forces behind contemporary terrorism, and in recent years a number of best-selling authors have illustrated how matters of faith can lead to the murder of innocents. For example, Karen Armstrong's book *Battle for God* explores fundamentalist movements that have surfaced in Judaism, Christianity, and Islam (the three major monotheistic faiths) and illustrates how adherents of religious ideology—especially those who demand a return of religion to a central role in daily life—have been responsible for many killings, assassinations, and other acts of terror over the past century.[3] Of these three, Islamist extremism has recently come to pose the most pressing challenge for global peace and security.

Many Muslims today consider the idea that Islam encompasses all aspects of life—including the political—to be a basic tenet of the religion.[4] According to a recent report by the U.S. Institute of Peace, Islamist extremist groups in Egypt, Lebanon, and the Palestinian Territories have been "deeply influenced by the Muslim Brotherhood, an organization established in 1928 by Hasan al-Banna. The works of al-Banna, particularly his letters and speeches, are among the standard references for Islamic thinkers and activists."[5] The works of Sayyid Qutb, particularly his revolutionary seven-volume interpretation of the Koran, have also had a deep impact on the thoughts and practice of radical Islamists. Both the Muslim Brotherhood and Jama'at-I Islami—a group founded in Pakistan by Sayyid Abul A'la Maududi—rejected the perceived Western idea of splitting religion and politics, declaring that doing so would corrupt the ideals of Islamic civilization.[6]

In several of his publications, John Esposito highlights the various dimensions through which religious ideology has played a prominent role in a variety of modern conflicts—including Bosnia, Kosovo, Chechnya, Rwanda, Somalia, Sudan, and Sri Lanka—and gives particular attention to the importance of jihad (which incorporates warfare with an individual effort to live a holy life) in contemporary Islamic movements.[7] According to Jarret Brachman, in recent years the term jihad has been leveraged by local groups on behalf of a global ideology filled with hatred. "The face of jihad has changed dramatically over the past century. For some, it has come to refer to the struggle to defend religious ideals against destructive forces. For others, jihad refers to a command by God to all Muslims to fight against the aggressors who seek to corrupt Islam—embodied and globally perpetuated by the West."[8] Maha Azzam agrees that Islamist extremists are characterizing jihad within the context of an ensuing struggle with secularism and westernization. She argues in a recent publication that "Islamist extremists breed on the politics and policies that are perceived by them as detrimental to Muslim interests, and which have remained unaltered for generations. A growing number among them believe they can influence this situation through a strategy of terror."[9]

Mark Juergensmeyer's best-selling book *Terror in the Mind of God* explores how and why the combination of religious conviction and hatred of secular society translates into the selection of potential terrorist targets. Although he illuminates the tenets of Islam that condone the use of violence, Juergensmeyer also highlights the ideological basis for American Christian militant groups, and shows that violent acts based on religious fervor are not the sole domain of Islamist terrorists.[10] And David Rapoport has published widely on the historical relationship between terrorism and religious ideology, noting that sacred terror has important differences from terrorism undertaken with secular intentions; terrorists undertaking action for religious means (whom he terms "sacred terrorists") always look to the past, at the beginning of a religious tradition, to justify their actions and dictate the means they shall use to achieve their vision of the future, while secular terrorists allow themselves to follow any and all successful paths.[11]

Secular terrorist groups—whose nonreligious ideology is geared more toward political goals, including ethnic separatism—offer their members an equally powerful motivation for taking up violent means to achieve their goals. From the Black Hand in Serbia before WWI, to Marxist revolutionaries in Italy and radicals (both left-wing and right-wing) in Germany during the 1970s, a diverse mix of political ideologies has played an important role in European terrorist movements throughout the last century.[12] An array of ethnic separatist movements around the globe—from India and Mexico to Sri Lanka and Turkey—have also offered powerful ideological motivations for individuals to entertain the use of terrorist tactics.[13] However, it should be noted that few revolutionary, ideological, utopian, or apocalyptic groups are based solely on one type of motivational knowledge. For example, the political violence in Northern Ireland since the late 1960s was driven by a mixture of political ideology, ethnic nationalism, and cultural and religious convictions.[14]

Leonard Weinberg recently noted that as rationalization and justification for the use of terrorist violence, secular and religious ideologies have certain properties in common. "Their common function is to absolve the terrorist and the terrorist group of responsibility for their acts by establishing distance between the perpetrator and the deed or by deflecting responsibility onto others. The violence is defensive in character because the other side initiated the conflict and is responsible for far more suffering than the terrorists are prepared to inflict to achieve their transcendent cause. The enemy is responsible for their own demise. All peaceful remedies have either been exhausted or were nonexistent in the first place; violence is the only option remaining. The other side is not really human. Rather, the other side constitutes an objective and inherently 'criminal' category in the population, so that acts of terrorism carried out against members of the category are not equivalent to attacking human beings. For bearers of revolutionary ideologies, such categories as 'bourgeoisie', 'capitalist exploiter', 'imperialist agent' or 'communist' are every bit as dehumanizing and self-justifying as 'infidel', 'apostate' and 'godless' for religiously motivated terrorists."[15]

From the sociological and psychological literature, a number of scholars have offered different—and sometimes even contradictory—descriptions of how these types of ideologies contribute to the formation of the "terrorist mindset." Robert Lifton, an expert on cults, notes that individuals come to see their chosen ideology—viewed as a set of emotionally charged convictions about people and their relationship to the natural or supernatural world—as ultimately more valid, true, and real than any other aspect of actual human character or human experience, and thus one must subject one's experience to that "truth." When this view of the world is put forth by a group with an absolute vision of truth, those who are not in the group are bound up in evil, are not enlightened, are not saved, and do not have the right to exist.[16] Psychologist Jerrold Post (1998) argues that terrorists have particular psychological natures that drive them to commit acts of violence, but admits that they are not psychopathic. He believes that terrorist actions stem from a need to satisfy this internal drive, and that ideological belief and justifications are used to cover up their wholly personal acts of violence.[17]

Sociologist Martha Crenshaw (1998) agrees with these other scholars in declining to ascribe abnormal pathology to terrorists, but argues that terrorists' actions are the product of a strategic, rational choice (often, but not always, fueled by a particularly powerful ideology).[18] Forensic psychiatrist Marc Sageman's research suggests that members of the transnational Islamist extremist movement are motivated to join terrorist organizations because of the social networks in which their loyalties to others develop. Indeed, he argues that "social bonds play a more important role in the emergence of the global Salafi jihad than ideology."[19] And psychologist Anthony Stahelski's research led him to develop a model of social psychological conditioning through which individuals are transformed into terrorists—in essence, a group with extremist ideologies first eliminates a new recruit's old social and personal identities, and then reconditions them to identify the group's enemies as evil subhumans or nonhumans who should be killed.[20]

In sum, a good deal of the literature in the study of terrorism agrees that ideological knowledge plays a critical role in motivating an individual to become a terrorist (though there is some disagreement on the way in which this transformation takes place). There is also some agreement among researchers that motivational knowledge transfer can take place at any one of a large variety of institutions and entities. Indeed, virtually anywhere that people gather—either physically or online—can potentially serve as a center for motivational learning. There are, however, types of common locations where hatred of "the other" may be taught; these include places of education, worship, and incarceration. In the realm of education, for example, Al-Azhar University in Cairo, Adbul Aziz University in Saudi Arabia, the Bandung Institute of Technology in Malaysia, and the Abu Bakar Islamic University in Pakistan have each earned a reputation as places of significant motivational knowledge transfer among potential recruits for Islamist extremist organizations.

Mosques can also serve as important centers of motivational knowledge transfer. Leaders of Islamist terrorist groups look for particularly devout Muslims—those who come not just to Friday prayers, but to prayers five times a day, every day—and work to develop their motivation for using violence to achieve social and political change. Mosques are important places where members of the Islamic community gather, and in most cases have nothing to do with terrorist indoctrination or recruitment. However, in more than a few cases, these institutions have been co-opted by firebrand leaders, spewing a message of hatred and violence that unfortunately appeals to the anti-Western sentiments of some Muslims.

For example, the Finsbury Park mosque in North London earned a reputation for its particularly radical brand of Islam. One of London's largest places of worship, this four-story mosque serves a diverse community of over two thousand Pakistanis, Bengalis, Algerians, and Egyptians—most of whom simply come to worship and take part in classes in Muslim culture, Arabic, and the Koran. However, among those known to have worshipped at the mosque are alleged shoe bomber Richard Reid and Zacarias Moussaoui, the alleged "20th hijacker" of September 11.[21] Further, the mosque's leader—Sheikh Abu Hamza—was arrested in 2004 and charged with a variety of terror-related offenses following a raid that discovered weapons, explosives, and other things uncommon for a place of worship.[22]

A year earlier, the United Kingdom's Charity Commission, which oversees places of worship in Britain, banned Abu Hamza from preaching at the Finsbury Park mosque after he praised Osama bin Laden and declared—among other things—that the crew who died in the Columbia space shuttle disaster had been punished by Allah.[23] Other examples include the Quds mosque in Hamburg, Germany, that brought together and inspired several al Qaeda recruits, including Mohammad Atta (the leader of the September 11 hijackers).[24] From Seattle, Washington (e.g., the Idris mosque and the now-closed Dar-us-Salaam mosque), to Albany, New York (e.g., the Masjid As-Salam mosque), U.S. authorities have launched investigations into allegations of extremist activities at mosques throughout the country. And the number of mosques that provide safe havens to Islamist extremists in the West pales in comparison to the vast array of mosques in Central and Southeast Asia, North Africa, and the Middle East.

In addition to these universities and mosques, a worldwide network of *madrasas* and *pesantren* (Muslim boarding schools)—many of which are Wahhabi-oriented[25] and funded by charities in Saudi Arabia and other Gulf countries—continues to play an important role in the growth of the jihadi terrorist network, at the very least by introducing students to Islamist radical ideology and activities.[26] For example, according to Zachary Abuza, the Al Mukmin madrasa in Ngruki, Indonesia, has played a central role in the development of the Islamist terrorist group Jemaah Islamiyah (JI). Established in 1972 by Abu Bakar Ba'asyir and Abdullah Sungkar, the founders of JI, the graduates of Ngruki are a who's who of Southeast Asian terrorists.[27]

According to research conducted by Peter Singer, "around 10–15% of Pakistan's madrasas are affiliated with extremist religious/political groups, who have co-opted education for their own ends. These schools teach a distorted view of Islam. Hatred is permissible, jihad allows the murder of innocent civilians including other Muslim men, women and children, and the new heroes are terrorists."[28] Following a visit to Pakistan's al-Haqqania madrasa in 2002, an hour or so east of Peshawar, *New Yorker* foreign correspondent Mary Anne Weaver described a vast, four-teen-acre complex with "scores of classrooms, administrative buildings, mosques and dorms, and a state-of-the-art computer room."[29] Under the leadership of Maulana Sami ul-Haq—one of the most powerful and most anti-American of Pakistan's religious militants—students at this madrasa study a core curriculum of Arabic and Islam, memorize the Koran, and develop a commitment to fighting a jihad against the enemies of Islam. At institutions like these, militant education breeds militants; a curriculum oriented toward hatred and violence produces violent graduates.

Prisons can also serve as centers of knowledge transfer in the terrorist world—indeed, FBI Director Robert Mueller recently referred to them as "fertile ground for extremists."[30] A variety of organizations are active in prisons throughout the U.S., from right-wing groups—like the Aryan Nations Church prison ministry (which preaches a violent flavor of Christian Identity ideology)[31] and the Confederate Knights of America—to religious organizations like the Islamic Society of North America (ISNA) and the Graduate School of Islamic and Social Sciences (GSISS).[32] According to Professor Michael Waller of the Institute of World Politics, white supremacist movements, religious extremists, and foreign-sponsored groups (including Imams of the global Wahhabi religious movement, which is sponsored by the Saudi Arabian government) have all penetrated the U.S. prison system.[33] In most cases, these groups contribute solely to motivational knowledge transfer and the indoctrination of new recruits. However, in a few cases, prisons have also served as important vehicles for the transfer of operational knowledge. For example, when members of the Irish Republican Army were captured and sent to British or Irish prisons, they were immediately debriefed by other inmates, who then smuggled the information (and lessons learned) to IRA members outside the prison walls. Particularly useful information passed on by the imprisoned terrorists could include how they were caught, what information the captors were looking for, what (if anything) might have gone awry with a planned attack being carried out, and who (if anyone) might have played a role in their capture.[34]

In sum, motivational knowledge transfer takes place at a significant variety of institutions and gathering places. While many of these serve far more benign purposes than terrorist recruitment, they are still places of concern when developing a global understanding of terrorism. Their most important link to the spread of terrorism is that they produce the willingness to kill. Once a student reaches this level of motivation, the acquisition of operational knowledge (the skill to kill) is all that is needed to become a *bona fide* terrorist. Thus, the next section of this chapter reviews the various types of operational knowledge found most frequently in the terrorist world, and explores some of the more prominent locations where this type of knowledge has been acquired by would-be terrorists.

CENTERS OF OPERATIONAL LEARNING

Given the aim of most terrorists—to inflict pain and damage in order to create fear among a target audience and compel some form of policy or behavioral change desired by the terrorists—it is clear why operational knowledge transfer is such an important topic within the study of terrorism. Terrorist organizations require a significant breadth of operational knowledge before they can be truly effective. Examples of the types of

knowledge needed include document falsification, sabotage, target vulnerability assessment, and artillery training. The most common and important places where significant operational learning (as well as indoctrination) has taken place are the various terrorist training camps scattered
throughout the globe. Ahmed Ressam, an Algerian who intended to set
off a suitcase bomb at Los Angeles International Airport on New Year's
Day 2000, admitted at his trial that he received training at the al
Qaeda–sponsored Khaldan camp in Afghanistan, learning how to fire
handguns, machine guns, and rocket-propelled grenade launchers, as
well as how to assemble bombs from TNT and the plastic explosive C4.[35]
He also talked of studying urban warfare, "how to block roads and storm
buildings," and "how to blow up the infrastructure of a country . . . such
installations as electric power plants, airports, railroads, large corporations, and military installations."[36]

According to research conducted in the 1990s by an officer of the U.S.
Marine Corps, a typical day at a PLO training camp began with early
morning physical fitness exercises, and as the day progressed, students
generally conducted a parade. Daily instruction included education in explosives and detonators, the art of setting mines in munitions dumps and
on bridges and vehicles, the rudiments of chemical and biological warfare, field command and escape tactics, marksmanship and camouflage,
and the use and employment of Soviet RPG rockets and shoulder borne
Strela missiles.[37] Clearly, life in a terrorist training camp was not your ordinary Boy Scout campfire outing.

In a remarkable 2003 *Foreign Policy* article, researchers Martha Brill Olcott
and Bakhityar Babajanov describe their analysis of ten notebooks that once
belonged to young men who were recruited for jihad and attended terrorist training camps in Central Asia (most likely Uzbekistan) during the
1990s.[38] They describe how students learned cartography (map-making),
the use of small firearms (mainly Soviet-era rifles and the occasional Egyptian rocket-propelled grenade launcher), tactics for targeting the enemy
(both on the ground and in the air), explosive device construction (including antipersonnel mines), and how to make poison using corn, flour, beef,
yak dung, alcohol, and water. While the motivational knowledge represented in these students' notebooks reflects a clear Islamist radicalist influence, it is equally interesting to note that, according to Olcott and Babajanov, "the teachers who used Russian terminology clearly had experience
with the Red Army and Soviet system of military instruction, and those
who used Arabic likely passed through terrorist camps in Afghanistan and
maybe even those of the Middle East."[39]

In 2002, *New York Times* reporters C.J. Chivers and David Rohde examined hundreds of documents collected from "terrorist training schools"
during the U.S. military assault on the Taliban, and found "signs that in

developing martial curriculums, the [terrorist] groups were cannily re-sourceful in amassing knowledge."[40] The documents included student notebooks, instructors' lesson plans, course curricula, training manuals, reference books, and memoranda—collectively, the same sorts of materials one would expect to find at a conventional military academy. Analysis of the documents revealed that students began their training by learning all about Kalishnikov rifles, the ubiquitous Soviet-era weapon used by many insurgent organizations around the world. Once the history, design, and operation of these weapons were mastered—mainly through rote memorization—students turned their attention to "PK machine guns, 82-millimeter mortars and the RPG-7, a shoulder-fired rocket effective against armored vehicles and trucks."[41] In this program of study, the next course was a sort of "infantry weapons 201," with some students learning sniper rifle skills and how to fine-tune a rifle sight at short range to ensure accuracy at longer distances, while others studied how to direct weapon fire at targets on the ground and in the air. Training in four-man unit deployments and formations—including wedges, columns, echelons, and lines—reflected similar techniques used by U.S. Marines and Army Rangers.[42] Demolition instruction was also provided, covering mines and grenades, pressure and trip wire booby traps, and the basic knowledge of electrical engineering that would allow students to figure out "the wiring, power sources and fuses required to spark an explosive charge."[43]

According to an archive of videotapes obtained by CNN in 2002, al Qaeda has also trained recruits in urban guerilla tactics. These tapes show how the group "replicated a small Western-style city on a hillside in eastern Afghanistan, using canvas and stone," and how trainees used explosives to destroy simulated houses, office buildings and bridges.[44] Also included on the tapes were "step-by-step instructions on how to use a surface-to-air missile" and "lessons on complex hostage-taking techniques and assassination operations."[45] And according to terrorist trial testimony and other sources, many training camps offer instruction in basic hand-to-hand combat skills, including the use of knives and martial arts.[46]

In addition to operational knowledge, terror training camps incorporate a number of psychological development processes that advance the ideological motivations that brought the students to the camps in the first place.[47] The physical isolation of the training camps is an important aspect to this process, in part because members come to rely on each other (and thus build bonds of mutual trust within the organization) for success and survival. At a minimum, one could argue that training camps offer more powerful forms of motivational knowledge transfer than any other institution discussed in this chapter. Thus, training camps for terrorism are obviously places of great concern for the civilized world. While these places are rich in motivational knowledge transfer, they are far more worrisome for their role in bringing enthusiastic learners (with a willingness to kill) together with experts in operational knowledge on how to kill. And contrary to the mainstream media's focus on the training camps of Afghanistan, these centers of learning can be found throughout the world.

A BRIEF HISTORY OF TERRORIST TRAINING CENTERS

The geography of former and current terrorist centers of learning includes the following, listed alphabetically rather than by order of importance:

Afghanistan and the Anti-Soviet Jihad

By some estimates, several thousand camps were established throughout Afghanistan between 1980 and 1989, providing military training and seminars in Islamic history and theology to Afghanis, Arabs, and others committed to the goal of driving Soviet forces out of the country. Training was provided by seasoned veterans from other armed services. For example, in 1986 Osama bin Laden established a base camp for non-Afghan fighters in the mountains southeast of Jalalabad, at which two former Egyptian servicemen and senior Egyptian Islamic Jihad members (Abu Ubaydah al-Banshiri and Abu Hafs al-Masri) led combat training and operations.[48] Other camps for the mujahideen were established across the Pakistani border, in and around the city of Peshawar and the tribal region of Waziristan. The curriculum at these camps typically included a broad range of learning objectives, including the operation of Stinger missiles, the production of explosives and poisons, vehicle driving and maintenance, basic engineering, farming, and even urban guerilla tactics.[49] These were harsh learning environments—mud huts, dusty classrooms, obstacle courses, mazes of barbed wire, trenches, and of course, no basic utilities.[50] Once the Soviets withdrew from Afghanistan, thousands of the combat-trained veterans returned home, some to enjoy comfortable environs and regular lifestyles, others to join Islamist groups elsewhere in the world, including the Chechen Mujahideen, the Armed Islamic Group in Algeria, the Abu Sayyaf Group in the Philippines, and Jemaah Islamiyah in Indonesia.[51]

Algeria, the Armed Islamic Group, and the GSPC

Beginning in the 1960s, Islamists in Algeria began training in urban guerilla tactics, for the purpose of driving the French colonial government out of the country. Political developments since Algerian independence eventually marginalized the extremists, who formed a number of organizations such as the Armed Islamic Group (GIA), the Salafist Group for

Preaching and Combat (GSPC), and the Al Takfir wal Hijra (Excommunication and Migration) movement (one of the most extreme jihadi groups, whose members seek to identify and target Muslim civilians and regimes that do not meet their standards of piousness). In the early 1990s, particularly with the return home of many veterans of the Afghanistan jihad, attacks against the government began to increase in number and lethality. Training camps both in Algeria and across the border in Tunisia were used to teach combat tactics, explosives production, and weapons handling to new recruits. After a decade of open civil war with the government, the Islamist radical organizations in Algeria have recently begun to abandon the cities in the north of the country and head south in search of opportunities to regroup, establish new training camps, and plan new attacks.

Bosnia and the Balkan Mujahideen

The war in Bosnia played an important role in providing training to members of the global Islamist jihad network. During the early 1990s, thousands of mujahideen left Afghanistan and other parts of Central Asia to fight alongside Bosnian Muslims against the Serbs. Weapons and fighters were smuggled through Croatia and other locations to support the Muslims in their struggle, and "on the job" combat training for new fighters was common. By 1994, major Balkan terrorist training camps included Zenica, Malisevo, and Mitrovica in Kosovo, where experienced veterans taught new recruits.[52] After the war, many foreign Islamist extremists chose to become Bosnian citizens, establishing normal lives (and, incidentally, providing convenient safe havens for the movement of jihadi elements to and from Europe), while others took their experience in search of a new place to continue the jihad.

Egypt, EIJ, Gama'at al-Islamiyaa, and the Muslim Brotherhood

During the 1990s, alumni of the Afghan jihad were blamed for a series of attacks in Egypt, including the 1997 attack in Luxor by Gama'at al-Islamiyaa ("the Islamic Group"), which killed fifty-eight tourists and four Egyptians.[53] The November 1995 attacks on an Egyptian diplomat in Switzerland and the Egyptian embassy in Pakistan were also attributed to Egyptian-born alumni of the Afghan training camps. However, most observers point to the much older Muslim Brotherhood as a prominent ideological source of Islamist extremist movements in Egypt and elsewhere. Founded in 1928, the Muslim Brotherhood produced the likes of Sayyid Qutb, who wrote the influential jihadist pamphlet *Ma'alim* (Guideposts), as well as many members of the Egyptian Islamic Jihad (EIJ)—including al Qaeda members Ayman al-Zawahiri (Osama bin Laden's deputy) and

Mohammed Atef (believed by many to be the strategic architect behind the attacks of September 11).[54] As early as 1940, the Muslim Brotherhood's militant wing—increasingly disenchanted with perceived corruption throughout the country's political system, and thus committed to armed revolutionary struggle—established guerilla training camps in the Mukatam Hills overlooking Cairo. Graduates of these camps then conducted a series of attacks, including the 1948 bombing of the Circurrel Shopping Complex and the assassination of Prime Minister Noqrashi Pasha, Judge Ahmed Al-Khizindaar, and several internal security officials.[55] After decades of mass arrests and financial crackdowns by the government's security forces, there are no longer any known terrorist training camps in Egypt, although the Muslim Brotherhood has continued to play a vital role in the spread of global jihad.

Indonesia and JI

Jemaah Islamiyah (JI) is a religious extremist organization that seeks to create a pan-Islamic state uniting Indonesia, Brunei, Malaysia, Singapore, and the Southern Philippines. Some estimates suggest that over a thousand Southeast Asian Muslims were trained by (and fought with) the Afghan mujahideen during the 1980s, returning home afterward with valuable combat knowledge, experience, and the belief that they contributed to the fall of a world superpower. JI's own training facilities include several camps located in the southern Philippines (see below) and Camp Jabal Quba on Mount Kararao, which provides courses in weapons and explosives.[56]

Japan and the Aum Shinrikyo

In 1993, the Japanese cult Aum Shinrikyo (or "Supreme Truth") built Satian 7, a nondescript building within the Aum complex at Mt. Fuji, which housed one of the most sophisticated chemical manufacturing facilities in the world. While new recruits were brought to the Aum complex (as well as Aum monasteries and other locations in Japan) mainly for ideological indoctrination, this particular building had only one purpose: to develop the group's capacity to manufacture sarin gas (a deadly nerve toxin), as well as VX, mustard gas, and phosgene gas, which the group used in several attacks on individuals and the general public around Japan.[57] Under the leadership of Masami Tsuchiya, a gifted chemist, the lab was capable of producing two tons of liquid sarin a day, and on March 20, 1995, the group released sarin in the Tokyo subway system, killing 12 people and injuring more than 5,500. When police raided Aum properties two days later, they found enough chemicals to kill an estimated 4.2 million people.[58] In 1998, Satian 7 became the first chemical production facility destroyed under the United Nations Chemical Weapons Convention.[59] While this unique center of operational knowledge transfer was used exclusively by members of Aum, its development and use certainly provides a model for other like-minded organizations.

Lebanon, AMAL, Hizballah, and the PLO

Between the founding of the state of Israel in 1948 and the Six Day War in 1967, the Palestinian refugee population in Lebanon grew to 350,000, providing an important recruiting ground for the recently formed Palestinian Liberation Organization (PLO). In 1968, the PLO began to launch guerilla raids against Israel from bases within Lebanon. Israeli reprisals against the PLO led to increasing Lebanese casualties, and a political rift between supporters and critics of the PLO's presence in the country contributed to ongoing religious tensions (particularly between Shia Muslims and Maronite Christians), which erupted into civil war in 1975 (a war that continued until 1990). For their part, the PLO provided arms and training to militias who supported their cause, the most prominent of which was Musa Sadr's Shiite group *Afwaj al-Muqawama al Lubnnania* (AMAL), or "Lebanese Resistance Detachments."[60] In 1982, after several years of internal chaos and cross-border attacks, Israeli Defense Forces crossed into Lebanon and began occupying the southern part of the country, resulting in a Shiite resistance force that came to be known as Hizballah.[61] This group—along with others, like the so-called Islamic Jihad—began using suicide bombers (often driving cars packed with explosives) to attack convoys of Israeli soldiers. Young men from the Palestinian refugee camps (and other places in the north of the country) were trained and brought into the theatre of conflict for such operations.[62] Several of these training camps were established in the Bekaa Valley (in eastern Lebanon), which has been under the control of Syrian forces since the 1980s.[63]

Libya and State-Sponsored or Sanctioned Training Camps

Until very recently, Libya's leader Muammar Qadaffi has viewed his country's destiny as being a revolutionary catalyst, a guide to the future that should sponsor every one of the faithful (particularly those faithful to Islam) as well as those opposed to imperialism.[64] As a result, Libya has compiled a well-documented history of extensive state sponsorship of terrorism—indeed, according to Christopher Boucek of the Royal United Services Institute in London, the employment of different terrorist groups by the Libyan government was an intrinsic feature of its foreign policy for a number of years.[65] As part of this effort, Libya has provided a safe haven for a variety of terrorist training camps since the early 1970s, including some used by groups committed to the spread of radical Islamist ideology. According to

Israeli terrorism expert Boaz Ganor, Libya opened its military bases to terrorist organizations and provided a variety of courses in military expertise to members of the PFLP (Popular Front for the Liberation of Palestine) and other Palestinian groups at Sinawin, Zuwarah, and Tubruq, and the Ras al Hilal facility, among other locations.[66] The group responsible for the May 1990 seaborne attack against Israel was trained at the Bilal Port Facility near Sidi. Bin Ghashir, just south of Tripoli, is said to have been used to train dissidents from Africa, Asia, and Latin America in terrorist/guerrilla tactics. In addition to Palestinian and Islamist terrorists, groups that have received training in Libya (particularly at the Seven April Training Camp) include the Irish Republican Army, the Basque separatist group ETA, Sierra Leone's Revolutionary United Front, Colombia's M-19, the Haitian Liberation Organization, the Chilean Manuel Rodriguez Patriotic Front, the Secret Army for the Liberation of Armenia, and the Japanese Red Army.[67]

Northern Ireland and the IRA

The IRA was founded on an island where weapons, even sporting guns, are closely controlled, licensed, and monitored, and where no great war has left the countryside littered with discarded military gear.[68] Nonetheless, through the cooperation of the Irish diaspora—and especially Irish Americans—a variety of weapons were imported, including the civilian version of the military's M-16, the Armalite, that could be purchased in America as a deer hunting rifle. Used on semiautomatic, the weapon proved ideal for poorly-trained gunmen, and the .223 cartridge could pierce the shell armor of British personnel carriers. At firing ranges constructed in isolated places, including abandoned mines and convenient cellars, new IRA recruits were trained on the Armalite—along with the AK-47, during the 1980s—as well as how to properly handle the explosive compound Semtex.[69] Although the IRA did not really use anything dramatic—no heavy weapons, no exotic explosives, no high-tech equipment that could not be bought at Radio Shack—they did prove ingenious in creating all sorts of explosive devices and traps, in the use of high-tech monitoring equipment, and in adapting their weapons to rural and urban conditions.[70] Many members improved their bomb manufacturing skills through knowledge acquired in their civilian occupations as electricians, and surprisingly, as pinball machine repairmen.[71]

Peru and Sendero Luminoso (the Shining Path)

One of the most ruthless terrorist groups in the world, Sendero Luminoso is based in the Peruvian countryside. Its forces have occupied villages, established revolutionary governments, and organized schools through which they have indoctrinated locals and evaluated their potential as new recruits. Training in and outside the schools has included guerilla strategy, the use of firearms and explosives, and on-the-job training in militant action against government forces, organized peasants, or other terrorists such as Tupac Amaru collaborators.[72]

The Philippines, the MILF, and the Abu Sayyaf Group

Three major JI terrorist training camps—Camp Vietnam, Camp Palestine, and Camp Hodeibia—were colocated in the Moro Islamic Liberation Front's (MILF) Camp Abu Bakar complex in Mindanao, the Philippines.[73] Research has pointed to al Qaeda involvement with both organizations, and these camps have, according to Philippine military intelligence, played host to several hundred trainers from the Middle East.[74] Abu Sayyaf, an organization with more criminal tendencies than jihadist sentiment, established a central base on Basilan's Mohadji mountain called Camp Abdurajak—one of at least nine Abu Sayyaf camps hidden in the jungles of the Philippines.[75]

Sri Lanka and the Tamil Tigers

Since the 1970s, one of the world's most fearsome organizations has been the Liberation Tigers of Tamil Eelam (LTTE), a terrorist group representing the minority Tamil community, fighting for an Eelam (or homeland) in the northern and eastern provinces of Sri Lanka. The LTTE is widely viewed as being at the cutting edge of insurgent and terrorist technology, military adaptation and innovation—for example, it is credited with the invention of (among other things) the speedboat suicide attack.[76] A unique, if macabre feature of its tactics has been the use of suicide commandos, both men and women, some in their early teens, for individual assassination as well as mass attacks.[77] Through intense training and conditioning, as well as societal isolation, the LTTE camps—many of them located in Jaffna and remote areas in the northern part of Sri Lanka—provide important centers of operational knowledge transfer. While several LTTE training camps are known to have existed in India—particularly in the state of Tamil Nadu—there are as yet no indications that this group has provided training for anyone other than Tamils committed to the goal of establishing a separatist state.

Sudan and Islamic Terrorist Groups

During the early 1990s, Osama bin Laden was exiled from Saudi Arabia and settled in Khartoum, the capital of Sudan. He brought with him a number of seasoned veterans from the Afghan conflict and established military training camps throughout the country. Some reports say more than twenty camps were built near Khartoum, Port Sudan, in the Damazin areas of eastern Sudan, and in the southern Equatoria Province, near the Ugandan border.[78] A recent report by the U.S. Institute of Peace indicates that "the Sudanese government has used its territory to provide safe haven, training bases, and staging areas to numerous terrorist organizations, including al Qaeda, Egyptian Islamic Jihad (EIJ), Hizballah, Hamas, Palestinian Islamic Jihad (PIJ), Abu Nidal, and Gama'at al Islamiyya. Operatives not only moved freely in and out of Sudan, but also established offices, businesses, and logistical bases for operations. Training camps were opened in the east of the country, which sent fighters from Lebanon, Afghanistan, and Algeria across the border into neighboring Eritrea and Ethiopia."[79]

Syria and Palestinian Terrorist Organizations

When Lebanon's civil war erupted in 1975, Syria (a predominately Sunni Muslim country) came to the aid of the Christians, who were being pounded by Shiite Muslim groups like AMAL.[80] According to the U.S. Department of State, several radical terrorist groups have maintained training camps or other facilities on Syrian territory over the last twenty years, including the Turkish separatist group PKK (Partiya Karkeren Kurdistan) and Palestinian groups like the Popular Front for the Liberation of Palestine (PFLP), the Abu Nidal Organization, and the Palestine Islamic Jihad (PIJ).[81] Many of the training camps have been located in the Syrian-controlled Bekaa Valley, in eastern Lebanon. One notorious example is the Ayn Tzahab terrorist training camp in Syria, allegedly supported by Iran and used for operational training for Palestinian terrorists, including Hamas and Palestinian Islamic Jihad operatives.[82]

Turkey and the PKK

According to Ely Karmon (1998), Islamist extremist groups in Turkey— including the Hizb ut-Tahrir (Islamic Liberation Party)—have been active since the 1960s, recruiting new members from poor towns and villages with a large Kurdish population (Dyarbakir, Silvan, Cizre, Kiziltepe, and others), especially among the young and unemployed.[83] Karmon's research cites how in 1993, a Turkish minister of the interior declared at a press conference that members of radical Islamist organizations underwent months of military and theoretical training in Iranian security installations, traveled with real and forged Iranian documents, had weapons and explosives of Iranian origin, and participated in attacks on Turkish citizens and also Iranian opposition militants.[84] However, while some Turkish terrorist organizations may have profited materially from Iranian backing in training, logistical support, weapons, and explosives, the more worrisome centers of terrorist knowledge are found among the training camps of the PKK.[85] Aside from the previously mentioned training camp in Lebanon's Bekaa Valley, the PKK has maintained centers of learning throughout southern Turkey and northern Iraq.

Uzbekistan and the IMU

During the Soviet era, the Fergana Valley of Uzbekistan became host to a number of underground mosques and religious schools, and over time, a supportive environment for Islamic radicalism allowed the establishment and maintenance of jihad terrorist training camps.[86] From this environment was launched the Islamic Movement of Uzbekistan (IMU), the most active group of its kind in Central Asia. While the IMU purportedly has used training camps and military bases in Afghanistan, Pakistan, and Tajikistan, as well as a "forward base of operations" in Batken, Kyrgyzstan, the group operates largely in the Fergana Valley on the Uzbek/Kyrgyz border, where it receives support and some protection from local inhabitants.[87]

The United States and Extremist Groups

In addition to faraway places like Indonesia, Sudan, and Uzbekistan, the United States has also played host to several terrorist training camps in recent decades. From Alabama to Oregon, centers of motivational—and sometimes operational—knowledge transfer are cause for increasing concern. In Northern Idaho, the Aryan Nations Church's twenty-acre gated fortress with guard towers provided a sanctuary in which Christian Identity adherents received weapons training, combat tactics instruction, and indoctrination. The closely related Covenant, Sword and the Arm of the Lord, headquartered on the Missouri-Arkansas border, amassed one of the largest private arms caches ever uncovered in American history on its 224-acre base, Zarepath-Horeb, including a thirty-gallon barrel of arsenic, at least one improvised armored vehicle, facilities for retooling machine guns out of semiautomatic weapons, grenades, RPGs (rocket-propelled grenades), silencers, and thousands of rounds of ammunition. Another U.S.-based extremist group, the Christian Patriots Defense League, established a perimeter of armed encampments around the American heartland to protect it from a planned incursion of troops from Africa, allegedly stationed on America's borders awaiting orders from the UN to invade.[88] And Timothy McVeigh, who was convicted and executed for his deadly 1995 attack on the Murrah Federal Building in Oklahoma City, was a frequent visitor to Elohim City (literally, the City of God), a Christian Identity enclave located nearby.[89]

There have also been recent attempts to establish Islamist extremist training camps in the United States. For example, in 2002 James Ujaama was indicted for attempting to turn a remote ranch in rural Oregon into an international training camp for jihad fighters. After hearing reports of gunfire and a large group of suspicious or unusual people in the area, the local sheriff informed the FBI, whose subsequent investigation revealed connections with the radical Islamist cleric Sheikh Abu Hamza al-Masri (who was recently charged in the U.K. with attempted murder and fomenting terrorism) and Haroon Rashid Aswat, a British citizen who was taken into custody after the July 7, 2005, terrorist attacks in London. For his part, Ujaama was sentenced to two years in prison in return for his cooperation with federal investigators.[90]

Without violating the crucial civil liberties of the U.S. (such as the freedom of association), widespread community vigilance must play a vital role in identifying and closing such training camps in this country in the future or preventing them from existing. The same can be said for all countries—such as those listed here—where terrorist centers of learning may exist.

CENTERS OF TERRORIST LEARNING: TODAY AND TOMORROW

The discussion above has focused mainly on historical examples of terrorist training camps, and in many cases (like Afghanistan, Libya, and Northern Ireland) these camps no longer exist. However, there are several contemporary centers of learning that also bear scrutiny. Some, like Pakistan and Chechnya, have been places of concern for some time. Others, like Iraq and parts of Africa, have only recently emerged on the counterterrorism analysts' radar screens.

Training Camps and Religious Schools in Kashmir and Pakistan

In June 2005, five members of a Pakistani community in Lodi, California, were arrested by authorities and charged with various offenses related to an FBI antiterrorism investigation. One of the suspects, twenty-two-year-old Hamid Hayat, admitted in a court affidavit that he had attended an al Qaeda–supported camp in Pakistan and that during his weapons training, photographs of "various high-ranking U.S. political figures, including President Bush, would be pasted on their targets."[91] Since 2002, according to terrorism expert Evan Kohlmann, "several suspected terrorist training camps affiliated with al Qaeda have surfaced along the Pakistani-Afghan border in Waziristan."[92] Terrorism expert (and CNN analyst) Peter Bergen agrees that there are likely to be several training camps in the country aimed at training Pakistanis for action in the disputed Kashmir region.[93] And in May 2005, India's security forces destroyed a terrorist training camp in Jammu and Kashmir's Doda district. They reported killing five terrorists in the operation, and recovering rifles, grenades, ammunition, a rocket-propelled grenade, and a wireless communication set.[94] However, Pakistan denies the existence of any terrorist training camps in its territory—despite videotapes obtained by ABC News in 2005 that contain images of al Qaeda training camps inside Pakistan. These tapes show fighters conducting a variety of exercises with automatic weapons, as they once did at similar camps in Afghanistan. The fighters are identified as coming from nine different countries in Africa and the Middle East, with many from Saudi Arabia.[95]

Following the ouster of the Taliban from Afghanistan in 2001, a good deal of U.S. attention (particularly in its hunt for Osama bin Laden and his colleagues) has been focused on its mountainous northern border with Pakistan—a region long known for providing safe haven for bandits and extremists. In fact, when the Pakistan Army deployed to the border region of North Waziristan in 2003, it was the first time in the country's fifty-seven-year history that the government had made any attempt to bring law and order to what it has called "tribal areas" of this "frontier region."[96] When Pakistan's President Pervez Musharraf initially lent his support in 2001 to the U.S. in fighting the Taliban, his decision was highly unpopular in his country, particularly in this region. However, two attempts by extremists to assassinate Musharraf in December 2003 helped remove any lasting doubts his administration may have had about the threat from Islamist militants in Pakistan, and his government has become a key ally in the global war on terrorism. Still, it is widely acknowledged that his government does not yet have complete control over all regions of Pakistan, and it these "ungoverned spaces" that lend themselves to the training of terrorists.

Most of the known or suspected terrorist training camps in Pakistan are reportedly located in the northern provinces, near the borders with Afghanistan and India, and in the northern region of Kashmir. Several groups operating in this region—including the most prominent Pakistani terrorist organization, Lashkar-e-Taiba—receive local support for their fight against the Indian police and soldiers in the southern part of Kashmir. Kashmir has also been an important center of learning for al Qaeda, primarily because of the specialized training experience available there. For example, while the Afghanistan camps offered training for a guerilla fight against conventional military forces, terrorist training in Kashmir has included actual penetration across the Indian border, sabotage actions, assassinations, and urban guerilla warfare.[97]

In addition to terrorist training camps, there has been growing concern in recent years about the kinds of teaching found at some of Pakistan's madrasas. Western and Pakistani officials estimate there are anywhere from twelve thousand to fifteen thousand madrasas in Pakistan, training about one million students.[98] Of these, only a small portion are considered to be affiliated with extremist groups. But if even 10–15 percent are, as suggested by Peter Singer of the Brookings Institution,[99] that is still roughly 1,200 to 1,500 centers of terrorist learning that we should be concerned about. Some madrasas have also been used as shelters or meeting points for militants, bases for clandestine operations by Taliban and al Qaeda supporters, or training grounds for their soldiers.[100] However, it is the role of these institutions in facilitating the spread of motivational knowledge that has become the cause of most concern. Following the July 7 attacks in London, it was reported that one of the suicide bombers—Shehzad Tanweer—had attended a madrasa in Lahore, Pakistan, where he is suspected of becoming indoctrinated in a particularly violent strand of religious ideology from the banned Islamist militant group Lashkar-e-Taiba.[101] Shortly afterwards, the Musharraf government launched a new initiative to monitor the teaching at madrasas, in an effort to ensure that these are no longer allowed to serve as places of radicalization. These schools will be required to register with the government, and their curricula will be assessed to ensure teachers are not promoting violence. In a further move to address the potential for terrorist knowledge transfer, Pakistan announced in August 2005 that it would close a number of refugee camps throughout its border with Afghanistan, where a large number of al Qaeda–linked militants fled after the U.S. invasion in 2001, and where a good deal of fighting has taken place since the security forces began combing the region for militants in 2003.[102] According to a statement made by Pakistan's president, "We certainly have a problem here, which we are trying to address very strongly."[103] His success or failure in addressing this problem will certainly have a lasting impact on the spread of motivational and operational knowledge in the terrorist world.

Chechnya and Anti-Russian Separatists

To understand the separatist conflict in Chechnya, it is first necessary to examine the political history of this region.[104] Chechnya, whose population is predominantly Muslim, was conquered by Russia in 1858 after the defeat of Imam Shamil and his fighters, who had sought to establish an Islamic state. In 1922, an autonomous Chechen region was established, which became the Chechen-Ingush Autonomous Soviet Socialist Republic in 1934. However, in 1944 Soviet dictator Josef Stalin deported the entire Chechen and Ingush populations to Siberia and Central Asia, citing alleged collaboration with Nazi Germany. Many thousands died throughout the forced migration and the years that followed. A significantly reduced population of Chechens was eventually allowed to return to their homeland in 1957. This history frames much of the contemporary animosity that exists between the Chechens and the Russians.

Following the collapse of the Soviet Union in 1991, Chechen rebel leader Dzhokhar Dudayev won a presidential poll and proclaimed Chechnya independent of Russia. In 1994, Russian President Boris Yeltsin refused to recognize the independence of Chechnya (citing a rise in organized crime, violence, and general lawlessness), and ordered troops into the breakaway region. Despite massive firepower, including aerial bombing throughout the region, the Russians were eventually worn down by the Chechen rebels—armed with rocket-propelled grenade launchers and operating in small guerrilla units—and withdrew (leaving behind some one hundred thousand dead) following the signing of a peace deal in 1996. For the next three years, a fragile peace endured, but in September 1999 a bomb attack on a Russian military housing complex in Dagestan and a series of apartment block bombings elsewhere in Russia (killing nearly three hundred people) were blamed on Chechen rebels. In response, then–Prime Minister Vladimir Putin ordered Russian forces to redeploy in Chechnya, where they have been fighting Chechen separatists ever since.

To most observers familiar with the region, it came as no surprise to see the Chechens adopt the same guerilla warfare tactics that were successful against the Soviets in Afghanistan. Indeed, Chechen commander Shamil Basayev and several of his senior military advisors had fought in that conflict along with Osama bin Laden and other Arab and Afghan mujahideen. In 1995, a group of veterans from the Afghanistan conflict, led by a Saudi citizen named Samer ben Saleh ben Abdallah al Swelem (known locally as Amir Khattab), arrived in Chechnya to assist the outgunned Chechen separatists in their struggles against Russian Federal Forces. Khattab and other members of the Afghan alumni had sworn an oath to the patron saint of the international jihad movement, Abdallah Azzam, to continue the defense of other threatened Muslim groups across the globe, and Chechnya became their choice of places to do this.[105] Khattab's so-called International Islamic Battalion (IIB) was instrumental in aiding Basayev and forcing the Russians to leave Chechnya a year later.

In the aftermath of the Russian withdrawal in 1996, Khattab and many of his rootless Arab jihadis stayed on in Chechnya. Others migrated to various parts of the world in pursuit of the global jihadi movement—including the United States. For example, Ahmed al Ghamidi, a Saudi who fought in Chechnya after studying engineering in Mecca, went on to become one of the 9/11 hijackers of United Airlines Flight 175, which hit the south World Trade Center tower. Another jihadi fighter in Chechnya, Nawaq al Hamzi, became one of the 9/11 hijackers on the flight that crashed into the Pentagon. And Ahmed al Haznawi, a hijacker on United Airlines Flight 93, which crashed in Pennsylvania on September 11, is reported to have left his home in the al Baha region of Saudi Arabia in 2000 telling friends he was going to train in an Al Qaeda camp in Afghanistan for jihad in Chechnya.[106] Meanwhile, another jihadi fighter from Chechnya—Mohammed Hamdi al Ahdal, a thirty-two-year-old Saudi citizen—was arrested in November 2003 after a lengthy investigation into the bombing of the *USS Cole* in Aden, Yemen, in 2000.[107]

For his part, Khattab married a local woman from neighboring Dagestan and established a series of training camps in southeastern Chechnya, largely with funding from Saudi charities like the Al Haramein foundation.[108] According to terrorism analyst Brian Williams, these camps "trained unemployed young Chechen men and Muslims from throughout the region for a never-ending jihad that was far greater in scope than the micro-republic envisioned by Chechnya's nationalist leadership. Ample proof of the danger these camps posed to Chechnya and the neighboring Russian Federation came in August and September of 1999 when Dagestani, Chechen, and Arab militants poured over the border from these camps and raided the neighboring Russian republic of Dagestan."[109] In August 2002, sweeps of the Chechen-inhabited Pankisi Gorge in Georgia by American-trained Georgian forces nabbed Saif al Islam el Masry, a member of al Qaeda's shura (council), and disrupted a plot by Arab jihadis training there to bomb or use improvised chemical weapons against Western (not Russian) targets in Russia and Central Asia.[110] As with other centers of learning, the precise number of jihadis trained at the camps in Chechnya remains unknown, but their contribution to the ongoing conflict in the region is widely accepted.

In one of several new guerilla warfare techniques, Khattab videotaped graphic attacks on Russian forces in the 1990s and packaged them together as videotapes called "Russian Hell," which were sold in Western mosques and Middle Eastern bazaars and now circulate on the Internet. In one video posted in the late 1990s, a Russian soldier is seen kneeling in front of a group of masked, shouting fighters, whose leader then steps forward and slits the soldier's throat. All the sights and sounds are captured in horrific detail, eerily reminiscent of the Iraqi videos we have come to know years later. Khattab also promoted the use of suicide bombings—a technique that has become all too common in other Islamist militant-related conflicts around the world. Prominent examples include the December 2002 attack on the headquarters of the Moscow-backed Chechen government; the May 2003 attack on a Chechen government building in the north of the republic; the June 2003 attack on a bus carrying military personnel stationed at Mozdok in North Ossetia near the Chechen border; the July 2003 bombing of a rock festival just outside Moscow; the August 2003 attack on a military hospital at Mozdok; the February and August 2004 attacks on Moscow's underground transport system; and the September 2004 siege of a school in Beslan, North Ossetia, which killed and wounded hundreds (many of them children), and which received widespread international attention and condemnation. Although Khattab and other Chechen leaders have been killed by Russian forces, the fighting continues; in July 2005, an armored police vehicle was blown up north of the Chechen capital, killing fifteen people.

In addition to acquiring and developing new knowledge in support of their struggle, Chechens are also facilitating the transfer of knowledge to other regions of the world. For example, in April 2005, a new magazine appeared on the Internet: *Sawt al-Qoqaz* ("The Voice of the Caucasus"). In the first issue, guerilla leader Shamil Basayev offers his views on the Chechen struggle, and describes the level of military cooperation between the various jihadi groups operating in the area. This issue also offers some lessons and experiences from the Chechen jihad, written by the well-respected militant Abu Omar Muhammad al-Sayf. A final plea is then made to Muslims across the world to come to the aid of the mujahideen fighting in the Caucasus.[111] Overall, the tactical innovations and soft target choices of the Chechen rebels (including the theater in Moscow and the school in Beslan) are providing examples for other terrorist groups to learn from. Thus, Chechnya can also be seen as a center of learning in the world of terrorism.

Iraq and the Anti-Coalition Insurgency

On March 22, 2005, the Pentagon announced that members of Iraq's First Police Commando Battalion had discovered and attacked an apparent training facility in the southwestern Salah ad Din province.[112] A few months later, on June 21, the Central Intelligence Agency issued a report suggesting that "Iraq may prove to be an even more effective training ground for Islamic extremists than Afghanistan."[113] Since May 2003, parts of Iraq have become new centers of terrorist learning—much of which could be called "on-the-job training." This training incorporates both motivational and operational learning. As terrorism experts Daniel Benjamin and Gabriel Weimann have argued, Iraq has become "a theater of inspiration" for a "drama of faith, in which the jihadists believe they can win by seizing cities and towns, killing American troops and destabilizing the country with attacks on the police, oil pipelines and reconstruction projects."[114] A mix of motivated Sunni extremists, former regime elements, and foreign fighters have caused a significant number of deaths (the majority of them Iraqi civilians) throughout the country, primarily through the use of explosives and light weaponry. As discussed earlier in this volume, their ability to conduct these attacks requires a certain breadth and depth of knowledge—knowledge that has been made available through a mixture of former Ba'ath party loyalists who were part of Saddam's army, foreign fighters (especially veterans of previous conflicts in Afghanistan and Bosnia), and the Internet.

For example, in 2003 several issues of the online al Qaeda publication *In the Shadow of the Lances* carried a series of articles by Sayf Al Adl (believed to be a high-ranking member of al Qaeda's military operations) that offered Iraqi insurgents tactical lessons learned from the battle against U.S. forces in Afghanistan.[115] His observations and advice include the following: "Converting the military force to small units with good administrative capabilities [and] to armed militias will render the mission of the enemy impossible. . . . Build covered trenches with more than one entrance inside the yards of homes to avoid bombardment or blockage of the entrance by falling rocks. This is in regard to city inhabitants or areas expected to be bombarded. These [trenches] help in hiding the location, and facilitates the operation of traps for any ground attack unit. Our second advice is to train on reconnaissance, traps, and raiding operations and to work in small groups, and avoid by all means working in large groups. . . . [Also, in a section regarding communications]: it is very important to have alternatives to advanced technology, down to old fashioned couriers."[116] Through this and other online publications, al Qaeda and other groups have provided both motivational and operational support for the Iraqi insurgency. In another example, a posting on the Syrian mujahid website Minbar Suria al-Islami (www.nnuu.org) during the summer of 2005 offered advice for those seeking to get into Iraq via Syria.[117] However, of even more importance to this discussion is the fact that knowledge transfer in Iraq is a two-way street: Insurgents are learning from other Islamist militants, and terrorists worldwide are learning from the successes and failures of the Iraqi insurgent groups.

While local support for the Iraqi insurgency varies from group to group, and little strategic coordination is likely between the groups, the ongoing conflict is providing a forum for new terrorist recruits to gain tactical and operational learning, particularly in the area of urban guerilla warfare. One group, which claims responsibility for many of the explosions, beheadings, and other attacks in Iraq, is led by Abu Musab al-Zarqawi, a veteran fighter who had run his own training camp in the western Afghan city of Herat before fleeing to northern Iraq during the 2001 U.S.-led war in Afghanistan. While initially, this group had no formal association with al Qaeda, on October 19, 2004, Zarqawi announced a new name for the group, formerly known as Tawhid wal Jihad (Unity and Holy War); it would now be called the Al Qaeda Committee for Jihad in the Land of the Two Rivers. This group, more than any other, has been a key source of knowledge transfer both in and out of the Iraqi theater of operations.

As described in chapter 1 of this volume, Iraq is providing an important center of organizational learning and adaptation, particularly in the realm of suicide bombings and in building and deploying improvised explosive devices (IEDs) with greater effectiveness. Recognizing that this kind of operational learning is useful not only among members of the Iraqi insurgency, instructions and lessons learned are being shared globally, via the Internet. In one example, a twenty-six-minute video posted to the infamous "al-Ansar" forum lays out in precise detail how to construct a suicide bomber's explosive belt, with tips on how to estimate the impact of an explosion, how best to arrange the shrapnel for maximum destruction, how to strap the belt onto the bomber's body, and even how to avoid the migraine headache that can come from exposure to the recommended explosive chemicals.[118] Other video clips include "Heroes of Fallujah," which shows several black-masked men laying a roadside bomb, disguising it in a hole in the dusty road, then watching as it blows up a U.S. armored personnel carrier, and a professional-looking promotional video called "All Religion Will Be for Allah." As a recent *Washington Post* article observed, "Never before has a guerrilla organization so successfully intertwined its real-time war on the ground with its electronic jihad, making Zarqawi's group practitioners of what experts say will be the future of insurgent warfare, where no act goes unrecorded and atrocities seem to be committed in order to be filmed and distributed nearly instantaneously online."[119] Thus, through videos of terrorist attacks and instructions on how to carry out your own attacks, insurgents in Iraq are demonstrating how the Internet can be useful for the spread of radical Islamist terror elsewhere in the world.

Websites have popped up throughout the Internet, depicting events in Iraq as a glorious struggle and characterizing the lethal deeds of terrorists as valiant efforts to drive out the aggressors and occupiers of an Islamic land. Some websites have posted images of Western hostages begging for their lives and being beheaded, accompanied by messages justifying such atrocities as serving the will of Allah. Even the Sunni extremist group Lashkar-e-Taiba, probably the largest militant group in Pakistan, has turned its attention away from its longtime focus on Kashmir, and is focusing on the struggle in Iraq. Its online Urdu publication has called for sending holy warriors to Iraq "to take revenge" for a host of alleged Western atrocities. More alarming to U.S. policymakers, a notice on the website of this group recently read, "Jihad against America has now become mandatory."[120]

In sum, according to the 2005 CIA report mentioned earlier, the conflict in Iraq has provided a real-world laboratory for testing and refining urban combat tactics, helping would-be terrorists learn how to carry out assassinations, kidnappings, car bombings, and other kinds of attacks that were never a staple of the fighting in Afghanistan during the anti-Soviet campaigns of the 1980s.[121] In some cases, new recruits to the Islamist extremist movement have been drawn to the Iraqi conflict for the sole purpose of learning how to conduct jihad. Indeed, one could argue that Zarqawi's organization might not exist without the opportunity to gather motivated individuals who could subsequently gain operational knowledge in the Iraqi theatre of combat. While some of these individuals will surely never leave Iraq alive, others will eventually return to their countries of origin or migrate to other parts of the world, taking with them valuable knowledge for conducting terrorist attacks. As such, Iraq can be considered one of many important centers of learning in the terrorist world.

The "Ungoverned Spaces" of Africa

Marine Corps General James L. Jones, commander of the U.S. and NATO (North Atlantic Treaty Organization) forces in Europe, recently commented that "the large, ungoverned spaces in Africa are very tempting" to terrorist organizations.[122] Indeed, recent intelligence reports have indicated that violent extremist groups are increasingly looking to sub-Saharan Africa as an attractive transit route for illegal materials and money laundering. According to a 2003 Congressional Research Service report, al Qaeda has already established a presence in several regions of Africa.[123] Further, organized criminal cartels have for decades taken advantage of a variety of security vulnerabilities throughout Africa, including porous borders and a limited law enforcement capacity. The extensive land and sea boundaries of many African states are often virtually unpatrolled. Many points of entry cannot be monitored by states with limited resources, resulting in opportunities for illegal immigration and constituting entry points for organized criminals. Customs and immigration services in African countries are often poorly trained, equipped, and paid. As such, they are readily circumvented or intimidated by the relatively sophisticated methods employed by drug dealers and others who can offer bribes and have access to speedboats and overwhelming firepower.[124] These same regional security vulnerabilities can also facilitate the activities of terrorist networks—indeed, according to Jonathon Schanzer, author of a recent book on al Qaeda, "If you can't seal your borders and there are areas that no one's watching, it leaves the opportunity for exploitation."[125]

Africa is already no stranger to global terrorism. Al Qaeda established its ability to strike at U.S. interests in Africa with the 1998 bombings of the

U.S. embassies in Kenya and Tanzania, killing 214 and wounding nearly 5,000. In November 2002, a suicide bomber rammed a truck into an Israeli hotel in the Kenyan port city of Mombasa, killing 15 people, while another attacker fired two surface-to-air rockets at a commercial Israeli airliner, narrowly failing in their attempt to bring the aircraft down. Other recent terrorist attacks in Africa include the 1997 mass murder of 62 people, mainly tourists, in Luxor, Egypt; a 2002 gas tank bombing in Djerba, Tunisia, that killed 21 and injured more than 30 others; and a series of suicide attacks in 2003, in which the group Salafia Jihadia killed 33 and injured more than 100 others throughout Casablanca, Morocco.

Terrorist networks have already been established in the Horn of Africa and the eastern coastal states of Kenya and Tanzania.[126] For example, reports have identified the Dabaab refugee camp on the Somalia-Kenya border as a training ground for Islamist extremists.[127] As mentioned earlier, Sudan has provided space for terrorist training and activities for many years. In addition, failed or failing states in central and western Africa have already provided opportunities for al Qaeda and criminal networks possibly affiliated with it to profit from various underground financial and trade networks.[128] General Charles Wald, Deputy Commander of U.S. European Command, has been warning Congress for some time that al Qaeda–affiliated groups are active in Mauritania, Mali, Chad, and Niger.[129] U.S. security think tanks have also listed Nigeria—where the presence of radical Islam is growing—as being among nations that have al Qaeda cells.[130] Clearly, the sociopolitical environment in some parts of this region is primed for the formation of al Qaeda–friendly groups. For example, in September 2004, a group of over forty armed Islamist militants, wearing red bandanas and crying "Allahu Akbar" (God is great), attacked two police stations in Borno state, northeastern Nigeria.[131] Meanwhile, economic globalization has brought an increasing presence of Western private interests throughout sub-Saharan Africa. From import-export companies to oil exploration to private security firms, the footprint of North American and European countries in Africa is significant and growing. For anti-Western extremists, this trend offers an increasingly rich target environment. Terrorists can also take advantage of the collateral benefits of globalization, particularly in the realms of finance and telecommunications.

Overall, the countries of sub-Saharan Africa are extremely vulnerable to being used as venues for terrorist training because of weak security, porous borders, and widespread corruption among border guards and other low-level officials susceptible to being bribed. To help remedy this alarming situation, the U.S. has recently launched a new initiative to enhance regional security and stability. In June 2005, the U.S. announced the Trans-Saharan Counterterrorism Initiative (built on the experiences of the earlier Pan-Sahel Initiative), through which the Pentagon will train thousands of African troops in battalions equipped for extended desert and border operations, and will link the militaries of different countries with secure satellite communications. The initiative, with funding of $100 million over five years, covers Algeria, Chad, Mali, Mauritania, Niger, Senegal, Nigeria, Morocco, and Tunisia—with the U.S. military eager to add Libya if relations improve.[132] Clearly, initiatives like these are needed anywhere there is a potential for terrorists to establish new centers of operational learning. Unfortunately, however, there is another, much larger "ungoverned space" that is proving increasingly valuable for knowledge transfer in the terrorist world.

The Internet: The Ultimate "Ungoverned Space"

In addition to traditional training camps and uncontrolled territories, recruitment and training by terrorist organizations have involved various forms of distance education—defined as instruction provided through print or electronic means to individuals in a geographic location separate from the instructor(s).[133] As described in chapter 1 of this volume, the distribution of literature has historically complemented face-to-face contact as primary vehicles for both recruitment and training of new supporters of terrorist organizations. In the twenty-first century, the Internet has become a primary vehicle for the distribution of both motivational and operational types of knowledge.

Indeed, terrorists are discovering what many Western institutions of higher learning have already recognized: images, audio and video recordings, and other forms of multimedia (distributed on CD-ROMs or via the Internet) offer powerful vehicles for motivational and operational knowledge transfer. Audio recordings have already played an historically important role in the world of Islamist extremists. Osama bin Laden is said to have been considerably influenced by the tape recordings of fiery sermons by Abdallah Azzam, a Palestinian and a disciple of Sayyid Qutb.[134] But the use of video recordings, widely distributed on the Internet, offers terrorist groups a much more powerful medium for motivating and training new cadres of members.

In late 1996, Babar Ahmad—a twenty-two-year-old computer whiz and mechanical engineering student at Imperial College in London—launched a website dedicated to promoting Islamist fighters in Bosnia, Chechnya, and Afghanistan.[135] Dubbed Azzam.com (in honor of Abdallah Azzam), the website rapidly became a prominent and influential platform for Islamist militants. Ahmad's website catered to English speakers, featured snazzy graphics, and couched its radical politics in a moderate tone by posting firsthand news reports from amateur correspondents around the world. International news organizations, including the BBC, often cited dispatches from Azzam.com and its sister websites when reporting on events in Chechnya and Afghanistan.[136] According to terrorism expert Evan Kohlmann, this was "the very first real al Qaeda website. It taught an entire generation about jihad. Even in its nascency, it was professional. It wasn't technically sophisticated, but it was professional looking, definitely more professional than any other jihadi websites out there."[137]

Almost a decade later, on June 29, 2005, a website used by Iraqi insurgent leader Abu Musab al Zarqawi's "information wing" released "All Religion Will Be for Allah"—a slickly produced video with professional-quality graphics and the feel of a blood-and-guts report of live-action war in Iraq.[138] In one chilling scene, the video cuts to a brigade of smiling young men. They are the only fighters shown unmasked, and the video explains why: They are a corps of suicide bombers-in-training. The video was offered to the world on a specially designed Web page, with dozens of links to the video, so users could choose which version to download. There were large-file editions that consumed 150 megabytes for viewers with high-speed access to the Internet and a scaled-down 4-megabyte version for those limited to dial-up access. Viewers could choose Windows Media or RealPlayer. They could even download "All Religion Will Be for Allah" to play on a cell phone.[139] These videos are not only providing motivational and operational knowledge. Their use by one terrorist group as a recruitment and training tool offers an important lesson for other terrorist groups to follow.

Among the myriad examples of motivational videos in the terrorist world, perhaps the most worrisome are those clearly designed to appeal to younger generations. For example, on August 8, 2005, a video titled "Cubs of the Land of the Two Sanctuaries" was posted to the militant radical Islamic web forum Tajdid.org.uk.[140] In the title of the video, the use of the word "cubs" suggests lion cubs, as militant radical Muslims commonly refer to themselves as lions, while the "Land of the Two Sanctuaries" is an Islamic term for Saudi Arabia, the two sanctuaries being Mecca and Medina. The video introduces a young girl, perhaps ten years old, with an AK-47 at her side. She is joined by a young boy, and together they begin speaking and gesturing in unison, waving pistols in the air as they recite the following speech: "We are terrorists, and terror is our way. Let the oppressors . . . and their masters know that we are terrorists and that we frighten. Prepare what force and equipment you can to terrorize the enemy of God. For terror is an obligation of the religion." While reciting lines such as, "We are terrorists, and terror is our way," the children place the pistols in front of their own chests. At other times they point the pistols up in the air, or toward the camera.

Other youth-oriented videos incorporate a militant Islamist flavor of hip-hop music known as "Terror Rap."[141] For example, in 2004 a British hip-hop group calling itself *Soul Salah Crew* (although their real identities are unknown) released a video entitled "Dirty Kuffar," featuring a masked "Sheikh Terra" dancing and rapping in front of the camera with the Koran in one hand and a gun in the other. Other Islamist extremist organizations, like Hizb ut-Tahrir—which seeks to overthrow Western governments in order to install Islamic fundamentalist leadership—have supported similar hip-hop groups, like "Soldiers of Allah" and "An-Nasr Productions." With catchy tunes and simple, easy-to-memorize lyrics, these videos appeal to a generation of hip-hop fans and provide an important means for terrorist groups to connect with a younger audience and gain support for their cause—and, in some cases, these individuals go on to seek knowledge in terrorist operations, either via training camps or the Internet.

Video games are also used by both Islamist extremist groups and American extremist groups as a means for both recruitment and training. For example, the Lebanese terrorist group Hizballah recently developed a video game called "Special Force," which gives players a simulated experience of military operations against Israeli soldiers in battles recreated from actual encounters in the south of Lebanon. The game—which anyone can download from the Internet and install on their home computer—is intended not only to entertain, but also to train children emotionally and mentally for military confrontation with their Israeli enemies. According to Madeleine Gruen, an intelligence analyst at the New York City Police Department's Counter Terrorism Division, "Special Force" was launched in February 2003 by Hizballah, and by the end of May more than 10,000 copies had been sold in the United States, Australia, Lebanon, Syria, Iran, Bahrain, and the United Arab Emirates.[142] Hizballah's approach, Gruen explains, was learned directly from the "first-person shooter" games developed by white supremacist groups in the U.S. For example, the racist organization National Alliance offers video games on its website with titles like "Nigger Hunt" and "Rattenjagt"—games with violent graphics, depicting real-life scenarios in which the player is the central character, killing Jews and other racial minorities.[143]

The global spread of Internet connectivity provides an increasingly useful mechanism for the terrorists to engage in distance learning activities. The invention and increasing availability of online language translation tools offers a unique and important dimension to the transfer of knowledge in the terrorism world. With these tools, the U.S. military-related websites—which offers scores of publicly available field manuals on everything from conducting psychological operations to sniper training and how to install Claymore antipersonnel mines—can be translated online and used to educate non-English-speaking terrorist-minded individuals. Further, the ability to rapidly transfer new information in electronic form to a global audience, simultaneously and in multiple languages, presents additional challenges to those seeking to curb the ability of terrorist organizations to train new members.

New online tools also offer terrorists the capability to conduct new kinds of attacks—the so-called cyberterror threat. The Internet offers a rich source of information for self-styled hackers or crackers to learn how to conduct a wide variety of cyberattacks against any private or public entity with an online presence. These resources are becoming increasingly sophisticated, and can enable a would-be terrorist to potentially crash a power grid or airport control tower, among other types of targets. A host of websites provide detailed step-by-step instructions for conducting denial of service attacks, packet sniffing, password cracking, buffer overflow attacks, network vulnerability testing, and so forth. Web surfers can download free software (like the SuperScan vulnerability scanning tool or the Ethereal packet sniffing program) for use in exploiting virtually any type of computer or network system. An entire world of hacker communities is supported online through chat rooms and other communication forums, where members share ideas and experiences, sometimes even boasting of their exploits in a perverse form of one-upmanship. Criminal hackers (an increasing concern of the FBI, Interpol, and many other agencies) most often use their technical knowledge in an effort to gain financial rewards. Terrorists may use the same knowledge and tools to gain financial rewards, but may also seek to cause real harm to economies, infrastructure, and people.[144] While private firms like CERT and Symantec scramble to keep up with the evolution and proliferation of Internet viruses and newly invented hacking techniques, the U.S. government has only recently issued its first national strategy for securing cyberspace.[145] To its credit, this document highlights the importance of multinational cooperation, particularly since many of the most active websites are hosted in countries beyond those that are committed to the global war on terrorism. Indeed, most countries recognize that it is counterproductive to allow the exchange of terrorist-related learning on their soil, and thus training camps are limited to a relatively small number of countries; yet these same countries do not yet seem to recognize that knowledge transfer may already be taking place in a virtual form, under their very noses. By allowing terrorist training websites to exist on Internet servers within their jurisdiction, these countries are in essence playing host to online centers of knowledge transfer in the terrorist world. As a result, governments are facilitating a vast "ungoverned space" that terrorist organizations are able and willing to take advantage of, as researcher Gabriel Wiemann describes in greater detail in the next chapter of this volume.

CONCLUSION

While this discussion is clearly not inclusive of all countries in which ter- rorist training camps have existed or exist today, it is representative of the multifaceted and geographically diverse world of knowledge transfer. Obviously, there are many other "ungoverned spaces" throughout the world—including regions of Latin America, Asia, and the Pacific—which demand our attention. The "centers of learning" described in this chapter have played an important role in transforming motivated individuals into dangerous terrorists. In addition to training camps and places of ongoing conflict, there are many centers of learning on the Internet that contribute to the global threat of terrorism. For example, the ongoing conflict in Iraq is not only providing a training and proving ground for Islamist extrem- ist terrorists—anyone, regardless of their political or religious ideology, can learn from the instructional videos and other materials that Zarqawi's group has made available online. As addressed in the next chapter of this volume, the role of the Internet in providing motivation and operational training of a new generation of terrorists should not be overlooked.

However, the Internet is mostly used to facilitate knowledge transfer that is primarily unidirectional. Truly effective learning, on the other hand, requires an open exchange between teachers and learners, so that ques- tions may be answered, new ideas and dimensions may be explored, and most importantly, a student's learning may be assessed. Real training for explosives requires experienced teachers and well-prepared students. Ac- cording to one military expert, "substantial instruction is required to con- struct anything more complicated than the most fundamental explosive weapons. Use of components such as mercury tilt fuses (common to car bombs), remotely controlled, and electromagnetic firing devices must be taught by experts to students already well versed in, and confident work- ing with, explosives."[146] Too many idle followers of website bomb-making instructions are likely to blow themselves and their families to bits.

Thus, this analysis indicates that physical training camps and "on-the- job" learning (through active insurgencies) will continue to play a crucial role in developing the operational capabilities of terrorist organizations for the foreseeable future. Most every significant terrorist organization has had to learn the catastrophic result of putting explosives in the hands of ill-equipped, inexperienced recruits. According to Bruce Hoffman, the term "own goal" was used in Northern Ireland to describe instances where an IRA member was assembling, transporting, or installing a de- vice that exploded prematurely. Thus, while websites and other online centers of learning appear to play an increasing role in the recruitment and training of terrorists, it is highly doubtful that they will ever truly take the place of training camps and other physical centers of motivational and operational learning. Further, as terrorism scholar J. Bowyer Bell observes, "Training camps are as much intended to raise morale and steel the faith as teach tactics and weaponry."[147] And as Marc Sageman and other researchers have observed, they also serve to build social networks—communities of like-minded individuals whose shared purpose and experiences build lifelong trust and a sense of "us, together against the world" among its members.

In prosecuting the global war on terrorism, we must therefore identify and monitor potential places for terrorist training camps, based on what past camps have had in common. The "large, ungoverned spaces" in Africa that General Jones referred to are attractive to terrorist organizations for a number of reasons. First, they are far away from population centers, which makes it harder for governments to gain human intelligence on the organization. It is, of course, equally important to avoid disturbing one's neighbors with the sounds of live combat training. Geographic isolation is also needed in order to foster and strengthen group identity formation and group cohesion. Overall, there are many good reasons why most all terrorist training camps are located in low population density areas.

Another element that is common to many training camps of the past has been the lack of a state government with the will or ability to close the camps down or prevent new ones from forming. Of particular concern are regions within poor states, where security can readily be purchased, where corruption is widespread, and where impoverished, disenfranchised youth are easy targets for recruiters promising a better way of life. It has also been recognized that the establishment of a terrorist presence is more common in the border regions between developing countries, where the lack of security forces or regular border patrols facilitates easy escape to neighboring states when necessary. Further, areas where the terrain is rugged and relatively inhospitable—whether from high, cavernous mountains as in Afghanistan, or from the dense vegetation cover found in much of Central and West Africa, southeast Asia, and Latin America—provide strategically useful staging and training grounds as well as transit routes for both criminals and terrorists. (However, given the absence of municipal services in these places, large amounts of food, water, and shelter are obviously needed, thus presenting a potential vulnerability in these camps that counterterrorist forces can exploit). Overall, as General Charles Wald observed in 2004, "we can't allow areas like that to become havens for terrorists."[148]

In addition to state incapacity, the historical record shows that state sponsorship—particularly in the extreme cases of Afghanistan, Libya, Syria, and Sudan—is a beneficial element for the establishment and maintenance of terrorist training camps. The U.S. will undoubtedly continue to exert diplomatic pressure on countries that choose to harbor or otherwise facilitate knowledge transfer in the terrorist world. Further, as the astute reader will notice, training camps are not always necessary for a country to become a place of knowledge transfer; as recent events in Iraq have clearly shown, a good deal of motivational and operational knowledge is being acquired "on the job" rather than through any formal curriculum or training regimen. As a result, there is great concern within the counterterrorism community that the extremists from Saudi Arabia, Pakistan, North Africa, Europe, and elsewhere who have gained operational experience in the Iraqi insurgency are returning home, intent on applying their knowledge toward terrorist attacks in their own countries. As CIA Director Porter Goss told a Senate meeting in February 2005, "the jihadists who survive will leave Iraq experienced in and focused on acts of urban terrorism. They represent a potential pool of contacts to build transnational cells, groups, and networks, in Saudi Arabia, Jordan and other countries."[149]

Centers of terrorist learning also require easy access to weapons and ammunition, including mortar rounds for heavy weapons training. The global arms trade thus has a role to play in preventing the proliferation of terrorist training. Counterterrorist efforts must also focus on the providers of training—organizational members with military combat experience who play a critical role as the knowledge experts upon whom the students rely. To sum up, at a minimum an operational center of learning needs operational space (preferably isolated), teachers (experts in professionally relevant knowledge), committed learners, time, money, and basic necessities.

Our understanding of terrorist training camps informs our appreciation of the global terrorist threat, and offers opportunities for successful counterterrorism efforts, while raising a number of questions for further research, including: Where are the centers of learning of the future? How do we find them? Who legitimizes knowledge in the terrorist world? Who are seen as "experts" in the kinds of knowledge useful in the terrorist world? What types of knowledge are terrorists seeking now? What are we doing to restrict access to operational knowledge (WMD, specific targets, etc.) that can be used against us? What can be done to undermine the value and credibility of knowledge centers and experts? What are the implications for intelligence services, covert special operational forces, or information operations? How can we learn what we need to know better, faster, and more effectively? Overall, as the terrorists apply their energies toward improving their level of organizational knowledge and operational sophistication (as described throughout this volume), we must respond by learning to recognize and disrupt the centers and developmental pathways of learning in the terrorist world. Our ability in and commitment to doing so may very well dictate the outcome of the global war on terror.

NOTES

I would like to thank Brigadier General (retired) Russell Howard, Major George Stewart III, and Dr. James Smith for their thoughtful guidance in revising this chapter. The views expressed are those of the author and not of the Department of the Army, the U.S. Military Academy, or any other agency of the U.S. Government.

1. Portions of this chapter were presented at the 2004 Joint Conference of the International Security and Arms Control Section of the American Political Science Association, and the International Security Studies Section of the International Studies Association (Washington, DC, October 29–30, 2004). Also, an earlier review of terrorist training camps (minus the descriptions of several countries, including Iraq, Kashmir, Chechnya, and Africa) appeared in *The Making of a Terrorist: Recruitment, Training and Root Causes*, vol. 2, ed. James JF Forest (Westport, CT: Praeger Publishers, 2005).

2. Leonard Weinberg, "Political and Revolutionary Ideologies," in *Making of a Terrorist: Recruitment, Training and Root Causes*, vol. 1, ed. James JF Forest (Westport, CT: Praeger, 2005).

3. Karen Armstrong, *The Battle for God* (New York: Alfred A. Knopf, 2000).

4. For example, see Maha Azzam, "Political Islam: Violence and the Wahhabi Connection," in *The Making of a Terrorist: Recruitment, Training and Root Causes*, vol. 1, ed. James JF Forest (Westport, CT: Praeger, 2005).

5. United States Institute of Peace, "Islamic Extremists: How Do They Mobilize Support?" Special Report no. 89 (Washington, DC: USIP, July 2002), 5–6.

6. Jarret Brachman, "Jihad Doctrine and Radical Islam," in *The Making of a Terrorist: Recruitment, Training and Root Causes*, vol. 1, ed. James JF Forest (Westport, CT: Praeger, 2005).

7. For example, see John L. Esposito, "Overview: The Significance of Religion for Global Order," in *Religion and Global Order*, ed. John L. Esposito and Michael Watson (Cardiff: University of Wales Press, 2000), 17–37; and John L. Esposito, *Unholy War: Terror in the Name of Islam* (New York: Oxford University Press, 2002).

8. Brachman, "Jihad Doctrine and Radical Islam."

9. Azzam, "Political Islam."

10. Mark Juergensmeyer, *Terror in the Mind of God: The Global Rise of Religious Violence* (Berkeley and Los Angeles: University of California Press, 2000). In particular, see 19–36 and 60–83.

11. See David C. Rapoport, "Fear and Trembling: Terrorism in Three Religious Traditions," *The American Political Science Review* 78, no. 3 (September 1984): 658–677; and David C. Rapoport, "Sacred Terror: A Contemporary Example from Islam," in *Origins of Terrorism: Psychologies, Ideologies, Theologies, States of Mind*, ed. Walter Reich (Baltimore: Woodrow Wilson Center Press, 1998), 103–130.

12. See Donatella della Porta, *Social Movements, Political Violence and the State: A Comparative Analysis of Italy and Germany* (London: Cambridge University Press, 1995); and Konrad Kellen, "Ideology and Rebellion: Terrorism in Western Germany," in *Origins of Terrorism: Psychologies, Ideologies, Theologies, States of Mind*, ed. Walter Reich (Baltimore: Woodrow Wilson Center Press, 1998), 43–58.

13. For example, see Peter Heehs, *The Bomb in Bengal: The Rise of Revolutionary Terrorism in India, 1900–1910* (Oxford University Press, 1996); and Rohan Gunaratna, *Sri Lanka's Ethnic Crisis and National Security* (Colombo: South Asian Network on Conflict Research, 1998).

14. John Darby, "The Historical Background," in *Northern Ireland: The Background to the Conflict* (Belfast, Northern Ireland: Appletree Press, 1983), 13–31; Marianne Elliott, "A Resentful Belonging: Catholic Identity in the Twentieth Century," in *The Catholics of Ulster: A History* (New York: Basic Books, 2002), 431–482; and J. Bowyer Bell, *The IRA, 1968–2000: Analysis of a Secret Army* (London: Frank Cass, 2000).

15. Weinberg, "Political and Revolutionary Ideologies."

16. See Robert J. Lifton, *Thought Reform: The Psychology of Totalism* (Chapel Hill: University of North Carolina Press, 1989); and Robert J. Lifton, *The Future of Immortality* (New York: Basic Books, 1987).

17. Jerrold M. Post, "Terrorist Psycho-logic: Terrorist Behavior as a Product of Psychological Forces," in *Origins of Terrorism: Psychologies, Ideologies, Theologies, States of Mind*, ed. Walter Reich (Baltimore: Woodrow Wilson Center Press, 1998), 25–40; and Jerrold Post, "When Hatred Is Bred in the Bone: The Socio-Cultural Underpinnings of Terrorist Psychology," in *The Making of a Terrorist: Recruitment, Training and Root Causes*, vol. 2, ed. James JF Forest (Westport, CT: Praeger, 2005).

18. Martha Crenshaw, "The Logic of Terrorism: Terrorist Behavior as a Product of Strategic Choice," in *Origins of Terrorism: Psychologies, Ideologies, Theologies, States of Mind*, ed. Walter Reich (Baltimore: Woodrow Wilson Center Press, 1998), 7–24.

19. Marc Sageman, *Understanding Terror Networks* (Philadelphia: University of Pennsylvania Press, 2004), 178.

20. Anthony Stahelski, "Terrorists Are Made, not Born: Creating Terrorists Using Social Psychological Conditioning," *Journal of Homeland Security*, March 2004, www.homelandsecurity.org/journal/Articles/stahelski.html.

21. See "Controversial Cleric of UK Mosque," *CNN*, 1 April 2003, www.cnn.com/2003/WORLD/europe/01/20/uk.hamzaprofile.

22. For the ongoing news reports on this story, see www.arabnews.com, www.bbc.com, and http://abu-hamza-news.newslib.com.

23. See "Abu Hamza: Controversial Muslim Figure," *CNN*, 7 May 2004, www.cnn.com/2004/WORLD/europe/05/27/uk.hamza.profile.

24. National Commission on Terrorist Attacks Upon the United States, *The 9/11 Commission Report* (New York: W. W. Norton, 2004): 160–165.

25. Founded by Mohammed ibn Abd Wahhab in the 1740s, Wahhabism seeks to purge what are viewed as corrupting influences in Islam and return it to its original orthodoxy. Non-Wahhabis are considered infidels, and failure to adhere to the faith's tenets draws severe punishment.

26. See, for example, Peter W. Singer, "Pakistan's Madrassahs: Ensuring a System of Education, not Jihad," Analysis Paper #14 (Washington, DC: Brookings Institution, November 2001).

27. See Zachary Abuza, *Militant Islam in Southeast Asia: Crucible of Terror* (Boulder: Lynne Rienner, 2003); see also International Crisis Group (ICG), *Al-Qaeda in Southeast Asia: The Case of the Ngruki Network* (Brussels, August 8, 2002), 7; and Zachary Abuza, "Education and Radicalization: Jemaah Islamiyah Recruitment in Southeast Asia," in *The Making of a Terrorist: Recruitment, Training and Root Causes*, vol. 1, ed. James JF Forest (Westport, CT: Praeger, 2005).

28. Singer, "Pakistan's Madrassahs."

29. Mary Anne Weaver, "A Land of Madrassahs," *APF Report* 20 (Alicia Patterson Foundation, 2002). Available online at www.aliciapatterson.org/APF2002/Weaver.

30. Greg Krikorian and Jenifer Warren, "Terror Probe Targets Prison in Folsom," *Los Angeles Times*, 17 August 2005.

31. See U.S. Congress. Senate, Committee on the Judiciary, "Testimony of John Pistole, Assistant Director of Counterterrorism, Federal Bureau of Investigation," *Terrorist Recruitment and Infiltration in the United States: Prisons and Military as an Operational Base*, 14 October 2003. See also Kevin Flynn and Gary Gerhardt, *The Silent Brotherhood: Inside America's Racist Underground* (New York: Free Press, 1989); and Anti-Defamation League, *Dangerous Convictions: An Introduction to Extremist Activities in Prison* (Washington, DC: ALD, 2002). Available online at www.adl.org/learn/Ext_Terr/dangerous_convictions.pdf.

32. See U.S. Department of Justice. "A Review of the Bureau of Prisons' Selection of Muslim Religious Services Providers," April 2004. Available online at www.usdoj.gov/oig/special/0404/.

33. J. Michael Waller, "Prisons as Terrorist Breeding Grounds," in *The Making of a Terrorist: Recruitment, Training and Root Causes*, vol. 2, ed. James JF Forest (Westport, CT: Praeger, 2005).

34. See Bell, *The IRA, 1968–2000*. See also David E. Smith, *The Training of Terrorist Organizations* (CSC Report, 1995). Available online at www.globalsecurity.org/military/library/report/1995/SDE.htm [accessed 24 July 2003].

35. Phil Hirschkorn, "Trials Expose Terrorist Training Camps," *CNN*, 18 July 2001.

36. Hirschkorn, "Trials Expose Terrorist Training Camps."

37. See Smith, "Training of Terrorist Organizations."

38. See Martha Brill Olcott and Bakhtiyar Babajanov, "The Terrorist Notebooks," *Foreign Policy* (March–April 2003), 30–40.

39. Olcott and Babajanov, "The Terrorist Notebooks," 33.

40. See C. J. Chivers and David Rohde, "Turning out Guerillas and Terrorists to Wage a Holy War," *New York Times*, 18 March 2002, A1.

41. Chivers and Rohde, "Turning out Guerillas."

42. Chivers and Rohde, "Turning out Guerillas."

43. Chivers and Rohde, "Turning out Guerillas."

44. See Nic Robertson, "Tapes Show al Qaeda Trained for Urban Jihad on West," *CNN*, 20 August 2002, www.cnn.com/2002/US/08/20/terror.tape.main.

45. Robertson, "Tapes Show al Qaeda."

46. See John J. Lumpkin, "Bin Laden's Terrorist Training Combined Math, Missiles," *Associated Press*, 9 October 2001. Available online at www.globalsecurity.org/org/news/2001/011009attack02.htm.

47. For more on this, please read chapter 1 of this volume, as well as *The Making of a Terrorist: Recruitment, Training and Root Causes*, vol. 2, ed. James Forest (Westport, CT: Praeger, 2005).

48. See Anonymous, *Through Our Enemy's Eyes* (Dulles, Virginia: Brasseys, Inc., 2003), 101.

49. Anonymous, *Through Our Enemy's Eyes*, 130–131.

50. See, for example, Chivers and Rohde, "Turning out Guerillas," 2002.

51. For more on Al Qaeda's terrorist training camps in Afghanistan, see Rohan Gunaratna and Arabinda Acharya, "The Al Qaeda Training Camps of Afghanistan and Beyond," in *The Making of a Terrorist: Recruitment, Training and Root Causes*, vol. 2, ed. James JF Forest (Westport, CT: Praeger, 2005).

52. Marcia Christoff Kurop, "Al Qaeda's Balkan Links," *Wall Street Journal Europe*, 1 November 2001.

53. See Saul Shay and Yoram Schweitzer, "The 'Afghan Alumni' Terrorism," International Policy Institute for Counterterrorism Report, 6 November 2000. Available online at www.ict.org.il.

54. Youssef H. Aboul-Enein, "Al-Ikhwan Al-Muslimeen: The Muslim Brotherhood," *Military Review*, July–August, 2003, 26–31.

55. Aboul-Enein, "Al-Ikhwan Al-Muslimeen," 28.

56. For more on these, please see the chapter by Kumar Ramakrishna in this volume, as well as Zachary Abuza, "Education and Radicalization: Jemaah Islamiyah Recruitment in Southeast Asia," and Kumar Ramakrishna, "Indoctrination Processes Within Jemaah Islamiyah," in *The Making of a Terrorist: Recruitment, Training and Root Causes*, ed. James JF Forest (Westport, CT: Praeger, 2005).

57. See David E. Kaplan and Andrew Marshall, *The Cult at the End of the World* (New York: Crown Publishers, 1996); Amy E. Smithson and Leslie Anne Levy, "Ataxia: The Chemical and Biological Terrorism Threat and the U.S. Response," Stimson Center Report No. 35 (Washington, DC: Henry L. Stimson Center, 2000); and Patrick Bellamy, "Aum Shinrikyo" (a terrorist group profile), www.crimelibrary.com/terrorists_spies/terrorists/prophet/28.html?sect=22.

VX gas was developed in the Porton Down Chemical Weapons Research Centre, Wiltshire, England. VX gas is a straw-colored, toxic liquid (boiling point 298 degrees Celsius) with the formula: methylphosphonothioic acid, S-[2-[bis(1-methylethyl)amino]ethyl]- O-ethyl ester. The "V" of VX signifies its long persistence—it is more dangerous and toxic than its cousins of the "G" variety like GA (Tabun) and GB (Sarin), which dissipate quickly and have only short-term effects. It is easily absorbed into the body, disrupts the passage of messages between nerves, and from nerves to muscles. The liquid form of VX is absorbed through the eyes or the skin of the victim. It takes an hour or two to take effect and its effects result in death. The gaseous form is more deadly than the liquid form and acts almost immediately on the victim. The effects are worst when it is inhaled and death is an end to the suffering. Inhalation at concentrations as low as 30 mg per cubic meter kills within fifteen minutes.

58. United Nations Office of Drugs and Crime, "Terrorism and Weapons of Mass Destruction," www.unodc.org/unodc/terrorism_weapons_mass_destruction_page002.html [accessed October 18, 2004].

59. United Nations Office of Drugs and Crime, "Terrorism and Weapons of Mass Destruction."

60. See Hala Jaber, *Hezbollah, Born with a Vengeance* (New York: Columbia University Press, 1997), 12.

61. Jaber, *Hezbollah*, 19–22.

62. Jaber, *Hezbollah*, 22–23.

63. See Magnus Ranstorp, "The Hizballah Training Camps of Lebanon," in *The Making of a Terrorist: Recruitment, Training and Root Causes*, vol. 2, ed. James JF Forest (Westport, CT: Praeger, 2005); see also "IDF Action in Syria," *Israel News Agency*, 5 October 2003. Available online at www.israelnewsagency.com

64. Bell, *The IRA, 1968–2000*, 184.

65. Christopher Boucek, "Libyan State-Sponsored Terrorism: An Historical Perspective," *Terrorism Monitor* 3, no. 6 (March 24, 2005).

66. Boaz Ganor, "Libya and Terrorism," *Survey of Arab Affairs—A Periodic Supplement to Jerusalem Letter/Viewpoints* 28 (1 June 1992), www.ict.org.il/articles/article3.htm.

67. Council on Foreign Relations, "Libya," profiled on its "Terrorism: Q&A" website at http://cfrterrorism.org/sponsors/libya.html; and Global Security, "Libya," profiled on their website at www.globalsecurity.org/intell/world/libya/facility.htm.

68. Bell, *The IRA, 1968–2000*, 182.

69. Bell, *The IRA, 1968–2000*, 180–185.

70. Bell, *The IRA, 1968–2000*, 184–185.

71. Smith, "Training of Terrorist Organizations," 25.

72. See Smith, "Training of Terrorist Organizations," 25; and Thomas Bedford and Frank Jones, "Sendero Luminoso: Origins, Outlooks and Implications" (Monterey, CA: Naval Postgraduate School, June 1986), 53.

73. Maria Ressa, *The Seeds of Terror: An Eyewitness Account of Al Qaeda's Newest Center of Operations in Southeast Asia* (New York: Free Press, 2003), 133–135.

74. Abuza, *Militant Islam*, 97.

75. Ressa, *Seeds of Terror*, 110.

76. Rohan Gunaratna, *Sri Lanka's Ethnic Crisis and National Security* (Colombo: South Asian Network on Conflict Research, 1998).

77. Manoj Joshi, "On the Razor's Edge: The Liberation Tigers of Tamil Eelam," *Studies in Conflict and Terrorism* 19, no. 1 (January–March, 1996), 19–42.

78. Alan Feur, "Jihad, Inc.: The Bin Laden Network of Companies Exporting Terror," *New York Times*, 13 February 2001, as cited in *Through Our Enemy's Eyes*, 2003, 126.

79. United States Institute of Peace, "Terrorism in the Horn of Africa," Special Report 113 (Washington, DC: USIP, January 2004). Available online at www.usip.org.

80. See Jaber, *Hezbollah,* 12–22.

81. U.S. Department of State, *Patterns of Global Terrorism,* 1993, www.hri.org/USSD-Terror/93/statespon.html.

82. See "IDF Action in Syria," *Israel News Agency,* 5 October 2003. Available online at www.israelnewsagency.com.

83. Dr. Ely Karmon, "Islamic Terrorist Activities in Turkey in the 1990s," *Terrorism and Political Violence* 10, no. 4 (Winter 1998): 101–121.

84. Karmon, "Islamic Terrorist Activities."

85. Ely Karmon, "Terrorism in Turkey: An Analysis of the Principal Players," International Policy Institute for Counterterrorism report, 1999. Available online at www.ict.org.il/articles/articledet.cfm?articleid=74.

86. For more on the history of this region, see Ahmad Rashid, *Jihad: The Rise of Militant Islam in Central Asia* (New Haven: Yale University Press, 2002).

87. Center for Nonproliferation Studies, "Islamic Movement of Uzbekistan," Monterey Institute of International Studies, Special Section: Terrorist Attacks on America. Available online at http://cns.miis.edu/research/wtc01/imu.htm.

88. James Aho, "Christian Fundamentalism and Militia Movements in the United States," in *The Making of a Terrorist: Recruitment, Training and Root Causes,* vol 1, ed. James JF Forest (Westport, CT: Praeger Publishers, 2005).

89. Aho, "Christian Fundamentalism."

90. For more on this story, see the series of investigative reports by the *Seattle Times,* including Mike Carter and Hal Bernton, "U.S. Complain Details Failed Plan for Terrorist Training in Oregon," *Seattle Times,* 9 August 2005.

91. "FBI: Al Qaeda plot possibly uncovered," *CNN,* 9 June 2005, www.cnn.com/2005/US/06/09/terror.probe/.

92. See the Counterterrorism Blog report at http://counterterror.typepad.com/the_counterterrorism_blog/2005/06/lodi_terror_cas.html.

93. "FBI: Al Qaeda plot possibly uncovered," *CNN,* 9 June 2005, www.cnn.com/2005/US/06/09/terror.probe/.

94. Press Trust of India, "Terrorist training camp destroyed, five terrorists killed," 27 May 2005. Availabe online at www.hindustantimes.com/news/181_1378250,000900010002.htm.

95. "New Questions About Al Qaeda Training Camps in Pakistan," *ABC News,* 8 June 2005. Available online at http://abcnews.go.com/WNT/Investigation/story?id=831750&page=1&CMP=OTC-RSSFeeds0312.

96. Khwaja Geedar Khan, "Peshawar: The Obdurant Bastion of Soviet-Era Mujahideen," *Terrorism Monitor* 2, no. 17 (9 September 2004).

97. For example, see "Kashmir Key to Al Qaeda's Strategy Versus US," *Global Policy Forum,* 19 June 2002. Available online at www.globalpolicy.org/wtc/analysis/2002/0619kashmir.htm.

98. Preston Mendenhall, "Pakistan's religious schools in spotlight again: Crackdown ordered, but madrasas promise backlash of hatred," *NBC News,* 25 July 2005, http://msnbc.msn.com/id/8698592/.

99. Singer, "Pakistan's Madrassahs."

100. Mendenhall, "Pakistan's religious schools."

101. Mendenhall, "Pakistan's religious schools."

102. Reuters, "Pakistan to close Afghan refugee camps near border," 6 August 2005, http://in.today.reuters.com/news/newsArticle.aspx?type=topNews&storyID=2005-08-06T184437Z_01_NOOTR_RTRJONC_0_India-211817-1.xml.

103. Mendenhall, "Pakistan's religious schools."

104. The following paragraph on the history of Chechnya draws on material from several BBC resources, including: "The First Bloody Battle," *BBC News,* 16 March 2000, http://

news.bbc.co.uk/1/hi/world/europe/482323.stm; "Timeline: Chechnya," *BBC News*, 20 July 2005, available online at http://news.bbc.co.uk/1/hi/world/asia-pacific/country_profiles/2357267.stm; and "Timeline: Russia," *BBC News*, 9 August 2005, http://news.bbc.co.uk/1/hi/world/europe/country_profiles/1113655.stm.

105. See Brian Glyn Williams, "The 'Chechen Arabs': An Introduction to the Real Al Qaeda Terrorists from Chechnya," *Terrorism Monitor* 2, no. 1, 15 January 2004.

106. *Observer* (UK), "The Men Who Brought the World to the Brink of War," September 23, 2001. Cited in Brian Glyn Williams, "The Chechen Arabs," *Terrorism Monitor* 2, no. 1, 15 January 2004.

107. Ahmed al Haj, "Yemen Arrests Suspected Al Qaeda Leader," *Associated Press*, 26 November 2003. Cited in Williams, "The Chechen Arabs."

108. al Haj, "Yemen Arrests Suspected Al Qaeda Leader."

109. al Haj, "Yemen Arrests Suspected Al Qaeda Leader."

110. Paul Quinn-Judge, "The Surprise in the Gorge. Al Qaeda Flourishes in Far-Off Spots," *Time*, 20 October 2002. Cited in Williams, "The Chechen Arabs."

111. Stephen Ulph, "The Voice of the Caucasus—A New Jihadi Magazine," *Terrorism Focus* 2, no. 8 (28 April 2005).

112. "Iraqi Commandos Strike Insurgent Training Site," *American Forces Press Service*, 22 March 2005, www.defenselink.mil/news/Mar2005/20050322_276.html.

113. Douglas Jehl, "Iraq May Be Prime Place for Training of Militants, CIA Report Concludes," *Washington Post*, 21 June 2005.

114. Daniel Benjamin and Gabriel Weimann, "What the Terrorists Have in Mind," *New York Times*, 27 October 2004.

115. Ben Venzke and Aimee Ibrahim, "Al Qaeda's Advice for Mujahideen in Iraq: Lessons Learned in Afghanistan," *IntelCenter Report V1.0*, 14 April 2003, www.intelcenter.com.

116. Venzke and Ibrahim, "Al Qaeda's Advice."

117. Stephen Ulph, "Syrian website calls for experienced mujahideen, as Aleppo becomes key point of departure for Iraq," *Terrorism Focus* 2, no. 13 (13 July 2005).

118. Susan B. Glasser and Steve Coll, "The Web as Weapon: Zarqawi Intertwines Acts on Ground in Iraq with Propaganda Campaign on the Internet," *Washington Post*, 9 August 2005, A01. Online at www.washingtonpost.com/wp-dyn/content/article/2005/08/08/AR2005080801018.html.

119. Glasser and Coll, "The Web as Weapon."

120. Daniel Benjamin and Gabriel Weimann, "What the Terrorists Have in Mind," *New York Times*, 27 October 2004.

121. Jehl, "Iraq May Be Prime Place."

122. Schrader, Esther, "U.S. Seeks Military Access in N. Africa," *New York Times*, 27 March 2004.

123. Congressional Research Service, *Nations Hospitable to Organized Crime and Terrorism* (Washington, DC: Library of Congress, Federal Research Division, October, 2003).

124. Congressional Research Service, *Nations Hospitable*.

125. Quoted in Council on Foreign Relations, "Africa: Terror Havens," website profile, 30 December 2003, www.cfr.org

126. House Committee on International Relations, Subcommittee on Africa, Princeton N. Lyman, "The Terrorist Threat in Africa," 1 April 2004.

127. For example, see United States Institute of Peace, "Terrorism in the Horn of Africa," *USIP Special Report 113*, January 2004. Available online at www.usip.org.

128. Lyman, "Terrorist Threat in Africa."

129. Douglas Farah and Richard Shultz, "Al Qaeda's Growing Sanctuary," *Washington Post*, 13 July 2004. Also, see Voice of America, "Terrorism in Africa" (editorial), 7 April 2004.

130. *Associated Press*, "U.S. Military Shows Interest in Africa," 25 February 2004, www.military.com/NewsContent/0,13319,FL_Africa_022502,00.html.

131. Elizabeth Blunt, "Nigeria's New Breed of Radical Islam," *BBC News*, 22 September 2004, http://news.bbc.co.uk/1/hi/world/africa/3679960.stm; and "Nigeria police hunt 'Taleban,'" *BBC News*, 22 September 2004, http://news.bbc.co.uk/1/hi/world/africa/3679092.stm

132. Ann Scott Tyson, "U.S. Pushes Anti-Terrorism in Africa: Under Long-Term Program, Pentagon to Train Soldiers of 9 Nations," *Washington Post*, 26 July 2005, A01. Also, see Rear Admiral Hamlin B. Tallent (Director of European Plans and Operations Center, EUCOM), testimony before Congress, 10 March 2005.

133. Debra J. Blanke and Gina M. Wekke, "Distance Education," in *Higher Education in the United States*, ed. James J.F. Forest and Kevin Kinser (Santa Barbara, CA: ABC-CLIO Press, 2002).

134. *9/11 Commission Report*, 55

135. Craig Whitlock, "Briton Used Internet as His Bully Pulpit," *Washington Post*, 8 August 2005, A01.

136. Whitlock, "Briton Used Internet."

137. Whitlock, "Briton Used Internet."

138. Glasser and Coll, "Web as Weapon."

140. " أشبال من بلاد الحرمين .. (فديو) .. حصريا على منتدى التجديد ولأول مرة " (Exclusively on Tajdid Forum for the First Time, Video: Cubs from the Land of the Two Sanctuaries)," 9 August 2005. Availabe online at www.tajdeed.org.uk/forums/showthread.php?s=8454388d52907025a6fa6157feb51bde&threadid=37270.

141. The following paragraph summarizes material from Madeleine Gruen, "Innovative Recruitment and Indoctrination Tactics by Extremists: Video Games, Hip Hop, and the World Wide Web," in *The Making of a Terrorist: Recruitment, Training and Root Causes*, vol. 1, ed. James JF Forest (Westport, CT: Praeger, 2005).

142. See Gruen, "Innovative Recruitment."

143. Gruen, "Innovative Recruitment."

144. However, it is doubtful that al Qaeda or any other group would actually want to "bring down the Internet." Indeed, according to Louise Richardson, the executive dean of the Radcliffe Institute, for all the concern about "cyberterrorism," the Internet is "far too valuable to al Qaeda" and other groups: "Al Qaeda could not function without the Internet." See Ruth Walker, "Terror online, and how to counteract it," *Harvard Gazette*, 3 March 2005, www.news.harvard.edu/gazette/2005/03.03/01-cyberterror.html.

145. *National Strategy for Security Cyberspace* (Washington, DC: The White House, 2002).

146. See Smith, "Training of Terrorist Organizations."

147. Bell, *The IRA, 1968–2000*, 180

148. Andrew Koch, "No Safe Haven in Africa," *Jane's Intelligence Review*, 9 November 2004.

149. Anna Badkhen, "Curbing Terrorism Stumbles over Bush's War on Terror," *San Francisco Chronicle*, 20 March 2005.

5

Virtual Training Camps:
Terrorists' Use of the Internet

Gabriel Weimann

"Oh Mujahid [holy warrior] brother, in order to join the great training camps you don't have to travel to other lands. Alone, in your home or with a group of your brothers, you too can begin to execute the training program. You can all join the Al-Battar Training Camp."

Al-Battar no. 1, the online manual of al Qaeda

When American forces in Afghanistan shut down al Qaeda terrorist training camps, the terror group moved its base of operations to the Internet. The Internet has become a valuable tool for the terrorist organization, not just to coordinate operations and launch attacks, but also to serve as a location for virtual training camps and a tool for indoctrination and recruitment. In reality, the Internet became for al Qaeda what experts call an "online terrorism university." The prospect of self-taught terrorism suggests that personal initiative and decentralization may soon provide additional elements of chaos to the already difficult task of tracking the web of terror groups and individuals. More than three hundred new pages of al Qaeda–related manuals, instructions, and rhetoric are published on the Internet every month. "It is not necessary . . . for you to join in a military training camp, or travel to another country . . . you can learn alone, or with other brothers, in [our arms] preparation program," announced al Qaeda leader Abu Hadschir Al Muqrin, and cited by *Der Spiegel Online*, the Internet version of the weekly German newsmagazine.[1]

Paradoxically, the very decentralized network of communication that the U.S. security services created (out of fear of the Soviet Union) now serves the interests of the greatest foe of the West's security services since the end of the Cold War: international terror. The roots of the modern Internet are to be found in the early 1970s, during the days of the Cold War, when the U.S. Department of Defense was concerned with reducing the vulnerability of its communication networks to nuclear attack. The Defense Department decided to decentralize the entire system by creating an interconnected web of computer networks. After twenty years of development and use by academic researchers, the Internet quickly expanded and changed its character when it was opened up to commercial users in the late 1980s. By the mid-1990s, the Internet connected more than eighteen thousand private, public, and national networks, with the number increasing daily. Hooked into those networks were about 3.2 million host computers and perhaps as many as 60 million users spread across all seven continents. The estimated number of users in the early years of the twenty-first century is over a billion.

With the enormous growth in the size and the use of the network, utopian visions of the promise of the Internet were challenged by the proliferation of pornographic and violent content on the Web, and by the use of the Internet by extremist organizations of various kinds. Groups with very different political goals—but united in their readiness to employ terrorist tactics—started using the network to distribute their propaganda, to communicate with their supporters, to foster public awareness of (and sympathy for) their causes, to teach and train their operatives, and even to execute operations.

By its very nature, the Internet is in many ways an ideal arena for activity by terrorist organizations. Most notably, it offers:

- easy access;
- little or no regulation, censorship, or other forms of government control;
- potentially huge audiences spread throughout the world;
- anonymity of communication;
- fast flow of information;
- interactive communication;
- inexpensive development and maintenance of a web presence; and
- a multimedia environment (the ability to combine text, graphics, audio, and video and to allow users to download films, songs, books, posters, and so forth).

These advantages have not gone unnoticed by terrorist organizations, no matter what their political orientation. Islamists and Marxists, nationalists and separatists, fundamentalists and extremists, racists and anarchists—they all find the Internet alluring. Today, almost all active terrorist organizations maintain websites, and many maintain more than one website and use several different languages. Websites are only one of the Internet's services used by modern terrorism: there are other facilities on the Net—including e-mail, chat rooms, e-groups, forums, and virtual message boards—that are used more and more by terrorists. Thus, for example, Yahoo! has become one of al Qaeda's most significantly useful bases of operation. They utilize several facets of the Yahoo! service, including chat functions, e-mail, and most importantly, Yahoo! Groups. Yahoo! Groups are electronic groups (e-groups) dedicated to a specific topic whereby members of the group can discuss the topic, post relevant articles and multimedia files, and share a meeting place for those with similar interests. Creating a Yahoo! Group is free, quick, and extremely easy, and several terrorist groups and their supporters have used several Yahoo! Groups.[2] Very often, the groups contain the latest links to other websites—serving as an online directory for information of interest to group members—and are sometimes the first to post communiqués to the public. This chapter examines the terrorists' use of the Internet as virtual training camps, as an online forum for indoctrination, and as a terrorist arsenal of manuals, instructions, and data.

RESEARCH ON TERRORISTS' USE OF THE INTERNET

The discussion provided in this chapter draws from a more general research project hosted and funded by the United States Institute of Peace that summarized seven years of monitoring terrorist presence on the Internet.[3] The population for this study was defined as the Internet sites of terrorist movements as they appeared in the period between January 1998 and July 2004. The U.S. State Department's list of terrorist organizations was used, which meets the accepted definition of terror.[4] Two earlier studies served as pilot studies for the present project: a systematic content analysis was applied to a sample of terrorist sites and this analysis was repeated after three years.[5] These exploratory studies provided both the methodological tools and the first evidence of the diffusion of terrorism into the Internet and its growing sophistication.

To locate the terrorist sites, frequent systematic scans of the Internet were conducted using the various keywords and names of hundreds of organizations in the database. First, the standard search engines (Altavista, Lycos, Infoseek, Yahoo, Magellan, and Google) were used. The first search, conducted in January 1998, yielded fourteen organizations and sixteen Internet sites. Another search, conducted in January 2002, yielded twenty-nine sites from eighteen organizations. Almost all organizations active in 1998 were also online in 2002. However, many of the Web addresses used by terrorist sites in 1998 had changed by 2003–2004 (mostly due to moves to different servers) when the third Internet scan was conducted. The scan of the Internet in 2003–2004 revealed hundreds of websites serving terrorists and their supporters. The Internet, as this research confirmed, is a very dynamic arena—websites emerge and disappear, change addresses, or reformat. Throughout the years of monitoring the terrorist presence in the Net, this project has helped researchers learn how to locate terrorist organizations' new websites, and how to search in chat rooms, forums, and websites of supporters and sympathizers for new "addresses" and links. This is often a Sisyphean effort, especially since in certain instances (e.g., al Qaeda's websites) the location and contents change almost daily.

This research notably revealed a proliferation of radical Islamic websites. This is not a methodological or ideological bias, but rather a significant trend that emerged through extensive analysis of terrorist websites throughout the study. Curiously, this trend points to an interesting contradiction: the freedom offered by the Internet is vulnerable to abuse from groups that, paradoxically, are themselves intensely hostile to uncensored thought and expression. Further, the research described in this chapter demonstrates how extreme anti-Western and antimodernity forces are using the most sophisticated tools of modern Western culture.

In sum, this research identified numerous, albeit sometimes overlapping, ways in which contemporary terrorists use the Internet.[6] Some of these parallel the uses to which everyone puts the Internet—information gathering, for instance. Some resemble the uses made of the medium by traditional political organizations—for example, raising funds and disseminating propaganda. Others, however, are much more unusual and distinctive—for instance, hiding instructions, manuals, and directions in coded messages or encrypted files. While clearly there is much to explore, this discussion will focus on the use of the Internet as a virtual training camp—using the computer-mediated channels to train, teach, direct, and coordinate terrorists.

DATAMINING THE INTERNET

The Internet may be viewed as a vast digital library. The World Wide Web alone offers about a billion pages of information, much of it free—and much of it of interest to terrorist organizations. Terrorists, for instance, can learn from the Internet about the schedules and locations of targets such as transportation facilities, nuclear power plants, public buildings, airports, and ports, and even counterterrorism measures. According to researcher Dan Verton, "al Qaeda cells now operate with the assistance of large databases containing details of potential targets in the U.S. They use the Internet to collect intelligence on those targets, especially critical economic nodes, and modern software enables them to study structural weaknesses in facilities as well as predict the cascading failure effect of attacking certain systems."[7]

Numerous tools are available to facilitate such data collection, including search engines, e-mail distribution lists, chat rooms, and discussion groups. Many websites offer their own search tools for extracting information from databases on their sites. Word searches of online newspapers and journals can likewise generate useful information for terrorists; some of this information may also be available in the traditional media, but online searching capabilities allow terrorists to capture it anonymously and with very little effort or expense. One captured al Qaeda computer contained the engineering and structural architecture features of a dam, enabling al Qaeda engineers and planners to simulate catastrophic failures.[8] According to Secretary of Defense Donald Rumsfeld, speaking on January 15, 2003, an al Qaeda training manual recovered in Afghanistan tells its readers, "Using public sources openly and without resorting to illegal means, it is possible to gather at least 80 percent of all information required about the enemy."[9]

In February 2002, a major financial institution in the United States received a report outlining the extent to which its website exposes it to potential attacks by al Qaeda and other terrorist organizations. The audit, produced by the security consulting firm Stroz Associates LLC, is one of the first of its kind in the private sector. It marks a growing trend by companies in the aftermath of the September 11 terrorist attacks to assess whether content on their websites increases their risk of being targeted by terrorist organizations. The amount of sensitive data uncovered by Stroz Associates at various corporate websites is startling—according to the report, "Many websites constitute a gold mine for potential attackers." This includes descriptions of physical locations of backup facilities, the number of people working at specific facilities, detailed information about wired and wireless networks, and specifications on ventilation, air conditioning, and elevator systems. Other sites give graphical representations of floor plans, cabling connections, and ventilation ductwork and offer photographs and maps. The FBI's National Infrastructure Protection Center (NIPC) issued a warning to all companies and government agencies to scour their public websites for sensitive information pertaining to critical infrastructure systems.

The website operated by the Muslim Hackers Club (a group that U.S. security agencies believe aims to develop software tools to launch cyberattacks on Western targets) featured links to U.S. sites that purport to disclose sensitive information such as code names and radio frequencies used by the U.S. Secret Service. The same website offers tutorials in creating and spreading viruses, devising hacking stratagems, network sabotage, and developing codes; it also provides links to other militant Islamic and terrorist web addresses. Specific targets that al Qaeda–related websites have discussed include the Centers for Disease Control and Prevention in Atlanta; FedWire, the money-movement clearing system maintained by the Federal Reserve Board; and facilities controlling the flow of information over the Internet.

Like many other Internet users, terrorists have access not only to maps and diagrams of potential targets, but also to imaging data on those same facilities and networks that may reveal counterterrorist activities at a target site. Terrorists can use the Internet to learn about counterterrorism: word searches of online newspapers and journals allow a terrorist to study the means designed to counter his actions, or the vulnerabilities of these measures. For example, recent articles reported on attempts to slip contraband items through security checkpoints. One report noted that at Cincinnati's airport, contraband slipped through over 50 percent of the time. A simple Internet search by terrorists would uncover this shortcoming and offer the terrorists an embarkation point for their next operation. Several reports in various Internet sites noted that U.S. law enforcement agencies were tracing calls made overseas to al Qaeda cells from phone cards, cell phones, phone booths, or Internet-based phone services. Exposing the targeting techniques of law enforcement agencies allows the terrorists to alter their operating procedures.

In April 2004, it was reported that Hezbollah has managed to penetrate computers of senior Israeli journalists and extract sensitive information from them, and even listen to phone conversations. The incident was exposed during the interrogation of Alam Koka, a senior Fatah al-Aqsa Brigades' operative from Samaria. An Israeli military court convicted Koka of involvement in terrorist activity and sentenced him to eighteen years in prison. Koka told his interrogators about his contacts with Hezbollah's computer experts, who taught him how to penetrate personal computers. According to Koka, he was instructed to use an Italian software program that enables breaking into computers that are connected to the Internet, which in turn also enables tapping in on phone lines. Koka added that his operator gave him several computer addresses of Israeli journalists. He claimed to have succeeded in breaking into the computer of one senior journalist, and had eavesdropped on his phone conversations for over ten days. In addition, he penetrated a number of e-mail addresses. Koka recorded all the conversations he listened to and sent them to his operator—a man who, according to Koka, is a member of the General Palestinian Intelligence Service in Ramallah and is knowledgeable about methods of interrogation and collecting information.

Finally, if you are a terrorist looking to acquire radioactive material in order to construct a dirty bomb, or you want to know what highways and railways are likely to be used for transporting high-level radioactive waste, or if you are seeking an antitank weapon to attack a nuclear shipment—there is an online answer to your search. On an official website of the state of Nevada, one can find a special guide with nineteen pages, twenty-seven figures, and seven tables.[10] The information was posted quite legitimately, as a report presented to a counterterrorism training symposium in 1996. The report's authors are in no way supporters of terrorists; they are a transportation consultant and an instructor at a university criminal justice department. The report appears to be part of Nevada's campaign to prevent the use of the Yucca Mountain site for the storage of high-level nuclear waste. By providing a detailed review of the methods for shipping high-level nuclear waste, the weapons that can be used to attack such shipments, the schematics of the containers the waste is transported in, the highways and railways used to transport high-level nuclear waste (not just within Nevada but throughout the United States), and analysis of the damage that would result from a variety of incidents, the report becomes (in the wrong hands) a real threat. Will terrorists find this information and try to make use of it? According to the Internet Haganah organization, they already have.[11] On the Islamist almoltaqa.org site, in a thread that began with a detailed discussion of how to construct explosives, there is a link to the Nevada site.

USING THE INTERNET TO NETWORK TERRORISTS

Most terrorist groups in the past have had a hierarchal pyramid structure similar to modern corporations or military organizations. They typically had a leader or various councils or ministries of senior officials, midlevel managers, and low level operatives. However, postmodern terrorists prefer the loose network structure, or "leaderless resistance," since they believe that a hierarchical structure is more vulnerable when facing state intelligence.[12] In the loose network structure, group members are organized into cells that have little or no contact with other cells or a central control or headquarters. Leaders do not issue orders to the cells, but rather distribute information via the media, websites, and e-mails that can be distributed and accessed anonymously. The advantage of this operational structure is that surveillance, penetration, or capture of operatives does not lead the intelligence agency to other cells or the central control structure. In addition, cell members can be dispersed quickly and the organization dismantled when one member is captured, due to the flexible and ad hoc nature of the organization.[13]

RAND Corporation experts on modern terrorism point to the emergence of new forms of terrorist organization attuned to the Information

Age, arguing that terrorists "will continue to move from hierarchical toward information-age network designs. More effort will go into building arrays of transnational internetted groups than into building stand alone groups."[14] This type of organizational structure is qualitatively different from traditional hierarchical designs. Drawing on CIA testimonies, a paper submitted by the National Communications System (NCS) concludes:

Many terrorist groups have undergone a transformation from strictly hierarchical organizations with designated leaders to affiliations of loosely interconnected, semi-independent cells that have no single commanding hierarchy, like Hamas and the bin Laden organization. Through the use of the Internet, loosely interconnected groups without clearly designated leaders are able to maintain contact and communication.[15]

Al Qaeda, for example, is a notably and deliberately decentralized, compartmentalized, flexible, and loosely-knit network. Al Qaeda has previously operated with an informal horizontal structure, comprising more than twenty-four constituent terrorist organizations, combined with a formal vertical structure.[16] Below Osama bin Laden was the "majlis al shura," a consultative council that directed the four key committees (military, religious, finance, and media), members of which were handpicked by senior leadership. The majlis al shura discussed and approved major operations, including terrorist attacks. Bin Laden and his two cohorts, Ayman al-Zawahiri and Mohammed Atef, set general policies and approved large-scale actions. Until the U.S. intervention in Afghanistan, al Qaeda acted in a manner somewhat resembling a large charity organization that funded terrorist projects to be conducted by preexisting or affiliate terrorist groups. Al Qaeda's strength lay in its reliance on a multicellular structure, spanning the entire globe, which gave the organization agility and cover. One French terrorism expert in recent years lamented, "If you have good knowledge of the [al Qaeda] network today, it's not operational tomorrow."[17] He compared its networks to a constantly changing virus that is impossible to totally grasp or destroy.

According to analysts Michele Zanini and Sean Edwards, "What has been emerging in the business world is now becoming apparent in the organizational structures of the newer and more active terrorist groups, which appear to be adopting decentralized, flexible network structures. The rise of networked arrangements in terrorist organizations is part of a wider move away from formally organized, state-sponsored groups to privately financed, loose networks of individuals and subgroups that may have strategic guidance but that, nonetheless, enjoy tactical independence."[18] But terrorists' organizational structures can be categorized roughly into traditional and new-generation groups. Traditional groups date to the late 1960s

and early 1970s; the majority were (and some still are) relatively bureaucratic and utilized autonomous cells as part of their organizational structure, but the operation of such cells is guided by a hierarchy through clear
reporting relationships and very little horizontal coordination. In contrast,
the newer and less hierarchical groups (e.g., Hamas, the Palestinian Islamic
Jihad, Hezbollah, Algeria's Armed Islamic Group, the Egyptian Islamic
Group, and al Qaeda's network) have become the most active organizations.[19] In these loosely organized groups with religious or ideological motives, operatives are part of a network that relies less on bureaucratic structure and more on shared values and horizontal coordination mechanisms
to accomplish its goals. To varying degrees, many modern terrorist groups
share the principles of the networked organization—relative flatness, decentralization and delegation of decision-making authority, and loose lat-
eral ties among dispersed groups and individuals.

Several reasons explain why modern communication technologies, especially computer-mediated communications, are so useful for modern
terrorists in establishing and maintaining networks. First, new technologies have greatly reduced transmission time, enabling dispersed organizational actors to communicate swiftly and to coordinate effectively. Second, new technologies have significantly reduced the cost of
communication. Third, by integrating computing with communications,
they have substantially increased the variety and complexity of the information that can be shared. The Internet connects not only members of the
same terrorist organizations but also members of different groups.

For instance, dozens of sites exist that express support for terrorism
conducted in the name of jihad. These sites and related forums permit terrorists in places such as Chechnya, Palestine, Indonesia, Afghanistan,
Turkey, Iraq, Malaysia, the Philippines, and Lebanon to exchange not only
ideas and suggestions but also practical information about how to build
bombs, establish terror cells, and carry out attacks. "Thus, information-
age technologies are highly advantageous for a netwar group whose con-
stituents are geographically dispersed or carry out distinct but comple-
mentary activities. IT can be used to plan, coordinate, and execute
operations. Using the Internet for communication can increase the speed
of mobilization and allow more dialogue between members, which en-
hances the organization's flexibility, since tactics can be adjusted more frequently."[20] The latest communications technologies are thus enabling terrorists to operate from almost any country in the world, provided they
have access to the necessary infrastructure. Some analysts have argued
that networked terrorists may have a reduced need for state support—indeed, governmental protection may become less necessary if technologies
such as encryption allow a terrorist group to operate with a greater degree
of stealth and safety.[21]

In the future, terrorists are likely to be organized to act in a more fully networked, decentralized, "all-channel" manner. Ideally, there is no single, central leadership, command, or headquarters. Within the network as a whole there is little or no hierarchy and there may be multiple leaders depending upon the size of the group. In other words, there is no specific heart or head that can be targeted. To realize its potential, such a network must utilize the latest information and communications technologies. As many experts have observed, the Internet is becoming an integral component of such organizations.[22]

SHARING INFORMATION, MANUALS, AND INSTRUCTIONS

"My dear brothers in Jihad," wrote a surfer in recent years who identified himself as Abu Jendal, "I have a kilo of acetone peroxide. I want to know how to make a bomb from it in order to blow up an army jeep, I await your quick response." About an hour later the answer came: "My dear brother Abu Jendal," answered a Hamas supporter who called himself Abu Hadafa, "I understand that you have 1,000 grams of Om El Abad. Well done! There are several ways to change it into a bomb." ("Om El Abad," the mother of Abad, is the Hamas nickname for the improvised explosive TATP—triacetone triperoxide). Abu Hadafa goes on to explain in detail how to change the homemade explosive into a deadly roadside bomb, and even attaches a file that teaches how to make detonators for the bomb.[23] However, this exchange was not between members of the military division of Hamas. Abu Jendal and Abu Hadafa are two anonymous Palestinians who, it seems, never met one another. The exchange was not encoded or concealed, but was published completely openly on the Internet site of the Az al din al Kassam Brigades, the military faction of Hamas.

Terrorists may use the Internet to provide information to fellow terrorists, including maps, photographs, directions, codes, and technical details of how to use explosives. The World Wide Web is home to dozens of sites that provide information on how to build chemical and explosive weapons. Many of these sites post the *Terrorist's Handbook* and *The Anarchist Cookbook*, two well-known manuals that offer detailed instructions of how to construct a wide range of bombs. Another manual, *The Mujahideen Poisons Handbook*, written by Abdel-Aziz in 1996 and "published" on the official Hamas website, details in twenty-three pages how to prepare various homemade poisons, poisonous gases, and other deadly materials for use in terrorist attacks. Below is an example of instructions provided in the manual (the information provided is purposely incomplete, so that it cannot actually be used).

Cyanides
  Name: Potassium Cyanide Chemical
  Appearance: Deliquescent crystalline salt Lethal
  Dose: ********
  Time to Death: 3–4 minutes
  Preparations: 1. Add **gm of ***** —found in printing shops to 3 gm of ******** or 3 gm of *****, and grind them both together in a beaker. 2. Heat: until it turns black. 3. Put about **ml of ***** into the beaker and mix. Allow the mixture to cool. 4. Filter. The KCN is dissolved in the water. 5. To obtain the powder form, evaporate the water.
  Precautions: Even though neither ***** nor ***** is poisonous, you MUST wear gloves and a gas mask during preparation and handling of cyanides. Do not touch it even with a gloved hand. Inhalation of its odor will lead to headaches, dizziness, fever and stomach pain. If by mistake it touches the mouth, give huge amounts of water and induce vomiting. Keep away from acid.
  Notes: It is notorious as an intensely powerful poison. By mouth, by injection or by skin. This is the most powerful chemical poison. If using skin penetration, you must dissolve in olive oil as it will penetrate the skin and hide the smell to some extent. It can also be used in most face creams—especially *****—for easy skin penetration.

This kind of information is sought out not just by sophisticated terrorist organizations but also by disaffected individuals prepared to use terrorist tactics to advance their idiosyncratic agendas. In 1999, for instance, a young man by the name of David Copeland planted nail bombs in three different areas of London: multiracial Brixton, the largely Bangladeshi community of Brick Lane, and the gay quarter in Soho. Over the course of three weeks, he killed 3 people and injured 139. At his trial, he revealed that he learned his deadly techniques from the Internet, downloading *The Terrorist's Handbook* and *How to Make Bombs: Book Two*. Both titles are still easily accessible. A search for the keywords "terrorist" and "handbook" on the Google search engine found nearly four thousand matches that included references to guidebooks, manuals, and instruction books. One site gives instructions on how to acquire ammonium nitrate, Copeland's "first choice" of explosive material.

In 2002, a brilliant chemistry student in Finland who called himself "RC" discussed bomb-making techniques with other enthusiasts on a Finnish Internet website devoted to bombs and explosives. Sometimes he posted queries on topics such as manufacturing nerve gas at home. Often he traded information with the site's moderator, whose messages carried a picture of his own face superimposed on Osama bin Laden's body, complete with turban and beard. Then RC set off a bomb that killed seven people, including himself, in a crowded shopping mall. The website frequented by RC, known as the Home Chemistry Forum, was shut down by its sponsor, a computer magazine. But a backup copy was immediately posted again on a read-only basis.

The Hamas organization, which claims responsibility for the lion's share of Palestinian suicide bombing attacks, has launched an Internet site that offers Muslims instructions in the production and assembly of explosives, rockets, and light aircraft. News of the site has spread throughout the West Bank and Gaza Strip. The instructions can be found on the website of Hamas's Izzedin Kassam military wing. The site, called "Military Academy," offers fourteen lessons in bomb-making as part of what the Islamic group said is a campaign to expand the pool of bomb-makers. The courses include lessons on the production of a belt filled with explosives that can be worn by a suicide bomber. Other courses demonstrate how to manufacture plastic explosives from RDX (research department explosive; hexahydro1,3,5-trinitro-1,3,5 triazine, which is also known as cyclonite), a material that is said to be difficult to detect. The Hamas online course also provides instructions on preparing regular bombs as well as methods to identify targets. Izzedin Kassam said the process of producing suicide bombs requires three people; they are a bomb expert, an electrician, and a tailor to sew the belt to the proportions of the suicide attacker. The Hamas site is interactive and those taking the course can correspond with the movement's bomb instructors. However, the military wing warned that those who miss one lesson would not be allowed to continue the course. The site said those who ask a question about a lesson that already was given would be removed from the course. Those taking the course would also be required to take tests after each stage.

A full volume of al Qaeda's manual is published online by the United States Department of Justice.[24] This manual was located by the Manchester (England) Metropolitan Police during a search of an al Qaeda member's home. The manual was found in a computer file described as "the military series" related to the "Declaration of Jihad." The manual was translated into English and was posted on the Department of Justice's website. However, it is wisely edited since, as declared there, "[the department] is only providing the following selected text from the manual because it does not want to aid in educating terrorists or encourage further acts of terrorism."

There are many "lessons" in this manual: Lesson Twelve, for example, is titled *Information Gathering Methods* and includes the following suggestions:

Information needed to be gathered through covert means is of only two types: First: Information about government personnel, officers, important personalities, and all matters related to those (residence, work place, times of leaving and returning, wives and children, places visited).

Second: Information about strategic buildings, important establishments, and military bases. Examples are important ministries such as those of Defense and Internal Security, airports, seaports, land border points, embassies, and radio and TV stations.

General security measures that should be taken by the person during the process of gathering information, whether about governing personalities or establishments, the person doing the gathering must take the following security measures. . . .

Another "lesson" describes recruitment methods and even details "Types of Agents Preferred by the American Intelligence Agency (CIA)," distinguishing between (a) "Foreign officials who are disenchanted with their country's policies and are looking toward the U.S. for guidance and direction"; (b) "The ideologist who is in his country but against his government and is considered a valuable catch and a good candidate for the CIA"; and (c) "Officials who have a lavish lifestyle and cannot keep up using their regular wages, or those who have weaknesses for women, other men, or alcoholic beverages." Lesson Four describes "Weapons: Measures related to buying and transporting them." In another part detailing safety measures, the "married brothers" are warned that they "should observe the following: (a) Not talking with their wives about Jihad work; and (b) The members with security risks should not travel with their wives. A wife with an Islamic appearance (veil) attracts attention." Other "lessons" relate to hiding places, using false documents, communication among "brothers," traveling (including instructions on what to do "when your travel to Pakistan is discovered"), meetings, "in case of being captured," and more.

Finally, the Internet can serve as a virtual training camp, as illustrated by al Qaeda's "Al Battar Training Camp." "Al Battar" takes its name from the "Sword of the Prophets," currently located in the Topkapi Museum in Istanbul. In an effort to maintain the tradition of victory that is associated with the phrase "Al Battar," the authors go into extensive detail each month, providing explicit directions in a wide range of topics that are essential for the well-prepared mujahid, or warrior. In early 2004, al Qaeda published the first issue of Al Battar Training Camp.[25] The introduction to the issue states:

Preparing [for Jihad] is a personal commandment that applies to every Muslim. . . . Because many of Islam's young people do not yet know how to bear arms, not to mention use them, and because the agents of the Cross are hobbling the Muslims and preventing them from planning [*Jihad*] for the sake of Allah—your brothers the Mujahideen in the Arabian peninsula have decided to publish this booklet to serve the Mujahid brother in his place of isolation, and he will do the exercises and act according to the military knowledge included within it. . . . The basic idea is to spread military culture among the youth with the aim of filling the vacuum that the enemies of the religion have been seeking to expand for a long time. Allah willing, the magazine will be simple and easy, and in it, my Muslim brother, you will find basic lessons in the framework of a military training program, beginning with programs for sports training, through types of light weapons and guerilla group actions in the cities and mountains, and [including] important points in security and intelligence, so that you will be able . . . to fulfill the religious obligation that Allah has set upon you.

The next article, by Mu'aadh Mansour, is titled "The Importance of Military Preparedness in Shari'a." The magazine also features a lengthy review by Al Baraa Al-Qahtani about the Kalashnikov rifle, and, following that, an old article by Sheikh Al-'Ayyiri himself, on the importance of sports in training Mujahideen. The sixth issue of Al Battar, published online in April 2004, contains detailed articles on cell organization and management, weapons training, physical fitness, and even wilderness survival training. In May 2004 the tenth issue of al Battar appeared on the Net. The main focus of this issue is how to properly conduct kidnapping operations. Various types of kidnapping are discussed, including "secret" and "public" kidnapping. The issue discusses hostage negotiations as well as how to implement the kidnapping operation. The first part explains the motives for kidnappings:

> Reasons for detaining one or more individuals by an enemy:
>   i) Force the government or the enemy to succumb to some demands.
> ii) Put the government in a difficult situation that will create a political embarrassment between the government and the countries of the detainees.
> iii) Obtaining important information from the detainees.
> iv) Obtaining ransoms. Such was the case with the brothers in the Philippines, Chechnya, and Algiers. Our brothers from Muhammad's Army in Cashmere received a two million dollar ransom that provided good financial support to the organization.
>   v) Bringing a specific case to light. This happened at the beginning of the cases in Chechnya and Algeria, with the hijacking of the French plane, and the kidnapping operations performed by the brothers in Chechnya and the Philippines.

Given the recent rise in kidnapping incidents throughout Saudi Arabia and Iraq, information such as this offers a particularly chilling example of how the Internet is being used for instruction in terrorist activities.

IDEOLOGICAL INDOCTRINATION

Most terrorist organizations use the Internet as a vehicle for ideological indoctrination. An impressive example of such use is the sophisticated website of FARC—the Revolutionary Armed Forces of Colombia. The

FARC websites appear in six different languages—Spanish, English, Italian, Portuguese, Russian, and German. The initial page of the main site in Spanish is extremely well designed: the graphics are bright and crisp and instantly portray the FARC's struggle against the Colombian government, including a map of Colombia and a colorful picture of two members of FARC, a young male and female, looking up and far off into the jungle, the man's arms around the shoulder of the woman, and the title "Desde Marquetalia Hasta la Victoria" (From Marquetalia Until Victory). Underneath the main graphic is a menu containing the choices: Home (Inicio), Woman (Mujer), Culture (Cultura), Boliviarian Movement (Movimiento Bolivariano), and This is Colombia (Asi es Colombia). Much of the information is the same in the various languages. However, there are some unique features of the Spanish site: the link to Calendar 2003 contains graphics of a calendar and a poster for the Bolivarian Movement, which includes a picture of Simon Bolivar and a quote from him: "There is no better way to achieve liberty than to fight for it." The Plenary Session of the Spanish site has pictures of FARC leaders and "documents and greetings to the central General Staff of the FARC-EP," which contains their political declaration, their law to tax the rich, their proposal to legalize drugs, and their rejections of the extraditions treaty, in addition to "greetings" aimed at nearly every possible domestic constituency.

Another example is al Qaeda's virtual magazine—"Sawt Al-Jihad" or "The Voice of Jihad"—which appeared first at http://www.cybcity.com/image900/index.htm and then moved to a different website. According to terrorism scholar Reuven Paz, the new magazine is supposed to appear twice a month and focuses on the use of violence as jihad's only way.[26] One "editorial" by Sheikh Naser al-Najdi, titled "Belief first: They are the heretics, the blood of each of them is the blood of a dog," implicitly calls for the killing of every American:

> My fighting brother, kill the heretic; kill whoever his blood is the blood of a dog; kill those that Almighty Allah has ordered you to kill. . . . Bush son of Bush . . . a dog son of a dog . . . his blood is that of a dog. . . . Shut your mouth and speak with your other mouth—the mouth of the defender against his attacker. Rhetoric might cause retreat.[27]

Another article follows the line of thought that prefers fighting to a political struggle for reforms. The author, Abu Abdallah al-Sa'di, argues with the reformers under the title "Explosion is not the way to reform." Al-Sa'di insists on viewing the "explosions" as an integral part of jihad. "This is the element that shook the armies of the Cross, and turned the life of the Jews into hell." And he asks, "Are the suicide operations merely explosions?" He concludes:

Why should we be surprised? Our times require such amazement. If people are too afraid to respond to the call for Jihad what should they do when their scholars are planting in them the seeds of disgrace and irrigate them with humiliation and collapse. They cover it with disguise of "wisdom and tranquility," telling them "explosion is not the way for reform."

In January 2004, the ninth issue of Sawt Al-Jihad was released online. This issue features an insightful commentary on bin Laden's latest speech and takes a clear stance supporting jihad in the mounting inner debate regarding armed jihad on the holy soil of Saudi Arabia. Louis Attyiat-Allah, an al Qaeda ideologist, provides a written analysis of bin Laden's latest speech. Attyiat-Allah criticizes al-Jazeera television for broadcasting only a small portion of bin Laden's speech, saying that this is one of the most important speeches for the coming times. Attyiat-Allah also writes in this website about a possible future attack on the same scale as 9/11, stating:

> The truth is that for a long time now, I was raising a simple yet specific and clear question to some people who have connections in al Qaeda, asking them if there is going to be a second, bigger attack. From the answers, some of the next attack's features were gathered, and the following are the most prominent:
> —It will be an innovative attack, in the sense that it will be completely unexpected, and impossible for them [the West] to even think about or picture its way of action, for it is unimaginable in the normal way.
> —It will be bigger, in the sense that the loss from which America and the Western World will suffer [will be bigger], because it will be very big and immeasurable.
> —Due to its greatness, it will change the global power balance.

This issue also contains a special section dedicated to recruiting women for terrorist attacks, in which women are encouraged to assist the warriors by all means. This issue's article, titled "Um Hamza, an Example for the Woman Holy Warrior," tells the story of the late Um Hamza by her husband, in which her virtues are detailed. "Um Hamza and Martyrdom: Um Hamza was very happy whenever she heard about a martyrdom operation carried out by a woman, whether it was in Palestine or Chechnya. She used to cry because she wanted a martyrdom operation against the Christians in the Arabian Peninsula." A copy of a letter handwritten by Um Hamza shortly before her death is displayed to the right on the webpage.

On 23 May 2004, al Qaeda released online issue seventeen of the Voice of Jihad. This issue consists of fifty-four pages in a newly formatted four-color version. Major topics contained in this issue include the implementation of "Madrid type" attacks in the U.S. and pending attacks in Saudi Arabia. The introductory portion of the magazine begins with a recap of world events from a fundamentalist jihad warrior perspective, and discusses the "abusive treatment" of the Iraqi prisoners at Abu Ghraib prison as well as the "payback" of this mistreatment via the "slaughter" of Nicholas Berg. They note that the video of Berg has ignited an antiwar sentiment in the U.S., which is consistent with their ambition to cause pressure from within the U.S. to end the "occupation." This issue also refers to the assassination of Iraqi Governing Council head Abdul Zahra Othman Mohammad (Izzedin Salim) in Baghdad on Monday, 17 May 2004, describing the action as a "blow to American occupying forces." Also addressed with disdain in this issue are the allegations that attempts are being made to "Christianize" Saudi Arabia.

PLANNING AND COORDINATION

Terrorists use the Internet not only to learn how to build bombs but also to plan and coordinate specific attacks. Al Qaeda operatives relied heavily on the Internet in planning and coordinating the September 11 attacks. Thousands of encrypted messages that had been posted in a password-protected area of a website were found by federal officials on the computer of arrested al Qaeda terrorist Abu Zubaydah, who reportedly masterminded the September 11 attacks. The first messages found on Zubaydah's computer were dated May 2001, and the last were sent on September 9, 2001. The frequency of the messages was highest in August 2001. To preserve their anonymity, the al Qaeda terrorists used the Internet in public places and sent messages via public e-mail. It is often simple to use the Internet in public facilities without being traced or identified; at many public libraries, nearly anyone can walk up to a terminal and access the Internet without presenting identification.

Another place al Qaeda members have accessed the Internet is in "hawalas," or storefront money exchanges that have been used to funnel money to bin Laden and al Qaeda. The U.S. government raided and shut down dozens of these "hawalas" in November 2001. Certain September 11 hijackers communicated using free web-based e-mail accounts provided by a popular Internet company. Such accounts can easily be opened with fake registration information, and they can be accessed from any computer connected to the Internet. It is known now that al Qaeda used the Internet to search for, and find, logistical information to use in planning the September 11 attacks. Some of the September 11 hijackers used the Internet to research the chemical dispersal capabilities of crop dusters, and their ringleader, Mohammed Atta, made his plane reservations online. U.S. officials in Afghanistan found information about manufacturing a nuclear bomb and files describing American utilities, downloaded from the Internet, in al Qaeda safe houses.

In May 2004, a detailed program to assassinate Saudi Arabia's Minister of the Interior, Prince Nayif Bin-Abd-al-Aziz, was discovered in a website of al Qaeda operatives in Saudi Arabia.[28] The plans, authored by Abu Hajar Abdel Aziz al-Moqrin—the former leader of al Qaeda in Saudi Arabia and the man who claimed responsibility for the attack on the residential complex in Saudi Arabia on May 29, 2004—outlined Prince Nayif's itinerary, manner and route of travel, personal security, and planned method of attack using rocket-propelled grenades. The detailed plans were found in Issue 11 of al Battar, the military-style training manual. Selected segments, translated from the Arabic text, give the following instructions:

The target: Nayef Bin Abdul Aziz. He will attend a reception of external security personnel in a secret visit of the queen at King Khaled International Airport.

Residence address: the Gardens—several palaces (the present palace in Arqa, also the Mother's palace, and several other palaces that he frequents).

Daily routine: He goes to sleep shortly before dawn, and goes to the ministry some days at 7 o'clock at night until eight thirty, resting in the evenings, and attending parties, and private meetings.

Number of guards: 8 persons

Typed of armament: light. The guards can be targeted as they descend from the car; they are near but not too close. The guarding crew varies the route at times. The target changes its car. Mostly uses the same car, which is not easy to approach since the highways are closed.

Route information: From Arqa palace to the airport, 40 kilos.

Route Description: From Arqa, take the western circular, then the northern circular, then the airport highway, with the probability of moving onto other roads.

Schedule: The departure time: at six at night. The arrival time: 25 minutes after 6.

The first stage: the specification of the target. This stage is complete.

The second stage: the collection of the information. This stage is complete also.

The third stage: Determining the way of killing (the explosives), and it will be with the explosions in the procession during the passing of the procession at the bottom of the bridge linking the northern circular and the eastern one, and on the sides of the highway at the turn, beginning with the emergence of the group of confirmation and the destruction, with the assurance of killing them, or it may be carried out with the use of anti-armament missiles.

In another example, Hamas activists in the Middle East use chat rooms to plan operations, and operatives exchange e-mail to coordinate actions across Gaza, the West Bank, Lebanon, and Israel. Instructions in the form of maps, photographs, directions, and technical details of how to use explosives are often disguised by means of steganography, which involves hiding messages inside graphic files. Sometimes, however, instructions are delivered concealed in only the simplest of codes. Hidden pages or phrases can be coded instructions for terrorist operatives and supporters. Messages can be hidden on pages inside sites with no links to them, or placed openly in chat rooms.[29] Al Qaeda used prearranged phrases and symbols to direct its agents.[30] An icon of an AK-47 can appear next to a photo of Osama bin Laden facing one direction one day, and another direction the next. Mohammed Atta's final message to the other eighteen terrorists who carried out the attacks of 9/11 is reported to have read: "The semester begins in three more weeks. We've obtained 19 confirmations for studies in the faculty of law, the faculty of urban planning, the faculty of fine arts, and the faculty of engineering."[31] (The reference to the various faculties was apparently the code for the buildings targeted in the attacks.)

The Internet can be used by terrorists to plan attacks that will interfere with elections, as demonstrated in several cases. In December 2000, the www.qoqaz.com site operated by al Qaeda members in Chechnya posted an audio recording directed to the Mujahideen in Saudi Arabia—a recording by Sheikh Abu Omar Al-Seif, a Saudi considered to be the deputy of Abu Al-Walid (a Saudi who is regarded as the commander of the Jihad in Chechnya). In this new recording, Sheikh Al-Seif states that the aim of the Mujahideen in Chechnya is to bring about Vladimir Putin's defeat in the upcoming March 2004 elections. The text includes the statement: "In this tape, I want to advise that it is no secret that there will be a presidential election in Russia in the coming months, and those months will be of the most significant ones. The Mujahideen are trying to escalate the operations in order to topple Putin, Allah willing. Putin is trying by any and all means to present himself during these months as a victor, in order to win the elections. These months will be difficult and important to this issue."

Another example of terrorist planning via the Internet was the March 11, 2004, Madrid bombings days before Spanish general elections. Since the Madrid bombings there has been considerable interest in a document found on radical Islamic websites by researchers at the Norwegian Defense Research Establishment (FFI). FFI's researcher Brynjar Lia came across the document in December 2003, on a website called "Global Islamic Media" that regularly posts various kinds of radical Islamist texts. Lia then skimmed the document and interpreted it as a strategy document intended for the Islamist resistance within Iraq. However, just after the Madrid bombings FFI researchers recalled the document and started analyzing it in more detail. The detailed reading provided many interesting new insights, particularly when coupled with details from the investigation of the Madrid attacks. The document recommends "painful strikes" against Spanish "forces" specifically around the time of the Spanish elections and there has naturally been much speculation about the relationship between this text and the Madrid events. According to the heading of the document, it was prepared by the "Media Committee for the Victory of the Iraqi People (Mujahideen Services Center)." This entity is previously unknown, but the reference to a "services centre" (markaz al-khidamat) echoes the "Services Bureau" (maktab al-khidamat), the organization from which al Qaeda grew in the late 1980s. The text contains a dedication to Yusuf al-Ayiri and several quotations from his books. Yusuf al-Ayiri was a key al-Qaeda ideologist and media coordinator who was killed by Saudi security forces in May 2003.

The main thesis proposed in the document is that America cannot be coerced to leave Iraq by military-political means alone, but the Islamist resistance can succeed if it makes the occupation of Iraq as costly as possible—in economic terms—for the United States. The document therefore offers a number of specific "policy recommendations" in order to increase the economic impact of the insurgency and the Jihadi campaign in Iraq. The most important of these recommendations consists of trying to limit the number of American allies present in Iraq, because America must not be allowed to share the cost of occupation with a wide coalition of countries. If the mujahideen can force U.S. allies to withdraw from Iraq then America will be left to cover the expenses on her own, which she cannot sustain for very long. The intermediary strategic goal is therefore to make one or two of the U.S. allies leave the coalition, because this will cause others to follow suit and the dominoes will start falling. The document then analyzes three countries (Britain, Spain, and Poland) in depth, with a view to identifying the weakest link or the domino piece most likely to fall first. The author provides a surprisingly informed and nuanced analysis of the domestic political map in each country. He argues that each country will react differently to violent attacks against its forces because of domestic political factors. Spain is presented as very vulnerable to attacks on its forces, primarily because public opposition to the war is almost total, and the government is virtually on its own on this issue. The author therefore identifies Spain as the weakest link in the coalition. The most interesting passage of the whole text is the author's concluding remarks regarding Spain (translated from Arabic):

> Therefore we say that in order to force the Spanish government to withdraw from Iraq the resistance should deal painful blows to its forces. This should be accompanied by an information campaign clarifying the truth of the matter inside Iraq. It is necessary to make utmost use of the upcoming general election in Spain in March next year. We think that the Spanish government could not tolerate more than two, maximum three blows, after which it will have to withdraw as a result of popular pressure.

The document's significance derives first of all from the way in which it might be linked to Madrid's dreadful events that killed 201 people and wounded 1,240. FFI's researchers think it is likely that the perpetrators of the attacks knew this online document in some way or another. There are three reasons for this: First of all, the document highlights Spain as politically the most convenient target of the coalition countries present in Iraq, and it specifically mentions the Spanish elections as a good time to strike. Second, the perpetrators may have adopted the overall strategy outlined in the document while altering the tactics somewhat and taking the campaign onto Spanish territory. Moreover, the fact that the document is addressed to global jihadists, and that it was posted on the "Global Islamic Media" website, indicates that its scope went way beyond the Iraqi battlefield. Third, the man who assumes responsibility for the attacks appears on a video under the name Abu Dujana al-Afghani, echoing a reference to the historical Abu Dujana on page two of the document.

CONCLUSION

Terrorists fight their wars in cyberspace as well as on the ground. As this discussion makes plain, terrorist organizations and their supporters maintain hundreds of websites, exploiting the unregulated, anonymous, and easily accessible nature of the Internet for various purposes. In a briefing given in late September 2001, Ronald Dick—assistant director of the FBI and head of the United States National Infrastructure Protection Center (NIPC)—told reporters that the hijackers of 9/11 had used the Internet, and "used it well." Since 9/11, terrorists have only sharpened their Internet skills and increased their web presence. Today, terrorists of very different ideological persuasions—Islamist, Marxist, nationalist, separatist, racist—have learned many of the same lessons about how to make the most out of the Internet. The great virtues of the Internet—ease of access, lack of regulation, vast potential audiences, fast flow of information, and so forth—have been turned to the advantage of groups committed to terrorizing societies to achieve their goals.

How should those societies respond? This is not the forum in which to attempt anything like a definitive answer, but two things seem clear. First, we must become better informed about the uses to which terrorists put the Internet and better able to monitor their activities. Journalists, scholars, policymakers, and even security agencies have tended to focus on the exaggerated threat of cyberterrorism and have paid insufficient attention to the more routine uses made of the Internet.[32] Those uses are numerous and, from the terrorists' perspective, invaluable. Hence, it is imperative that security agencies continue to improve their ability to study and monitor terrorist activities on the Internet and explore measures to limit the usability of this medium by modern terrorists.

Second, while we clearly must defend our societies better against terrorism, we must not in the process erode the very qualities and values that make our societies worth defending. The Internet is in many ways an almost perfect embodiment of the democratic ideals of free speech and open communication; it is a marketplace of ideas unlike any that has existed before. Unfortunately, the freedom offered by the Internet is vulnerable to abuse from groups that, paradoxically, are themselves often hostile to uncensored thought and expression. But if, fearful of further terrorist attacks, we circumscribe our own freedom to use the Internet, then we hand the terrorists a victory and deal democracy a blow. The use of advanced techniques to monitor, search, track, and analyze communications carries inherent dangers. Although such technologies might prove very helpful in the fight against cyberterrorism and Internet-savvy terrorists, they would also hand participating governments, especially authoritarian governments and agencies with little public accountability, tools with which to violate civil liberties domestically and abroad. It does not take much imagination to recognize that the long-term implications could be profound and damaging for democracies and their values, adding a heavy price in terms of diminished civil liberties to the high toll exacted by terrorism itself.

NOTES

This chapter is based on a research project funded by the United States Institute of Peace, Washington, DC, where the author was a Senior Fellow in 2003–2004.

1. Cited in T. Westerman, "Terror Training Online: Al Qaeda Franchises Out," *International News Analysis*, 23 April 2004, http://inatoday.com/terror%20training%20online%2042304.htm.

2. See Rita Katz and Josh Devon, "WWW.JIHAD.COM: E-Groups abused by jihadists," *National Review Online*, 14 July 2003, www.nationalreview.com/comment/comment-katz-devon071403.asp.

3. Gabriel Weimann, *WWW.Terror.Net: How Modern Terrorism Uses the Internet*, USIP Special Report 116 (Washington, DC: United States Institute of Peace, 2004); Gabriel Weimann, *Cyberterrorism: How Real Is the Threat?* USIP Special Report (Washington, DC: United States Institute of Peace, 2004); Gabriel Weimann, *Terror on the Internet: The New Arena, the New Challenges* (Washington: United States Institute of Peace Press, 2006).

4. Alex P. Schmid and Albert J. Jongman, *Political Terrorism* (Amsterdam: North-Holland Publishing, 1988); and Gabriel Weimann and Conrad Winn, *The Theater of Terror* (New York: Longman Publications, 1994).

5. Yariv Tsfati and Gabriel Weimann, "Terror on the Internet," *Politika* 4 (1999), 45–64 (Hebrew); and Yariv Tsfati and Gabriel Weimann, "WWW.Terrorism.com: Terror on the Internet," *Studies in Conflict and Terrorism* 25, no. 5 (2002): 317–332.

6. Weimann, *WWW.Terror.Net*.

7. Dan Verton, *Black Ice: The Invisible Threat of Cyber-Terrorism* (New York: McGraw-Hill Osborne Media, 2003).

8. Barton Gellman, "Cyber-attacks by Al-Qaeda feared," *Washington Post*, 27 June 2002, A01.

9. From "Citing Al Qaeda Manual, Rumsfeld Re-Emphasizes Web Security," *Inside Defense.com,* 15 January 2003, www.insidedefense.com.

10. The official website of the state of Nevada is at www.state.nv.us.

11. See the Internet Haganah report at http://haganah.us/harchives/000385.html

12. Simson L. Garfinkel, "Leaderless resistance today," *First Monday* 8, no. 3 (2003), http://firstmonday.org/issues/issue8_3/garfinkel/index.html.

13. Bruce Hoffman, "Plan of Attack," *Atlantic Monthly,* June 2004, www.theatlantic.com/issues/2004/07/hoffman.htm.

14. John Arquilla, David F. Ronfeldt, and Michele Zanini, "Networks, Netwar and Information-Age Terrorism," in *Countering the New Terrorism,* ed. Ian O. Lesser, Bruce Hoffman, John Arquilla, David F. Ronfeldt, Michele Zanini, and Brian Michael Jenkins (Santa Monica: RAND Corporation, 1999), 41.

15. National Communications System, "The Electronic Intrusion Threat to National Security and Emergency Preparedness (NS/EP) Internet Communications" (Washington, DC: Office of the Manager, National Communications System, December 2000), 28–31.

16. See Paul J. Smith, "Transnational Terrorism and the al Qaeda Model: Confronting New Realities," *Parameters,* Summer 2002, 33–46.

17. Cited in Steven Erlanger and Chris Hedges, "Terror Cells Slip Through Europe's Grasp," *New York Times,* 28 December 2001, 1.

18. Michele Zanini and Sean J. A. Edwards, "The Networking of Terror in the Information Age," in *Networks and Netwars,* ed. John Arquilla and David Ronfeldt (Santa Monica: RAND Corporation, 2001), 29.

19. U.S. Department of State, *2000 Foreign Terrorist Organizations Report* (Washington, DC: Office of the Coordinator for Counterterrorism, 2000).

20. Zanini and Edwards, "Networking of Terror," 36.

21. Kevin J. Soo Hoo, Seymour E. Goodman, and Lawrence T. Greenberg, "Information Technology and the Terrorist Threat," *Survival* 39, no. 3 (1997): 135–155.

22. cf. Arquilla et al., "Networks, Netwar and Information-Age Terrorism," 48–53; and Arquilla and Ronfeldt, *Networks and Netwars.*

23. Reported by Amit Cohen, "Hamas Dot Com," in *Maariv Online,* 2 July 2003, www.maarivenglish.com/tour/Hamas%20Dot%20Com.htm.

24. Available online at www.usdoj.gov/ag/trainingmanual.htm.

25. Available online at www.hostinganime.com/battar/b1word.zip.

26. Reuven Paz, "Sawt al-Jihad: New Indoctrination of Qa'idat al-Jihad," *Occasional Papers Published by PRISM,* volume 1, no. 8 (2003). Available online at www.e-prism.org.

27. Paz, "Sawt al-Jihad."

28. The American Northeast Intelligence Network reported this finding (on 2 June 2004) online at www.homelandsecurityus.com.

29. Maria T. Welch, "Accumulating Digital Evidence Is Difficult," *Post Standard,* 11 September 2002, D–9, 11.

30. Timothy L. Thomas, "Al Qaeda and the Internet: The Danger of 'Cyberplanning,'" *Parameters,* Spring 2003, 112–123.

31. Yossi Melman, "Virtual soldiers in a Holy War," *Ha'aretz,* 17 September 2002, www.haaretz.com.

32. Weimann, *Cyberterrorism.*

6

✛

The Media as a Showcase for Terrorism

Cindy C. Combs

If terrorism is seen as political theater performed for audiences . . .
clearly the mass media plays a crucial role. Without massive news coverage the terrorist act would resemble the proverbial tree falling in the
forest.

Brigitte L. Nacos, "Accomplice or Witness:
The Media's Role in Terrorism" (2004).

There is no universally accepted definition of terrorism today. In fact,
there is not even a single definition accepted by the differing agencies
of a government engaged in a "war" on terrorism. However, most defini-
tions have at least one common element: the targeting of an audience
broader than the immediate victims in order to bring about some type of
political/social change.

Given this focus on reaching an audience, it is hardly surprising that the
role of the media in the context of terrorism is a contentious subject. Many
of today's terrorists have learned an important lesson about this technological age: media, particularly the Internet and the television, can be a
formidable link between the terrorist and his/her audience. According to
Brian Jenkins, an expert on terrorism, "terrorists want a lot of people
watching and a lot of people listening, not a lot of people dead. . . . Terrorists choreograph dramatic incidents to achieve maximum publicity,
and in that sense, terrorism is theater."[1] If this is the case, then the media
serve as a "showcase" for the theater of terrorism today.

The media have, to varying extents in differing cultures, become a tool
of modern terrorists, offering a "showcase" through which those carrying

out terrorist acts can impress and threaten an audience, recruit and train new members, and support and coordinate an emerging network of followers. The role of the media as a "showcase"—which by definition offers structure and support with a clear display of items arranged to attract the attention of an audience—offers useful insights into one method of "teaching terror" in the twenty-first century.

In order to understand the use of the media as a "teaching tool" for terrorism today, it is important to examine at least two important facets: the audience for which the showcase is designed, and the response sought from that audience. Clearly, all of those viewing the media do not share the same cultural, economic, political, religious, or demographic traits. Therefore, if the "showcase" is to be effective, it must be designed to have divergent appeals to differing audiences. The "effectiveness" of the showcase could be evaluated in terms of the responses sought and obtained from those divergent audiences. So it becomes necessary to clarify both the types of audiences targeted and the types of responses sought, in order to assess the role of the media as a "showcase" by which terrorism is taught.

There is also one other perspective of the relationship between the media and terrorism that must be a part of this analysis. Many terrorism scholars have identified a *symbiotic relationship* between terrorists seeking attention from an audience and news organizations, which seek dramatic stories to increase their readership and ratings. A symbiotic relationship is, according to *Webster's Dictionary of the English Language,* "the intimate association of two dissimilar organisms from which each organism benefits."[2]

Clearly, terrorists seeking attention and the media searching for dramatic events can benefit from an association. The intimacy of the association and the degree to which each benefits will depend on a variety of factors, including the goals sought by each "organism" and the limitations of the systems in which both operate. Thus, a look at the role of the governments involved in shaping the way in which media can interact in the event, as well as an examination of the goals of the media and the terrorists, may help to clarify the relationship that exists between these dissimilar organisms.

Two final points need to be clarified before we examine the audiences and goals of the media/terrorist relationship: the appropriate application of the term "symbiotic" to describe that relationship; and the relevance of the term "showcase" in explaining what terrorists are putting on display. Both points are critical in accurately interpreting the dynamic interaction between the media and terrorism today.

THE MEDIA AND TERRORISM: A SYMBIOTIC RELATIONSHIP?

The relationship between terrorism and the media is accurately described as "symbiotic" most of the time, but not always. To be symbiotic, the relationship must be intimate, not casual or conflictual, and must benefit both organisms. If the media choose—for personal, professional, or legal reasons—not to publicize or to critically publicize a terrorist event, then at least one of the partners in this relationship is not benefiting. If the individuals carrying out the terrorist acts choose to target (capture, kill, torture) members of the media, then the "benefit" to one partner is also not clear. Thus, the relationship will be symbiotic much of the time, since both organisms benefit from the attention of the audience, but this will not always be the case.

The mutually beneficial status of any relationship depends, in part, on the extent to which the two entities understand each other. While both can benefit by working in tandem without planning, it is also true that either entity can thwart the goals/desires of the other by intent. Since terrorism, as currently defined, needs an audience, it also needs the media, and would not therefore intentionally thwart the media's desire to report or "showcase" a terrorist event. However, terrorists could withhold information about a pending terrorist event or about individuals responsible for such events, thus diminishing the "beneficial" relationship. Similarly, media may refuse to report threats that might cause panic, or to publish pictures that might cause pain, thereby diminishing the "benefits" to the terrorists of the relationship.

So the symbiosis of the relationship is not universal, but depends to some degree on the extent to which the two entities understand each other, and to which their goals/desires converge. Each uses the other, to some extent, and therefore is partially responsible for the outcome that their relationship achieves. Unfortunately, many of today's terrorists have learned well how to use the media as an effective tool, offering sufficient "benefits" in terms of audience appeal to make the relationship symbiotic. In fact, some individuals involved in terrorist acts have successfully *targeted* the media, using the acts to attract attention and to shape coverage. Islamist militants linked to al Qaeda in Pakistan lured the *Wall Street Journal* reporter Daniel Pearl with the offer of an interview, where he was then abducted and killed, generating a story that claimed international headlines for days. Letters infected with anthrax were mailed to several newsrooms in the United States, causing national panic and making headlines for weeks. Clearly, some of those carrying out terrorism today understand the media and are willing to use them ruthlessly.

Terrorists benefit from what has been called an "amplification effect," when their activities are broadcast through the media to a much larger audience than would be available on the spot where the action occurs. For instance, insurgents carried on rural guerrilla warfare in several countries—including Angola and Mozambique—for more than a decade, without receiving much attention from the rest of the world. But when a similar number of Palestinians carried their warfare into the urban centers of Europe and the Middle East, their actions and their causes became dinner table conversation for TV audiences around the world, because in the urban centers of Europe and the Middle East, the terrorists were within reach of TV newsmen and their cameras.

The same level of understanding and manipulation is not as clear in terms of the ability of the media to anticipate terrorist events or to use terrorist sources to generate news not of benefit to terrorist groups. In the evaluation of information-gathering and reporting generated by the events of September 11, 2001, the media have been criticized by some of its own members for failing to understand the threat that terrorism constituted and to use that knowledge to make terrorism a front-page story without waiting for an event to provoke the coverage.

Coverage of the events of 9/11 was beneficial, in some respects, to both the network of terrorists responsible for the events and to the media, since a worldwide audience listened and looked for weeks to the coverage. But information about al Qaeda and about the growing threat of terrorism against the United States was not treated by the media as "news" until the terrorist attacks. This makes credible the critiques by recent analysts that the media were "asleep" in terms of providing the public with information about the threat of terrorism before 9/11. The media, then, may not be causing terrorism, and may even be the victim of terrorist attacks; but they have too often been a passive partner, at least in a symbiotic relationship with terrorism, allowing the terrorists to determine when to reap "benefits" from the relationship.

This confluence of interest between the media—who thrive on sensational news—and terrorists—who are only too happy to provide the sensational events—raises questions about the possible complicity of the media in today's terrorism. Scholars researching terrorism have suggested that the media today are in fact a contributing factor, a weapon in the hands of modern terrorists. A quick survey of the opinions of a few of these experts is illuminating:

—*Dr. Frederick Hacker*, a California psychiatrist who served as a negotiator in terrorist incidents, notes that "if the mass media did not exist, terrorists would have to invent them. In turn, the mass media hanker after terrorist acts because they fit into their programming needs: namely, sudden acts of great excitement that are susceptible, presumably, of quick solution. So there's a mutual dependency."

—*Walter Laqueur*, chairman of the International Research Council of the Center for Strategic and International Studies, stated that "The media are a terrorist's best friend. . . . (T)errorists are the super-entertainers of our time."

—*Professor Raymond Tanter*, political scientist at the University of Michigan, makes the relationship dilemma a bit clearer in his statement: "Since the terror is aimed at the media and not at the victim, success is defined in terms of media coverage. And there is no way in the West that you could *not* have media coverage because you're dealing in a free society."[3]

Within Professor Tanter's comments there is a critical point that must be made regarding the role of the media in terrorism. Censorship in any form is anathema to most free societies. Democratic systems instead assume that the media can exercise voluntary self-restraint where necessary in reporting such events. But the media are not convinced that restraint is either necessary or desirable. Conflict still rages over the extent of the public's "right to know" in the coverage of terrorist events. Executives of most of the major news companies maintain that television's "right to report" is absolute, asserting that it is better to report than not report. ABC's William Sheehan stated that he did not think it was the media's job "to decide what people should not know." According to Sheehan, "the news media are not the reason for terrorism even though they may sometimes become part of the story."[4]

Which is the more accurate picture of the role of the media with respect to terrorism today? Is it the responsible means by which the public is kept informed on events and individuals who are interacting in the international arena? Or are the media willing tools in the hands of clever and ruthless individuals and groups carrying out terrorist acts? If it is indeed true that the media are responsible for amplifying the effects of terrorist attacks, to what extent are the media responsible for the effects of that amplification? If terrorists have to move to increasingly more spectacular crimes in order to satisfy the increasingly jaded palette of TV audiences sated with violence, to what extent are the media responsible for whetting that appetite?

The relationship between terrorism and the media does not flow in a single direction; rather, terrorism reacts to and utilizes the media in a fashion similar to that in which the media react to and use (to attract readers and viewers) the terrorist events. This interactive relationship has allowed serious charges of *complicity*—a legal charge indicating active participation of a primary or secondary nature—in terrorist events to be leveled at the media by law enforcement and government counterterrorism officials.

The interaction of the media with terrorists in the Hanafi Muslim siege in Washington, D.C., in March 1977, offers numerous examples of the active role of some media in terrorist events. Live broadcasts from the scene continued throughout the siege, and zealous journalists kept a vast audience enthralled by the live footage and frequent interviews with the hostage-takers. While law enforcement complained about the problems caused for them by the strong media presence, the comments of one of the hostages, who was also a journalist, sum up well the problematic relationship of media and terrorism during an event:

> As hostages, many of us felt that the Hanafi takeover was a happening, a guerrilla theater, a high impact propaganda exercise programmed for the TV screen, and . . . for the front pages of newspapers around the world. . . . Beneath

the resentment and the anger of my fellow hostages toward the press is a conviction gained . . . that the news media and terrorism feed on each other, that
the news media and particularly TV create a thirst for fame and recognition.
Reporters do not simply report the news. They help create it. They are not objective observers, but subjective participants.[5]

This description of the relationship between media and terrorism is not
inconsistent with the one presented earlier: a symbiotic joining. The important point here is not that media and terrorists both need an audience,
and feed off the attention from that audience. Instead, it is important to
note that, where terrorists have in recent years taken a very *proactive* role
in this relationship, by causing the events, the media remain in their historically *reactive* role, reporting the events that occur without seeking to
shape either the news or the policy that is the target of the attack. The media in democratic systems have often taken the position that their role is
just to report the news, not to shape either policy or the news itself. Yet by
this passive, reactive role, the media have allowed themselves to be tools
of terrorists, thereby becoming a tool that does in fact attempt to shape
policy and make news. The complications in this role remain unresolved,
and are compounded by the terrorist use of the media as a "showcase" for
effective terrorist techniques today.

THE MEDIA AS A "SHOWCASE" FOR TERRORISM

A "showcase" is a "glass-fronted cupboard, fitted with shelves, in which
goods are set out on view for sale or objects for exhibition."[6] If terrorists
are intentionally using the media as a "showcase," then—like any good
vendor—they will be careful to display their causes, their actions, and
their leaders in the best possible light, with the display designed to offer
information in formats designed to evoke the desired response from their
viewing audience.

Terrorism is a crime of theater. In order for terrorism to be effective, the
terrorists need to be able to communicate their actions and threats to their
audience as quickly and dramatically as possible. Statistically, terrorist incidents worldwide are insignificant—both in terms of the number of dead
and injured, and in terms of the number of incidents reported annually—
compared to the number injured or killed in wars, famines, natural disas-
ters, or even auto accidents. But massive media coverage of individual terrorist attacks reaches a vast audience, creating an impact far beyond that
which the incident, in the absence of this media, could be expected to effect. Without intensive media coverage, it could be argued that few would
know of terrorist actions, motivations, and actors. Hence, the "showcase"

in which terrorism is displayed amplifies the effect of the single act of terrorism dramatically.

Theater is a form of "showcase," in which not only the talents of the actors are illuminated, but also those of the playwright, producer, director, sound and lighting experts, costume designer, and many others, whose effective techniques make the "play" a success. Since terrorism is a crime of theater, it is logical to assume that, in showcasing the terrorism, highlights will fall on the actors, the plot or cause for which all of the action occurs, those who produced/directed/wrote the script for the action, and the support staff who make all of the action flow.

Just as no theater, or theater billboard, can focus on all of these aspects simultaneously, terrorists using the media for a showcase for their acts must carefully select the items to be displayed, choices that will depend in large measure on the audiences (supporters/collaborators, enemies, the general public) to be drawn to the "play" and the response sought in that audience (fear, support, anxiety, excitement, etc.). Since all of the prospective audiences can have access to the display in the media, important decisions with regard to the display in the showcase rest on the type of audience targeted and the type of responses desired from those audiences. Showcasing demonstrably effective terrorist actions for an audience of potential supporters and/or collaborators has become an effective and essentially cost-free teaching technique for terrorists today.

TARGET AUDIENCES FOR TERRORIST MEDIA "SHOWCASES"

There are at least three different audiences for which most terrorist media "showcases" are designed: *current and potential supporters, the general public,* and *enemy publics.* Each of these target audiences is offered a different view, designed to convey a different message and thus to evoke a different response. Let us briefly examine each of these potential audiences in terms of the showcase structure most often utilized.

Current and potential supporters are most often drawn to the media window of the Internet. Most active terrorist groups today have established their presence on the Internet, with hundreds of websites existing worldwide utilized by terrorists and their supporters, according to a recent study by the United States Institute of Peace.[7] These websites use slogans to catch attention, often offering items for sale (such as T-shirts, badges, flags, and video or audio cassettes). Frequently the websites are designed to draw local supporters, providing information in a local language and giving information about the activities of a local cell as well as those of the larger organization. The website is, thus, a recruiting tool as well as a basic educational link for local sympathizers and supporters.

The general public (including the *international public*), while not directly involved in a specific conflict, often has some interest in the issues involved, and is actively sought as an audience in most terrorist events today. Terrorists will use the media to offer information about the cause for which the action is being taken, as well as historical background material about the organization and individuals involved in the cause, seeking to draw sympathetic understanding and even support from this audience.

It is also this audience, however, which must be made to fear the consequences of *not* changing the policy or system that is the target of the attack. If terrorism is defined by the creating of a mood of fear, this is the audience that must be made to feel that fear most intensely.

The third type of audience, *the enemy public,* includes not only the state but frequently the citizens of the state against which the terrorist act is being committed. While the enemy that is the target is not always clearly defined, at least one governing regime, or the policy of one regime, is usually a clear target, since terrorism by definition is seeking to cause some type of political/social change. The enemy public, then, is the audience that the terrorist "showcase" is intended to demoralize and humiliate as well as threaten, thereby weakening public support for the targeted regime by facilitating a change in public opinion.

Thus, terrorist events may be showcased in the media to impact at least three definable audiences. The critical difference is the type of reaction that the display is designed to evoke. These responses can be described as the *goals* of the terrorists in their intentional interaction with the media. The extent to which that goal is achieved will depend in part on the goals of the media in this interaction. Remember that the relationship *can be* symbiotic, and that the media *can be* a showcase for terrorist activity, but that neither of these may be the case. If the goals of media and terrorists converge and are compatible, the relationship may be symbiotic and an effective showcase may be achieved. If not, then the display may carry a different message from the intent of the terrorists and the impact on the audience may not produce the desired effect.

It is important, therefore, to examine the definable goals of terrorists with regard to the media, and those of the media with regard to terrorist activity. While generalizations here must be made carefully, scholars of terrorism have in recent decades agreed on several basic goals for each group, which deserve scrutiny to determine points of potential agreement and others of possible stress for this tenuous relationship. Perhaps it would be more accurate to say that terrorism and the media may share some goals, which impacts the nature of their relationship. An examination of the goals of terrorists, the goals of the media, and the goals of democratic governments reveals some insights into the complex relationship that exists between these three actors.

TERRORIST GOALS REGARDING MEDIA

In the view of several of the experts, terrorists have goals that the media can help them achieve. These include, but are certainly not limited to: publicity and propaganda, favorable understanding of their cause, legitimacy, identity, recruitment, mobilization, networking, data mining, sharing information, planning and coordination, fundraising, psychological warfare, and destabilization of the enemy. Let us briefly examine a few of these goals of terrorists in order to determine more clearly the stakes in this very dangerous relationship.

1. Publicity and Propaganda

Since terrorism is an act of theater, and requires an audience, most terrorist groups welcome the opportunity to acquire "free" publicity. Getting information out to a large, even a global audience, about the cause for which the acts are being committed is a vital part of the act itself. Press coverage that makes the world aware of the "problem" that the individual or group is seeking to resolve is clearly advantageous. This publicity can offer both tactical (short-term) and strategic (long-term) gains for the operation itself, and in some cases to the cause for which the terrorist act is being committed.

Tactical gains in publicity are usually measured in terms of getting information concerning demands that must be met (within a specified time frame) to more than just the law enforcement officers at the scene. If the general public can be made aware of the demands, and the consequences threatened for lack of fulfillment, then pressure to comply may be put on the legal officers by a concerned public. Strategic goals can be met by increasing that large audience's awareness of the "justice" of the cause for which the act is being committed, and the seriousness of the "problem" that the terrorists are trying to rectify.

2. Favorable Understanding of Their Cause

This is a vitally important goal of most terrorists today. Everyone wants to be understood, and an individual or group that is clearly breaking important laws and norms of behavior has an intense desire for their audience to understand why they are carrying out these acts. Sympathy for their personal suffering, and more importantly, for their cause, can be generated by a press willing to convey their message. If terrorists live with images of their world that are unlike those of most of this audience, then it is critically important to them that they convey to that audience the justice for which they struggle, and the reasons that have driven them to carry out acts of terrorism.

3. Legitimacy, Identity, and Recruitment

When numerous groups exist that share a similar general "problem" focus, then a group may carry out bombings or assassinations simply to establish a separate and credible identity. Certainly in areas such as Northern Ireland and Israel this has been the case, as splinter groups commit
acts of terrorism whose tactical goal seems to be establishing a separate
identity.

In order to recruit effectively, groups must convey a clear sense of purpose and identity to those who might be seeking similar political goals.
Proving to be both committed and effective in kidnapping, bombing, assassination, and other dramatic terrorist events can be a very useful tool
in the recruitment of new members to a group's cause. In addition to news
broadcasts and other forms of event coverage, terrorists are increasingly
turning to the World Wide Web to demonstrate their legitimacy to potential recruits. Using the Internet, terrorist organizations can seek "con-
verts" by using the full panoply of website technologies (audio, digital
video, etc.) to showcase the presentation of their message, as well as capture information about the users who browse their websites. Those most
interested in the organization's cause, or most likely to be useful in carrying out its work, can be contacted, or more skilled groups can utilize new
technologies such as electronic bulletin boards and issue-specific chat
rooms to reach out and draw in potential recruits.

In addition to media broadcasts of militant group statements claiming
responsibility for attacks and calls for jihad, terrorist organizations can use
the web to actively seek recruits, providing them with detailed instructions
on how to get involved. The SITE Institute, a Washington, D.C.–based terrorism research group, provided disturbing details of al Qaeda's Internet
recruitment drive launched in 2003 to recruit fighters to travel to Iraq and
attack U.S. and coalition forces there. Those regarded as potential recruits
were inundated with religious decrees and anti-American propaganda,
and given training manuals on basic skills for successful terrorism. These
recruits, as they progressed through a maze of secret chat rooms, were
given instructions on how to travel to Iraq, to take part in the "jihad" for
which they were being recruited.

4. Mobilization and Coordination

Media coverage of terrorist events can mobilize supporters to come join
the fight. In particular, the power of the Internet to rally activists was illustrated by the global response to the arrest of Abdullah Ocalan, the
leader of the Kurdish group PKK, whom the Turkish authorities have accused of terrorism. When Ocalan was arrested, tens of thousands of Kurds

throughout the world demonstrated to protest his arrest, in response to websites urging supporters to protest. Terrorist groups have become increasingly adept at using the Internet to plan and coordinate their activities across all borders.

Al Qaeda members relied heavily on their use of the Internet in planning and coordinating the attacks of September 11, 2001. Abu Zubaydah, the reported mastermind of these attacks, had on his computer thousands of encrypted messages posted in a password-protected area of a website, messages dating from May 2001 until September 2, 2001. From the analysis of federal investigators, it is clear that the Internet was a vital channel for coordination of these attacks. Hamas supporters in the Middle East use chat rooms to plan and coordinate operations, exchanging e-mails across Gaza, the West Bank, Lebanon, and Israel. Maps, photographs, directions, and technical details of how to use explosives are often sent in this exchange, sometimes encrypted but not always. The Internet has proven to be an excellent showcase by which information about targets, tactics, training opportunities, travel options, and a host of other useful details for mobilized supporters is displayed.

5. Data Mining and Information Sharing

The media, particularly in the form of the Internet, act as a useful source of strategic information for terrorists today. Terrorists can learn—via newspapers, television, and the World Wide Web—a vast array of details about targets like transportation facilities, nuclear power plants, airports, banks, and other public buildings, including information about security and other counterterrorism measures. According to the United States Secretary of Defense, in a speech on January 15, 2003, an al Qaeda training manual recovered in Afghanistan informed its readers: "Using public sources openly and without resorting to illegal means, it is possible to gather at least 80 percent of all information required about the enemy."[8]

The Internet also acts as a vehicle for knowledge transfer from one group of terrorists to others. A website operated by the Muslim Hackers Club, for example, offers tutorials in creating and spreading viruses, sabotaging networks, and devising hacking stratagems. One computer captured from an al Qaeda supporter held engineering and structural features of a dam, downloaded from the Internet, which enabled al Qaeda planners and engineers to simulate catastrophic failures. Through the Internet, then, terrorists have access not only to maps and diagrams of potential targets but also to counterterrorism measures in place at those targets, and often training manuals on how to plan attacks on the facilities.

The Internet also has many sites that offer information on how to create devastating weapons. While some of the better-known manuals—such as

The Terrorist's Handbook and *The Anarchist Cookbook*—have been available in print (legally and illegally) for some time, there are new additions to this library of "how-to" books for terrorists. *The Mujahideen Poisons Handbook*, for example, explains how to make various poisons, poisonous gases, and other deadly weapons, and is available on the official Hamas website. The so-called *Encyclopedia of Jihad*, created by al Qaeda, is also available on the Internet, and offers instructions on everything from establishing and operating an underground network to carrying out violent attacks.

6. Networking and Fundraising

Individuals and groups seeking to carry out terrorist attacks successfully not only need recruits and information; they also need the ability to network, so that activities for "common cause" can converge rather than conflict. Clearly, the media are playing an important role in displaying information and instruction to would-be terrorists. The World Wide Web is also facilitating the networking of increasingly unstructured terrorist organizations. Groups engaging in terrorism today are becoming increasingly decentralized in terms of leadership. Most of them—including the more visible groups like Hamas and al Qaeda—since they cannot fight a conventional war successfully against modern military technology and strength, have evolved to engage in a form of netwar, with semi-independent cells with no single command structure.[9] The Internet is essential for maintaining connections between these cells, which often exist not only in different cities but in differing countries throughout the world.

Modern communication technologies have made this "networking" relatively fast and effective, fairly low-cost, and diverse, with an increasing variety and complexity of information that can be shared across oceans and borders. Another obvious example of successful networking today is in news broadcasts, newspaper and journal interviews, and websites in which individuals express their support for a jihad. Of particular concern, these websites allow terrorists in Chechnya, Palestine, Indonesia, Afghanistan, Turkey, Iraq, Malaysia, and the Philippines to exchange ideas, practical information, and support for planned attacks. Lacking this format for networking, many recent attacks would have been much more difficult to achieve.

Active groups engaging in terrorism require funding, and the media—particularly the Internet—have been an excellent showcase for appeals for such funding. Hizb ut-Tahrir, a Sunni extremist group, for example, has established websites from Europe to Africa that ask supporters to assist the cause of jihad. Like those sponsored by fighters in Chechnya, the websites display numbered bank accounts to which supporters can contribute. Even with the recent UN Convention on Financing Terrorism, it is difficult to monitor these sites and accounts, which are closed and re-opened under a different name very swiftly. Although the United States, in the wake of the attacks on 9/11, seized or froze the assets of several charities that allegedly used the Internet to raise money for al Qaeda, the ability to stop the flow of funds via the Internet to terrorist organizations is difficult, time-consuming, and not demonstrably successful.

7. Psychological Warfare

Since terrorism is an act of theater for an audience, it is, by nature, a form of psychological warfare, since it is intended to create a mood of fear in that audience, not to destroy an enemy by military force. The ability of a terrorist group to spread disinformation, deliver threats intended to spread a mood of fear and helplessness, display horrible images of recent actions like the beheading of a victim or the explosive destruction of a subway—all of this greatly increases the ability of the group to wage psychological warfare. The brutal murder of Daniel Pearl by the group that held him was shared with the world by a videotape, and was played repeatedly on several websites even after the television media had played it for a day.[10]

Each "successful" terrorist event can be a significant tool in the psychological warfare waged by terrorists, as well as a significant learning tool that other terrorists may imitate. Al Qaeda's network has been extraordinarily successful in its use of multimedia propaganda, producing pre-recorded videotapes and audiotapes, CD-ROMs, DVDs, photographs, and written announcements, which are disseminated regularly to news agencies around the world. On its websites, the attacks on the World Trade Center in New York are visually displayed as part of an assault on the U.S. economy. According to the message on these websites, the effectiveness of this attack was demonstrated by the weakening of the U.S. dollar, the decline of the U.S. stock market, and a purported loss of confidence worldwide in the U.S. economy. The visual picture of the destruction of the World Trade Towers and the message claiming long-term damage carry a powerful message to supporters, but also to that international audience that is encouraged to be afraid and to believe that their government could not, and still cannot, protect them from such attacks.

A chilling attempt at "psychological warfare" occurred in the spring/summer of 2004, as citizens of various countries with civilian or military support personnel involved in Iraq were kidnapped—and in some cases executed—by a variety of different unknown groups. Nicholas Berg, a twenty-six-year-old American, was beheaded and a video of this event was posted on a website that received global attention. It is interesting to note, however, that although the execution of Fabrizio Quattrocchi, an Italian hostage apparently shot in the back of the head by members of another group, was also videotaped, the Arabic Al-Jazeera television channel, to which the tape was given, decided not to broadcast the images as they were "too disturbing."[11] Two Pakistanis were executed by yet another group, but with apparently no effort to create a worldwide media event with a videotape.

In each case, a demand was issued to the country of which the hostage was a citizen. The demands were for a pullout of troops, support staff, or civilian contractors from Iraq by the hostage's country, often accompanied by a request that the country exert pressure on the U.S.-led occupation forces to withdraw.

Two important details need to be emphasized here. The first is that the impact of the "psychological warfare" tactic was erratic, and depended in part on the willingness of the media to be a "showcase." Al-Jazeera's refusal to publish the video of the Italian hostage's execution may have impacted Italy's decision not to comply with the demand for withdrawal of its troops. But several other nations did comply with the demands for withdrawal in order to secure hostages' release, even without a visually "disturbing" display. So it is difficult to assess the success of this particular gambit.

The second point is that these kidnappings, executions, and videos were carried out by a variety of largely unknown groups, perhaps seeking identity or recognition. The negative response by the Arabic media network may have deterred the use of this weapon, since recognition was being withheld by the cultural media, but the emergence of similarly motivated cells of Iraqis offers insights into a new facet of netwar. These groups, while not formally networked with a structured leadership system, clearly shared a common goal (the removal of occupation forces and their support systems from Iraq) and a common strategy (taking of hostages, vocalizing of demands for removal of non-Iraqis from Iraq, and occasionally execution of hostages in dramatic fashion). There was no sense of coordination, but the collaborative efforts of these cells resulted in the removal of at least some of the non-Iraqi forces. This was a netwar engagement in which the media played a significant role in the battle.

8. Destabilizing the Enemy

A goal often cited by terrorist groups has been to cause damage to the enemy by generating a sense of unrest, enhancing a fear that the government is unable to offer security and stability to its people. Since terrorism is an act designed to create a mood of fear, the press can be seen by terrorists as a valuable tool in the achievement of this goal. If the media can be used, as noted above, to amplify fear, to spread panic, and to make the population feel insecure, then the terrorists will have achieved an important goal.

SUMMARY OF TERRORIST GOALS AND THEIR AUDIENCES

Most of the terrorists' goals have been directed at specific audiences. The international audience of public opinion would be the primary target by which the first two goals, publicity and the development of a favorable understanding, are achieved. Clearly, this is the audience that needs to understand, in a positive way, why certain acts are committed, and the "righteousness" of the cause and those who work for it. This understanding will, from the perspective of the terrorists, inhibit public support for actions against the group and may increase the base of the second audience, those who are potential supporters. Thus, in this portion of the showcase display, terrorists will seek to display only that which will build positive understanding, sympathy, and even support, but not fear and anger.

The next four goals are achieved through a focus primarily on the audience that comprises potential and current supporters. For this audience, websites are designed to establish the identity and the legitimacy of a group trying to attract new members and to reassure the existing membership of the value of the commitment they have made. This is also the audience targeted for mobilization and coordination, with slogans, videos, and audiotapes calling for action. Information is collected and shared in formats designed to make the carrying out of a terrorist attack seem feasible, and the fundamentals of networking and fundraising are built across national borders.

The last two goals can be achieved when the audience includes members of the "enemy public." This is the audience that must be made to feel fear, so that they will change their policies. If the government can be challenged to react—by changing the policies in ways that meet the demands of the terrorists—or even to overreact—by radically crushing civil liberties or victimizing innocent people by profiling, for example—then the terrorist goal of "destabilizing" the system is at least partially achieved.

Different forms of media have different levels of use to terrorist organizations. For the most part, all audiences will not visit all websites, so it is possible on the Internet (to some degree) to "target" one audience type and to effectively exclude (by passwords, mazes, and a variety of other tools) most other audience members. This is less true of other media formats, since newspapers, magazines, television, radio, movies, and such have relatively few limits on access, except for the purchase price. Thus, successfully targeting only one audience with a particular display from the media is much more difficult in all mediums except the Internet, making goal achievement with such displays much more problematic.

MEDIA GOALS IN TERRORIST EVENTS

While both the media and the terrorist want, in a general way, to produce exciting news for as large an audience as possible, this only establishes that both *may* be able to benefit from a terrorist attack. In order to assess whether the media are truly a "teaching tool" for terrorist groups, a closer look at specific media goals in such events is useful.

1. Getting a "Scoop"

In a world with fast-breaking news, twenty-four hours a day, being the first to report the news is a crucial goal. High-tech communications make it possible, and increase the pressure, to transmit news stories "real time"—that is, as the event actually happens. This leaves little option for editing or carefully evaluating the impact of such a news release on the situation. In such situations, this may mean that stopping to discuss the impact of their reporting with public safety officers, noted as part of several goals of the law enforcement community, may be costly to the journalists, who stand to lose that "scoop" to a less scrupulous reporter.

2. Dramatic Presentation of News

The media, in this fierce competition for public attention, clearly need to make the presentation of the event dramatic as well as timely. During the hijacking of TWA Flight 847 in June 1985, ABC broadcast extensive interviews with the hijackers and the hostages. Indeed, in one dramatic reel, a pistol was aimed at the pilot's head in a staged photo-op for the interviewers. The media argue that the intense scrutiny they give to each aspect of the event actually protects the hostages. This assumes that the primary goal of the act is to communicate a cause, drawing support from this explication. If drama is needed to demonstrate the seriousness of the cause, however, then the lives of hostages could be jeopardized by news media seeking drama. If killing a hostage, or a planeload of hostages, becomes the price of "drama," then media may be held responsible for raising the stakes in the hostage "game."

3. Protection of Rights

The media have a strong commitment to the public's "right to know" about events as they occur. Usually, this does not mean that the media see their role as being in opposition to law enforcement. Most media seek to be professional and accurate, being careful not to give out disinformation, and playing as constructive a role as possible in the event. Freedom of speech is not an absolute and inviolable value; most democracies have experienced times when civil liberties, including free speech, have had to be curtailed in the interests of national security. As one scholar notes, the conflict that is discussed here between the media and law enforcement "is between our commitment to unhindered public discourse and the need for public security."[12]

The concept of censorship of the press in most democracies in unacceptable; the idea of voluntary restraints by the press on itself is advocated, but difficult to evoke in a form that is flexible yet effective enough to satisfy all concerned. If democracies give up free speech in order to stop terrorism, then regardless of the "success" of this effort, the terrorists win, since the government and its citizens lose a fundamental part of their system. But an absolutely free press can cost lives. In the hijacking of TWA Flight 847 mentioned earlier, radio broadcasts alerted the hijackers that the captain of the plane was transmitting information to authorities on the ground. The hijackers then killed the captain. The press was free, and the cost was the life of the pilot.

4. Personal Security

The Committee to Protect Journalists, based in New York, notes that more than three hundred journalists have been murdered since 1986 as a result of their work. In 1995 alone, according to this group's records, forty-five were assassinated.[13] Thus, one of the goals of members of the media is increasingly to be able to protect themselves, both during and after terrorist operations. Journalists who interview terrorists are at risk, and those who fail to satisfy terrorists' goals of favorable understanding and publicity may be vulnerable to attack by the terrorists and their sympathizers. On January 23, 2002, *Wall Street Journal* reporter Daniel Pearl was kidnapped in Karachi, Pakistan, by members of an organization with links to al Qaeda. Its members murdered and beheaded him, and shared a videotape of the murder on many websites.

SUMMARY OF GOALS OF MEDIA
WITH RESPECT TO TERRORISM

The media, then, want to be the first to have the "big" story, and prefer dramatic news over the peaceful settlement of disputes, since drama sells newspapers and magazines much faster than quietly happy stories. The public—that large audience desired by both terrorists and the media—is attracted more easily to death and drama than to peacefully cheerful endings. Therefore, it is in the interest of the media as well as the terrorist to provide drama to that audience.

Both terrorists and the media claim to believe that the public has "a right to know" about what is happening in their world. From that perspective, the goals of the media and the terrorist converge, *unless* the government provides information about the "happening" and its meaning to their world for the media that does not match what is being provided by the terrorists in their propaganda or interviews. If there is a divergence on this goal between media and terrorist, then, it must come from a larger knowledge base of the issues than those carrying out the terrorist act have. As noted earlier, the symbiosis of the relationship depends on the understanding that each entity has of the other.

The goal of "personal security" is one on which the terrorist and the media often do *not* converge. As was made obvious in the case of Daniel Pearl, the media's desire to achieve the first and second goals may put them at risk of losing the fifth, vitally important one. In fact, as the terrorists achieve their last two goals—psychological warfare and systemic destabilization—it can be argued that the media lose their security goal. At this point, the relationship is clearly not symbiotic.

CASE STUDY: BIN LADEN'S TAPES

A brief look at the skillful use of the media by one of the world's best known terrorists, Osama bin Laden, makes many of the preceding "goals" clear. It also raises interesting questions about the impact of the media on a terrorist crisis.

As Judith Miller so aptly put it, "With his turban and camouflage jacket, his ornate Arabic and harsh vows of continued terror against America, Osama bin Laden revealed in his speech the instinctive cunning that has made him such a formidable foe."[14] Referring to one of his taped speeches, in which bin Laden articulated once again his call for jihad, she noted that the speech gave this al Qaeda leader his most visible platform, since it was broadcast worldwide over a popular Arabic satellite channel and rebroadcast many times by CNN and many other networks.

Using this platform, bin Laden expressed righteous indignation over the suffering of Iraq and of Palestine. With his pledge to end the eighty years of "humiliation and disgrace" that Muslims have endured since the demise of the Ottoman Empire, and to re-create the caliphate (the Muslim empire that was based for about five hundred years in Iraq), bin Laden made his appeal for understanding among the common Arab men of the region.

His timing of this platform appearance was excellent. Al-Jazeera, the Arabic network, had followed bin Laden's instructions to delay release of the tape until after the start of the American bombing in Afghanistan. Using the West's media weapon very effectively, bin Laden issued his global statement just as President Bush was trying to declare war on terrorism. In his taped address, bin Laden suggested that the world was divided, not between those who stood with America in rejecting terrorism and those who stood against her, but in terms of people who were "faithful" to Islam, and the "infidels" who opposed him.

While this was not the first call by bin Laden to jihad against America—it was in fact the fourth such call—the video shown around the world in early October 2001 was by far the most effective in terms of communicating his message to a broad audience. He used the media to secure a platform with a worldwide audience, to emotionally explain the cause for his anger and his anguish, and to paint the enemies of his jihad in ways that shook the alliance that President Bush was trying to form. Ahmed Abdullah, another of bin Laden's "lieutenants" and the head of al Qaeda's media committee, is believed to have arranged the filming and transmission of many of bin Laden's propaganda videos.[15]

CONCLUSION

Technological progress in communications systems has made the media potentially significant weapons in the terrorist arsenal. Whether the media are "the terrorist's best friend," an unwitting ally, or a convenient "teaching tool," it seems clear that the media play a significant role in the "propaganda by the deed" that is modern terrorism. The line between reporter of terrorist events and participant in these events, between impartial journalist and partisan advocate, is often quite thin and easily, if unintentionally, crossed.

Studies suggest that violent behavior can be "learned" and that "copycat" behavior among individuals and groups is common. To the extent that the media serve as a showcase for terrorism, in a symbiotic relationship, then the media may be actively involved in the learning processes of emerging terrorists. This does not mean that anyone truly believes that the media plan, or deliberately suggest, terrorist attacks to groups or individuals. But the actions of the media have been scrutinized intensely in recent years to determine whether media coverage of terrorist events caused, for instance, terrorists to choose one particular choice of action over another (for example, bombings over hijackings).

Further, it is not unreasonable to assume that the "showcased" portrayal of terrorist events in the news may actually motivate (or, at the very least, inform) terrorist behavior. This does not suggest that journalists are intentionally involved in the global increase in terrorist incidents. Although journalists have sometimes interfered in situations to a degree that may have altered the course of the event, this is the exception rather than the rule.

Three hypotheses of Schmid and de Graff (1982) are useful when discussing the impact of the media in the displaying of terrorist events before an audience.[16] The first, called the *arousal hypothesis,* suggests that unusual or unique media content can increase a person's desire to act aggressively; that, in fact, any news story detailing some form of aggressive behavior can increase the potential for more aggressive behavior from members of the media's audience. A second hypothesis concerns what is termed *disinhibition.* This hypothesis suggests that violence portrayed in the media weakens the inhibition of the viewer to engage in similar behavior, which in turn increases the person's readiness to engage in aggressive behavior.

These are hardly as radical a set of concepts today as they were in 1982 when Schmid and de Graff suggested them. Indeed, a great deal of time and attention has been devoted to determining whether the media encourage violent behavior in viewers, particularly young people.[17] Results of research into these hypotheses have been mixed, but have generated sufficient concern for the Attorney General of the United States to issue a not-too-veiled warning to the television networks, strongly suggesting that they initiate self-regulation systems for limiting TV violence, before the government decides that it must regulate the industry on this issue.

The third hypothesis suggested by Schmid and de Graff involves the *social learning theory.* This is premised on the belief that all behavior is learned by observation. Thus, if television depicts successful terrorist acts, then viewers will learn all about them; this will in turn increase the likelihood of terrorism. The media would thus be engaged in training individuals in terrorist behavior each time it reported such acts.[18]

Obviously, other factors beyond the scope of this chapter influence the decision of an individual or group to engage in terrorist activities. While the media may have some impact, it is clearly erroneous to assume that the actions of the media cause terrorist events to happen, even by the coverage of previous events. Hijacking incidents did not become less frequent because of limited press coverage—on the contrary, press coverage was extensive, while the reduction in the number of incidents can more likely be attributed to the enactment of several aerial hijacking conventions, and the subsequent closing of most safe havens for hijackers by the "extradite or prosecute" provisions in international agreements.

It is possible to infer from a variety of studies on this issue that the media can impact terrorists by what Schmid and de Graff term a *"built-in escalation imperative"*[19] that requires that terrorists must commit more and more bizarre and cruel acts to gain media attention. Since kidnapping failed to generate continued media attention, even though many times the ransom demands were met, terrorists turned increasingly to the use of assassination. When the shooting of a single citizen failed to generate media coverage (as it did between 1985 and 1989), bombs that resulted in multiple deaths became the weapon of choice.

A relationship certainly exists between terrorists and the media. The strength and direction of that relationship is dependent upon many variables, and is thus rarely a suitable target for intervention by the government. Indeed, intervention could skew the relationship in an undesirable direction. As Schmid and de Graff noted, "the assertion of insurgent terrorists that democratic states are not really democratic would gain credibility if the freedom of the press were suspended."[20] So the media may be offering *arousal, disinhibition,* and even *social learning* opportunities for modern terrorists. Since all of these may generate more exciting news, but may also destabilize the system in which the media operate, it is hardly surprising that, during the last decade of the twentieth century, efforts were made by both media and government to find solutions to this unintended impact without emasculating the news media.

The standards suggested by the media during the last decade of the twentieth century call for balanced coverage, which avoid the use of provocative catchwords and phrases. There has been agreement, as well, on the need to avoid offering terrorists a "showcase" for their propaganda. But as noted earlier, the Internet provides an almost unfettered option for media "showcasing," which, even if the television networks and the entertainment industry refuse to use it, will surely allow the public to be targeted with demonstrably successful effects. This leaves media that cooperate with efforts to limit the "showcasing" in a situation where they can—and do—lose audiences to the Internet for news, interviews, graphic pictures, and titillating details about the most recent terrorist attacks. Such an approach requires the media to abandon their first three goals to achieve the final one of security—a difficult position to take in today's competitive media market.

Ted Koppel, anchor of ABC television's "Nightline," suggested that American media operate at the outer boundaries of what their European allies would view as acceptable. He noted that American television is particularly vulnerable to misuse, pointing out that since terrorism by definition tends to be dramatic and involves acts that are pictorial, the visual media are even more likely to be used, without restrictions, as a showcase for terrorist events.[21] Some contend that TV news broadcasts of ongoing terrorist events amount to "social pornography" by catering to unhealthy desires of the public to be shocked and horrified—as long as it is someone else's horror being broadcast. Arguments have also been made that global terrorism would decrease if television brought its coverage under control in this context. But what kind of controls can a democratic society afford to impose on its media? What are the dangers of such controls? How effective would either voluntary or involuntary controls on media coverage of terrorism be in reducing either the number or the violence of terrorist events?

Even if print and visual media forums were placed under restrictions (thereby reducing freedoms and helping terrorists achieve one of their goals without a shot being fired), it is clear that the World Wide Web will continue to offer open access to audiences, information, recruits, technology, networking, financing, and a host of other needs of any "theater" production. The media, particularly through the Internet, will remain an active participant in all stages of terrorism, from recruitment to action to pictorial evidence of jobs well done. Deciding which goals of the media— and of the systems in which they operate—must be met, and the acceptable cost for meeting them, will be a challenge governments in the twenty-first century *must* face successfully, or the terrorists will win another curtain call before a captive audience.

NOTES

1. Brian Jenkins, "High Technology Terrorism and Surrogate War: The Impact of New Technology on Low-Level Violence," in *Contemporary Terrorism: Selected Readings,* ed. John D. Elliott and Leslie K. Gibson (Gaithersburg, MD: International Association of Chiefs of Police, 1978), 24.

2. *Webster's Dictionary of the English Language* (Lexicon Publications, Inc., 1991), 923.

3. Cindy C. Combs, *Terrorism in the Twenty-First Century* (Upper Saddle River, NJ: Prentice-Hall, 2002), 138.

4. Neil Hickey, "Gaining the Media's Attention," in *The Struggle Against Terrorism* (New York: The H. W. Wilson Company, 1977), 117.

5. Alex P. Schmid and J. de Graff, *Violence as Communication: Insurgent Terrorism and the Western News Media* (Beverly Hills, CA: Sage Publications, 1982), 42.

6. *Webster's,* 921.

7. Gabriel Weimann, *WWW.Terrorism.Net: How Modern Terrorism Uses the Internet* (Washington, DC: U.S. Institute of Peace, 2004), 1. Also, please see the chapter by Gabriel Weimann in this volume.

8. Weimann, *WWW.Terrorism.Net,* 7.

9. For more on the concept of netwar, see John Arquilla and David Ronfeldt, *Networks and Netwars: The Future of Terror, Crime and Militancy* (Santa Monica: RAND, 2001).

10. Weimann, *WWW.Terrorism.Net,* 5.

11. Agence France Presse, "Three Japanese Hostages Freed in Iraq," *Rense.com,* 12 May 2004, 2

12. John E. Finn, "Media Coverage of Political Terrorism and the First Amendment: Reconciling the Public's Right to Know with Public Order," *Violence and Terrorism: 98/99* (Guilford, CT: Dushkin/McGraw-Hill, 1990), 168.

13. Combs, *Terrorism,* 153

14. Judith Miller, "Bin Laden's Media Savvy: Expert Timing of Threats," *New York Times,* 9 October 2001, A1.

15. Combs, *Terrorism,* 154

16. Schmid and de Graff, *Violence as Communication.*

17. cf. Sissela Bok, *Mayhem: Violence as Public Entertainment* (Reading, MA: Addison-Wesley, 1998).

18. Schmid and de Graff, *Violence as Communication,* 172

19. Schmid and de Graff, *Violence as Communication,* 172.

20. Schmid and de Graff, *Violence as Communication,* 174.

21. Rushworth Kidder, "Manipulation of the Media," *Violence and Terrorism 98/99* (Guilford, CT: Dushkin/McGraw Hill, 1998), 151–154.

7

✛

The Technical Challenges of Nuclear and Radiological Terrorism

Annette Schaper

Nuclear terrorism is a scenario widely discussed since September 11. The events of September 11 have made it clear that mass murder can be a terrorist's objective, although before then it was thought that terrorists were technically incapable of producing and operating nuclear weapons. It was also widely held that their interest in nuclear weapons was low, as compared to other terrorist means. After the events of September 11, this view was revised: mass murder can be a terrorist's objective. Nuclear weapons are particularly suited to maximizing the number of casualties, and a nuclear explosion would be a next step in the escalation of terror. This chapter will investigate to what extent nuclear terrorism is likely and what role knowledge transfer will play.

In principle, two different scenarios of nuclear terrorism must be distinguished: the first is the explosion of a nuclear device causing mass casualties comparable to that of the Hiroshima bomb; the other is radiological terrorism—for example, spreading highly radioactive materials with the aid of conventional explosives or other means. Accordingly, this chapter is organized in two parts, each addressing one of these scenarios in detail.

A NUCLEAR EXPLOSION CAUSED BY TERRORISTS?

In order to create a nuclear explosion, terrorists need the theoretical knowledge of how to ignite a nuclear explosive and the relevant materials. Both know-how and material acquisition are not trivial and pose special challenges to the would-be terrorist.

Acquisition of the Ignition Technology

During the Second World War, thousands of scientists and additional staff contributed to the creation of the first crude nuclear explosive devices in the Manhattan project. The American government recruited the best scientists, and enormous logistical and financial efforts were made. This leads many observers to ask, would terrorists today be in a position to construct such a nuclear explosive device without comparable efforts?

There is, however, one important difference: the physicists of the Manhattan project did not even know if a nuclear explosion would be possible, and years were spent on basic research and essential inventions. They had to produce the nuclear material themselves. Furthermore, the operating procedures had to be developed and studied. Today, not only are the principles of nuclear weapons known, but the fundamental theories are also published in detail and are, to some extent, even available on the Internet.[1] These publications are not officially authorized and might contain mistakes in the detail. However, they are based on information that has been declassified and that can be used to reveal and understand the physical facts of nuclear explosions.[2]

Condemnation of declassification is of no use—it is merely a consequence of the inevitable scientific progress that has been made since the beginning of the nuclear age. Since those beginnings, the academic discipline of nuclear physics has been established, many textbooks written, numerous nuclear plants designed, and the functioning of nuclear weapons thoroughly researched. Moreover, many countries had ambitions to develop nuclear weapons during the 1950s and 1960s. Therefore, scientists have studied the relevant underlying theories for decades. The physics of a crude nuclear explosive device is simple when compared to the physics of a nuclear reactor. After a few years, an average physics student will have sufficient knowledge to understand such a device. There was no way to avoid the essential theoretical foundations becoming publicly known. Moreover, regulations implementing exaggerated secrecy have counterproductive effects: they can impede nuclear disarmament and its verification,[3] they can be misused to hide mismanagement, corruption, and mistakes, and they can be used to influence political decisions.[4] However, they are to some extent useful in protecting information that facilitates the proliferation of nuclear weapons.[5]

The information that is and must be kept secret relates to engineering. Many laborious steps lay between a basic understanding of the operating principles and an actual technical blueprint. It is not enough just to understand the theory. Terrorist organizations would have to acquire special abilities and techniques in order to build even a simple nuclear explosive device. These include, for example, the generation of shock waves with the aid of high explosives, the handling of fuel, electronics, and radioactive material, radiochemistry, and the precision mechanics of metallic uranium or plutonium. Information on even these subjects can be found in detailed specialist publications that are available not only in libraries but also on the Internet. In principle, it is possible to study these publications and use them as a basis for acquiring the relevant capabilities. However, many crucial details are kept secret, especially those that are based on experimental measurements rather than theory. Terrorists will need to invest substantial development effort in order to work out the details.

In principle, there are two different ignition techniques—the *implosion method*, and the *gun type method*. In the first method, a hollow sphere of plutonium or highly enriched uranium (HEU) is imploded to create a so-called *overcritical* mass. When a neutron enters this mass, a *chain reaction* is started that will lead to a nuclear explosion. In the case of plutonium, such a starting neutron will practically always be present, as plutonium generates initial neutrons through the high rate of *spontaneous fission*. HEU has a lower rate of spontaneous fission and thus a lower *neutron background*. Therefore, in the case of HEU, neutrons will have to be added artificially at the right point in time in order to start the chain reaction. A comparatively high compression can be achieved using the implosion method, which means that large overcritical masses can be achieved with relatively small amounts of material.

The production of a warhead with this method requires complete mastering of the technique of generating precise spherical shock waves. This in turn requires experimental preliminary studies involving many conventional explosions for which terrorists would probably take several years. There is no information in the public domain that explains the experimental results in detail; however, there are publications that describe typical experimental settings and measurements for shock wave experimentation with other materials. The terrorists would need quite expensive equipment, and even more importantly, they would need an experimental site that is hardly mobile, and they would need protection from unwanted detection for several years. This would only be possible with the knowledge and the approval of the state in which the experiments take place.

The other method, the *gun-type method*, is technically less sophisticated: two subcritical masses of HEU are shot at one another to generate an overcritical mass. This method was used by South Africa to build six warheads. It should be noted that only HEU is suitable for this method. This is due to the time that passes until maximal overcriticality is reached. Using the gun-type method, this period of time is on the scale of milliseconds and far longer than the few microseconds (thousandths of a millisecond) needed using the implosion method. If plutonium were used, the chain reaction would start too early, due to its high neutron background, leading to a small detonation on the scale of a conventional explosion. Compression cannot be achieved by using the gun-type method. Thus, larger masses of several tens of kilograms are necessary and only a relatively small overcriticality can be achieved. Nevertheless, this method can be sufficient to generate a nuclear explosion on the scale of the Hiroshima bomb. States and terrorists would only choose this method if they were sure of having access to sufficient HEU. However, with respect to its sophistication, this method is the most attractive to terrorists. The Hiroshima bomb has never been tested, because its designers were sure that it would work.

Nevertheless, the method is not entirely trivial: It is not sufficient to simply "drop" one part of HEU onto the other. Although HEU generates fewer spontaneous neutrons than plutonium, they occur too frequently to allow such a long period of time for the combination of the two parts. The danger of early ignition would be far too high. The combination has to be achieved as quickly as possible—that is, within a few milliseconds. The terrorists would have to develop a technique to shoot the two parts at each other in a gun barrel, without them getting stuck. This presents a substantial engineering challenge, considering the large masses involved. It would presumably require months if not years of preliminary experimental tests. Similar to the information on the implosion method, the information on the gun-type method that is available in the public domain is only very general and does not give precise details. Therefore, also with this method, the terrorists will have to do the experiments themselves. But the task is less difficult, and in principle, it remains possible for a highly motivated and financially well-endowed terror organization to acquire the technical abilities necessary to manufacture an ignition mechanism for a nuclear explosive device. Various specialists would have to acquire the necessary knowledge and skills in university studies abroad.

Revelations about the preparations undertaken for the attacks against the World Trade Center show that terrorists are prepared to go this far to achieve their aims. The experimental base could hardly be mobile, as for both methods, a test site would be needed to carry out conventional explosions, together with some research labs and offices. The work could only be done under the supervision of highly qualified physicists.

However, it must be emphasized that for the development of the ignition mechanism, the handling of plutonium or highly enriched uranium is not yet required. Thus, hiding the base would be comparatively easy. Research into conventional explosives is usually carried out in a military environment, and, therefore, is hardly accessible for outsiders, for obvious reasons. Nevertheless, cover and protection by a state are required, as the existence of a base and the experiments carried out in it would be noticed by nearby residents. Once a state comes under suspicion, it will always face the risk of secret services discovering the base. In the now abandoned South African nuclear weapons program, the development of the ignition technology represented only a small part, requiring a correspondingly small amount of effort,[6] and a fraction of this effort would probably be sufficient for terrorists.

Procurement of Fissile Materials

Thus far, this chapter has focused on the development of ignition technology. However, it is significantly more difficult to get hold of the nuclear fuel. Nuclear material exists in many different forms. Of these, only metallic plutonium or HEU can be used directly in nuclear weapons, without having to be processed further. As a rough estimate, beginners would need at least 20 kg HEU or 10 kg plutonium in order to build one warhead using the implosion method, as was used for the Nagasaki bomb.[7] A simpler construction principle was applied to the gun-type method used for the Hiroshima bomb. Using this method, plutonium does not work and an estimated 50 kg of uranium is needed for one bomb. A terrorist group would only choose the gun-type method if it was sure of having access to enough HEU. But then it would benefit from the easier design requirements.

Globally, there are about 250 tons of military plutonium and about 1,700 tons of military HEU, along with additional civil stocks. Obviously, this and other nuclear material is subject to strict security measures. Additionally, nuclear material located in non–nuclear weapon states is subject to controls by the International Atomic Energy Agency (IAEA), called "safeguards." Safeguards are designed to detect a theft as early as possible, to leave enough time for the international community to agree on a line of action before a bomb is operational. Thus, it is very unlikely that a theft of weapon-usable material could go undiscovered in a non–nuclear weapon state. Terrorists would have to circumvent not only the physical protection but also the material accountancy and the safeguards. International safeguards trigger discipline in material accountancy and protection, and thereby change the overall security culture in a state with civilian nuclear energy.[8] Terrorists would need to study the safeguards and material protection in detail and to conspire with a lot of staff involved, both technical and administrative. This need for a conspiracy with many people involved raises the likelihood for detection.

The situation is somewhat different in states that possess nuclear weapons and are not subject to international controls. An important incentive for discipline in material accountancy and for transparency to the international community is lacking. The largest part of weapons-usable materials is in the hands of these states.

For many years, Russia has posed a special concern with regard to the security of nuclear material. It seems that an exact overview of stocks has been lost or never existed in a sufficiently accurate form. Moreover, many plants and deposits are not sufficiently secure. It is not known whether terrorists or third party states have already managed to get hold of nuclear material. However, it is certain that several attempts have been made in the past, some involving Osama bin Laden. Several cases were uncovered during the mid-1990s, where smugglers stole weapon-ready nuclear material, sometimes in kilogram amounts.[9] In 1998, Russian government members revealed that plans had been made to steal 18.5 kg of HEU from one of the nation's largest nuclear weapon plants. The plan was stopped before the material had left the plant.[10]

It is, however, perfectly possible that thefts have been carried out on other occasions that have never been discovered. It is not known whether potential thieves of nuclear material, smugglers, and recipients have already made contact. Thus, it is possible that a terrorist cache of sufficient nuclear material to build a weapon already exists. However, we have no indication that this is really the case.

The problem of insecure nuclear material is not only confined to Russia. Even in the U.S., complaints about the limited security surrounding weapon-ready material have repeatedly been filed, even though much stricter and more modern regulations concerning the physical protection of nuclear material are in place.[11] One instance where security concerns arose came from an event in October 2000, when a group of "terrorists," made up of army and navy personnel, managed to get hold of sensitive nuclear material from the Los Alamos laboratories during the course of a training exercise.[12] In the first decades after the invention of nuclear weapons, the recording of nuclear materials was still very incomplete. The U.S. Department of Energy published a detailed account of the history of American plutonium production in 1996.[13] It was demonstrated that 2.5 tons of plutonium are "missing," which means that the stocks taken by measurement and the number calculated from historical documents differ by 2.5 tons. This material has not necessarily been lost or stolen—this number could just indicate the extent to which the early recording of material was inexact. However, what becomes clear is that it is not possible to determine whether material has been taken away in the past. It can be assumed that such inaccuracies are even worse in Russia.

Metallic plutonium is difficult to process, due to its radiotoxic properties and its reactivity. A terrorist group would be taking on substantial risks— of accidents and of health—as it would be unable to gain practical experience of processing plutonium. However, it is assumed that many are willing to put up with these risks. The handling of metallic uranium is slightly easier, and can be practiced in advance with natural uranium. Natural uranium cannot be used for a nuclear weapon, but its mechanical and chemical properties are the same as those of highly enriched uranium. Therefore, it is well suited for studying the machining and the fabrication of the uranium parts of a nuclear weapon. Natural uranium is available in many countries in large quantities, and it is far less intensively controlled than weapons-grade material. A worldwide inventory does not exist and is hardly feasible, because uranium mines can be found in many countries.

A dedicated terrorist group therefore can do a lot of the "homework" in advance—for example, mastering the ignition technique and handling uranium. This homework, however, is detectable, unless it takes place under the protection of a state. In case this preparation work has been done already, then an operational weapon can be assembled quickly, once enough plutonium or HEU comes its way. Not much more studying would be necessary. And there is no way to detect this final assembly.

Acquisition of Weapon-Usable Fissile Materials by Own Production

It can be ruled out that a terrorist group has the capability to produce plutonium or HEU by its own means. At most, only a state with appropriate resources could carry out such an endeavor, and it is doubtful whether such a program could be kept hidden for long. Large-scale nuclear plants are necessary, the procurement and operation of which could not be kept a secret. All procedures for the enrichment of uranium or for plutonium reprocessing leave traces in the environment. In case of suspicion, these activities could be traced immediately as all plants, at least in non–nuclear weapon states, are subject to IAEA safeguards.

The production of uranium or plutonium needs extraordinarily high efforts, as can be illustrated by the fact that Iraq had employed thousands of staff members for years during the 1980s in order to manufacture HEU under cover. Nevertheless, only small amounts of HEU were produced. At that time, the IAEA inspections were less thorough, and the extent of the production activities was only discovered after the 1991 Gulf War.

Meanwhile, IAEA safeguards have been tightened, and it is regarded as improbable that a similar case could go undiscovered today. On May 15, 1997, the IAEA and its member states adopted new safeguards arrangements (known as the Additional Protocol) for strengthening the effectiveness and improving the efficiency of the safeguards system.[14] As a consequence, activities leading to the production of HEU or plutonium are likely to be revealed much earlier in time. After the Iraq scandal, with activities being detected at such a late stage, the industrial states now cooperate in observing international procurement activities. Moreover, other pieces of information—for example, from intelligence or from satellite imagery—are provided for evaluation. The technique of collecting and collating scattered pieces of information and their interpretation has improved immensely. The IAEA maintains a database in which such information is collected and registered. Therefore, the IAEA is capable of drawing attention to suspicious facts at a very early stage.[15] Routine inspections can be complemented with special inspections where appropriate. The civil nuclear activities of most countries are transparent.

These reforms, if implemented, will make it very difficult even for a state to secretly produce weapon-usable nuclear materials, without being detected at an early stage. Nevertheless, it is possible that such a state could launch an attempt and collaborate with a group of terrorists and supply them with bomb-grade materials. A state that clandestinely tries to produce HEU or plutonium has two options for how to proceed: one option is simply to expel the IAEA, but this would automatically provoke the international community. An example of this is North Korea, whose acquisition activities are well known. However, North Korea's actions have raised suspicions over its intentions, and political measures are being sought to cope with it. The clandestine nature of its effort is already lost, to a certain extent, in this case. However, it is extremely unlikely that Pyongyang would cooperate with terrorists or that terrorists could get access to this material.

The other option would be an attempt to fool the IAEA safeguards, but it would be much more difficult. The state would need a civilian cover for its activities. It then must study the safeguards system very carefully, which is only possible by participating in IAEA safeguards activities. This has happened in the past—for example, in the case of Iraq. Prior to the first Gulf War, Iraq had planned to divert its HEU between two inspections. The Iraqi experts knew exactly how the inspectors would proceed and which loopholes the safeguards system had left. Their acquisition scenarios made use of this knowledge in order to fool the safeguards system. In a comparable case, the state would try not to implement the Additional Protocol and proceed the same way. In case the Additional Protocol is already implemented when the decision is made to go nuclear, this fooling is extremely difficult, especially in cases when there is no history of earlier attempts. In case of such earlier attempts, there would already be a network of potential suppliers and a theoretical knowledge base that eventually might be used clandestinely for preparations. Nevertheless, any suspicion would trigger special inspections, according to the Additional Protocol, which inevitably would discover the activities. The state therefore would be dependent on the discretion of all members of the network.

An example of a network that existed for years and supplied several countries with knowledge and enrichment technology was led by Pakistan's chief scientist, Dr. A. Q. Khan, and was discovered in February

2004.[16] Khan confessed to Pakistani security officials that he had transferred nuclear-related technologies to Iran, Libya, and North Korea, but denied that he had received any support from the Pakistani government. While it is doubtful that the Pakistani government did not know about the deals, it is remarkable that the network remained undiscovered for so long. Theoretically, it is possible that a group of well-organized and well-equipped terrorists would manage to connect with such a network and might be able to purchase knowledge and technology. Nevertheless, the terrorists would need to convert this knowledge and technology in a production industry, either enrichment or reprocessing. This in turn would not be possible without the protection of a state. This means that again, the situation would in fact be state proliferation. And it is theoretically possible that a state would pass on nuclear materials to terrorists, although it is more likely that a state would keep a clandestine nuclear option for its own purposes.

A state under suspicion of nuclear proliferation and of supporting terrorists is Iran. Iran has almost completed the construction of an enrichment plant that it claims is for civilian purposes only. This has been discovered only recently because Iran has not yet signed the Additional Protocol; otherwise its activities would have become known much earlier. However, Iran has not yet produced at least substantial amounts of weapons-grade nuclear materials, and it may be doubted whether it would pass them on to terrorists. Nevertheless, a solution must be found soon in order to prevent the situation from escalating.[17]

Another possible state source could have been South Africa. Before South Africa signed up to the Non-Proliferation Treaty in 1991 and submitted to IAEA safeguards, it had produced large amounts of plutonium in its secret nuclear weapons program. Meanwhile, these stocks have been completely accounted for.[18] It can be assumed, with a reasonable degree of certainty, that there are no more undeclared hiding places. Today, an undiscovered theft is just as unlikely as in the other non–nuclear weapon states. However, some amounts might have been covertly sold in the past, and they might be in the possession of criminals today. It has been reported, for example, that bin Laden attempted to procure HEU of South African origin in 1993–1994.[19] It is unknown whether he had any success.

RADIOLOGICAL WEAPONS AND SABOTAGE

A variant of nuclear terrorism that is technically much less challenging would be the use of a radiological weapon (a "dirty bomb") instead of a nuclear explosive device.[20] Such a weapon is detonated by a conventional explosion and distributes highly radioactive material. Several blocks of a city could thus be made uninhabitable for many years. Plutonium and HEU, which are used in nuclear weapons, are not only difficult to obtain but are also not very radioactive. Therefore, they are not suitable for a radiological weapon.

Spent fuel elements are more radioactive than plutonium and HEU, and are produced by all civil nuclear power stations. However, theft of spent fuel elements is extremely difficult; because of their high radioactivity, they would quickly release a lethal dose of radiation if not adequately shielded. Moreover, they are very heavy and bulky. The theft of such elements would require the use of an appropriate form of transport. In Germany, spent fuel is transported by rail in specially designed, shielded containers. It is very difficult but not entirely impossible to imagine terrorists organizing a raid to capture and remove such containers. In non–nuclear weapon states, all spent fuel elements are registered by the IAEA and a theft would almost certainly be quickly discovered.

A terrorist would find it much easier to get hold of radioactive sources from other applications. There are numerous radioactive sources in various applications, but most of them are too weak to cause more than psychological damage. Only a few applications use sources with a high enough radioactivity to make more devastating damage possible. Only a small fraction of these radiological sources are in use, but they pose most of the risk. They include cobalt-60 sources—sources in hospitals used for cancer treatment, radioisotope thermoelectric generators, abandoned seed irradiators, industrial irradiators, and well-logging sources. The materials that pose the greatest security risk are Co-60 (cobalt), Cs-137 (cesium), Ir-192 (iridium), Sr-90 (strontium), Pu-238 (plutonium), Am-241 (americium), and Cf-252 (californium).

Depending on their application, these sources come in various forms, quantities, and shieldings. Some of them are not very mobile; others are so radioactive that they would cause immediate harm to an unprotected thief. Nevertheless, these materials can be found in a large number of research laboratories, industries, and hospitals all over the world. They are dealt with in commercial use, and they are transported worldwide. Their protection is generally mediocre, and thieves might be able to steal these types of sources. No reliable inventories of these materials exist, and a large percentage of them are no longer in use, have been discarded, or are lost. Although the number of abandoned or not well-protected sources is high, only a small percentage of them pose a serious security risk—but they are the ones that might be used for a radiological weapon. In the United States, as many as 375 radioactive sources were reported lost, stolen, or abandoned in a single year.[21] Similar numbers can be assumed in many other industrialized states. Specific details about these sources are scarce because they are regarded as commercial secrets.

The technical challenge for terrorists to acquire and to detonate a radiological weapon is not comparable to that of a complete nuclear bomb. A simple conventional explosive would be sufficient just to disperse the radioactive material and to destroy its shielding. The knowledge that terrorists would need to obtain includes the following: they would need to know the standards of radiation protection in order to protect themselves from the radioactivity; they would need to know the basics of shielding from radioactivity; and they would need to know where to get a radioactive source—for example, either to steal or to buy one, or to find an orphaned one. In contrast to those who try to minimize the risk and who want to learn the location and protection of all existing sources, it would be sufficient for terrorists to find and get just one source. Finally, they would need to know the basics of their conventional explosive. In most cases, they would not need to repackage the radioactive material.

There are indeed orphaned sources that are a serious concern, especially those that are strewn throughout the former Soviet Union, most of them left behind by the Russian army during its return to the Russian Federation. In the 1970s, Soviet scientists working with the military developed scores of radioactive sources and dispatched them to the countryside in order to deliberately expose plants to radiation and measure the effects.[22] All of the experiments used Cs-137 in a shielded canister containing enough radioactivity to contaminate a small city. The material is highly dispersible—ideal for terrorists who seek to construct a radiological weapon. Meanwhile, international nuclear experts have searched for the devices, and found some in Georgia and Moldova. But there is no accountancy, and it is unclear how many are still out there or whether terrorists are searching for them, too. Radioactive sources have turned up repeatedly on the black market. They are also known to have been acquired by Chechen rebels in the Russian Federation.[23]

Depending on where it was detonated, a radiological weapon would initially cause few casualties, and technically it cannot be regarded as a weapon of mass destruction. Nevertheless, the psychological impact of such an explosion and its social and economic consequences would be enormous, and the contamination would have dreadful long-term consequences. In a computer simulation of a dirty bomb attack on New York City, the detonation of 3,500 curies of cesium chloride in Lower Manhattan would spread radioactive fallout over sixty city blocks. Immediate casualties would be limited to victims of the immediate blast. The aftereffects, including relocation and cleanup, would cost tens of billions of dollars.[24] Radiological weapons have never been used, so simulations such as these provide much of what we know about the potential impact of their use. However, it is thought that in 1980, Iraq produced and tested conventional bombs filled with radioactive material, presumably from spent fuel elements.[25]

Nuclear plants have frequently been the focus of terrorist and criminal interest. Attempts at invading, attacking, or threatening nuclear power stations have been reported in Argentina, the Russian Federation, Lithuania, South Africa, South Korea, and even the United States and France.[26] Not all such attempts are classified as large-scale acts of terror, as some of them are "only" sabotage attempts by discontented staff or bomb scares in nuclear power stations. There have, however, been cases of threatened suicide attacks by plane hijackers—for example, in November 1972, when three hijackers threatened to bring a plane down on a nuclear research plant in Oak Ridge, Tennessee.[27] Another widely discussed scenario involves a passenger plane, with full fuel tanks, being crashed into a nuclear power station.

The containment design of German nuclear power stations takes into account the possibility of a combat aircraft crashing but not of a plane with full fuel tanks. An IAEA spokesperson confirmed that this also applies to other countries' designs.[28] The containment would probably not withstand such an attack. The core of the reactor is unlikely to be hit but the cooling system might be destroyed. If the emergency cooling system, which is designed to flood the reactor in such a situation, were to fail, it could lead to overheating of the core and a Chernobyl-type catastrophe. Whole regions would be rendered uninhabitable. However, to succeed in releasing the radioactive contents of a nuclear power station, terrorists would have to be capable of hitting the reactor shield vertically—in a nosedive—rather than just scraping it from the side. This is a far greater challenge than directing a plane into a high building, and is very unlikely.

A more likely scenario is sabotage of a nuclear plant with the aid of insiders. The Chernobyl accident was caused by fatal errors of the personnel during an experiment. Similar actions might be conducted deliberately by malevolent staff, either for nonpolitical reasons (such as psychological problems), or by political motivation and collaboration with terrorists.

CONCLUSION

In sum, terrorist acquisition of nuclear materials and knowledge is fraught with difficult challenges. While it is easy to understand the basics of a nuclear weapon because a considerable amount of information is available, the main element in acquiring nuclear capability consists of engineering, whose details are not available. The terrorists would have to conduct experiments that are likely to be detected unless they are protected by a state. Further, they would be dependent on international procurement networks. A terrorist group that operates independently from any government would hardly be able to acquire a working nuclear weapon. The only exception is a group that has done a lot of homework in the past, when it was still under protection. This group could quickly accomplish the final assembly when it gets hold of the nuclear material.

A more likely scenario of nuclear terrorism is the detonation of a radiological weapon. Its preparation does not need sophisticated skills and knowledge but just the acquisition of a high-level source. The effects are less severe than that of a nuclear explosion, but nevertheless, the psychological terror would be tremendous. In order to prevent nuclear terrorism, the focus must be on the protection of nuclear materials by international collaboration and education.

NOTES

1. Examples are: Carey Sublette, "Nuclear Weapons Frequently Asked Questions" (Version 2.25) 9 August 2001, www.fas.org/nuke/hew/Nwfaq/Nfaq0.html; and Gerhardt Locke, *Aufbau und Funktionsweise von Kernspaltungswaffen, Bericht INT 25* (Euskirchen, 1982). Another site that offers many resources and links is "The Nuclear Weapon Archive—A Guide to Nuclear Weapons," http://nuclearweaponarchive.org.

2. U.S. Department of Energy, Office of Declassification, Restricted Data Declassification Policy 1946 to the Present (RDD-7), 1 January 2001, www.osti.gov/opennet/rdd-7.pdf. The following publication is among the first concerning the function of nuclear weapons to be declassified: Robert Serber, *The Los Alamos Prime—The First Lectures on How To Build an Atomic Bomb* (Berkeley, 1982) (written in 1943, declassified in 1965).

3. Russia, for example, refused to publish the composition of the plutonium that stems from Russian disarmed nuclear weapons. In this way, the international cooperation for the inclusion of this material in civil disposal programs is impeded.

4. Edward Teller's lobbying of Ronald Reagan with regard to SDI is an example of the latter.

5. Annette Schaper, "Looking for a Demarcation Between Nuclear Transparency and Nuclear Secrecy," PRIF Reports No. 68 (Peace Research Institute Frankfurt, 2004), www.hsfk.de/publication_detail.php?publicationid=2467&language=en.

6. David Albright and Corey Hinderstein, "South Africa's Nuclear Weaponization Efforts: Success on a Small-Scale," *ISIS-Working-Paper*, 13 September 2001, www.isis-online.org/publications/terrorism/safrica.pdf.

7. This estimate is based on the assumptions that the implosion would not be perfect, the material would be partially lost in the production process, and a reflector would probably be used. It is assumed that the HEU is more than 90 percent enriched.

8. Annette Schaper, "The Case for Universal Full Scope Safeguards on Nuclear Material," *The Nonproliferation Review*, 5, no. 2 (Winter 1998): 69.

9. Annette Schaper, "Nuclear Smuggling in Europe: Real Dangers and Enigmatic Deceptions," in *Illegal Nuclear Traffic: Risks, Safeguards, and Countermeasures: Proceedings of the International Forum, Science for Peace Series*, Vol. 4, edited by Vladimir Kouzminov and Maurizio Martellini (Venice: UNESCO, 1998). Most cases that were discovered and published in Germany and Central Europe in the 1990s turned out to be harmless, as the material used was not weapon-ready.

10. Matthew Bunn, "The Next Wave: Urgently Needed New Steps to Control Warheads and Fissile Material" (Washington, DC: Carnegie Endowment for International Peace and Harvard Project on Managing the Atom, April 2000). Available online at http://ksgnotes1.harvard.edu/BCSIA/Library.nsf/pubs/Nextwave.

11. President's Foreign Intelligence Advisory Board, *Science At Its Best, Security At Its Worst: A Report on Security Problems at the Department of Energy* (the Rudman Report) (Washington, DC: President's Foreign Intelligence Advisory Board, June 1999). Available online at www.fas.org/sgp/library/pfiab.

12. Stephen J. Hedges and Jeff Zeleny, "Mock terrorists breached security at weapons plants," *Chicago Tribune,* 5 October 2001, www.chicagotribune.com/news/nationworld/chi-0110050267oct05.story.

13. U.S. Department of Energy, *Plutonium: The First 50 Years. United States plutonium production, acquisition, and utilization from 1944 to 1994* (Washington, DC: Department of Energy, February 1996).

14. IAEA, "Model Protocol Additional to Existing Safeguards Agreements Between States and the International Atomic Energy Agency for the Application of Safeguards," September 1997, INFCIRC/540.

15. K. Chitumbo, "Information Analysis in the Strengthened Safeguards System," keynote presentation at the Symposium on International Safeguards: Verification and Nuclear Material Security, Vienna, 29 October—2 November 2001.

16. Center for Nonproliferation Studies, "Pakistan, Khan, and the Nuclear Black Market," December 2004. Available online at www.nti.org/f_wmd411/f2i6.html.

17. The pros and cons of different means of persuading Iran to abandon its enrichment are not discussed in this article.

18. Adolf von Baeckmann, Garry Dillon, and Demetrius Perricos, "Nuclear Verification in South Africa," *IAEA Bulletin* 37, no. 1 (March 1995).

19. Kimberly McCloud and Matthew Osborne, "WMD Terrorism and Usama Bin Laden," *CNS Report,* 14 March 2001, http://cns.miis.edu/pubs/reports/binladen.htm; A. Brownfeld, "Bin Ladin's activities exposed in New York trial," *Jane's Terrorism & Security Monitor,* 14 March 2001, http://newsite.janes.com/security/ international_security/news/jtsm/jtsm010314_1_n.shtml.

20. Charles Ferguson, Tahseen Kazi, and Judith Perera, "Commercial Radioactive Sources: Surveying the Security Risks," Occasional Paper No. 11 (Monterey: Center for Nonproliferation Studies, 2003); Gregory J. Van Tuyle, Tiffany L. Strub, Harold A. O'Brien, Caroline F. V. Mason, and Steven J. Gitomer, "Reducing RDD Concerns Related to Large Radiological Source Applications," LA-UR-03-6664 (Los Alamos, September 2003).

21. Ferguson, Kazi, and Perera, "Commercial Radioactive Sources," 17.

22. Jo Warrick, "Hunting a Deadly Soviet Legacy," *Washington Post,* 11 November 2002, A01.

23. William C. Potter and Leonard S. Spector, "The Real Sum of All Fears," *Los Angeles Times,* 11 June 2002.

24. Michael A. Levi and Henry C. Kelly, "Weapons of Mass Disruption," *Scientific American,* November 2002, 78.

25. Glenn Zorpette and Steve Miller, "Unconventional Nuclear Weapons," *IEEE Spectrum Online,* November 2001, www.spectrum.ieee.org/WEBONLY/publicfeature/nov01/nterr.html

26. Oleg Bukharin, "Problems of Nuclear Terrorism," *The Monitor: Nonproliferation, Demilitarization and Arms Control,* Spring 1997, 1; Oleg Bukharin, "Upgrading Security at Nuclear Power Plants in the Newly Independent States," *Nonproliferation Review* (Winter 1997), 28; *Three Mile Island Alert.* "Nuclear Plant Terrorism: Securing Reactors from Sabotage and Terrorism," online at www.tmia.com/security (updated July 2004). Three Mile Island Alert is a nonprofit citizens' organization dedicated to the promotion of safe-energy alternatives to nuclear power and is especially critical of the Three Mile Island nuclear plant.

27. Gavin Cameron, "Nuclear Terrorism: Reactors & Radiological Attacks After September 11," *IAEA Special Session on Combating Nuclear Terrorism,* 30 October 2001. Available online at www.iaea.org/worldatom/Press/Focus/Nuclear_Terrorism/cameron.pdf.

28. William J. Kole, "Global atomic agency confesses little can be done to safeguard nuclear plants," *Associated Press,* 19 September 2001.

II
CASE STUDIES

8

✛

Al Qaeda's Lose and Learn Doctrine: The Trajectory from Oplan Bojinka to 9/11

Rohan Gunaratna

Every terrorist group has a life cycle. In the fight against terrorist networks, both knowing and understanding the enemy are vital. Our knowledge and understanding of how a terrorist group transmits its knowledge and expertise from generation to generation, group to group, and individual to individual, are likely to determine its longevity and threat. While knowledge is relevant information, it is also necessary to understand how the enemy thinks. Al Qaeda's watershed operation to target America's most iconic landmarks in September 2001 developed from a failed operation, code-named Oplan Bojinka. Oplan Bojinka was developed by Ramzi Ahmed Yousef, the first World Trade Center bomber, and his uncle Khalid Sheikh Mohammed—alias KSM, alias "Mokhtar" [The Brain]—whose objective was to nearly simultaneously destroy twelve U.S. airliners over the Pacific in January of 1995.

Within a month of his capture in Rawalpindi, Pakistan, in March 2003, Khalid Sheikh Mohammed (identified by U.S. authorities as the mastermind of 9/11) told his American interrogators that the genesis of 9/11 was Oplan Bojinka. To develop 9/11, KSM claimed that he used the vast experience he gained in late 1994 by casing airline and airport security in Asia in support of Oplan Bojinka. It was the first terrorist operation in which KSM was directly involved in the planning and coordination. While KSM personally traveled and tested airport security on a flight from Manila to Seoul, his nephew Ramzi Ahmed Yousef, the bomber of the first World Trade Center attack, tested security on a flight from Hong Kong to Taipei.[1] Before they could achieve their goal, however, the U.S.

government and its allies disrupted Yousef's network. Yousef, the planner, was arrested in Pakistan; Abdul Hakim Murad, in the Philippines; and Wali Amin Khan Shah in Malaysia. All of them were rendered to the U.S. and sentenced. However, KSM evaded capture. As a result, disrupting the Oplan Bojinka cell did not prevent the flow of knowledge and experience. KSM eventually joined al Qaeda, and converted Oplan Bojinka into the plan for 9/11.

THE CONTEXT

Terrorist groups systematically develop their ideological motivation and operational capabilities—human expertise and material, essential for conducting terrorist attacks. The development of human expertise, knowledge, and experience—through a process of losing and learning, spanning several years—is the most crucial. Even if one cell operative is arrested, another cell operative carries the knowledge and experience forward, improving and using it to advance the terrorists' interests. By apprehending a single terrorist or breaking a cell, a government may disrupt an operation, but it may not be successful in preventing the next attack. Drawing upon the Oplan Bojinka case study, the first half of this chapter will examine how terrorists are able to suffer disruption, recover, learn, reorganize, and strike. The second part of this chapter will examine how government and industry perceive the terrorist threat and respond to it.

The al Qaeda organization[2] adheres to—and encourages its members to rigidly adhere to—a lose and learn doctrine. In the course of its long and difficult fight against the enemy, al Qaeda leaders agree that it will suffer personnel or infrastructure losses. As there is an inherent risk involved in planning, preparing, and executing terrorist attacks, al Qaeda acknowledges that a member will serve as long as he is alive and free, and thereafter, the remaining members will carry on the fight. Al Qaeda accepts as inevitable that some of its operations will fail and lead to the loss of some of its best and most valued assets. Provided its members can learn from mistakes and avoid repeating those mistakes, al Qaeda doctrine suggests that its cadre must not consider a loss real or permanent. In essence, al Qaeda builds its lessons learned into its operational experiences.

Despite being the world's most hunted terrorist group, al Qaeda has been able to survive and succeed. Due to its adherence to the lose and learn doctrine, al Qaeda is rapidly learning from its past and present operations, whether successful or failed; it is unlikely to repeat its mistakes. In an ever-changing counterterrorism environment, the key to a terrorist's success is for the terrorist to know his own strengths and weaknesses as well as the opponent's strengths and vulnerabilities. By studying its own successes and failures, al Qaeda is constantly learning from government security and countermeasures. By constantly maximizing its successes and minimizing its failures, al Qaeda will adapt its practices to survive and succeed. By adhering to the lose and learn doctrine, al Qaeda will remain dynamic, agile, and flexible. If al Qaeda can learn faster than government law enforcement and intelligence agencies, it will stay ahead of the learning curve. The group will survive and succeed under different and difficult circumstances.

THE ORIGINS OF 9/11

On February 26, 1993, Ramzi Ahmed Yousef—a graduate of al Qaeda's Al-Sadda training camp[3]—executed his first successful terrorist strike on the American homeland.[4] A rental truck packed with powerful explosives was detonated in an underground parking lot below the World Trade Center, killing six bystanders, injuring fifteen hundred, and causing havoc in downtown Manhattan. In addition to advising him over the phone, KSM wired US$660 to Yousef on November 3, 1992, to support the operation.[5] Subsequently, the FBI disrupted another associated cell, led by Dr. Omar Abdel Rahman alias the Blind Sheikh, which was planning to destroy New York landmarks. Both operations were loosely, although not directly, linked to Osama bin Laden, and while they were not official al Qaeda operations, the terrorists and supporters operated in the al Qaeda milieu.

After the bombing of the World Trade Center in February 1993, Yousef relocated to the Philippines and developed a plan with KSM to bomb twelve U.S. airliners over the Pacific. To test airport and aviation security, they decided to rehearse the operation in airports in Hong Kong, Taiwan, Korea, and the Philippines. In his 2003 debriefing, KSM claimed that he poured out the contents of fourteen contact lens solution bottles and then filled them with concentrated nitromethane, an inexpensive explosive chemical, readily available in the Philippines.[6] He described how he had carefully removed the tops of the contact lens solution bottles without breaking the plastic seals, and then returned the tops after filling the bottles. While he traveled through airport security carrying thirteen of the nitromethane-filled bottles in his bag, Yousef carried one. KSM and Yousef decided not to check any luggage, since they did not plan on doing so during the actual operation. To test his ability to clear airport security carrying a detonator, KSM decided to carry a bolt, which he taped to the arch of his foot and then covered with a sock. When searched by airport authorities, he was asked to undress, but while he was asked to remove his shoes, the police did not insist that he take off his socks. To deceive airport security, both men also decided to wear clothing with metal in it, such as buttons and accessories, and jewelry.

KSM said he and Yousef also placed condoms in their bags to support their cover story that their main purpose in traveling to the Philippines was to meet women.[7] He did not have a visa for the Philippines and claimed that he was told at the Korean Embassy that he did not need a visa. When asked about purchasing his ticket one day before traveling, he explained that his Philippine visa was about to expire and that he had to leave the Philippines and travel to another country in order to renew his visa. Upon arriving in Seoul, he was denied entry because he did not have a visa, and was held for ten hours at the immigration office before being deported back to the Philippines. Having realized that he might be searched, KSM disposed of his false identity card down the toilet in Seoul.

Upon reflection, KSM admitted to authorities that he made some mistakes during the rehearsal. For instance, he accidentally left a copy of the plan for Bojinka in his bag, which contained all twelve of the targeted flights as well as the time the bombs were to have exploded. Although the document went undetected, KSM vowed not to repeat such mistakes again.

For his rehearsal, Yousef boarded Philippines Airlines Flight 434 from Manila to Narita, Tokyo (via Cebu, Philippines), on December 12, 1994. From the components he carried on board—nitromethane in contact lens solution bottles, a detonator in his shoe, and a Casio watch with a timer—he improvised an explosive device, placed it under his seat, and deplaned in Cebu. Although the explosion made a hole in the fuselage, resulting in the death of one passenger and injuries to several others, the plane did not explode.

Afterward, while Yousef continued to refine the effectiveness of a miniature explosive device, an accidental fire led the police to raid his apartment in Manila. The police arrested Abdul Hakim Murad, al Qaeda's first pilot, who had trained in six aviation schools: Peshawar Flying Club in Pakistan; Emirates Flying School in Dubai; Alfa Tango Flying School, San Antonio, Texas; Richmore Aviation, Schenectady, New York; Coast Aviation Flying School, New Bern, North Carolina; and the California Aeronautical Flying School.[8] The cell in Manila had also engaged in learning about helicopters and aircraft in the Philippines.[9]

Further investigations revealed that Yousef and Murad had discussed crashing a commercial airplane into CIA headquarters in Langley, Virginia. Murad's debrief by the Philippine National Police records this plan: "What the subject has in his mind is that he will board any American commercial aircraft, pretending to be an ordinary passenger. Then he will hijack said aircraft, control its cockpit, and dive it at the CIA Headquarters. There will be no bomb or explosive that he will use in its execution. It is simply a suicide mission that he is very much willing to execute. All that he needs is to be able to board the aircraft with a pistol so that he could execute the hijacking."[10]

Yousef was subsequently arrested in Pakistan, while another member of the operational cell—Osama Asmurai, alias Wali Amin Khan Shah, a man linked to Osama bin Laden—was arrested in Malaysia. They were all brought to the U.S. for trial. Thus, with the exception of KSM, the U.S. government was successful in capturing all of the terrorists involved in Oplan Bojinka. Despite attempts to arrest him in Qatar and Brazil, the U.S. government failed to successfully target and neutralize KSM, a key player in Oplan Bojinka. Although Yousef and his associates were arrested, a revengeful KSM was undeterred by the loss of his nephew and continued to develop his operational capabilities, putting his vast, varied, and rich experience into practice. Having studied both the mistakes and successes of Oplan Bojinka, KSM designed and executed 9/11 by minimizing the failures and maximizing the successes of Oplan Bojinka. On his return to Afghanistan in 1996, KSM met with Osama bin Laden and proposed an operation "that would involve training pilots who would crash planes into buildings in the United States."[11] This proposal eventually would become the 9/11 operation.

OTHER HIJACKINGS

The idea of crashing aircrafts into strategic, high-profile, and symbolic targets was not unique to KSM or al Qaeda. Indeed, examples of this tactic could be found in both Asia and the Middle East. Similar to the operation in the Philippines, which was detected and disrupted, another operation was initiated from Algeria almost during the same period, and reached an advanced stage before being successfully neutralized in France. On December 24–26, 1994, the Algerian Armed Islamic Group (GIA) hijacked an Air France flight from Algiers to France. French authorities deceived the terrorists into thinking the plane did not have enough fuel to reach Paris, and diverted it to Marseilles.[12] A French antiterrorist force stormed the plane, freed the plane's 173 passengers, and killed all four terrorists. During the hijacking, an anonymous informant warned the French consulate in Oran, Algeria, that the plane would be used as a "flying bomb that will explode over Paris."[13] The French authorities believe that the terrorists' intention was to crash the aircraft into the Eiffel Tower. The GIA later avenged the loss of its "martyrs" by murdering four Roman Catholic priests in the Algerian city of Tizi-Ouzou.

The organizational and individual links between al Qaeda and GIA are sketchy. What is known is that GIA recruits were trained in al Qaeda camps both in Afghanistan and in Sudan, the home of al Qaeda's head-quarters between 1991 and 1996.[14] Investigations revealed that Ramzi Ahmed Yousef, the Oplan Bojinka planner, was closely associated with Algerian and Egyptian terrorists, initially during his training in Afghanistan in 1993. Yousef's co-conspirator Abdul Hakim Murad told authorities that after the Philippines operation to bomb twelve U.S. airliners over the Pacific, Yousef planned "to go to France, Egypt, and Algeria."[15] Murad added that: "The purpose was to train those Muslim brothers on using a Casio watch as a timing device and making chemical mixtures for compound bombs, as well as to share his expertise on eluding detection by airport x-ray machines in order to smuggle liquid chemical bombs. Furthermore, France has a lot of Algerians . . . [and] these Egyptians and Algerians have no experience on making these bombs and do not know the basics of smuggling liquid bombs through the airport."[16] Like al Qaeda, a group with guerrilla experience against the Soviets, many Middle Eastern and Asian groups lacked an understanding of operating in the urban environment. In the early 1990s, they were learning by trial and error to conduct urban terrorist attacks using explosives. There is insufficient information to conclude that the hand of al Qaeda was present in the hijacking of the French Airbus. However, KSM is likely to have known of it, especially the outcome of it. Nonetheless, the al Qaeda leadership (including KSM) is very likely to have benefited from the operational knowledge and expertise of an operation that was staged by an associated group.

In another example, Pakistani members of Harkat-ul-Ansar (HUA) hijacked Indian Airlines Flight 814 while en route to New Delhi, India, from Kathmandu, Nepal, on December 24, 1999. The Airbus A-300 aircraft carried 174 passengers and fifteen crew members. About thirty minutes after takeoff, an armed masked person stood up and announced the hijacking. At about the same time, four other hijackers wearing red masks took up positions throughout the plane. Although they demanded to be flown to Lahore, Pakistan, Pakistani officials refused permission to land there and the plane was flown instead to Amritsar, India. However, the plane was not refueled before taking off again. After the plane made an emergency landing in Lahore, food, water, and fuel were provided. The plane took off again and landed in Dubai on December 25, where 27 passengers were released in exchange for food and fuel. The plane then departed for Kandahar, Afghanistan, where it remained until December 31, when the Indian government released Maulana Masood Azhar (the General Secretary of HUA) and Ahmed Saeed Omar Sheikh from custody, along with two other terrorists. Although there is no evidence to link al Qaeda to this hijacking, links can be established on the basis of personal acquaintances of the released terrorists with Osama bin Laden. Intelligence reports indicated that two of the released prisoners—Azhar and Sheikh—before reappearing in Pakistan, spent time in Afghanistan, and probably with Osama bin Laden. It was not known whether the hijackers went to a particular training camp, but a *New York Times* report indicated that U.S. Special Forces and the CIA discovered four ticket stubs from the flight, two boarding passes, an Indian Airlines Airbus 300 safety procedure card, and a handwritten list of the plane's passengers in an abandoned camp in Kabul. The specific identity and ownership of the camp are not known at this time. The camp also contained notes on nuclear and biological weapons,[17] an issue that the Indian Central Bureau of Investigation (CBI) raised with the FBI in December 2001.[18]

DESIGN AND IMPLEMENTATION OF 9/11

In the design and the implementation of the 9/11 operation, KSM considered all the lessons he learned from Oplan Bojinka and other relevant operations. Having studied in the U.S., KSM knew how to mount an operation within the U.S. KSM taught many of the pilots and musclemen basic English and important phrases, as well as how to read a phone book, make travel reservations, and use the Internet and encoded communication.[19] In the same way that KSM had studied the airline schedules in East Asia, he ensured that the suicide pilots knew to analyze U.S. airline schedules in order to identify flights that would be in the air at the same time. In much the same way that KSM had tested airport and airline security during the rehearsals for Oplan Bojinka, 9/11 hijacker Walid Muhammad Salih Bin Attash (alias Khallad) flew in January 2000 aboard a U.S. airliner from Kuala Lumpur to Hong Kong with a box cutter concealed in his toiletries bag.[20] The second test was conducted inside the United States, where Mohammad Atta, Marwan al Shehhi, and Ziad Jarrah were able to carry box cutters onto their rehearsal flights.

In the same way that KSM and his nephew had engaged in test runs for Oplan Bojinka, the 9/11 hijackers conducted multiple cross-country surveillance flights. Traveling first class on board the same type of aircraft they would pilot on 9/11, Marwan al Shehhi flew from New York to San Francisco and on to Las Vegas on May 24; Ziad Jarrah, from Baltimore to Los Angeles and on to Las Vegas on June 7; and Mohammad Atta, from Boston to San Francisco and on to Las Vegas on June 28, 2001.[21] Gradually, the flight rehearsals resembled the actual operation. Jarrah flew the Hudson Corridor, a low-altitude hallway along the Hudson River that passed several New York landmarks—including the World Trade Center—in early June 2001.[22]

In much the same way that KSM, Yousef, and other Oplan Bojinka terrorists used deception, the 9/11 hijackers practiced deception. By wearing jewelry purchased in Bangkok, they created the impression to airport and aircraft officials (as well as to the passengers) that they were rich Saudi tourists. KSM befriended two bar girls ("Precious" and "Rose"), and used Rose to open a bank account and to buy a mobile phone for his use. However, KSM refrained from having sex with either of them, and drank only nonalcoholic beer.[23] Similarly, by visiting bars and nightclubs, the 9/11 hijackers created the impression that they were interested in women and a generally American singles lifestyle.

However, the 9/11 operation also had several features that were improvements on Oplan Bojinka. To begin with, the organizational and operational security were much better. To increase the chances that the 9/11 operation would succeed, KSM ensured that one half of the hijackers, based in Florida, reported to Mohammad Atta (the operational commander) while the rest, based in Paterson, New Jersey, reported to his deputy Hawaz Al Hazmi.[24] Functioning as a cut-out, Ramzi bin al-Shibh, the 9/11 logistics coordinator in Hamburg, Germany, used encrypted email to communicate with the hijackers and KSM.

UNDERSTANDING THE THREAT

Governments and the public are content when terrorist cells are broken and operations disrupted. Nonetheless, as terrorist groups are learning organizations, the strategic threat is still persistent. Any operation, whether successful or failed, demonstrates a continuing level of threat. To reduce the threat, the U.S. government and the private sector did not develop an appropriate response. As a result of the disrupted Oplan Bojinka operation, the U.S. investigative and intelligence agencies were aware of the growing threat—they knew that terrorists were keen to attack high-profile, strategic, and symbolic targets, and were particularly interested in aviation. During the mid-1990s, the CIA's annual National Intelligence Estimates warned: "As an open and free democracy, the United States is particularly vulnerable to various types of terrorist attacks. Several kinds of targets are especially at risk: National symbols such as the White House and the Capitol, and symbols of U.S. capitalism such as Wall Street; power grids, communications switches, water facilities, and transportation infrastructure—particularly civil aviation, subway systems, cruise lines, and petroleum pipelines; places where large numbers of people congregate, such as large office buildings, shopping centers, sports arenas, and airport and other transportation terminals."[25]

The report added: "We assess that civil aviation will figure prominently among possible terrorist targets in the United States. This stems from the increasing domestic threat posed by foreign terrorists, the continuing appeal of civil aviation as a target, and a domestic aviation security system that has been the focus of media attention. We have attempted to penetrate security at U.S. airports in recent years. The media have called attention to, among other things, inadequate security for checked baggage. Our review of the evidence obtained thus far about the plot uncovered in Manila in early 1995 suggests the conspirators were guided in their selection of the method and venue of attack by carefully studying security procedures in place in the region. If terrorists operating in this country are similarly methodical, they will identify serious vulnerabilities in the security system for domestic flights."[26]

Referring to Oplan Bojinka, Keith O. Fultz, Assistant Comptroller General of the GAO's (General Accounting Office) Resources, Community, and Economic Development Division, informed the Senate Committee on Commerce, Science and Transportation in 1996 that: "According to information that was accidentally uncovered in early January 1995, this bombing was a rehearsal for multiple attacks on specific U.S. flights in Asia. Officials told us that they rarely have the advantage of a detailed, verifiable plot to target U.S. airliners. They also said that the terrorists were aware both of airports' vulnerabilities and of how existing security measures could be defeated."[27] He added: "Aviation security is a shared responsibility of the FAA and the airlines and airports. FAA has mandated additional security procedures as the threat has changed; however, the domestic and international aviation system has numerous vulnerabilities. For example, conventional X-ray screening of checked baggage has performance limitations and offers little protection against a moderately sophisticated explosive device. . . . The threat of terrorism against the United States has increased, according to the intelligence community. The experts believe that aviation is likely to remain an attractive target for terrorists well into the foreseeable future. Until the early 1990s, the Federal Bureau of Investigation (FBI), the State Department, FAA, the Department of Transportation (DOT), and airline officials had maintained that the threat of terrorism was far greater overseas than in the United States. However, the World Trade Center bombing and the recent convictions of individuals charged with plotting to bomb several landmarks in the New York area revealed that the international terrorist threat in the United States is more serious and more extensive then previously believed."[28]

Reporting on the terrorist threat was consistent the following year. The FAA (Federal Aviation Administration) publication "Criminal Acts against Civil Aviation 1997" stated: "The fact that the number of incidents against civil aviation has declined over the past five years, and longer, may be interpreted as an indication that the threat is decreasing. This, however, is not true, as several events in the past few years attest. The September 1996 conviction of Ramzi Yousef for his plan to place explosive devices on as many as 12 U.S. airliners flying out of the Far East is proof that a threat to aviation exists. Yousef was also convicted of placing a device on a Philippine Airlines plane in December 1994 as a test for his more elaborate plan. One person was killed in this incident. Other examples of the continuing threat include the bombing of the Alas Chiricanas Airline plane in Panama in July 1994, in which 21 people died; the commandeering of the Air France flight in Algeria in December 1994 by members of the Armed Islamic Group; and the hijacking of the Ethiopian Airlines plane that crashed into the Indian Ocean in November 1996. There is every reason to believe that civil aviation will continue to be an attractive target to terrorist groups. The publicity and fear generated by a terrorist hijacking or bombing of an airplane can be a powerful attraction to a group seeking to make a statement or promote a particular cause. . . . Increased awareness and vigilance are necessary to deter future incidents—be they from terrorists like Ramzi Yousef or non-terrorists bent on suicide, as occurred in Brazil in 1997. It is important to do the utmost to prevent such acts rather than to lower security measures by interpreting the statistics as an indication of a decreasing threat."[29]

Although the U.S. government had no precise and accurate information of a suicide attack on U.S. targets at home using aircraft, the increasing threat to the U.S. homeland, the vulnerability of aviation, and the use of suicide operations were clear. The analysis needed to look at the complete threat spectrum was lacking. In February 1997, the White House Commission on Aviation Safety and Security reported: "The Federal Bureau of Investigation, the Central Intelligence Agency, and other intelligence sources have been warning that the threat of terrorism is changing in two important ways. First, it is no longer just an overseas threat from foreign terrorists. People and places in the United States have joined the list of targets, and Americans have joined the ranks of terrorists. The bombings of the World Trade Center in New York and the Federal Building in Oklahoma City are clear examples of the shift, as is the conviction of Ramzi Yousef for attempting to bomb twelve American airliners out of the sky over the Pacific Ocean. The second change is that in addition to well-known, established terrorist groups, it is becoming more common to find terrorists working alone or in ad-hoc groups, some of whom are not afraid to die in carrying out their designs."[30]

The case of the disrupted Oplan Bojinka, combined with subsequent threat information, suggests that the U.S. government did not respond adequately. Although information was partial, as in most cases, the threat was clear. Murad cooperated with the FBI by divulging terrorist intentions. On April 10, 1995, Murad told the FBI that the plan of the Manila cell included an operation to fly a plane into the CIA headquarters.[31] The threat of terrorists flying commercial aircraft (with or without explosives) into U.S. targets was thus known. Potential targets included the U.S. Consulate in Karachi, Pakistan; U.S. nuclear power plants; and a variety of U.S. government buildings, including CIA headquarters and the Pentagon.[32] Although Yousef did not cooperate with authorities following his capture, a letter on his computer disk warned that future attacks would be more precise and that they would continue to target the World Trade Center if their demands were not met. The CIA specialists who studied Oplan Bojinka recognized that members of Yousef's cell were still at large. "We believe that the threat is not over. We still have not identified all of the members of Yousef's network, nor do we know their present location. We also do not know how many are trained in making bombs or have the capability to carry out other types of terrorist attacks."[33]

THE THREAT FROM THE AL QAEDA NETWORK

In the second half of the 1990s, the threat to the continental U.S. from the bin Laden network became apparent. Toward the late 1990s, both open source and classified reporting identified the threat even more clearly. After bin Laden moved from Sudan to Afghanistan in May 1996, a move precipitated by the U.S., the threat to the U.S. increased. In August 1996, bin Laden issued a public fatwa titled "Declaration of War against the Americans Occupying the Land of the Two Holy Places." Authorizing attacks on Western military targets in the Arabian Peninsula, bin Laden declared: "It is a duty now on every tribe in the Arab Peninsula to fight, jihad, in the cause of Allah and to cleanse the land from those occupiers. Allah knows that their blood is permitted to be spilled and their wealth is a booty; their wealth is a booty to those who kill them. . . . Your brothers in Palestine and in the land of the two Holy Places are calling upon your help and asking you to take part in fighting against the enemy—your enemy and their enemy—the Americans and the Israelis. They are asking you to do whatever you can, within one's own means and ability, to expel the enemy, humiliated and defeated, out of the sanctities of Islam."[34]

On February 23, 1998, bin Laden issued another fatwa, declaring it a religious duty of all Muslims "to kill the Americans and their allies—civilians and military—and plunder their money when and wherever they find it . . . in any country in which it is possible." The statement, an expansion of his 1996 fatwa, came after bin Laden met with other Middle Eastern and Asian terrorist leaders in Afghanistan. After forming the World Islamic Front for Jihad Against the Jews and the Crusaders, they jointly agreed that "the ruling to kill the Americans and their allies—civilians and military—is an individual duty for every Muslim who can do it in any country in which it is possible to do it." The 1998 fatwa thus stated that: "We—with God's help—call on every Muslim who believes in God and wishes to be rewarded, to comply with God's order to kill the Americans and plunder their money wherever and whenever they find it. We also call on Muslim ulema, leaders, youths, and soldiers to launch the raid on Satan's U.S. troops and the devil's supporters allying with them, and to displace those who are behind them so that they may learn a lesson."[35]

On May 28, 1998, bin Laden told ABC News: "Our battle with the Americans is larger than our battle with the Russians. . . . We predict a black day for America and the end of the United States as United States, when it will become separate states, and will retreat from our land and collect the bodies of its sons back to America, Allah willing. Once again, I have to stress the necessity of focusing on the Americans and the Jews, for they represent the spearhead with which the members of our religion have been slaughtered. Any effort directed against America and the Jews yields positive and direct results, Allah willing. It is far better for anyone to kill a single American soldier than to squander his efforts on other activities."[36]

In response to al Qaeda's bombing of U.S. embassies in East Africa, and the resulting U.S. missile strikes on al Qaeda training camps in Afghanistan in August 1998, the blind Sheikh Dr. Omar Abdel Rahman issued a new call to arms. Smuggled out of his American prison cell with the help of his paralegals and lawyer Lynne Stewart, his fatwa addressed all Muslims: "[The Jews and Christians] are the ones that are fighting every Muslim resurrection in the whole world, they act to spread prostitution, usury, and other kinds of corruption all over the land. Oh, Muslims everywhere! Cut the transportation of their countries, tear it apart, destroy their economy, burn their companies, eliminate their interests, sink their ships, shoot down their planes, kill them on the sea, air, or land. Kill them when you find them, take them and encircle them, paralyze their every post. Kill those infidels. . . . Allah will torment by your hands those who wish to kill you; Allah will put shame upon them, he will blow wind in the chests of the believers and show the anger of their hearts."[37]

Bin Laden and Sheikh Rahman were associates with compatible ideologies. During that period, one of the blind Sheikh's sons was serving with bin Laden in Afghanistan as a trainer, and appeared on television seated next to bin Laden. Al Qaeda millennium bomber Ahmed Ressam later recalled that Sheikh Rahman's fatwa was distributed widely throughout the Afghan military training camps in 1998–1999.[38] The threat posed by bin Laden and his network to the United States was becoming increasingly apparent. On June 2001, bin Laden sent a message to his followers worldwide: "[T]o all mujahideen . . . it's time to penetrate America and Israel and hit them where it hurts the most."[39]

THE U.S. RESPONSE TO THE THREAT

Gradually, the threat became more specific. Based on intelligence, the U.S. government issued several warnings from October through December 1998 that Bin Laden posed a threat to aviation in the U.S.[40] The FAA warned U.S. airports and airlines in late 1998 about a possible terrorist hijacking at a metropolitan airport in the Eastern United States, and urged a high degree of vigilance against threats to U.S. civil aviation from Osama bin Laden's terrorist network. The first of the three FAA circulars, issued on October 8, 1998, instructed airports and airlines to maintain a "high degree of alertness" based on statements made by bin Laden and other Islamic leaders and intelligence information. Bin Laden, the circular states, had praised one of the bombers arrested in a failed 1995 plot to blow up U.S. civilian airliners in the Far East. Another unnamed Islamic leader had stated that "militants had been mobilized to strike a significant U.S. or Israeli target, to include bringing down or hijacking aircraft." The report continues, "The arrest and pending extradition of the bin Laden cadre raises the possibility of a U.S. airliner being hijacked in an effort to demand the release of incarcerated members." In a December 8, 1998, circular, the FAA "strongly recommends a high degree of vigilance" based on "the potential for retaliation for U.S. cruise missile strikes in Afghanistan and Sudan." In a December 29, 1998, bulletin, the FAA references Osama bin Laden's fatwa when it states, "In light of these inflammatory statements, there is continuing concern that bin Laden and terrorist groups comprising his terrorist network are preparing to conduct further terrorist attacks against U.S. interests, including U.S. aviation." In its publication 'Criminal Acts against Civil Aviation 2000,' the FAA stated: "Although Bin Laden is not known to have attacked civil aviation, he has both the motivation and the wherewithal to do so. Bin Laden's anti-Western and anti-American attitudes make him and his followers a significant threat to civil aviation, especially U.S. civil aviation." The FAA report also pointed out that: "Increased awareness and vigilance are necessary to deter future incidents—be they from terrorist or non-terrorists. It is important to do the utmost to prevent such acts rather than to lower security measures by interpreting the statistics as indicating a decreasing threat."[41]

On July 17, 2001, the Federal Aviation Administration re-emphasized the threat of potential hijackings. The FAA announcement, issued two months before 9/11, stated: "The terrorist threat level in the United States over the next decade will remain as high as it is and will probably rise. The expanding geographical range of terrorist activity is increasingly evident. Members of foreign terrorist groups, representatives from state sponsors of terrorism, and radical fundamentalist elements are present in the United States. . . . With respect specifically to the threat to civil aviation in the United States, it must be seen in the context of the broader threat. The events in Asia in early 1995 showed that the terrorists persisted in planning to attack aviation even when there were other targets in the area identifiable with the United States, and even when they knew that the security measures protecting aviation had been strengthened. Publicity about problems with U.S. domestic civil aviation security measures increases the potential for attacks here. Civil aviation targets may be chosen by terrorists even if alternative, and (in their view) softer targets are available, especially since an attack on aviation seizes the public's imagination to a degree equaled by few other types of attack."[42]

There were several other specific reports of varying strengths that indicated the use of aviation to mount a terrorist attack. For instance, an FBI agent in the Oklahoma City FBI field office sent a memo to his supervisor in May 1998 warning that he had observed "large numbers of Middle Eastern males receiving flight training at Oklahoma airports in recent months."[43] The memo, titled "Weapons of Mass Destruction," further states that this "may be related to planned terrorist activity" and speculates that "light planes would be an ideal means of spreading chemicals or biological agents."[44] Later in 1998, the FBI received reports that a terrorist organization might be planning to bring students to the U.S. for flight training.[45] The FBI was aware that people connected to this unnamed organization had performed surveillance and security tests at airports in the U.S. and had made comments suggesting an intention to target civil aviation.[46]

In sum, both the U.S. government and U.S. aviation industry had knowledge of al Qaeda pilot training in the United States more than two years prior to September 11, 2001. An investigation in the Southern District of New York into the case of *USA v. Ihab Mohamed Ali* revealed that the defendant, an accused al Qaeda operative, received pilot training in Oklahoma in 1994.[47] Nonetheless, there was little done to strengthen aviation—both aircraft and airport—security to reduce the threat. The U.S. leaders did not fully understand terrorist thinking, nor recognize the urgent need to develop appropriate security measures in order to detect terrorist operations and protect the U.S.' national infrastructure from terrorist attack. In the face of a determined al Qaeda seeking to attack the United States homeland, the government failed at an operational level either to target the terrorists or to harden the targets. The airlines, screening companies, and airports had sufficient notice to reasonably foresee that terrorists would use weapons to hijack civilian airliners in the United States and fly these planes into high-profile targets. Despite a recurrent and a growing threat and multiple and frequent warnings, the U.S. government did not appreciate the threat adequately to develop a timely and an appropriate response. The case of al Qaeda, which learned and applied lessons from Oplan Bojinka, thus illustrates how terrorist groups can be more capable of organizational learning than government agencies.

CONCLUSION

Lean and mean terrorist organizations have the capacity to learn from their mistakes and successes. Inherently, government bureaucracies lack that ability. The type of warnings issued by the government had limited or no effect on the ground. Furthermore, the government publicly identified the weaknesses in the aviation security system. In June 2000, a Government Accounting Office report stated: "The United States and other countries have a number of safeguards in place to prevent attacks against commercial aircraft. Among the most important of these are the checkpoints at airports where passengers and their carryon items are screened for dangerous objects, such as guns, and explosives. Historically, however, screeners who operate checkpoints in the United States have had difficulty in detecting dangerous objects, missing as many as 20 percent during tests, and numerous reports—including two by presidential commissions—have detailed significant problems with screeners' performance. The report's principal findings take great concern with the long-standing problems and program delays which have impaired improvements in screener performance. Major problems include low wages, rapid turnover, and inadequate training."[48] Although the U.S. government identified the problems, there was little action taken to correct the gaps and loopholes in security. According to the FAA and the aviation industry, the GAO report added, "this turnover is largely due to the low pay and few, if any, benefits screeners receive, as well as the daily stress of the job. It is not unusual for the starting wages at airport fast-food restaurants to be higher than the wages screeners receive. For instance, at one airport GAO visited, screeners' wages started as low as $6.25 an hour, whereas the starting wage at one of the airport's fast-food restaurants was $7 an hour. The human factors associated with screening—those work-related issues that are influenced by human capabilities and constraints—have also been noted by the FAA as problems affecting performance for over 20 years."

"GAO examined pre-board passenger screening practices in Belgium, Canada, France, the Netherlands, and the United Kingdom—five countries recommended by FAA and industry representatives. . . . [Although] the countries did not make data on the performance of their screeners available to GAO, the performance of screeners in at least one country was better than in the United States. Joint testing by FAA and this country, using consistent procedures and test objects, demonstrated that the other country's screeners were able to detect the objects at better than twice the rate of U.S. screeners."[49] Until the loss of nearly three thousand lives and billions of dollars on September 11, 2001, the U.S. government did not correct the flaws in its aviation security system. In essence, it did not exhibit the attributes of a learning organization, able to scan the environment, capture knowledge, analyze and learn from that knowledge, and develop strategy in response to the threat. This is in marked contrast with the organizational learning capabilities demonstrated by al Qaeda.

Al Qaeda's adherence to its lose and learn doctrine has far-reaching security implications. Al Qaeda's mandate is not only to see that it succeeds as a group. As al Qaeda is the proclaimed "pioneering vanguard of the Islamic movements,"[50] it disseminates knowledge and expertise to its associated groups worldwide. Drawing from its global best practices, al Qaeda improves and instills its tried and tested experiences among its associated groups. As a group, al Qaeda is a teaching institution tested by fire in the post 9/11 environment. As several tens of thousands of non–al Qaeda recruits have been trained in al Qaeda camps in Afghanistan and in al Qaeda–sponsored camps worldwide, al Qaeda's lose and learn doctrine will no doubt be increasingly practiced by its associated members.[51]

NOTES

1. Debriefing of Khalid Sheikh Mohammed, Central Intelligence Agency, April 2003.

2. The correct name of the Al Qaeda organization led by Osama bin Laden and deputy Dr. Ayman Al Zawahiri is Tanzeem Qadat al Jihad, a group formed by the merger of Al Qaeda and the Egyptian Islamic Jihad in June 1999. In this chapter, I will refer to Tanzeem Qadat al Jihad as Al Qaeda.

3. Debriefing of Abdul Hakim Murad, Special Investigations Group, National Police Commission, February 13, 1995, 1. Murad said that Yousef trained for six months in Afghanistan in 1993. For more on this, please see the *Report of the National Commission on Terrorist Attacks Upon the United States (The 9/11 Commission Report)*, 507, note 8. National Commission on Terrorist Attacks Upon the United States. (Washington, DC: Government Printing Office, 2004). Available online at www.gpoaccess.gov/911.

4. A claim of responsibility by the "Fifth Battalion of the Liberation Army" was delivered to New York media and was signed by "Abu Bakr al-Makki," meaning the father of Bakr from Mecca in Saudi Arabia.

5. Definition of Khalid Sheikh Mohammed, www.wordiq.com/definition/Khalid_Sheikh _Mohammed. Accessed on October 15, 2004.

6. Debriefing of Khalid Sheikh Mohammed.

7. Debriefing of Khalid Sheikh Mohammed.

8. Debriefing of Abdul Hakim Murad, Special Investigations Group, National Police Commission, February 13, 1995, 2–3. For more on this, please see the National Commission on Terrorist Attacks Upon the United States, *Final Report of the National Commission on Ter-*

rorist Attacks Upon the United States (The 9/11 Commission Report), 507, note 8. (Washington, DC: U.S. Government Printing Office, 2004). Available online at www.gpoaccess.gov/911.

9. Both KSM and Yousef rented a chopper from Airlink International Aviation School and thereafter an aircraft, ostensibly to impress a dentist working at Sheafa Dental Clinic at M. Adriatico St. in Ermita, Manila. Abdul Hakim Hasim Murad, After Debriefing Report, Philippine National Police, January 20, 1995, 3.

10. Abdul Hakim Hasim Murad, After Debriefing Report, 4.

11. *Report of the National Commission on Terrorist Attacks*, 149.

12. Senate Intelligence Committee, 18 September 2002; Thomas Sancton, "Anatomy of a Hijack," *Time*, December 26, 1994.

13. Sancton, "Anatomy of a Hijack."

14. Algeria threatened to sever diplomatic relations with both Iran and Sudan because of their sponsorship of GIA training in Iran and Sudan in the early 1990s.

15. Debriefing of Abdul Hakim Murad, Special Investigations Group, National Police Commission, February 13, 1995, 1.

16. Debriefing of Abdul Hakim Murad.

17. "Bombay terrorist reveals links with IC 814 hijackers," *Rediff.com*, www.rediff.com/news/2001/dec/07ter.htm.

18. U.S. Department of Transportation, *Criminal Acts Against Civil Aviation* (Washington, DC: U.S. Department of Transportation, 1999).

19. "Staff Statement No. 16 Prepared for the 9/11 Commission on Terrorist Attacks," *New York Times*, June 17, 2004.

20. "Staff Statement No. 16."

21. "Staff Statement No. 16."

22. "Staff Statement No. 16."

23. Chronology of Activities of Rose Mosquera, Philippines National Police, January 1995, 1–2.

24. "Staff Statement No. 16."

25. "CIA Warned of US Attack in 1995," *CBS News.com*, April 16, 2004.

26. "CIA Warned of US Attack in 1995."

27. Senate Committee on Commerce, Science and Transportation, Testimony of Keith Fultz, "Immediate Action Needed to Improve Security," August 1, 1996.

28. Testimony of Keith Fultz.

29. U.S. Department of Transportation, "Criminal Acts Against Civil Aviation."

30. White House Commission on Aviation Safety and Security, February 12, 1997.

31. Interview with an FBI agent, November 2004.

32. *U.S. v. Yousef*, Docket No. 98-1041 (2nd Cir. 2003); *Report of the National Commission on Terrorist Attacks*, 491; and Central Intelligence Agency, "Ramzi Ahmed Yousef: A New Generation of Sunni Islamic Terrorists," 1995, 3.

33. Central Intelligence Agency, "Ramzi Ahmed Yousef," 7.

34. "Declaration of War Against the Americans Occupying the Land of the Two Holy Places," *Al Quds Al Arabi*, August 1996.

35. World Islamic Front for Jihad Against the Jews and the Crusaders, February 23, 1998.

36. "Hunting Bin Laden," *Frontline*, PBS, May 1998.

37. Sheikh Omar Abdel Rahman (writing from an American prison cell), fatwa, August 1998.

38. Interview with Mike Elsner, 9/11 lawyer, Charleston, North Carolina, November 2004.

39. See the CNN web page at www.cnn.com/2001/WORLD/europe/06/21/video.bin-laden/index.html.

40. Ralph Ranalli, "Bulletin Warned Airports in '98," *Boston Globe*, May 26, 2002.

41. U.S. Department of Transportation, "Criminal Acts Against Civil Aviation."

42. Department of Transportation, Federal Aviation Administration, 14 CFR Part 108 [Docket No. FAA-2001-8725; Formerly Docket No. 28978; Amendment No. 108-18], July 17, 2001.

43. Oklahoma FBI Report, May 18, 1998.

44. Oklahoma FBI Report, May 18, 1998.

45. Interview with Mike Elsner.

46. Interview with Mike Elsner.

47. *USA v. Ihab Mohamed Ali*, United States District Court, Southern District of New York, May 1999.

48. GAO, "Long-Standing Problems Impair Airport Screeners' Performance," June 2000.

49. GAO, "Long-Standing Problems."

50. Reuven Paz, *Tangled Web: International Islamist Networking* (Washington, DC: The Washington Institute for Near East Policy, 2002).

51. See chapter 1 of this volume for a sample list of groups whose members are known to have received training in al Qaeda's camps in Afghanistan.

9

✛

Learning to Survive: The Case of the Islamic Resistance Movement (Hamas)

R. Kim Cragin

Author's note: Since this chapter was written, Palestinian President Yasser Arafat has passed away, leaving significant questions as to the direction of al-Fatah and the Israeli-Palestinian peace process. In addition, Hamas won a majority of seats in the January 2006 parliamentary elections. Due to timing, neither of these events were taken into account as part of this chapter.

In his best-selling book *Inside Terrorism*, Bruce Hoffman noted that "The terrorist campaign is like a shark: it must keep moving forward—no matter how slowly or incrementally—or die."[1] This metaphor is apt. It is easy to imagine the predatory terrorist organization, like a shark, constantly searching for new prey. Yet questions still exist as to what exactly it means for terrorist groups to continue to move forward. Some argue that in the never-ending search for media attention, terrorist groups believe that they must conduct increasingly spectacular attacks. Understood in this context, terrorists' learning is active, driven by the organizations' desire to reach out to new and perhaps even distant audiences. Still others suggest that terrorist groups are not inherently innovative organizations and that learning takes place inasmuch as one generation of terrorists passes on knowledge (for example, about improvised explosive devices) to the next. Only a period of escalation and counterescalation with state security forces can cause terrorists to truly innovate.

These suppositions hold significantly different implications for the study of terrorist organizations, and lead to several research questions: How do terrorists derive legitimacy? How does legitimacy (or the pursuit of legitimacy) motivate them? What is the role of media attention in the operational evolution of a terrorist group? Do terrorists plan ahead? Do they learn from the past? Or are they mostly concerned with the immediate problem of avoiding counterterrorism forces? Exploring questions such as these contributes to our understanding of terrorist groups' decision making. Although this chapter does not propose to answer all of these questions, it does examine how one particular terrorist organization methodically, and through twenty years of planning, built up its membership, support, and legitimacy, only to lose it over a period of a few years. The chapter then discusses how this group has struggled to regain its legitimacy in the face of significant counterterrorism activities, and how their efforts demonstrate the attributes of a learning organization.

This case study examines the Palestinian terrorist group, *Harakat al-Muqawama al-Islamiyya*, commonly known by its Arabic acronym, Hamas. Since Hamas first issued its charter in August 1988, it has come under increasing pressure from Israeli security forces.[2] Israeli counterterrorism activities include arrests, deportations, assassinations, and most recently, the building of a security fence between Israel proper and the Occupied Territories. The Israeli government has also targeted Hamas' families as part of its counterterrorism policies. For example, the Israeli military has demolished the homes of Hamas suicide bombers as a deterrent to new or potential volunteers. Similarly, in the mid-1990s, the Israeli government reacted to suicide attacks by closing off Palestinian workers' access to the Israeli economy in an effort to turn public opinion against the terrorists. And yet Hamas has managed to survive Israel's attempts to eradicate it.

Palestinian authorities have also sought to undermine Hamas. For example, after the Oslo Accords in 1993 and the Palestinian national elections, Yasser Arafat attempted to undermine the role of Hamas in the Palestinian national struggle. These efforts included closing down Islamic charities as well as arresting Hamas activists. And yet, ten years later, Arafat was perceived by the Palestinian people as a corrupt and inadequate leader, while Hamas has managed to survive.[3]

As this case study reveals, Hamas' ability to sustain itself as a revolutionary organization is owed in some part to what can be termed "strategic learning," a concept discussed in chapter 3 of this volume. At the highest, most strategic level of organizational learning, terrorists use their own worldview to interpret how international and domestic systems operate as well as how these systems might react to various forms of violence. As terrorists engage in strategic learning, therefore, they adapt their activities in order to prompt or account for these expected reactions. This learning is a form of knowledge transfer that lies beyond the realm of tactical learning (e.g., how to build and deploy explosive devices), yet it is vitally important. While tactical learning might include the interpretation of information with regard to the best use of a particular weapon, strategic learning includes examining the operational environment and gaining an understanding of the impact that an attack against any given target might have on society. Strategic learning also includes decisions that terrorist groups make in managing both internal and external constituencies. As terrorism researchers Horacio Trujillo and Brian Jackson observed:

> strategic learning has led some terrorist groups to complement their violent activities with "legitimate" political wings or even programs to provide educational, health care, and other social services to the communities in which they are based or from which they draw support. In this way, the interpretation stage of the learning process plays a particularly critical role in the development of terrorist groups' strategies and in thus directing the actions that they will ultimately choose to carry out.[4]

Hamas' leaders have made strategic decisions on a full range of challenges, including if and when to engage in terrorist attacks, the stance that Hamas should take on the Oslo Accords and the wider peace process, and how to respond to the assassination of key personnel. In making these decisions, Hamas' leaders had to take into account international reaction and Israeli counterterrorism response, as well as their relationship with Palestinian society. Indeed, Hamas' relationship with the larger Palestinian society is rooted in both its ability to confront Israel and its social and welfare services. While many Palestinians perceive that the Palestinian leadership and international community have failed to provide adequate services—such as infrastructure, education, and medical care—Hamas has been able to fill this void. This relationship between a terrorist group and local communities, therefore, is arguably just as important to our understanding of organization learning as the back-and-forth between terrorist and counterterrorism forces. In the case of Hamas, sometimes leaders interpreted the information on these issues correctly and made the requisite adjustments to help their organizations survive and expand. But other times, Hamas' leaders made mistakes that threatened the survival of their organization. In examining Hamas, therefore, this chapter attempts to further our understanding of how terrorist organizations learn—even from the mistakes they make—and what it takes to survive.

PHASE I: THE BUILDING PROCESS (1973–1988)

Hamas' ideology emerged out of the Muslim Brotherhood movement in the West Bank and Gaza Strip. The Muslim Brotherhood was founded in the late 1920s by Hassan al-Banna in Egypt.[5] Al-Banna was, in fact, a schoolteacher and not a religious intellectual or scholar. During his time at al-Azhar University in Cairo, however, he was influenced by early political Islamists, such as Jamal al-din al-Afghani. Political historian Anthony Black wrote the following of al-Afghani:

> Al-Afghani was the catalyst of modernism, which he imbued with a spirit that would become fundamentalism. In al-Afghani, the currents of modernism were fused into a more wide-ranging internationalist and aggressive political project. While he embraced European philosophy and science, he took a confrontational political stance towards the West. He was the pinnacle of the modernists and the foundation of the fundamentalists—a genius of a kind.[6]

Differences would later emerge between al-Banna and the Islamist intellectuals, especially after World War II. For one, Hassan al-Banna's Muslim Brotherhood was a mass movement, rooted in Egypt's rural poor. Al-Banna attempted, through the Muslim Brotherhood, to change the Muslim community from within, primarily through religious education and mosques. Thus, al-Banna's grassroots approach contradicted the writings of political Islamists, who fundamentally believed that the correct forms of Islam could only be practiced in the context of an Islamic political system.[7]

Hamas, in the early years of its existence, followed the pattern set out by Hassan al-Banna and the Muslim Brotherhood. Hamas has its organizational roots in Gaza's al-Mujamma al-Islami, also known as the Islamic Center, which opened in 1973. Sheikh Yassin used al-Mujamma to draw together the eventual founders of Hamas, including Isa al-Nashshar, Dr. Ibrahim al-Yazuri, Abdulfattah Doukhan, Dr. Abdul Aziz Rantisi, Mohamad Hassan Shama'a, and Salah Shehade. Drawing on the experience of the Muslim Brotherhood in Egypt, these initial founders apparently focused on building an Islamic grassroots movement in the Gaza Strip. To do this, they opened mosques, youth centers, and schools (especially kindergartens) that emphasized Islamic reform in the Gaza Strip and eventually the West Bank. Yassin and his followers gained some ground during this time—approximately 1973 to 1978—and managed to get control of the important Engineers Association and Islamic University in Gaza. It was not enough, however, to sustain a widespread political movement.

Part of the reason for the slowness of the Islamic movement to take hold in the West Bank and Gaza Strip (WBGS) was that Yassin and his followers were not the only Palestinian faction in the WBGS to build their legitimacy on social welfare networks. Following the Israeli occupation of the WBGS in 1967, the social network structure in Palestinian towns and villages began to collapse. Various factions attempted to fill this void, including Arafat's al-Fatah, the Democratic Front for the Liberation of Palestine (DFLP), the Popular Front for the Liberation of Palestine (PFLP), and the Israeli Military and Civil Administrations.[8] By the late 1970s the al-Fatah–controlled Palestine Liberation Organization (PLO) had won the battle over the provision of social services to the Palestinian people. Most of the charitable contributions and aid coming from the Muslim world were filtered through the PLO on its way to the residents of the West Bank and Gaza. Yassin and his followers simply did not have the funds to compete with the PLO in this arena.

Notably, the Israeli Civil and Military Administrations attempted to counter the PLO's growing influence by encouraging an indigenous alternative in the form of municipal elections. The first elections were held on April 12, 1972.[9] But this attempt was generally unsuccessful, as nominees were perceived as collaborating with the Israeli occupying force. Similarly, the Israeli Administrations also tried to foster nonviolent alternatives to the Palestinian nationalists. In this context, Islamic Center leaders registered their organization with the Israeli military authorities that administered the Gaza Strip in 1978.[10] This registration explains a common argument made by some that the Israeli government in effect "sponsored" Hamas in an effort to undermine Arafat and Palestinian nationalism. But this was not true sponsorship, in that the IDF (Israeli Defense Forces) did not provide training, weapons, or strategic direction.

It is clear that Hamas' founders attempted, from its earliest years, to build a foundation of support within the Palestinian community before it launched its militant activities. Indeed, this period of building lasted almost fifteen years, from 1973 to 1987. Questions remain, however, as to when and why Hamas' founders decided to make the transformation into a terrorist organization. The next section of this chapter explores this transformation and how it affected the relationship between Hamas and the Palestinian community.

PHASE II: ADOPTING TERRORIST TACTICS (1988–1999)

In examining the strategic learning of Hamas' leadership, one key question is whether Hamas' leaders planned to engage in terrorist activities from the group's inception in 1973. It is doubtful that we will ever have a complete answer to this question. Published interviews with Hamas members themselves tend to imply that the answer is "yes." Yet it is in the interest of Hamas leaders to make their decision making appear as forward thinking and as strategic as possible, if only to substantiate Hamas' existence to Palestinians. In contrast, the IDF and Israeli Civil Administration allowed the Islamic Center to register as a legitimate charitable organization in 1978. This registration appears to indicate that the Israelis, at least, did not believe that the group would later evolve to become engaged in militant activities.

The most likely answer is that Sheikh Yassin and his followers initially molded their group in the image of the nonmilitant Egyptian Muslim Brotherhood. But by the late 1970s, it became clear to Yassin and his followers that the secular nationalists—primarily Arafat and al-Fatah—had convinced the Palestinian community that they were the legitimate force to counter the Is-raeli occupation. The nationalists gained legitimacy from both their social networks *and* their ability to successfully attack Jewish and Israeli targets. Thus, if Yassin and his followers were going to compete with al-Fatah, they needed to adopt a militant campaign as well.[11] This is an important example of strategic learning, in which an organization examines its operational en-vironment, and changes its behavior in order to survive. Hamas' adoption of a more militant set of strategic objectives led to a series of events that re-sulted in the IDF arresting Sheikh Yassin for weapons trafficking in 1983.[12]

Approximately four years later, on December 8, 1987, a popular uprising broke out in the Palestinian territories. This uprising would come to be known as the *Intifada* or "throwing off." Hamas' eventual leaders were ap-parently as taken aback by the Intifada as other Israeli and Palestinian leaders alike. But a new generation of leadership was emerging in Hamas, which argued for the use of terrorist tactics against the Israelis. These in-dividuals, who wanted to take advantage of the uprising and harness it for their own movement, included Isa al-Nashshar, Abdul Aziz Rantisi, Salah Shehade, Ibrahim Moukadema, Ahmad al-Milh, Ismail Abu Shanab, Moussa Abu Marzouq, Mahmoud Zahhar, Imad Alamy, Amad Nemr, and Sayyed Abu Musameh. On December 9, 1988, leaders of the Islamic Cen-ter gathered in Gaza to determine the role they would take in the In-tifada.[13] They decided to take a role in directing the protests; Hamas issued its first leaflet under that name in January 1989.

In the early years of the Intifada, Hamas issued approximately thirty dif-ferent leaflets.[14] These leaflets coordinated demonstrations, boycotts, and other political protest activities. But Hamas did not conduct or sponsor any terrorist attacks at this time. Indeed, Hamas did not declare jihad against Is-rael until October 1990. Hamas leaders apparently made the decision to ini-tiate terrorist attacks in response to the killing of seventeen Palestinians at Haram al-Sharif in Jerusalem by Israeli soldiers.[15] Two months later, Hamas members conducted their first terrorist attack against Israel, stabbing three Israelis to death on December 14, 1990—three years after the beginning of the Intifada. In an interview, Hamas' current political leader, Khaled Mishaal, identified this stabbing as a "huge operation."[16] In retrospect, these attacks seem almost harmless when compared to the scores of casual-ties that Hamas has inflicted on Israelis in recent years. Yet, they repre-sented an important shift by the group, away from social activities and stone throwing, and toward true terrorism. This evolution appears to have been driven by a combination of factors in the political environment as well as the organization's desire to sustain itself.

Another critical decision made by Hamas during the early years of the Intifada was to voice criticism of Saddam Hussein. After Hussein invaded

Kuwait, Arafat's rhetoric implied support for Saddam Hussein.[17] In an apparent effort to differentiate itself from al-Fatah and the nationalists, Hamas' leaders criticized Iraq's invasion of Kuwait. Hamas benefited from this decision, as many Gulf States diverted aid funds from the PLO to Hamas.[18] Hamas was able to use these funds to expand its infrastructure and charitable networks.

During this time period, Hamas leaders also established a militant wing: al-Qassam, led by Sheikh Salah Shehade. Although al-Qassam remained relatively small, with never much more than 100 members, it has been responsible for most of Hamas' terrorist activity. Prime Minister Rabin reacted with force to Hamas' entrance into the world of terrorism. In December 1992, after Hamas members kidnapped an IDF soldier, Rabin had approximately 415 Hamas members arrested and deported from the Occupied Territories into southern Lebanon.[19] It was not unusual for the Israeli government to deport Palestinian terrorists or activists at that time. The general thought was that the deportees would disperse into the Western world and return—normally after seven years—more moderate in their outlook. Thus, the 1992 deportation was likely an effort, on the part of Rabin, to stamp out a violent sect of Hamas before it gained momentum. But Hamas' members refused to disperse. Instead, they remained at Marj al-Zahour, Lebanon, for approximately twelve months, accumulating sympathy from the international community and Palestinians alike.

The 1992 deportations would prove to be a key turning point for Hamas. Until 1992, it appears that Sheikh Yassin and a select few confidants did most of the planning and strategic decision making for Hamas. Yet, at the time of the deportations, Yassin was once again in jail, while approximately 400 of Hamas' top activists were gathered in an isolated location with literally nothing to do other than consider Hamas' future direction. In addition, the 1992 deportation brought Hamas' leaders into Hizballah territory. Hizballah's leaders have historically articulated support for the Palestinian cause.[20] But since 1992, evidence suggests that Hizballah has provided at the very least tactical and logistical support to the Palestinian terrorist organizations. For example, Hamas members have trained in Hizballah camps in southern Lebanon.[21] Newspapers also reported the interception of a weapons transfer from Hizballah to a Palestinian terrorist organization in 2001.[22] Finally, evidence exists of knowledge transfer between these groups, in particular with regard to improvised weapons, such as homemade claymore devices. Some experts argue that the relationship between the two groups that formed during the 1992 deportation period pushed Hamas toward a more violent terrorist campaign. The degree of Hizballah's influence or impact on Hamas during the deportations is unclear. But it is clear that Hamas' leaders in Marj al-Zahour took the opportunity presented by the deportation to solidify the group's move toward terrorism.

Hamas members conducted their first suicide attack in March 1993. Hamas leaders state that the decision to adopt the tactic of suicide bombings was made in response to Baruch Goldstein's shooting of Palestinian Muslims praying at a mosque in Hebron in February 1993.[23] Hamas' leaders argued at the time that they would only use suicide bombings in retaliation for the assassination of its members or for extreme violence perpetrated against Palestinians by the Israelis. These statements indicate that the decision to adopt the tactic of suicide bombings was made at the highest level of Hamas' leadership. Hamas' leaders apparently determined that anger within the Palestinian community had reached a level, as a result of the Goldstein attack, that they would accept suicide attacks against Israeli civilians. The statements justifying Hamas' use of suicide bombings in retaliation for the assassination of its members similarly illustrate an interpretative step in Hamas' decision-making process: gratuitous use of suicide bombers would not be acceptable to Palestinians, but their limited use for revenge was tolerable. Figure 9.1 displays the distribution of suicide bombings perpetrated by Palestinian terrorist groups from when Hamas began to employ the tactic until the June 2003 *hudna*, or ceasefire. It is clear that after its first suicide attack, Hamas used this tactic on a consistent basis to maintain pressure on the Israeli government and populace until 1997. From 1997 to 1999, however, a review of the historical data reveals a significant dip in Hamas' use of the tactic. An important question for Hamas' strategic learning, then, is: what accounts for this dip?

Part of the explanation for Hamas' use and then suspension of suicide bombings comes from the relationship between Hamas and the wider Palestinian community. Significantly, the period between 1993 and 1998,

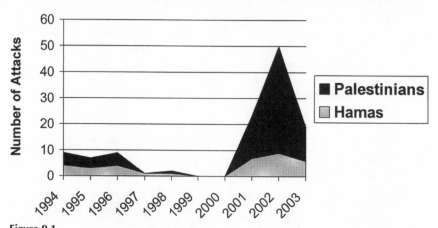

Figure 9.1.

Note: Data from the RAND Terrorism Chronology and RAND-MIPT Incident Database, available online at www.tkb.org.

when Hamas expanded its terrorist campaign against Israel, also marked the height of the peace process. The peace process placed Hamas in a difficult position. Although its leaders had now—since the beginning of the Intifada—joined the nationalists' fight for an independent Palestine, Hamas' true identity was that of an Islamist alternative to the nationalists, not a partner. But the nationalists retained the support of a majority of the Palestinian people. This support only increased as the Palestinian Authority (PA) received control over Palestinian cities—including Gaza, Jericho, and Ramallah—and Yasser Arafat was elected President. Hamas' leaders believed that they should not challenge al-Fatah directly, because they did not want to be seen as inciting civil war just as the Palestinians were beginning to win independence. This belief limited Hamas' ability to project itself as a legitimate alternative to the PLO. For example, on November 18, 1994, Hamas members clashed with Palestinian policemen outside a mosque in Gaza. The result was a series of riots throughout Gaza in support of Hamas, including an attempt by the rioters to tear down the newly built Palestinian Authority prison. Instead of encouraging these riots, Hamas leaders took steps to calm the rioters in an effort to avoid being seen as causing strife within the Palestinian community.[24]

This balance between challenging the PLO and not undermining the wider nationalist movement was difficult for Hamas' leaders to maintain. The difficulty is further highlighted in the debate that occurred in the Hamas leadership on whether or not Hamas would participate in the national parliamentary elections. Several known Hamas members declared their intentions to run as independents in the 1995 elections, including Imad al-Falouji, Ismail Haniye, Khaled el-Hindi, Said Namrouti, and Nasser Muzaini. But the Hamas leadership did not want to legitimize the secular Palestinian Authority through its own participation in the national elections. Instead, Hamas chose only to participate in local elections, including those for municipal governments, university student governments, and professional associations. Having made this decision, Hamas put pressure on its members to withdraw from the parliamentary elections. Three of these individuals withdrew (Haniye, el-Hindi, and Namrouti); al-Falouji was expelled.[25] But twelve others would go on to form the Khalas party that same year: it was an Islamic political party, comprised of former Hamas members, which advocated a political solution to the conflict with Israel.

Despite the efforts of Hamas' leaders to avoid civil war, their decision to continue support for terrorism (regardless of the ongoing peace process) caused a rift with the Palestinian community. This rift most likely accounts for the dip in Hamas' use of suicide bombings in 1998 and 1999. For example, in January 1996 Israel assassinated Yahyah Ayyash, the key bomb maker for Hamas. Hamas' leaders responded by launching three suicide bombings against Israeli civilians: one in Tel Aviv and two in Jerusalem. Polls taken at the time demonstrate that Hamas' leaders miscalculated the Palestinian people's response to these attacks. For example, the Center for Palestine Research and Studies found that approximately 70 percent of Palestinians polled opposed suicide bombings and 59 percent called for President Arafat to take action to prevent future attacks.[26]

Through a failure in strategic learning—specifically, failing to recognize and adapt to important changes in the operational environment—Hamas reached a crisis of legitimacy in the late 1990s. This crisis was a direct result of Hamas' leaders miscalculation of the Palestinian community and their support—or lack thereof—for the use of suicide bombings against Israeli targets. This mistake was critical for a number of reasons: it threatened the pool of potential recruits for Hamas, it undermined passive support for the group, and perhaps most importantly, it provided Arafat with enough public support so that he could systematically arrest key Hamas leaders in the WBGS. The momentum that Yassin and other early founders had been building for a period of twenty-five years threatened to dissolve altogether. Hamas now faced a struggle not to gain support as an alternative to Arafat's al-Fatah, but to simply survive.

PHASE III: LEARNING TO SURVIVE (1999–2004)

The period between 1999 and 2004 marks the most volatile period for Hamas. The group faced internal pressure from within the Palestinian community as well as extensive counterterrorism pressure from the Israeli security services. The combination of internal and external pressure forced Hamas to adjust its leadership structure. To do this, Hamas' leadership first had to shore up its dissolving local support. Hamas' efforts to do so can be seen through its internal propaganda campaign. For example, in response to criticism by Palestinians on Hamas' use of suicide bombings, Salah Shehade—the commander of al-Qassam—issued a communiqué that justified Hamas' use of this tactic. Shehade argued that Hamas did not manipulate its young followers to become martyrs, but instead applied strict requirements. New recruits had to be devout Muslims, with regular attendance at the local mosque. They also had to have a university education and not be the sole (male) provider of household income.[27] What is interesting about this communiqué is not so much the rules themselves, as the fact that Hamas' leaders felt the need to articulate their rules to the Palestinian population. It demonstrates a new awareness on the part of Hamas' leaders that they had misinterpreted or at least underestimated the response of the Palestinian community to Hamas' suicide bombings.

Hamas' campaign to regain support benefited from an increasing dissatisfaction among Palestinians with the peace process. From 1993 to 2000, most of the international aid to the WBGS was filtered through the Palestinian Authority. But President Arafat was gaining a reputation for cronyism and corruption in the Occupied Territories. At the same time, Hamas continued to benefit financially from its rhetorical support for Kuwait during the first Gulf War. In contrast to Arafat and al-Fatah, Hamas distributed approximately 95 percent of its funds throughout the Palestinian population to those in greatest need.[28] Thus, the group gained a reputation for fairness in contrast to the corruption of the Palestinian Authority. The group's leaders were able to argue that they were a legitimate alternative to Arafat and the PA in the area of social services. In addition, Palestinians were disillusioned with the peace process itself. This disillusionment eventually yielded the second "al-Aqsa" Intifada in September 2000.

The al-Aqsa Intifada was a boon for Hamas in the terms of public support. It gave Hamas one more opportunity to demonstrate to the Palestinians that it could both confront Israel and provide services better than the nationalists. Yet at the same time, the al-Aqsa Intifada prompted the Israeli security apparatus to step up its counterterrorism activities. In particular, the Israeli security services began to focus increasing amounts of energy on removing Hamas' decision-making structure. The evolution of Hamas in response to these opportunities and challenges offers important insights into a terrorist organization's capacity for strategic learning.

Despite frequent arrests, deportations, and assassinations, Hamas had managed to retain its leadership structure throughout most of the period of this study. Up until the al-Aqsa Intifada, Hamas' leaders had made a few changes, mostly to account for geography and/or their expanding base. For example, in January 1988, once the Islamic Center's leaders decided to publicly launch Hamas, Sheikh Yassin placed Jamil Hamami in charge of the West Bank branch of Hamas.[29] Yassin apparently did this in an effort to alleviate command, communication, and logistical difficulties between the two separate Palestinian territories. Similarly, after the 1992 deportation, Hamas divided leadership responsibilities between individuals inside and outside the Palestinian territories. A permanent political branch remained outside of the WBGS for continuity purposes. Finally, Hamas also adjusted its command structure during the al-Aqsa Intifada. Prior to the Intifada, most tactical decisions were left in the hands of operational cell leaders, while strategic direction was provided by Sheikh Yassin and his deputy, as well as the heads of Hamas' West Bank and Gaza Strip branches. The Israeli security apparatus, however, excelled at finding these midlevel operational leaders and preempting attacks. Hamas, therefore, began to designate multiple cells for the same attack in the spring of 2001, so that if the Israeli security services eliminated one cell, another could step in to take its place without instructions from regional leaders.[30] These steps indicate another type of learning on the part of Hamas, as it attempted to maintain its capabilities in the face of significant Israeli countermeasures.

Hamas' ability to adapt strategically to changes in its operating environment reflects some attributes of organizational learning. However, unlike other terrorist groups examined in this volume, the hierarchical nature of Hamas has persisted. Although Hamas' leaders made some structural adjustments, the actual strategic decision making remained in the hands of a few key founders. Sheikh Yasin retained the spiritual (and indeed functional) leadership of Hamas, with Ismail Abu Shanab as his deputy. Khaled Mishaal was the political head of Hamas in exile. Abdul Aziz Rantisi remained head of Hamas' strong Gaza faction, and Salah Shehade was the leader of al-Qassam, also based in Gaza.[31] Indeed, between 1994 and the second Intifada, the Israeli security services focused on arresting or killing field-level operatives rather than Hamas' leadership, with a few exceptions.[32] Beginning with the al-Aqsa Intifada, however, Israeli security forces began a determined campaign aimed not only at Hamas' upper echelon, but also at emerging leaders in different Palestinian communities. Table 9.1 provides a partial list of Hamas members assassinated by security officials between 1973 and 2003.[33]

A cursory review of this list reveals that since September 2000, the Israeli military has managed to eliminate the individuals who have retained strategic leadership over Hamas throughout its existence. As a result, central figures such as Ismail Abu Shanab and Abdul Aziz Rantisi—who had learned and evolved throughout the lifetime of the organization—are no longer available to direct Hamas. What is less obvious from this list is that the Israelis also targeted young emerging leaders—such as Muhamed Taher or Raed Abu Ziad—who might have replaced the older generation of terrorists. In fact, as some observers would argue, this is precisely what Israel needed to do when combating a learning, adapting terrorist organization. Although it is too early to tell the medium- or long-term impact that the assassination of its established and emerging leaders will have on Hamas, the number of terrorist attacks inside Israel has decreased since April 2004. Many in Israel attribute this decrease to the security fence that Israel has begun to build, plus its aggressive targeting policy.

The last time that Hamas faced a decisive threat against its leadership was in 1992, during the deportation of approximately four hundred individuals into southern Lebanon. At that time, Hizballah stepped in to provide assistance—and many say guidance—to the Palestinian terrorist or-

Table 9.1. Targeted Assassinations by Israeli Security Forces

Date Assassinated	Name	Affiliation
March 1986	Saeb Zahab	Muslim Brotherhood
March 1986	Jawad Abu Sulmiyeh	Muslim Brotherhood
January 1996	Yahyah Ayyash	Al-Qassam
*September 1997	*Khaled Mishaal	Hamas
November 2000	Ibrahim Bani Odeh	Hamas
December 2000	Abbas Uthman al-Uyowi	Hamas
January 2001	Mahmoud Madani	Al-Qassam
September 2001	Saleh Darwaza	Hamas
September 2001	Jamal Mansour	Hamas
October 2001	Abed Rahman Hamad	Al-Qassam
October 2001	Ahmed Marshoud	Hamas
October 2001	Ayman Halawe	Al-Qassam
November 2001	Mahmoud Abu Hanoud	Al-Qassam
November 2001	Ayman Hashaika	Al-Qassam
January 2002	Bakr Hamdan	Hamas
June 2002	Yasser Rizik	Hamas
June 2002	Suheil Abu Nahal	Hamas
July 2002	Muhamed Taher	Al-Qassam
July 2002	Salah Shedhadeh	Al-Qassam
August 2002	Nassr Jarar	Al-Qassam
February 2003	Raed Abu Ziad	Al-Qassam
March 2003	Ibrahim Makadmeh	Hamas
*June 2003	*Abdul Aziz Rantisi	*Hamas
June 2003	Mahmoud Issa	Hamas
August 2003	Ismail Abu Shanab	Hamas
March 2004	Hassan Zahut	Al-Qassam
March 2004	Sheikh Yasin	Hamas
April 2004	Abdul Aziz Rantisi	Hamas
April 2004	Khaled Kharyush	Al-Qassam

*Denotes botched assassination attempt.

ganization. It is possible that the same could occur as Hamas attempts to recover from the loss of its key leaders. For example, in March 2004 Hamas members slipped out of the Gaza Strip and attacked a key Israeli port in Ashdod.[34] This attack was significant because it was one of the few times that Hamas has hit a strategic target inside Israel, rather than civilians. Some believe that the choice of target was Hizballah's, and that the group urged Hamas' leaders to shift its focus away from civilians and toward economic and political targets. If this supposition holds true, Hamas' existing leaders could learn more from Hizballah's past experience and success against the Israeli government, and from this learning evolve once again into a major threat to Israel.

CONCLUSION

In sum, Hamas' leaders faced a number of strategic decisions over a thirty-year period. Initially, the Islamic Center leaders chose to develop their support networks through a system of schools and charitable organizations. They also chose to join the Intifada, criticize Saddam Hussein's invasion of Kuwait during the Gulf War, and sponsor terrorist attacks against Israeli civilians. Each of these decisions helped to ensure Hamas' survival as a terrorist organization. But it does not mean that Hamas' leaders did not make strategic mistakes. It is arguable that the Islamic Center's leaders sacrificed some popular support in their slow move toward the adoption of terrorist tactics and the establishment of what we now know as Hamas. Additionally, the decision to continue with suicide bombings, despite a lack of support within the Palestinian community in the mid-1990s, proved almost fatal to the group. Each of these examples demonstrates that terrorists' success depends, in part, on their ability to learn how to assess local support and adjust accordingly. As described previously in this volume, environmental monitoring and adaptation are key attributes of a learning organization.

Terrorism experts often look at learning in the context of technology or tactics. It is relatively simple to trace changes in tactics, where terrorists might have once failed but adapt in a later generation. It is also easy to identify the introduction of a new technology, such as rocket-fired grenades or remote-detonated devices. And, indeed, terrorists themselves invest in training camps or media that assist them in passing on this knowledge to new members. But, importantly, learning also incorporates the ability of terrorists to adjust at a more strategic level. This includes their choice in targets as well as the methods of attacking these targets. A learning organization must also constantly assess the operating environment and adapt to changes within it. As seen in the case of Hamas, this includes interpreting and managing the organization's relationship with sympathetic communities. While the experience of Hamas suggests that strategic learning is difficult for terrorists to pass on to a new generation of leaders, the degree of learning that takes place is critical to the overall success of a terrorist organization's goals.

NOTES

1. Bruce Hoffman, *Inside Terrorism* (New York: Columbia University Press, 1998), 162.

2. Hamas, "The Charter of Allah: The Platform of the Islamic Resistance Movement Hamas," in *The 1988–1989 Annual on Terrorism,* ed. Y. Alexander and H. Foxman (Netherlands: Kluwer Academic Publishers, 1990).

3. Yasser Arafat passed away in November 2004. He was seventy-five years old.

4. See chapter 3 of this volume, "Organizational Learning and Terrorist Groups," by Horacio R. Trujillo and Brian A. Jackson.

5. Robert Mitchell, *The Society of Muslim Brothers* (London: Oxford University Press, 1969), 16.

6. Anthony Black, *The History of Islamic Political Thought* (New York: Routledge, 2001), 304

7. Ibrahim M. Abu-Rabi, "Intellectual Origins of Islamic Resurgence in the Modern Arab World," in *SUNY Studies in Near Eastern Studies*, ed. Said Amir Arjomand (Albany: State University of New York Press, 1996), 128.

8. Khalil Nakhleh, *Indigenous Organizations in Palestine: Towards a Purposeful Societal Development* (Jerusalem: Arab Thought Forum, 2004), 36–41.

9. Jerusalem Media and Communications Center (JMCC), *Israeli Military Orders in the Occupied Palestinian West Bank: 1967–1992*, 2nd ed. (Jerusalem: JMCC, 1995), 76.

10. Ghassan Charbel, "The Khaled Interview (7 Parts)," *Dar al hayat*, December 5, 2003, interview 2 of 7.

11. This pragmatic shift paralleled a ideological change in the Islamist movement away from the moderate thinking personified by al-Banna towards the more revolutionary writings of Sayyid Qutb, who advocated confrontation with secular governments.

12. Charbel, "The Khaled Interview," interview 2 of 7.

13. Ziad Abu Amr, "Hamas: A Historical and Political Background," *Journal of Palestine Studies* 23, no. 4 (1993), 10.

14. Lisa Taraki, "The Islamic Resistance Movement in the Palestinian Uprising," *Middle East Report*, 1989, 30.

15. International Crisis Group (ICG), *Dealing with Hamas* (Brussels: ICG, 2003), 2.

16. Charbel, "The Khaled Interview," interview 1 of 7.

17. In fact, Arafat attempted to play mediator, but he also commented that the Iraqis and Palestinians were in the "same trench." For example, see "1990: Gulf War Brings Dilemma for Arafat," *The Daily Telegraph (UK) Guide to the History of the Mideast Conflict*, www .telegraph.co.uk [accessed October 18, 2004].

18. Yohanan Ramati, "Islamic Fundamentalism Gaining," *Midstream* 39, no. 2 (1993): 2.

19. Ali Jarbawi and Roger Heacock, "The Deportations and the Palestinian-Israeli Negotiations," *Journal of Palestine Studies* 26, no. 3 (1993): 32.

20. See, for example, quotations from Sheikh Nasrallah, Secretary-General of Hizballah, reprinted in "Lo, the Party of God Still Vows Victory," *Time* 142, no. 6 (9 August 1993): 33.

21. Shaul Mishal and Avraham Sela, *The Palestinian Hamas* (New York: Columbia University Press, 2000), 64.

22. Johanna McGeary, "Hamas: Popular, Extreme, and an Alternative to Arafat," *Time* 158, no. 26 (17 December 2001): 52.

23. Roger Gaess, "Interviews from Gaza: What Hamas Wants," *Middle East Policy* 9, no. 4 (2002): 107.

24. Khaled Hroub, *Hamas: Political Thought and Practice* (Washington, DC: Institute for Palestine Studies, 2000), 56.

25. Al-Falouji ran Hamas' newspaper al-Watan. The information on Hamas members who wanted to participate in the Palestinian national elections was taken from a Palestinian periodical, *Al-Raseed* 3, no. 48, 8 January 1995.

26. Center for Palestine Research and Studies (CPRS). 1996. Public Opinion Poll #22. Online at www.pcpsr.org/survey/cprspolls/96/poll22c.html#suparmed [accessed March 3 2002].

27. This communiqué was posted on the Hamas website, titled "Zionists Are Our Enemies, Jihad Is Our Way to Freedom," www.palestine-info.net.

28. Serge Schmenmann, "Cradle to Grave: Terror Isn't Alone as a Threat to Mideast Peace," *New York Times*, 3 March 1996, D1, 4.

29. Abu Amr, "Hamas: A Historical and Political Background," 10.

30. McGeary, "Hamas: Popular, Extreme, and an Alternative to Arafat," 52.

31. Charbel, "The Khaled Interview," interview 3 of 7; and Paul Hilder, "The Nail in the Wood: An Interview with Ismail Abu Shanab," Open Democracy Ltd., 9 April 2003, www.opendemocracy.net [accessed 9 March 2004].

32. Arieh O'Sullivan, "Hamas Activists Arrested," *Jerusalem Post*, 23 April 1997, 1.

33. This is a representative (not a complete) list, compiled from various open sources.

34. Ze'ev Schiff, "Hizballah Had a Role in Ashdod Bombing," *Ha'aretz*, 28 March 2004.

10

+

Renew to Last: Innovation and Strategy of the Revolutionary Armed Forces of Colombia (FARC)

Román D. Ortiz

Traditionally, the Revolutionary Armed Forces of Colombia (FARC) has been considered to be an exceptionally long-lived insurgent organization, typically defined as the "oldest guerilla movement in Latin America." In support of this distinction, it is said that the group has remained active for at least forty years, if its creation is established from the time it assumed its current name in 1966; it is older still if one links its creation to the armed activities of liberal and communist guerillas during the time of "La Violencia" (1947–1954).

However, the truth is that this perception of longevity does not correspond to reality. In fact, when compared to other armed groups within the region and beyond, the historical trajectory of Colombian insurgents does not particularly stand out as unique. For example, the Shining Path was formally created in 1968, launched its current armed campaign in 1980, and remains active today in certain regions of Peru. Other Latin American armed groups have not had such long periods of existence, but certainly their evolution is measured in decades and not in years. The National Liberation Sandinista Front (FSLN) was founded in 1961, and prolonged its insurrection campaign in Nicaragua for nearly two decades before assuming power in 1979. A similar trajectory is seen among groups in El Salvador, integrated under the National Liberation Farabundo Martí Front (FMLN), which became involved in armed activities during the early 1970s and surrendered its weapons after signing a peace agreement with the government of this Central American republic in 1992.

Outside Latin America, there are even more significant examples of long-lasting armed movements. In Europe, the Basque separatist group

Euskadi Ta Askatasuna ("Basque Homeland and Liberty" or ETA) began its terrorist campaign against the Spanish government in 1968 and is still active. Similarly, the Provisional Irish Republican Army (PIRA) was officially born in 1969 and ended its armed activities after the Good Friday agreements in 1998. Nonetheless, its origins may be seen much earlier if we take into account the first opportunity upon which the nationalist movement of this island used the name Irish Republican Army (IRA), which occurred with the Easter Uprising in 1916. In Africa, a noteworthy case is the guerilla movement National Unity for Total Independence of Angola (UNITA), created in 1966 as a movement against Portuguese colonialism, and which later started to combat the independent government of Luanda until the signing of a demobilization agreement in 2002. Certain groups linked to Palestinian nationalism have shown similar longevity, as seen in the case of the Palestine Liberation Popular Front (FPLP), active since 1967. And the same may be said of contemporary armed organizations in the Far East, such as the New People's Army (NPA) in the Philippines, formally founded in 1969. In truth, the NPA's roots may be traced to the Anti–Japanese Army guerillas (Hukbalahap or Huk) organized by the Communist Party in the Philippines in 1942 to fight against Japanese occupation of the archipelago. Overall, a review of the world's insurgent groups reveals that FARC is not all that exceptional from a historical perspective.

However, it must be noted that the historic evolution of FARC has not followed the conventional pattern expected from revolutionary organizations of this nature. In principle, the active life of an armed group can typically be divided into three basic stages. During the first period (of a purely formative nature), the founding core of the movement tries to find a strategic and political niche in order to ensure its survival and growth over the long term. This is a particularly critical phase, given that vast majorities of violent organizations are unable to survive through this phase and thus disappear due to the impossibility of finding resources to support their war, along with increased pressure from the State or a lack of internal cohesion within the leadership. A second period corresponds to the development or accumulation of political and military resources, until movements arrive at the culminating point that leads either to an insurgent victory over the State or to a government reaction (and thus limiting the expansion of the organization). Certainly, this growth stage is not necessarily linear, and may alternate with moments of crisis, stages of stagnation, and periods of accelerated growth. Lastly, for those organizations that are unable to impose themselves upon the State they combat, a third stage emerges—one of decay or decline, in which these movements may be militarily annihilated, a peace agreement for demobilization may be negotiated, or the group may simply languish indefinitely after being marginalized from the center of the strategic environment. From this perspective of expected patterns, it can be said that the historic behavior of the Colombian guerrilla has certain peculiarities when compared to the majority of insurgent organizations.

In this sense, it must be emphasized that FARC has enjoyed an extremely prolonged period of expansion, with results that to a certain degree are paradoxical. On one hand, the organization has grown in a sustained manner, to the point of becoming a strong political and military actor with a presence in almost the entirety of Colombia's territory.[1] However, at the same time this prolonged period of expansion has not led the armed movement to the culminating point of an insurrection process conducive to taking power or forcing a reaction from the State to eliminate the armed group as a main strategic actor. In this sense, the evolution of FARC must be analyzed as the result of the combination of a group of factors that allowed the consolidation of a powerful armed organization; yet, at the same time, such factors obstructed any possibilities of taking power—a contradiction that, rightly so, has been defined as the sustainability of an insurrection process without the perspective of revolutionary success.[2] Undoubtedly, a series of strategic environment characteristics then played an essential role in determining this peculiar evolution. The industrialization and liberalization of the Colombian economy reduced the productive and demographic importance of rural areas, thereby decreasing the strategic importance of an armed group of an essentially rural nature. At the same time, the urbanization process of the Colombian population reduced the extension of the social base accessible to insurgents, and generalized a political and social culture among the people that was radically separated from the socialist and agrarian ideology of FARC. Finally, the gradual modernization of the State offered the Andean government increasingly stronger tools to preserve public order and manage social conflicts. In this manner, the perspective of a rural revolution in Colombia began to appear increasingly distant until it became only an illusory possibility.

Yet, at the same time, another series of factors combined to allow FARC, instead of vanishing, to consolidate itself as a key strategic actor capable of establishing a solid predominant presence over substantial segments of Colombian territory, and put the survival of democracy in this Andean republic at risk. In this sense, the rugged geography and the vast dimensions of the Colombian territory offered insurgents favorable spaces to build their military and financial infrastructure, safe from the pressure from state security forces. At the same time, a lack of continuity in national security policies in Bogotá facilitated the expansion of FARC.[3] In fact, the organization took advantage of several periods of negotiation with the government—such as that promoted by the administration of Belisario Betancur in the mid-1980s—to accumulate resources that later allowed the organization to better resist periods of intense military pressure against insurgents, such as that which occurred during the Gaviria administration at the beginning of the 1990s. Likewise, FARC benefited from the existence of a security environment that forced the State to disperse its resources to confront a long list of national security threats ranging from other guerrilla groups—for example, the Foquist National Liberation Army (ELN) and the Maoist People's Liberation Army (EPL)—to drug cartels and the emerging paramilitary groups. In the midst of such a complex environment, Colombian authorities initially gave FARC only marginal attention, while concentrating on confronting other threats at the time perceived as more urgent. This strategic conduct by the State provided the organization—headed by Pedro Antonio Marín, also known as "Manuel Marulanda," or "Tirofijo"—with the opportunity to grow without facing strong government opposition. Lastly, the decision by the guerrilla movement to become involved in drug trafficking played a key role in its expansion process, not only due to the enormous volume of resources placed in the hands of the organization, but because it allowed the armed group to gain influence over peasant sectors dedicated to the production of narcotics and to come into contact with international networks involved in illegal drug trade, weapons contraband, and money laundering.

Overall, the advantages taken by FARC from the opportunities created by the lack of continuity in Colombian security policies and by its involvement in the illegal economy of drug trafficking were only possible thanks to the organization's capacity to adapt to the changes in the strategic environment and to introduce changes in its repertoire of political and military actions. That is, FARC's survival and expansion have been possible thanks to its notable capacity for learning. From a certain standpoint, it might seem strange that an organization created in the mid-1960s in the form of a small rural insurgent group could develop sufficient learning capacity to survive and grow in such a different environment as the globalized world of the 1990s. To explain this evolution, it is necessary to examine a series of characteristics of the organization that combined with the evolution of the Colombian and international strategic environment to allow the growth of the group's innovative potential.

FARC IDEOLOGY AND LEARNING CAPACITY

To begin with, it is necessary to consider the mixed nature of FARC ideology as an element that opened this organization to new ideas. Actually, despite the fact that the organization formally declared itself as Marxist-Leninist and maintained ties to the Colombian Communist Party (PCC), it cannot be said that its political message and strategic behavior are an exclusive result of the group's pro-Soviet socialist ideology.[4] In truth, the social origin and ideological profile of the group's founders established, from the beginning, an important distance with respect to communist orthodoxy. In contrast with the majority of Latin America guerrilla movements, whose leaders came from urban middle-class sectors, the founding nucleus of FARC was comprised of individuals of peasant origin, with little political education and more commitment to agrarian-oriented claims than to a struggle for a socialist society. Additionally, this sector had a very heterogeneous ideological composition. With origins in a series of insurgent cores—organized during the period of "La Violencia" (1946–1953)—which became known as Independent Republics, initial FARC militancy included communist sectors; however, it also included splinter groups from the liberal party.[5] These two politically different groups were forced together in order to confront the waves of sectarian violence promoted by the most radical sectors of the Colombian Conservative Party during the 1940s and 1950s. Thus, from its creation, FARC's ideological foundations involved a mixture of Marxist ideology and a powerful agrarian orientation, as well as a strong nationalist and anti-imperialist sentiment—an ideological combination that drove the organization to define its political views as "Bolivarian" in the 1990s. The absence of a narrowly defined ideological structure allowed the group to explore different political, financial, and military options. In other words, the dynamic nature of their ideology made it easier for the insurgents to be open to innovative solutions and to take advantage of opportunities emerging in the strategic environment. In fact, ideological flexibility as a favorable factor for operational innovation is made more visible when FARC's strategic trajectory is compared with other groups that followed a more rigid ideological path. Thus, while FARC assessed its involvement in drug trafficking from a pragmatic standpoint and decided to enter into the business during the early 1980s, ELN—with a less flexible Marxist ideology—rejected this possibility because of the criminal nature of the drug trade. Undoubtedly, this different attitude with respect to drug trafficking had a determining impact on the evolution of both groups, with the organization headed by Marulanda prospering and expanding while the "elenos" (ELN members) were condemned to a slow process of financial and military decay.

Certainly, this does not mean that the political and military behavior of FARC has not followed certain basic ideological guidelines that, without doubt, have set limits to its strategic repertoire, establishing which courses of action are acceptable and which are not. In fact, throughout its history, the organization has orchestrated its insurrection campaign following the principles of the Vietnamese version of the Maoist People's War (also known as War of Interlocking, or "Dau Trang" in its original language). On the basis of this idea, FARC combined different military tactics—guerrilla warfare or mobile warfare as allowed by the conditions of the operative environment—together with political and peasant mobilization aimed at the destruction of the State and the taking of power. Certainly, selecting this type of insurrection strategy—to a great extent, the result of the peasant origin of the group's founding nucleus and of the pro–Soviet communism influence at its center—established certain basic guidelines for the guerrilla organization's strategic behavior. However, FARC adopted the principles of People's War in a sufficiently flexible manner to allow for the adoption of certain innovations inspired by other insurrection conflicts. This was seen, for example, in their consistent demand to establish demilitarized zones as a condition prior to any negotiation with Colombian authorities. The rationale for this approach, which has actually been considered by the organization since the 1990s, became stronger after observing the experiences of the National Liberation Zapatista Army (EZLN), which was granted territory by the Mexican government as a condition to advance negotiations to resolve the Chiapas rebellion. As a result, FARC sought (and obtained) the creation of the so-called Demilitarized Zone as a condition for talks with the Pastrana administration (between 1998 and 2002). This area of forty-two thousand square kilometers provided a political infrastructure and military base for the Colombian armed group.

Additionally, FARC's innovation capacity throughout the decades has been stimulated by a lengthy tradition of self-sufficiency in military and financial terms. Indeed, throughout history Colombian insurgents have been extremely cautious in not developing relationships of dependence that might affect their strategic autonomy. Undoubtedly, the roots of such orientation must be found in the remote environment where the organization was created and in the peasant origins of its founding members. In fact, the insurgent enclaves of FARC origins were located in particularly remote areas of the central ridge of the Andean mountains. Rural communities had settled in these areas, isolated from the country's urban centers and developing a long history of insurrection linked directly to the Thousand Day War (1899–1902) between Colombian liberals and conservatives. Founders of FARC thus brought with them a lengthy tradition of economic and military self-sufficiency. From a productive standpoint, the region had traditionally maintained a subsistence agriculture economy with scarce integration into the national market. Regarding the military aspects, the armed groups that operated in this area during the Thousand Day War were part of the guerrilla movement created by the Liberal Party after the defeat of its regular forces in the battle of Palonegro. However, they enjoyed considerable autonomy regarding the direction of their operations and logistics. In this sense, the founding circle of FARC received a strategic inheritance marked by a strong inclination toward financial and military autonomy, a legacy that the new insurgent group inevitably incorporated into its organizational culture.

This emphasis on financial and military autonomy drove the organization to explore new ways to reduce its dependence on foreign sources and maintain the capacity to generate its own financial and technological resources. Inevitably, this strategic direction implied a sustainable innovative effort within the leadership of FARC. Thus, in the financial field, the growing involvement of the guerrilla movement in drug trafficking was the result of the pursuit of financial self-sufficiency that necessitated a robust learning process. Initially, toward the beginning of the 1980s, insurgents became involved in drug trafficking by providing military protection to drug traffickers in exchange for a percentage of the value of the drugs produced or transported.

However, this type of association provided relatively limited economic benefits; moreover, the organization had to depend on the management of this illegal trade by drug cartels. Consequently, in the late 1990s, FARC decided to independently produce its own narcotics and develop its own networks to market them. This decision forced the organization to learn how to be effective in activities such as cocaine production, trafficking, and laundering of substantial assets. In other words, the demand for financial autonomy served as a powerful driving force to stimulate technological innovation.

Likewise, the obsession over avoiding dependence upon foreign weapons vendors motivated the organization to develop a growing capacity to manufacture its own military equipment. As a result, FARC developed a series of mortars—beginning with very rudimentary and imprecise versions, and later advancing to the manufacturing of 80 and 120 mm mortars with a level of reach and precision that is very close to those industrially manufactured. In a similar manner, insurgents have made efforts to independently manufacture land mines. Thus, FARC members have developed a type of weapon that is simple to manufacture and very efficient. Additionally, they have tried to devise systems to synthesize high explosives from basic chemical products to be used in land mines.

In strategic terms, this capacity to independently produce military equipment has had a key role in FARC's capacity to resolve logistic and tactical problems when it became impossible to rely on the arms black market to satisfy this type of need. For example, FARC resolved its shortage of ammunition for certain types of machine guns and assault rifles by developing the capacity to recharge and reuse the cartridges fired by these weapons. In addition, in the face of the increasing need to respond to the growth of the Colombian Air Force, FARC has not only continued trying to purchase missiles on the black markets, but has also engaged in efforts to design and produce anti-aircraft weapons autonomously. In fact, the discovery of an anti-aircraft rocket in 2003, together with its instructions manual, in the Department of Putumayo, demonstrated the advances made by the guerrilla organization in the manufacturing of this type of weapon.

At the same time, the learning capacity of FARC seems to have been strengthened owing to the emphasis of the organization on improving the education and training of its militants. In fact, the substantial investments made by the guerrilla organization for the training of its members enabled innovative activities in two ways. On one hand, it expanded the base of technicians available to the group as it increased the number of militants with the education necessary to work on the development of different innovations. On the other hand, this allowed the dissemination of new techniques throughout the structure of the organization, including those learned by the insurgent leaders through their contacts with other illegal organizations as well as locally developed techniques. As part of the efforts to attain these objectives, the organization has tried to increase the number of its members with professional qualifications in fields such as medicine, engineering, architecture, and so on. To accomplish this, it has resorted to two main strategies. First, it has tried to recruit university students or others from these professional fields. Second, within the organization the insurgent leadership has given great importance to training in techniques and tactics useful for waging war. Further, the organization has invested a substantial amount of resources toward sending some of its members to universities throughout the country, so that the organization may benefit from their knowledge after they complete their studies. For this purpose, training centers have been established to provide lengthy training programs in which FARC has invested substantial human and material resources. In fact, it is not unusual to see the development of three-month courses, attended by dozens of guerrillas removed from their usual duties in order to receive training in new weapons or techniques.

As one would expect, the contents of these training courses have changed in order to meet the strategic needs of the organization. Thus, in the beginning of the 1990s, FARC's leadership established a broad training program aimed at preparing the organization to implement a military doctrine referred to as the New Method of Operations (NMO), which entailed the development of major mobile warfare operations such as extensive ambushes or attacks against fortified bases. For this purpose, FARC created the Hernando González Military School in Llanos del Yarí (Department of Caqueta), where a significant number of insurgent leaders were trained.[6] At the end of the 1990s, when the organization was forced to abandon mobile warfare and gradually return to guerilla warfare,[7] the organization's training courses were refocused on the tactical needs of this new stage of the conflict. Consequently, militants received training in specific guerilla warfare tactics—mine warfare, sniping, etc.— and special emphasis was placed on anti-aircraft defense training. At the same time, the stated intention of the organization to take the war to the cities implied an increase in training for intelligence gathering, special operations, the use of explosives, and other types of tactical resources particularly suitable for the practice of urban terrorism.

INTERNATIONALIZATION AS A SOURCE OF LEARNING

In general, a strategic culture aimed at self-sufficiency and substantial investments in training would have had a relatively minor strategic relevance had the organization not accessed learning sources abroad. In other words, FARC's innovative capacity was significantly enhanced as a result of increasing international links between the organization and criminal networks, terrorist groups, and guerrilla movements outside of Colombia. Certainly, for an armed group arising from isolated peasant sectors in the central Andean ridge, the establishment of such international relationships was a lengthy and complex task. Nevertheless, this effort was supported by two types of network ties that FARC used to its advantage: on one hand, relationships were established with ideologically aligned radical regimes and revolutionary groups; on the other hand, operational links were established with criminal groups through FARC's illegal business dealings, particularly in the international drug trade.

To begin with, international contacts of the Colombian guerrillas were established during the Cold War through trips such as those made by Luis Edgar Devia (also known as "Raúl Reyes") to the former German Democratic Republic during the 1980s, prior to becoming one of the outstanding members of FARC leadership. However, these old ties have been maintained over several decades and explain certain learning opportunities that have enabled FARC to introduce innovations into its tactical repertoire. Such is the case of relations with Libya, which allowed the organization to send fifteen FARC militants to receive training in the country for the purpose of manning its small fleet of light airplanes and helicopters (used by the insurgents in liaison and logistic support missions). Likewise, according to certain sources, relations between FARC and Vietnam enabled the exchange of experiences in the military field, providing the guerrillas important knowledge in the areas of special forces and sapper operations.

More specifically, the development of the New Method of Operations would have been incomprehensible without taking into account the cooperative relationships established by FARC with similar groups in other countries. In particular, the organization received considerable support from former militants of the Salvadoran FMLN. In fact, some major operations conducted during the mid-1990s—such as the attack on the Las Delicias military base—were identical copies of attacks carried out by Salvadoran insurgents during the civil war of this Central American country.[8] Simultaneously, Colombian guerrillas received support from revolutionary militants of Chilean nationality, who themselves had received training in Cuba and had participated with FSLN in the insurrection that ended with the regime of Anastasio Somoza in Nicaragua. In fact, certain instructors of FARC's Hernando Gonzales Military School belonged to this group of Chilean communists, who were the hard core of the Manuel Rodríguez Patriotic Front (FPMR). Thereafter, the decision of the guerrilla organization to wage war in the cities was accompanied by a new series of international contacts aimed at obtaining advice on the strategy and tactics of urban terrorism. Thus, at the end of the 1990s, authorities detected the presence of members of the Japanese Red Army (JRA) in the north of Colombia, who allegedly trained FARC in various capabilities related to terrorism.

Most importantly, the qualitative leap in FARC's technological capacity to perform urban attacks was the result of the organization's relations with the Provisional Irish Republican Army (PIRA). The relationship between the Irish and the Colombians was detected in 2001 when three important PIRA militants were arrested in the Bogotá airport. This incident uncovered a long relationship between FARC and PIRA, which had materialized through both the transfer of technology for the manufacturing of military equipment and tactical training to conduct attacks. As a result, in mid-1998, FARC began to use improvised mortars, using gas cylinders filled with explosives—a design replicated from weapons used by PIRA in Northern Ireland.

Years later, in 2002, Colombian insurgents initiated the use of a new type of booby traps in houses where searches would be conducted, with devices similar to those used by Irish separatists against British forces. In a similar manner, some of the most spectacular FARC attacks have been inspired by tactics previously tested by PIRA. For example, in August 2002, an attack against the Colombian presidential palace—using mortar grenades triggered by remote control—was an expanded version of a similar attack carried out by Irish terrorists against the British Prime Minister's office on Downing Street in 1991. Also, the strategy of placing explosives in automobiles and detonating them from a distance when the vehicles approached military control posts, was used by FARC several times in Arauca—a copycat of attacks launched by PIRA in Northern Ireland at the beginning of the 1990s.

FARC also took advantage of its relationships with international criminal networks involved in drug trafficking, which helped it refine the management of its finances and gain access to new sources of military equipment suppliers. Accordingly, the development of money laundering techniques and the establishment of economic structures designed to support the organization's armed activities were strategies easily learned by Colombian insurgents through their involvement in the drug trade. Additionally, international connections with drug mafias expanded FARC's relationships with the clandestine weapons market, since the illegal drugs and arms trafficking networks tend to be closely connected.

Thus, in 2000, authorities discovered the existence of an arms trafficking network used by FARC—a network that involved Desi Bouterse (the former dictator of Suriname) and Leonardo Dias Mendoça, an associate of the well-known Brazilian drug baron Luis Fernando Da Costa, also known as "Fernandiño Beira Mar." Through this network, Colombian guerrillas purchased from American and Russian traffickers enormous shipments of weapons, including assault rifles, machine guns, and rockets. During the same year, another major illegal arms operation was revealed, which had enabled FARC to purchase 8,500 Russian AK-47 assault rifles in Jordan, using as intermediaries the then-head of the Peruvian Intelligence Service, Vladimiro Montesinos, along with the aforementioned "Fernandiño Beira Mar." Soon after they were discovered, these networks were significantly disrupted by the removal from office and imprisonment of Montesinos (as a result of a number of corruption scandals) and the arrest of "Fernandiño" by Colombian military forces during the "Black Cat" operation. But these network connections offered clear evidence of the strategic role of drug trafficking in the acquisition of military equipment by FARC.

All learning and innovation efforts by Colombian insurgents were sustained by their enormous capacity to collect financial resources. In fact, FARC's economic strategy was a key factor in obtaining the modernization of the organization, while at the same time providing evidence of its enormous capacity to adapt. Since its creation, FARC has directed its financial activities toward attaining maximum self-sufficiency, in an attempt to avoid dependence on foreign support sources, in contrast with other Latin American guerilla movements—such as FMLN—that had developed close ties with countries of the Soviet bloc. Consequently, the group tended toward the practice of criminal activities—extortion, kidnapping, etc.—as financial sources.[9] However, the great qualitative leap—in financial terms—took place at the beginning of the 1980s, through the involvement of the organization in drug trafficking.[10] By 1998, relatively conservative estimates noted that FARC could be earning close to $140 million in taxes each year collected from drug traffickers for production and transportation through areas under insurgent control. Overall, since the late 1990s, income derived from FARC drug trafficking has multiplied, as the organization has ceased to be a mere collector of percentages on drug production and has become a producer and seller of its own narcotics. In fact, certain estimates indicate that FARC supplied the aforementioned "Fernandiño" with approximately twenty tons of cocaine per month until his arrest by Colombian military forces.

In the meantime, the organization escalated its extortion and kidnapping activities. The traditional payment demands to cattle raisers—referred to as "vaccines"—were gradually extended to practically any active business in the areas of guerrilla influence. In general, the benefits derived from extortion took a qualitative leap by the 1990s as a result of two factors; on one hand, the expansion of guerrilla pressure on large multinational companies in the country, forcing the companies to pay large sums of money to protect their interests; on the other hand, the efforts of the organization to develop a large-scale extortion strategy, by standardizing information-gathering processes on victims, exercising pressure on victims, and collecting payment—a trend that led to the promulgation by the FARC Secretariat of the so-called "Law 002," demanding contributions from all individuals or corporations with assets in excess of $1 million. As a supplement to this massive extortion campaign, the organization developed an overwhelming capacity to kidnap those rejecting its demands. In fact, by the 1990s FARC became the main kidnapping group in Colombia, committing more than 38 percent of the 1,875 extortive kidnappings that occurred in 2002. As such, extortion and kidnapping became two mutually supported activities. On one hand, the information and resources invested by insurgents in the extortion campaign were used to select kidnap victims and negotiate their ransom. On the other hand, group abductions increased the credibility of the threats and drove those undecided to give in to extortion. In such a manner, drug trafficking, extortion, and kidnappings—together with other types of minor income sources such as cattle theft or corruption—converted FARC into the richest guerrilla organization in the history of Latin America. Hence, since early 2000, Colombian insurgents have enjoyed resources of approximately between $500 million and $1 billion a year.

On this basis, FARC has developed an economic structure with an outstanding capacity for survival despite the pressures from the Colombian State.[11] This sound financial base of the insurgency is the result of two factors. First, the organization has found its financial sources in illegal businesses difficult to disrupt. Therefore, for example, extortion has proven to be a very resilient practice in spite of the efforts to eradicate it, since the decision of victims to reject extortion depends on their strong or weak conviction that the State can or will protect them. Thus, even in areas where insurgents have been expelled, memories of FARC power result in many of those threatened preferring to pay extortion demands, inasmuch as they feel security improvements are temporary and they must still fear rebels. Something similar may be said of drug trafficking. The retreat of the guerrillas as a consequence of military force pressure and the massive campaign to eradicate crops makes it more difficult for the organization to collect payments from coca growers. However, to the extent that insurgents are now directly involved in the drug trade, they only need to preserve a limited number of crop fields in order to grow sufficient coca to derive an enormous volume of benefits through its sales.

On the other hand, insurgents have made great efforts to diversify their finance mechanisms for the purpose of eliminating any dependence on a single source, particularly a source that could be strangled relatively easily through government action. Consequently, the guerrillas have kept cocaine trafficking, extortion, and kidnapping as their main financial sources. In addition, they continuously pursue alternative income sources. In fact, FARC has tried to diversify its narcotics production by seeking to control poppy crops and become involved in heroin production. Additionally, it has explored other activities, such as the exploitation of gold mines and public fund fraud.

As a result, the insurgency has developed an economic network to guarantee a substantial flow of economic resources, even amid the strong pressures sustained since President Alvaro Uribe Velez took office. This strong financial base is the key to the growth of FARC's innovative potential in two directions. First, the abundance of economic resources has provided the group with the means to acquire any legal or illegal goods and services suitable for strengthening its capacity to sustain a military and political campaign against the Colombian State. As an example, the large purchases of weapons carried out by FARC or its use of foreign advisers—Irish, Salvadoran, etc.—served the purpose of refining the organization's military performance. Second, the availability of unlimited financial resources has allowed the organization to invest in long-term innovative processes, assuming the inevitable uncertainties of the outcome of such efforts. This has been the case, for example, with efforts to build the group's capacity to manufacture—autonomously—weapons systems of increasing complexity. In fact, FARC developed the capacity to experiment with long-range mortars or anti-air rockets without being concerned about the availability of funds to acquire any type of materials necessary for this work or to sustain an unlimited amount of failed tests.

Lastly, a final ingredient influencing the innovative capacity evidenced by FARC has been the strength of its organizational structure and the stability of its leaders. Moreover, in its origins, the group implemented the tradition of the Colombian Communist Party by establishing a highly bureaucratic structure marked by strong discipline.[12] In fact, after its formal creation in 1966, FARC gave maximum priority to the establishment of the organization's apparatus, creating a Central General Staff in 1973 and completing internal group regulations in 1978. On this basis, the guerilla leadership proved stable, yet at the same time, open to change. Consequently, the group of guerrilla founders maintained a dominant position within the movement, with Manuel Marulanda as its top leader, together with other historical leaders such as Luciano Marín Arango, a.k.a. "Iván Márquez," and Rodrigo Londoño Echeverri, a.k.a. "Timoleón Jiménez." Notwithstanding this, FARC also allowed the simultaneous incorporation into the leadership of younger members with better political education, such as Luis Edgar Devia Silva, a.k.a. "Raúl Reyes," and Guillermo León Sáenz Vargas, a.k.a. "Alfonso Cano," as well as those with knowledge on more modern military action, such as Luis Suárez, a.k.a. "Mono Jojoy." Accordingly, the evolution of the organization's leadership was safe from divisions that characterized other Colombian armed groups, such as ELN. In fact, the continuity of organizational leaders and the solid hierarchy of the group prevented internal ruptures, to the point that it is difficult to speak of any schisms during the long history of FARC, with the exception of the division of the Ricardo Franco Front from FARC during the mid-1980s.

FARC's organizational strength had an important impact on the group's learning capacity. First, organizational strength and leadership continuity allowed FARC to develop long-term plans that favored the development of long-term innovation processes. In fact, strategic changes—such as the implementation of the New Method of Operations or the use of urban terrorism—were undertakings that Colombian insurgents were able to carry out solely due to their capacity to plan and invest resources over the long term. Concurrently, the flexibility of FARC's leadership in introducing members of the younger generation of leaders side-by-side with its founders resulted in an essential motivation for guerrilla modernization. Actually, since the early 1980s, new recruits to FARC from the urban middle classes, radicalized by the experience of the Nicaraguan revolution, have played an important role in the modernization of FARC. It was this group—from which Reyes and Cano came—that promoted substantial changes to the insurgents' political message, decided to become involved in drug trafficking, and modernized the FARC's military strategy.

In other words, without this generation of members entering the organization and their ascent to the top of the organization, FARC would not have become the insurgent machinery that destroyed the stability of the Colombian state during the 1990s. However, the strong bureaucracy and rigidity of the organizational structure also introduced limits to the group's innovative capacity. The group's strict discipline tended to stagnate its behavior in both political and military terms, limiting possibilities to adapt to changes in the strategic environment. At the same time, an excessive hierarchy established barriers to the circulation of information and ideas between the base and its commanders. Consequently, there was a reduction in the capacity of leaders to perceive the tactical needs of the field units and to receive suggestions on the introduction of potential innovations regarding their manner of operating.

STRATEGIC ENVIRONMENTAL INFLUENCES ON GUERRILLA INNOVATION

This set of FARC features—ideological blend, tendency toward self-sufficiency, investments in training, internationalization, and financial potential and organizational strength—gave shape to the innovative capacity of this organization. However, without doubt the practical results of FARC's efforts to modernize its repertoire of operations were influenced by the strategic context. In fact, the success of insurgents upon introducing changes in their political and military conduct depended on their innovative skills for taking advantage of the ideas and resources offered by the strategic environment to develop solutions for the challenges faced by them. In other words, FARC's modernization dynamics operated as an equation in which the group's learning capacity was superimposed over environmental conditions facilitating certain types of changes and, at the same time, making other changes impossible. On the basis of this combination of innovative capacity and opportunities provided by the environment, it may be said that the development of the organization has passed through at least three phases, and it could be close to entering a fourth phase. To begin with, the organization went through a formative phase between the 1960s and the 1970s. During this period, the group established the foundations of its organic structure and its ideology, while at the same time it initiated its political and military deployment throughout Colombian territory. In the meantime, FARC maintained very poor national and international connections. Under such conditions, there were no significant innovations in insurgent activities during this period, but rather a slow accumulation of forces as the group became consolidated. In some ways, FARC's leadership during these years was involved in designing and building the mechanisms that would later allow it to grow and adapt to the strategic environment where it intended to operate.

The second stage in FARC's evolution could be placed between the early 1980s, when the organization began forging contacts with drug traffickers, and the mid-1990s, when it launched mobile warfare in the south and east of Colombia. Undoubtedly, this period corresponded to a process of accelerated FARC modernization based on two key factors: the incorporation of individuals from the urban middle class, who contributed substantially to refining the political and military behavior of the organization; and increasing access by the organization to an unlimited amount of financial resources derived from drug trafficking. During this period, the insurgents also found a particularly favorable national and international environment for their modernization process.

In fact, Colombian society was in the midst of an urbanization and industrialization process facilitating guerrillas' access to individuals with technical education (engineers, pilots, etc.) as well as to industrial goods (chemical products, electronic equipment, etc.) susceptible of incorporation into their operations. Concurrently, the international environment marked by the dynamics of the Cold War allowed the guerrillas to consolidate their relations with countries of the Eastern Bloc, finding opportunities to improve the training of their militants and exchange political and military experiences. As a result of all the above factors, by the mid-1990s, FARC had introduced substantial innovations to its political and military strategy. First, it had strengthened its political message by developing a proposal to radically transform the state and society. In addition, it had expanded its structure with the creation of a political arm named the Clandestine Communist Party of Colombia (PCCC) and a mass organization called the Bolivarian Movement for New Colombia. Lastly, it had increased the sophistication of its military capabilities, in preparing to launch a mobile war campaign.

During its historic evolution, it may be said that FARC entered into a new phase between 1996, when it began to conduct mobile warfare, and 2002, upon the breaking of talks with the administration of President Andrés Pastrana and the inauguration of President Alvaro Uribe. Without doubt, this period was marked by the impact of FARC's completed modernization process on the strategic environment. The increase in insurgent military capacity, the multiplication of its financial resources, and the renewed capacity to project its political message turned FARC into a formidable threat against the Colombian State. However, simultaneously, the organization began to have growing problems in adapting to the changes in its operational environment. Namely, the learning and innovative capabilities of the organization became insufficient for the group to face the new challenges. The reason for these problems arose from the increasing distance between the strategic culture of the organization and the political and social realities of Colombia.

In essence, the group had its origins in an essentially rural country with scarce social mobility and deficient political participation mechanisms. And yet, by the end of the 1990s, Colombia was a mostly urban country with a significant middle class and established democratic institutions. This was an environment that posed almost insurmountable adaptation problems for a rural-oriented insurgency with communist and agrarian roots. However, the post–Cold War international environment offered certain additional opportunities for the strengthening of the organization in financial and military terms. In fact, an increase in the demand for cocaine in the new markets of Eastern Europe and the expansion of heroin production in Colombia provided FARC with new options to increase the volume of income from drug trafficking. At the same time, changes in the illegal arms market gave the Colombian guerrilla organization new opportunities to strengthen its military capacity. Thus, the growth of the black market in arms after the end of the Cold War made it feasible for Colombian insurgents to find an uninterrupted supply of military equipment.[13] Additionally, the appearance of clandestine networks to exchange operational experience and technical expertise between terrorist groups and criminal organizations offered the insurgents channels through which they could expand their fighting capability.

Thus, FARC found opportunities to perfect its financial and military structures. However, it was unable to enter into a process of accelerated innovation or make a qualitative leap that would allow it to adapt to the profound changes in the Colombian strategic environment. For example, while FARC modernized its propaganda mechanisms by incorporating the use of the Internet, it maintained an ideological message filled with obsolete ideas of an agrarian and anti-imperialist nature. Likewise, the organization developed the capacity to independently manufacture increasingly sophisticated weapon systems—anti-aircraft rockets, mortars, etc.— yet continued to practice rural guerilla warfare and proved unable to successfully launch an armed campaign in the cities.

As of 2006, this growing divergence between FARC's profile and the evolution of the Colombian strategic environment has become more acute. The guerrilla organization has continued to be incapable of modernizing its ideological message and military tactics or adapting them to a country with a predominantly urban population and with firm democratic institutions. At the same time, the international campaign against terrorism, launched after the 9/11 attacks in the U.S., began to debilitate international channels that FARC had used to increase its financial potential and modernize its military capacity. In particular, the new emphasis on the war against drugs and the war against the illegal arms trade has decreased the opportunities for Colombian insurgents to accumulate resources and acquire new technologies. In other words, while FARC has historically adapted on many tactical levels, it may not be able to adapt to the present strategic environment, because it has become financially dependent on network relationships and activities (e.g., the drug trade and illegal arms trafficking) that have become targets of the global war on terrorism. In these circumstances, the organization thus seems condemned to gradually lose its capacity for innovation that had allowed it to take enormous qualitative leaps adapting to the changes in the strategic environment and increasing its capabilities to exert political and military pressure on the Colombian state. Yet, the truth is that the loss of learning capacity and the reduction of strategic flexibility often have a devastating impact on the future expectations of an insurgency, reducing its possibilities to obtain resources, weakening its capacity to challenge the State, and lastly, converting it into a marginal actor. This might be the future of FARC.

NOTES

1. Camilo Echandía, *El Conflicto Armado y las Manifestaciones de la Violencia en las Regiones de Colombia* (Bogotá: Presidencia de la Républic–Oficina del Alto Comisionado para la Paz, 1999); and Alfredo Rangel, "Las FARC-EP: una mirada actual," in *Reconocer la guerra para construir la paz*, ed. Malcolm Deas and María Victoria Llorente (Bogota: Cerec-Uniandes-Norma, 1999), 21–52.

2. Eduardo Pizarro, *Insurgencia sin Revolución. La Guerrilla en Colombia en una Perspectiva Comparada* (Bogotá: Tercer Mundo Editores-IEPRI, 1996).

3. Román D. Ortiz, "El Estado Colombiano Frente a las FARC: Buscando respuestas a una nueva amenaza insurgente," in *Terrorismo y Seguridad*, ed. Reinaldo Botero (Bogotá: Planeta-Semana, 2003).

4. Thomas Fischer, "La Constante Guerra Civil en Colombia," in *Sociedades en guerra civil. Conflictos violentos de Europa y Latin America*, ed. Peter Waldman and Fernando Reinares (Barcelona: Paidos, 1999), 255–276.

5. Eduardo Pizarro, *Las FARC 1949–1966. De la Autodefensa de Masas a la Combinación de Todas las Formas de Lucha* (Bogotá: Tercer Mundo Editores-IEPRI, 1992).

6. Eduardo Pizarro, *Una democracia asediada. Balance y Perspectivas del Conflicto Armado en Colombia* (Bogotá: Norma, 2004).

7. Thomas Marks, *Colombian Army Adaptation to FARC Insurgency* (Carlisle: Strategic Studies Institute, U.S. Army War College, 2002).

8. David Spencer, "A Lesson for Colombia," *Jane's Intelligence Review* 9, no. 10 (1997): 474–477.

9. Alfredo Rangel, "Parasites and Predators: Guerrillas and the Insurrection Economy of Colombia," *Journal of International Affairs* 53, no. 2 (2000): 577–601.

10. Angel Rabasa and Peter Chalk, *Colombian Labyrinth. The synergy of drugs and insurgency and its implications for regional stability* (Santa Monica: RAND, 2001).

11. Jeremy McDermott, "Financing Insurgents in Colombia," *Jane's Intelligence Review* 15, no. 2 (2003): 16–19.

12. Juan Guillermo Ferro and Graciela Uribe, *El Orden de la Guerra. Las FARC-EP: Entre la Organización y la Política* (Bogotá: Centro Editorial Javeriano, 2002).

13. Kim Cragin and Bruce Hoffman, *Arms Trafficking and Colombia* (Santa Monica: RAND National Defense Research Institute, 2003).

11

The Making of the Jemaah Islamiyah Terrorist[1]

Kumar Ramakrishna

In January 2003, the Singapore Government published an authoritative analysis of the Jemaah Islamiyah (JI or "Islamic community") threat in Southeast Asia. The report shows that JI, which originated in Indonesia, seeks to establish a *Daulah Islamiyah Nusantara*, or an archipelagic Islamic Southeast Asian state incorporating Indonesia, Malaysia, the southern Philippines, and inevitably, Brunei and Singapore.[2] The report also shows how over the years JI has established linkages not only with regional radical Islamic terrorist groups such as the Kumpulan Militan Malaysia (KMM) and the Moro Islamic Liberation Front (MILF), but also with al Qaeda. In fact, al Qaeda and JI had planned to mount truck bomb attacks against American and other Western targets in Singapore in December 2001/January 2002 or April/May 2002.[3] When these planned attacks on well-guarded diplomatic and commercial institutions were thwarted by Singapore's intelligence services in December 2001, JI shifted emphasis in early 2002 to so-called "soft targets" such as shopping malls, hotels, bars, and nightclubs. The end result was the horrific terrorist strikes on 12 October 2002 that obliterated two exclusive Bali nightspots frequented by an Australian and European clientele, Paddy's Bar and the Sari Club. Two hundred two civilians—mostly young Australian tourists—perished.[4] The Bali attacks were followed up ten months later by another attack on the J. W. Marriott Hotel in Jakarta, killing 12 people and injuring 150.[5]

As this chapter was being written (in September 2004), days away from the third anniversary of the September 11 terrorist attacks in New York and Washington, D.C., yet another JI bomb attack occurred in Jakarta, this time targeting the Australian embassy. Nine people were killed and more than

180 injured, most of them ordinary Indonesians. As in the Bali and Marriott attacks, it appears that this latest terrorist strike involved a suicide bomber. Initial speculation suggests that the attack on the embassy was planned by a senior Malaysian JI bomb maker, Azahari Husin (killed in November 2005), and executed by a squad involving a "new generation of JI cadres" from South Sumatra.[6] It would appear therefore, that JI, despite its numbers having been decimated by counterterror action by regional governments, retains the capacity to mount significant terrorist attacks. Indonesian Police officials recently noted that "JI still had a few hundred kilograms of explosives in its possession."[7] More importantly, however, from a systemic perspective, the fact that new recruits from South Sumatra were involved clearly indicates that the organization is regenerating and continues to seek opportunities for further terrorist action against U.S., Western and friendly regional government interests in the region.[8]

As counterterrorism success ultimately depends on the ability to prevent terrorist organizations from regenerating, this chapter seeks to unearth the dynamics behind the JI regeneration process.[9] Particular emphasis is placed on aspects of knowledge central to the formation and maintenance of JI, and the complex processes by which ordinary young Muslim men are transformed into indoctrinated JI militants. Clearly, this transformation is multidimensional and far more complex than simple media stories or government reports would lead us to believe. The analysis presented in this chapter indicates that the intersection of four broad factors is especially important in the creation of new cohorts of trained and indoctrinated JI: the radical Islamist ideology of Qaedaism; the historical, political, and sociocultural backdrop of Southeast Asia and especially Indonesia, the world's largest Islamic country; the individual makeup of JI terrorists; and what we may call the "ingroup space" within which individual terrorists are enmeshed. Any analysis of the long road toward becoming a JI terrorist must begin with an examination of the wider historical backdrop of Islam in Southeast Asia, and in particular, in Indonesia, where JI first emerged.

THE HISTORICAL CONTEXT

Beginning around the fourteenth century, Islam came to Southeast Asia by way of West and Central Asian traders who took pains to ensure that religious considerations were not permitted to get in the way of commercial exchange. Over time, Islam—especially in the rural hinterlands of Southeast Asia—accommodated existing traditions deriving from other faiths, such as Hinduism and Buddhism. In this way, unique Southeast Asian varieties of Islam emerged, which Azyumardi Azra, a leading Indonesian Islamic scholar, considers to be "basically, tolerant, peaceful, and smiling."[10] This is not to imply, however, that Southeast Asian Islam has been without its harder-line fundamentalist strains. From the sixteenth to the eighteenth centuries, significant intellectual cross-fertilization took place between *Haramayn*-based clerics and Malay-Indonesian students and *ulama*, and one result of this interaction was the emergence, in the late eighteenth century, of the so-called Padri movement in West Sumatra in Indonesia. The Padris were a reform movement that emphasized a return to the "pure and pristine Islam as practiced by the Prophet Muhammad and his companions (the *salaf*)." Significantly, the Padris were quite willing to resort to forceful methods, including *jihad*, to compel fellow Muslims to return to the so-called fundamentals of Islam. This was a significant development in Southeast Asian Islam at the time. In fact it has been suggested that the Padri movement bore striking similarities to the Wahhabis in Saudi Arabia.[11]

Another important reformist current (emanating from Cairo in particular), which may be termed "modernist Islam" or "Islamic modernism," began appearing in Indonesia in the early twentieth century. The modernists thought in pan-Islamic terms, and ultimately sought to revitalize Islamic civilization in the face of global Western Christian ascendancy. To this end, within Southeast Asia, they tried to "purify" Islam of the traditional beliefs, customs, and Sufi-inspired practices that had been absorbed over the previous centuries.[12] Significantly, as part of their revivalist motif, the modernists sought an accommodation between Islamic revival and modern science and technology.[13] Modernist Islam spawned Indonesian Muslim mass organizations such as Muhammadiyah in 1912 and Al-Irsyad a year later.[14] Muhammadiyah, for instance, "advocated the purification of Islam through the literal adoption of the lifestyle and teachings of the Prophet and the analytical application of the Koran and the Sunnah to contemporary problems."[15] However, over the decades Muhammadiyah has been "domesticated," and today accommodates "local concerns, including the adoption of Sufi practices."[16] However, harder-edged, less compromising Islamic modernist streams persist. In 1923, another reform movement drawing inspiration from Islamic modernism—the Islamic Union (Persis)—emerged in East Java. Persis focused most of its energy and resources into propagating "correct" doctrine and practice. Persis has been described as by far the most "puritan" of Indonesian reform movements.[17]

After World War II, Masjumi (The Council of Indonesian Muslim Associations) emerged as the main Islamic modernist political party. Its key leaders, such as Mohammad Natsir and A. Hassan, were linked with Persis. In fact, Persis formed the "backbone" of Masjumi throughout its existence.[18] Throughout the 1950s, Masjumi leaders locked horns politically with the Indonesian Communist Party (PKI) and President Sukarno, a secular nationalist who opposed attempts to make Islamic or *shariah* law the basis of the

Indonesian constitution. Sukarno banned Masjumi at the end of the 1950s, following the involvement of some of its leaders in a short-lived U.S.-backed rebel government in Sumatra.[19] While Masjumi was dissolved in 1960 and two years later its leaders incarcerated for alleged political misdeeds,[20] the Masjumi/Persis ethos did not disappear. It persisted in the form of the Dewan Dakwah Islamiyah Indonesia (DDII) and in the parallel Darul Islam (DI) movement. The DDII was set up in February 1967 by a Masjumi/Persis clique of activists led by Mohammad Natsir. Rather than seeking political power outright, DDII sought to engage in *dakwah* (or proselytizing) in order to turn Indonesians into better Muslims. To this end, it set up a network of mosques, preachers, and publications. It has been suggested that the reason for the DDII's bottom-up Islamization stance was because its leaders had realized—following the failures of Muslim politicians to enshrine the so-called Jakarta Charter in the Indonesian constitutional debates of 1945 and 1959—that a top-down Islamization approach simply would not appeal to the vast masses of nominal Indonesian Muslims, and thus the bottom-up approach of *dakwah* was a better way of transforming society.[21] DDII was characterized especially by a fear of Christian missionary efforts among Indonesian Muslims. Over time, it became increasingly drawn to Saudi-style Wahhabism.[22] In fact, the DDII subsequently established close ties with the Saudi-based World Islamic League (Rabitat al-Alam al-Islami), and Natsir even became a vice-president of this organization, entrusted with Rabitat funding activities in Indonesia.[23]

Residual Masjumi/Persis sentiments survived in yet another ideological permutation: the oldest postwar radical Islamic movement, Darul Islam. The DI revolt commenced in 1947, led by a charismatic Masjumi Javanese activist called S.M. Kartosuwirjo.[24] Kartosuwirjo violently rejected the secular state vision and religiously neutral *Pancasila* ideology of secular nationalists Sukarno and Mohammad Hatta. Kartosuwirjo proclaimed instead an Islamic State in Indonesia (NII) based on *shariah* law in August 1949, and the DI/NII forces waged *jihad* against the Republican regime throughout the 1950s. By 1962, however, the DI revolt that had spread from its West Java epicenter to Aceh in the west and South Sulawesi in the east was crushed, and Kartosuwirjo was captured and executed. DI thereafter splintered into several factions and went underground.[25] While DI failed to attain its political goal of an Indonesian Islamic State, it nevertheless "inspired subsequent generations of radical Muslims with its commitment to a *shari'a*-based state and its heavy sacrifices in the cause of *jihad*."[26]

The Political Backdrop

As it turned out, all these cross-cutting historical influences—the Islamic modernist strain that sought civilizational revitalization through a fusion between Salafi fundamentalism and the fruits of modernity; the related Persis, Masjumi, and DDII movements; and the violent DI struggle—formed the essential background of what came to be known as JI. The co-founders of JI, Abdullah Sungkar and Abu Bakar Bashir, were born in Java in the 1930s and educated in modernist schools, and by the 1950s were leaders in a Masjumi-linked student organization, Gerakan Pemuda Islam Indonesia (GPII). They were also strong DI sympathisers and admirers of Kartosuwirjo, and were committed to keeping the vision of *Daulah Islamiyah* (the Islamic State) in Indonesia alive. Following the October 1965 coup that eventually led to the emergence of Suharto and the New Order regime in Indonesia, Sungkar—who had met and begun collaborating with Bashir in 1963—became chairman of the DDII Central Java Branch, and with the advent of the archsecularist Suharto, commenced campaigning with Bashir openly for an Islamic state in Indonesia.[27] Among other things, they set up a clandestine radio station—*Radio Dakwah Islamiyah Surakarta*—in Solo, Central Java, in 1967. *Radio Dakwah* openly broadcast calls for *jihad* in Central Java, and was eventually shut down in 1975. More significantly, Sungkar and Bashir also oversaw the establishment of the Al-Mukmin Islamic boarding school in 1971, which was moved to the village of Ngruki (east of Solo) two years later.[28] Al-Mukmin became a center of symbolic resistance to the New Order regime. It refused to fly the Indonesian flag or display presidential icons, for example, and when in the 1980s Suharto decreed that *Pancasila* ideology must be the underlying foundational principle (*azaz tunggal*) for all social organizations, including Muslim entities, Al-Mukmin's leadership publicly objected.[29]

Sungkar and Bashir engaged in more than symbolic resistance, however. As a DDII activist, Sungkar understood the rationale for *dakwah* and the necessity for Islamizing the individual Muslim as a prelude to Islamizing the wider society. However, he later decided that rather than unstructured proselytizing, what was needed was more focused propagation of the Islamic faith through a vanguard *jamaah* (religious community or community). In this, Sungkar was inspired by the second Caliph, Umar bin Khattab, who had apparently observed: "No Islam without *jamaah*, no *jamaah* without leadership and no leadership without compliance."[30] This imperative to place the *dakwah* process on a more organized, systematic basis was something Sungkar appears to have picked up from the Egyptian Muslim Brotherhood movement. Sidney Jones of the International Crisis Group has pointed out the influence of Brotherhood founder Hassan al-Banna on Sungkar and Bashir in the 1970s.[31] In the Brotherhood conception, the struggle toward the realization of an Islamic State depended on several steps: first, moral self-improvement; second, becoming part of a family of like-minded individuals (*usroh*) committed to "guide, help and control" one another and thus stay on the right path; third, coalescing the various *usroh* to form the wider *Jemaah Islamiyah*; and finally, coalescing the various *Jemaah* into an Islamic State. In fact, Sungkar and Bashir sought to organize the Al-Mukmin alumni into an *usroh* network. Martin van Bruinessen calls this collection of *usroh* a network of committed young Muslims, "some of them quietist, some of them militants, all of them opposed to the Suharto regime, organized in 'families,' that together were to constitute a true community of committed Muslims, a *Jama'ah Islamiyah*."[32] Sungkar and Bashir, moreover, being themselves sympathetic to the older and wider DI ideological diaspora, decided subsequently to affiliate the early JI network of ideological communes with the already existing DI. Consequently, JI officially became part of the Central Java DI in Solo, in 1976. Both Sungkar and Bashir swore an oath of allegiance to the DI Central Java leader Haji Ismail Pranoto, better known as Hispran.[33] Sungkar and Bashir introduced to the relatively unstructured DI—with its imprecise notions of what an actual Islamic State ought to be like—some of the ideas they themselves imbibed from the Egyptian Muslim Brotherhood.[34]

This institutional affiliation with DI and contact with veterans of the DI revolt may have played a part in radicalizing Sungkar and Bashir—in the sense of enabling them to accept at some subliminal level the utility of violence in pursuit of the *Daulah Islamiyah*. Hence, in February 1977, both men set up the Jemaah Mujahidin Anshorullah (JMA), which some analysts believe to be the precursor organization to today's terrorist JI network.[35] Furthermore, they became involved in the activities of a violent underground movement called Komando Jihad. This organization sought to set up an Islamic state in Indonesia and perpetrated the bombings of nightclubs, churches, and cinemas. Incidentally, Komando Jihad was to a large extent a creation of Indonesian intelligence and was set up to discredit political Islam in Indonesia and legitimize the New Order's subsequent crackdown on "less radical and non-violent Muslim politicians."[36] In 1978, both Sungkar and Bashir were detained for nine years for their involvement in the Komando Jihad. They were released in 1982, but following the Tanjong Priok incident two years later in which the security forces killed one hundred Muslims, both were charged yet again for subversion. This prompted them and several of their followers to decamp to Malaysia in 1985.[37] According to one account, they arrived illegally in Malaysia without proper documentation, settled in Kuala Pilah, about 250 kilometers southeast of Kuala Lumpur, and stayed at the home of a Malaysian cleric for about a year. While in Malaysia, Bashir adopted the pseudonym Abdus Samad, while Sungkar took on the *nom de guerre* Abdul Halim.[38] Over the years, both men—through the financial support base generated by their effective preaching activities—were able to buy property of their own in other parts of the country. Wherever they went, they set up Quran reading groups, and were invited to preach in small-group settings in Malaysia and even in Singapore. In 1992, they set up the Luqmanul Hakiem *pesantren* (Islamic board-ing school) in Ulu Tiram, in the southernmost Malaysian state of Johore. Luqmanul Hakiem was a clone of Al-Mukmin back in Solo. Bashir later told the Indonesian magazine *Tempo* that in Malaysia he set up "As-Sunnah, a community of Muslims."[39] In this way, the original Sungkar/Bashir net-work of *usroh* communities was transnationalized, establishing roots in In-donesia's neighbors, Malaysia and Singapore. It was also during the Malaysian exile that the mature JI ideology of what may be called Global Salafi Jihad evolved.

The Ideological Framework: From the "Near Enemy" to the "Far Enemy"

By the time Sungkar and Bashir arrived in Malaysia in 1985, they had be-come committed "radical Islamists." In order to understand this transfor-mation, some elaboration on the role of ideology is needed. Islamic funda-mentalism (or Salafi Islam) is no monolithic phenomenon. Salafi Muslims—who take the injunction to emulate the Companions of the Prophet very seriously—may express this piety simply in terms of *personal* adherence to implementing *shariah*-derived standards of worship, ritual, dress, and overall behavioral standards. The majority of Salafi Muslims, in fact, may be considered more technically as "neo-fundamentalists" who possess neither "a systematic ideology" nor "a global political agenda."[40] Islamism, on the other hand, "turns the traditional religion of Islam into a twentieth-century-style ideology."[41] In other words, when Salafi Muslims see it as an *added* obligation to actively seek recourse to political power in order to impose their belief system on the society at large, then they become not simply Muslims but rather *Islamists*. Daniel Pipes puts it aptly when he observes that Islamists seek to "build the just society by regimenting peo-ple according to a preconceived plan, only this time with an Islamic orien-tation."[42] Despite regional variations, Islamists worldwide share the com-mon belief that seeking political power (so as to Islamize whole societies) is the only way Islam as a faith can revitalize itself—and recapture the former preeminent position it enjoyed vis-à-vis the West. Modern Islamist move-ments include the Muslim Brotherhood in the Middle East and the Jama'at-I Islami in the Indian subcontinent, as well as many of the Iranian ideo-logues of the 1979 Revolution that brought down the Shah. These Islamists sought to construct "ideological systems" and "models" for "distinctive polities that challenged what they saw to be the alternative systems: na-tionalism, capitalism and Marxism."[43] In short, while the average Salafi Muslim emphasizes individual spiritual and moral transformation as the key to Islamic revitalization, the Islamist, as Pipes suggests, seeks *power* as the means to this end.[44] It is entirely possible, moreover, that in pursuing political objectives Islamists—like other political activists seeking to implement an ostensibly religious agenda—may lose touch with the ethical core of the very faith they are seeking to preserve and champion.[45] This process of ethical or moral disengagement facilitates terrorist acts, as described later in this chapter.

By 1985, both Sungkar and Bashir had been Islamists for years, in the sense that ultimately, they sought the setting up of an Islamic State based on the *shariah* in Indonesia. But what did they feel about the use of force in pursuit of this objective? In truth a latent ambiguity within their ideological systems over the role of violence seems to have existed for years. Both men had been aware of the potential of *dakwah* for gradually Islamizing Indonesian society from the bottom up; Sungkar had after all been the chairman of the DDII Central Java branch while Bashir had majored in *dakwah* at the Al-Irsyad Islamic university in Solo.[46] As noted, this belief in *dakwah* had also led them to set up Al-Mukmin in Solo in 1971. At the same time, however, they were long-term sympathizers with the Kartosuwirjo argument that Islamizing the polity by force was the only feasible approach. They even affiliated the nascent JI movement with Hispran's DI and were involved in the Komando Jihad. It would seem that the period of incarceration from 1978 and subsequent targeting by the New Order regime may have been the "tipping point" in terms of bringing them to their final insight that *dakwah* in the absence of *jihad* would be inefficacious. In other words, they became not merely Islamists but *radical* Islamists who believed in *jihad* as the means to actualize an Islamized Indonesia. The Indonesian journalist Blontank Poer observes in this respect that the *jihadi* emphasis in the overall strategy of Sungkar and Bashir became more developed after the shift to Malaysia in 1985.[47] In this sense, the Sungkar-Bashir radicalization experience mirrors that of the Egyptian Muslim Brotherhood activist Sayyid Qutb, who was "increasingly radicalized by Gamal Abdel Nasser's suppression of the Brotherhood." Cairo's repression prompted Qutb to transform "the ideology of [Muslim Brotherhood founder Hassan] al-Banna and [Jama'at-I Islami founder Mawlana] Mawdudi into a rejectionist revolutionary call to arms."[48]

By the 1980s, moreover, Islamist ideas from the Middle East and the Indian subcontinent had been translated and were in circulation in Southeast Asia.[49] These mingled and fused with the individual experiential and ideational trajectories of Sungkar and Bashir. Thus, the injunctions of al-Banna and Mawdudi to set up a "vanguard" community to serve as the "dynamic nucleus for true Islamic reformation within the broader society"[50] were long accepted by the Indonesian clerics. Moreover, Sungkar and Bashir would have viscerally embraced Sayyid Qutb's absolutist, polarized view of the world:[51]

There is only one place on earth which can be called the home of Islam (Dar-ul-Islam), and it is that place where the Islamic state is established and the Shariah is the authority and God's limits are observed and where all Muslims administer the affairs of the state with mutual consultation. The rest of the world is the home of hostility (Dar-ul-Harb).

Thus it could be said that in the latter half of the 1980s and into the 1990s, the Indonesian JI émigré community in Malaysia believed in several core tenets:

- Islam possesses exclusive authenticity and authority;
- Committed Muslims must keep God at the center of every aspect of life;
- God loves but tests his truest disciples; he also reserves for them eternal rewards in the life to come;
- Science and technology must be harnessed but within an Islamic rather than a Western context; and
- The profane world is an abomination to God; he only accepts the prayers and good works of Muslims who adhere strictly to the demands of the *shariah*, the Quran, and the Sunnah.

To be sure, some of these tenets would not have been unusual to mainstream Salafi Muslims. Other Sungkar/Bashir precepts, however, clearly incorporated politically driven Islamist thinking:

- Deviation from the path of true Islam and emulation of Western models has resulted in worldwide Muslim weakness;
- *Shariah* provides the ideal blueprint for a modern, successful Islamic society capable of competing with the West and restoring Muslim identity, pride, power, and wealth;
- Alternative systems—such as democracy, socialism, *Pancasila*, capitalism, other religions, and Islam as practiced by the majority of the Muslim community—are not acceptable to God and are destructive; and
- True Muslims cannot with good conscience accept a political system that is not based on the *shariah*.[52]

Finally, by the early 1990s the Sungkar-Bashir ideological framework represented a *radical* Islamist vision because it included the explicit willingness to resort to *jihad* in pursuit of the goal of an Islamized Indonesia. It should be noted that apart from the DI legacy as well as the more recent radicalizing effect of direct New Order repression, Sungkar, Bashir, and others in the JI orbit were also likely exposed to the ideas of the Egyptian radical Mohammad al-Faraj, executed by Cairo in 1982 for his role in the assassination of President Anwar Sadat.[53] Faraj, himself influenced by the works of al-Banna, Mawdudi, and Qutb, brought their incipient absolu-tizing ideas to their ultimate extremist conclusion. Unequivocally reject-ing the efficacy of *dakwah* as a means of Islamizing *jahili* (un-Islamic or im-moral) society,[54] Faraj argued that the decline of Muslim societies was due to the fact that Muslim leaders had hollowed out the vigorous concept of *jihad*, thereby robbing it of its "true meaning."[55] Faraj, in his pamphlet the *Neglected Obligation*, argued that the "Qu'ran and the Hadith were funda-mentally about warfare," and that the concept of *jihad*, in contrast to the conventional wisdom, was "meant to be taken literally, not allegori-cally."[56] He argued that *jihad* represented in fact the "sixth pillar of Islam," and that *jihad* calls for "fighting, which meant confrontation and blood."[57] Faraj held that not just infidels but even Muslims who deviated from the moral and social dictates of *shariah* were legitimate targets for *jihad*. Faraj concluded that peaceful means for fighting apostasy in Muslim societies were bound to fail, and ultimately the true soldier of Islam was justified in using "virtually any means available to achieve a just goal."[58] Given their own recent experiences at the hands of the Suharto regime, Sungkar and Bashir would have endorsed, at some deeper level, the ideas of Faraj on the necessity for a literal understanding of *jihad*, as well as his wider argument that *jihad* represented the highest form of devotion to God.[59] This is precisely why, in 1984–1985, when the Saudis sought volunteers for the *jihad* in Afghanistan against the invading Soviets, Sungkar and Bashir willingly raised groups of volunteers from among their follow-ing.[60] The Afghan theater was seen as a useful training ground for a future *jihad* in Indonesia itself.[61]

As it turned out, in an interesting case of the tail wagging the dog, rather than Afghanistan being seen as a training ground for a *jihad* aimed at setting up an Indonesian Islamic state, that conflict became the source of ideas that transformed the original Indonesia-centric vision of Sungkar and Bashir. To be sure, prior to the 1990s, the radical Islamist ideology driving JI may be termed as "Salafi Jihad."[62] The aim of the JI émigré com-munity in Malaysia, led by Sungkar and Bashir, was ultimately to wage a *jihad* against the Suharto regime—in Faraj's terms, the so-called "near en-emy"—and set up a Salafi Islamic state in Indonesia. However, returning Indonesian and other Southeast Asian veterans of the Afghan *jihad* ex-posed Sungkar and Bashir to fresh thinking on this issue. In Afghanistan, the Southeast Asian *jihadis* had been inspired to think in *global* terms by the teachings of the charismatic Palestinian *alim* (singular for *ulama*) Ab-dallah Azzam. Azzam, a key mentor of Osama bin Laden, had received a doctorate in Islamic jurisprudence from Al-Azhar University in Cairo, had met the family of Sayyid Qutb, and was friendly with Sheikh Omar Abdul Rahman. Sheikh Omar Abdul Rahman—better known as the

"Blind Sheikh"—was the spiritual guide of two key Egyptian radical Islamist terrorist organizations, the Egyptian Islamic Jihad (EIJ) and the
Egyptian Islamic Group (EIG), and would later be implicated in the 1993
World Trade Center bombing in New York. When the Soviets withdrew
from Afghanistan in 1989, Azzam—who had played a big part in recruiting non-Afghan foreign mujahideen worldwide, including Southeast
Asia, for the anti-Soviet *jihad*—began to set his sights further. He argued
that the struggle to expel the Soviets from Afghanistan was in fact "the
prelude to the liberation of Palestine and other 'lost' territories." As he put
it in his writings:

> Jihad is now . . . incumbent on all Muslims and will remains [sic] so until the
> Muslims recapture every spot that was Islamic but later fell into the hands of
> the *kuffar* [infidels]. Jihad has been a *fard 'ain* [individual obligation] since the
> fall of al-Andalus [Spain], and will remain so until all other lands that were
> Muslim are returned to us . . . Palestine, Bukhara, Lebanon, Chad, Eritrea, So-
> malia, the Philippines, Burma, Southern Yemen, Tashkent and al-Andalus. . . .
> The duty of jihad is one of the most important imposed on us by God. . . . He
> has made it incumbent on us, just like prayer, fasting and alms [zakat].[63]

However, Azzam (unlike Faraj) did not sanction *jihad* against "apostate"
Muslim governments in Egypt, Jordan, and Syria. His understanding of *ji-
had* was a traditional one in the sense of evicting infidel occupiers from
Muslim lands. He did not wish to see a Muslim wage *jihad* against another
Muslim. However, after his death in a car bomb explosion in Peshawar in
November 1989, the Afghan Arab mujahideen community—and Osama
bin Laden in particular—again accepted the Faraj argument that targeting
Muslim governments seen as apostate was perfectly legitimate.[64] Subse-
quently, at the beginning of the 1990s, once American troops arrived in
Saudi Arabia and in Somalia, both Muslim territories, "a more global analy-
sis of Islam's problems" occurred. As Marc Sageman concisely explains:

> Local *takfir* (hypocrite) Muslim leaders were seen as pawns of a global power,
> which itself was now considered the main obstacle to establishing a transna-
> tional *umma* (Muslim community) from Morocco to the Philippines. This in
> effect reversed Faraj's strategy, and now the priority was jihad against the
> "far enemy" over the "near enemy."[65]

Sageman observes that this gradual shift in strategic targeting philosophy—within what by the early 1990s had become al Qaeda—took place
during Bin Laden's Sudanese exile during that decade, as well as in con-
temporaneous parallel discussions within radical Islamist circles in New
York leading to the 1993 New York World Trade Center attack, and in Algeria and France just before the wave of bombings in those countries.[66]

These shifts in global radical Salafi ideology post-Afghanistan were not lost on Sungkar and Bashir. In addition to their discussions with returning Indonesian veterans of the Afghan war, both men also met with international *jihadi* groups in Malaysia. Consequently, by 1994, Sungkar and Bashir were no longer talking about establishing merely an Islamic state in Indonesia. Over and above this, they were now talking of establishing a *"khilafah* (world Islamic state)."[67] In this construction, a "world caliphate uniting all Muslim nations under a single, righteous exemplar and ruler" is the ultimate goal.[68] It is no coincidence, then, that at about this time Sungkar and Bashir reportedly made contact with Egyptian radicals associated with the Blind Sheikh.[69] Moreover, in the early 1990s, Sungkar and Bashir disassociated themselves from the Central Java DI movement because of serious doctrinal differences with regional DI leader Ajengan Masduki, who had apparently embraced Sufi teachings on nonviolence and tolerance. Sungkar and Bashir, casting off the overarching DI appellation, resurrected the name Jemaah Islamiyah.[70] This is the JI known today, infused with the post-Afghanistan neo-Faraj ethos of Global Salafi Jihad that henceforth took it upon itself to wreak "vengeance against perceived Western brutality and exploitation of Muslim communities."[71] This is the JI whose current spiritual leader, Bashir (Sungkar passed away in 1999), publicly declared that he supported "Osama bin Laden's struggle because his is the true struggle to uphold Islam, not terror—the terrorists are America and Israel."[72]

By the turn of the century, the virulent ideological strain of Global Salafi Jihad infusing JI had matured, and radical Islamist writers like Azzam, Qutb, and Faraj featured prominently on JI reading lists.[73] The outlines of this virulent ideology—with its global, anti-Western focus—were aptly encapsulated by the chilling statement apparently issued by JI immediately after the September 2004 bomb attack in Jakarta, which declared:

We (in the Jama'ah al-Islamiah) have sent many messages to the Christian government in Australia regarding its participation in the war against our brothers in Iraq. However, it didn't respond positively to our request; therefore we have decided to punish it, as we considered it the fiercest enemy of Allah and the Islamic religion. Thanks to Allah, who supported us in punishing [the Australians] in Jakarta when a brother successfully carried out a martyrdom operation using an explosive-laden car in the Australian embassy. Many were killed and injured besides [causing] great damage to the embassy. This is only one response in a series of many coming responses, God willing. Therefore, we advise all the Australians to leave Indonesia; otherwise, we will make it a grave for them. We also advise the Australian government to withdraw its troops from Iraq; otherwise, we are going to carry many painful attacks against them. Car bombs will not stop, and [our] list contains many who are ready to die as martyrs. The hands that attacked them in Bali are the same hands that carried out the attack in Jakarta. Our attacks and our Jihad will not stop until we liberate all the lands of the Muslims.[74]

In sum, as in all extremist militant organizations, the JI worldview encapsulates ideology and a historical perspective of perceived persecution, fueling intense grievances that motivate terrorist recruitment, training, and operations—including suicide attacks like those JI have perpetrated over the last several years. The role of ideology as a central form of knowledge in the world of the JI terrorist is similar to that in other religious extremist groups around the world. However, while the existence of an ideology is an important factor in the indoctrination of terrorists, it is not at all sufficient. After all, simple exposure to Global Salafi Jihad ideology—or, in the shorthand of British journalist Jason Burke, "al Qaedaism," has not resulted in the radicalization of all Muslims.[75] This is what Sageman calls the "fundamental problem of specificity"—why some and not all? From this perspective, it becomes clear that additional factors must also be accounted for in developing a complete understanding of how the JI terrorists view the world and their place within it.

MEDIATING FACTORS IN THE FORMATION OF JI TERRORISTS

From an extensive review of the literature on religious extremist organizations, particularly from the social science disciplines, three factors can be identified that appear to mediate the impact of Qaedaism: sociocultural space, individual factors, and ingroup space. While much has been written on each of these general terms, the following discussion highlights the ways in which research and scholarship in these fields can help us understand the formation of the JI terrorist.

Sociocultural Dimensions of Knowledge Formation

To begin with, how does the sociocultural space within which JI operates in Southeast Asia contribute to the terrorist construction process? Olufemi A. Lawal, drawing on anthropological research, identifies a few dimensions of culture that can be used to analyze different societies, including power distance, uncertainty avoidance, and individualism/collectivism.[76] Lawal notes that in high power-distance societies, "peoples accept as natural the fact that power and rewards are inequitably distributed in society."[77] Moreover, in collectivist societies, individuals are expected to be loyal to the ingroup and subordinate personal goals to those of the collective. In an age of globalization and the erosion of traditional social structures and processes, moreover, certain societies may feel particularly "threatened by uncertainty and ambiguity."[78] Following Lawal's analysis, it may be suggested that individuals in high power-distance, ambiguity-intolerant, and collectivist milieux would be "collectively" programmed for *potential* recruitment into terrorist organizations, especially religiously inspired ones. This is because such individuals, as Lawal suggests, would be relatively more likely to accept that all authority and "power [have] been naturally concentrated in the hands of a leader."[79] Being ambiguity-intolerant (as discussed later in this chapter), moreover, they would desire deeply, at some subconscious level, to accept that leader's clear and unambiguous interpretations of wider social and political developments. Finally, being cultural collectivists, they would tend to deem it their individual duty and proof of loyalty to the ingroup to execute the leader's instructions.[80]

Lawal notes in his essay that "non-Western and developing societies" tend to display high power-distance and collectivist orientations.[81] Certainly elements of Lawal's analysis appear to hold in the case of Southeast Asia. Barry Desker has pointed out the revered status of Hadrami Arab migrants in Southeast Asia, who were regarded as "descendants of the Prophet" and "whose command of Arabic was perceived as giving them an insight into the religious texts."[82] These Hadrami Arab migrants helped to introduce Wahhabi elements into Southeast Asian Islam.[83] It should be noted in this respect that the families of both Sungkar and Bashir have Yemeni roots.[84] Moreover, the most recent two decades or so of Islamic revival have resulted in the further Islamization of Indonesia's state and identity along Middle Eastern lines. Hence, Patricia Martinez observes that among many ordinary Southeast Asian Muslims today, a "core-periphery dynamic" exists, resulting in the tendency to canonize the Middle Eastern–trained and/or Arabic-speaking local *alim*:

> The core periphery dynamic, with the heartland of Islam as core and Southeast Asian Muslims as periphery, gives rise to an infantile religiosity among many ordinary Southeast Asian Muslims [who cannot] read the huge corpus of theology, philosophy, exegesis and jurisprudence that is the rich heritage of a Muslim [but] most of which is in Arabic.[85]

Martinez points out that as a result, many Southeast Asian Muslims "rely on the mediators of Islam—those who are *ulama*—to interpret and guide." The result?

> What transpires then is the abdication by many ordinary Muslims of the ability to decide and define how Islam will evolve in their particular milieu, *giving power to the guardians of tradition and the final arbiters of law and life—the ulama and those who claim to be authoritative* [emphasis added], and whose fidelity is not only to literal and selective applications of text and tradition but also to how this coheres in the heartland, the Middle East.[86]

The power distance hypothesis is also relevant in the hierarchically ordered Javanese cultural context. Many traditional *pesantren*, which are found in rural Java and in some cities, are usually run as the "social and intellectual fiefdoms of charismatic *syeikh*"—that is, "pilgrims who have returned to Java after an extended period of study in Mecca or Medinah." Tim Behrend observes that such "*syeikh*" enjoy high status in Indonesian society. Indeed, they play a critical personal role in "constructing the religious psyche" of *pesantren* students. Such *pesantren* alumni form extensive social networks long after graduation and even play significant roles in the polity and society later.[87]

The role of the *syeikh* in knowledge transfer in Indonesian society has particular salience for understanding terrorist-related knowledge transfer. In fact, Indonesian society can be conceived of structurally as a collection of overlapping Salafi and Islamist social networks built around influential religious figures. In the case of JI, this role was played by Sungkar and Bashir. Further, as alluded to above, the remote sociocultural roots of JI can be traced back to the highly Islamist Persis/Masjumi/DDII/DI "network of networks," whose ideological hub would comprise key Islamist figures in Indonesian history, such as Mohammad Natsir and Kartosuwirjo. Even though after 1960 the Persis-dominated Masjumi was never reconstituted as a political party, "its constituency has remained a recognizable entity, held together by a dense network of relationships, friendship, intermarriage, education, and all sorts of institutions."[88] As an illustration of the sociocultural embeddedness of today's JI, convicted Bali bomber Imam Samudra—as well as several of his followers from Serang, Java—hail from families associated with Persis.[89]

In addition, Darul Islam ideas and attachments continue to circulate within communities in West Java and South Sulawesi. Greg Fealy argues that "former DI areas have proven a rich source of new members for the JI and are likely to remain so in the future."[90] Of the ideological streams directly related to JI since 1971, more than three thousand alumni have passed through the Al-Mukmin *pesantren* in Solo.[91] These, along with the alumni of spinoff JI "Ivy League" *pesantren*—such as Al-Islam in East Java, Al-Muttaqien and Dar us-Syahadah in Central Java, and the now-closed Luqmanul Hakiem in Ulu Tiram, Malaysia—have formed linked networks of relatively like-minded (albeit geographically dispersed) *usroh* communities.[92] In fact a recent study has discovered that more than a hundred marriages involving JI leaders and members exist, integrating families in Malaysia, Indonesia, and (to some extent) the southern Philippines.[93] It appears that a related network of Islamist *pesantrens*—centered on Pesantren Hidayatullah in Balikpapan, East Kalimantan—is also sympathetic to the JI cause.[94] The JI terrorist network in Southeast Asia has therefore emerged from a complex, historically enduring, and interwoven sociocultural fabric centered in Indonesia.

However, within this milieu there is significant disagreement over the relative merits of *dakwah* and *jihad*, informed by a combination of doctrinal and individual experiential differences. As observed earlier, within the Al-Mukmin diaspora, some are "quietists" while others are "militants." Greg Fealy similarly points out that "not all JI members are engaged in terrorism, and the network also has groups conducting peaceful religious education and welfare functions."[95] The International Crisis Group takes pains to assert that to "have gone to a JI-linked *pesantren* does not make one a terrorist."[96] The issue here, however, is not whether an Islamist community believes it can achieve its political vision by violence. The issue is whether that community is Islamist in the first place. It has been said that Bashir does not himself publicly advocate violence against the Indonesian state. In this respect, through his Muslim Mujahidin Council (MMI), formed in August 2000, Bashir and other Islamists have sought to agitate for an Islamic State through ostensibly peaceful *dakwah*. Nevertheless, it is not the means that is at issue but the ultimate vision. Bashir's worldview is sharply polarized: Christians would have to accept the status of a minority *dhimmi* community with protected but restricted rights in an Indonesian Islamic State.[97] Muslims would tolerate but not embrace Christians, and would "not seek to mingle with them."[98] In addition, even as sympathetic an observer as Tim Behrend is compelled to concede that Bashir's message is "not simply anti-Zionist or anti-Israeli, but very deeply and personally anti-Jewish."[99]

Is this a problem? Social psychologists explain that "ethnocentrism and stereotyping" are part of the normal way individuals process information emanating from the environment. "The human mind groups people, as well as objects, into categories" that enable individuals to "simplify the present and predict the future more effectively."[100] However, as Neil Kressel argues, it is "a small step from categorization" to "stereotyping and favoritism for one's group." In a nutshell, "taken to extremes," ethnocentrism and stereotyping can foster prejudice.[101] All individuals, unfortunately, are prejudiced to some extent toward various "outgroups." J. Harold Ellens laments that "prejudice is a devastating force in our political and social order" that emerges from "a very sick psychology at the center of our souls."[102] Willard Gaylin feels that the prejudiced individual is coolly dismissive of (and indifferent to) the sensibilities and sufferings of the outgroup.[103] It does not stop there, however. Within the larger pool of prejudiced individuals there is a smaller number, whom Gaylin considers *bigots*, who are "strongly partial to one's own group, religion, race, or politics." Importantly, rather than being passively indifferent, bigots are *actively* "intolerant of those who differ."[104] The bigot, Gaylin informs us, would "support legislation and social conditions that deprive the minority of its autonomy and its right to be respected."[105] Finally, it is from the smaller sociocultural pool of bigots that the *haters* emerge. While a "bigot may feel malevolence whenever he thinks of the despised group," he "is not obsessively preoccupied with them."[106] On the other hand, hatred "requires both passion and a preoccupation with the hated group."[107] In this vein, Aristotle once pointed out that while the "angry man wants the object of his anger to suffer in return, hatred wishes its object not to exist."[108] Gaylin notes that there could be "significant slippage" between the bigots and the haters.[109] Significantly, however, Gaylin is forthright in condemning not just hatred but the other transition points to this end-state:

> Prejudice and bigotry also facilitate the agendas of a hating population. They take advantage of the passivity of the larger community of bigots, a passivity that is essential for that minority who truly hate to carry out their malicious destruction.[110]

This short exposition on prejudice, bigotry, and hatred is important to our understanding of knowledge transfer within the world of the JI terrorist. Bashir once told an Indonesian intelligence official that as a preacher he likened himself to a "craftsman" who sells "knives," but is not responsible for what happens to them.[111] As the foregoing analysis suggests, however, Bashir's remarks are disingenuous, as rhetoric matters a very great deal. Gaylin hits the nail on the head:

> As recently as the summer of 2002, the *New York Times* reported an interview in which a professor of Islamic law explained to a visiting reporter: "Well of course I hate you because you are Christian, but that doesn't mean I want to kill you." Well, the professor may not wish to kill the reporter, but the students he instills with his theological justifications of hatred may have different ideas about the proper expressions of hatred.[112]

In short, it is within the "culture of hatred" that "monstrous evil can be unleashed." When "everyday bias is supported and legitimated by religion," the "passions of ordinary malcontents will be intensified and focused."[113] The fact of the matter is that Bashir and others like him have helped shaped pockets of sociocultural space within Southeast Asia that breed the prejudice, bigotry, and ultimately hatred that foster JI extremism and violence. For example, Singaporean Malay/Muslim journalists who managed to visit Al-Mukmin in January 2004 noted how "anti-western and anti-American sentiment was woven into the daily teachings and routines of students, some as young as 15."[114] In particular, students were taught to believe that some countries "feared Islam's progress and were openly destroying the faith."[115] In addition, students were programmed into believing that "Americans and Jews were 'infidels',", and so were "Muslims who did nothing."[116] Significantly, posters and signs proclaiming *jihad* were prominently displayed "on walls, lockers and walkways leading to class-rooms," spouting messages like "Jihad, Why Not?" and "No Prestige with-out Jihad."[117] Moreover, students were spotted wearing T-shirts with im-ages of Osama bin Laden, Saddam Hussein, and the Chechen militant leader Shamil Basayev.[118] A few months earlier, an *Asian Wall Street Journal* reporter had even observed fifteen-year-old students practicing preaching in a mixture of *Bahasa Indonesia* and Arabic, telling classmates about the "importance of upholding strict Islamic law and defending their faith from attacks by infidels." Their classmates responded by pounding their wooden desks and exclaiming: "God is Great," "Hang the Jews," and "America . . . terrorist!"[119] In essence, Al-Mukmin was clearly acting as a dissemination center of Global Salafi Jihad or Qaedaist ideology, shaping a burgeoning culture of hatred.

While not all JI supporters or sympathizers may be directly involved in the planning, support, and/or execution of terror attacks, in truth they can all be strung out along Gaylin's continuum, with prejudice at one ex-treme, bigotry in the middle, and hatred at the other extreme. Under cer-tain circumstances—to be elaborated upon later in this chapter—preju-diced Islamists may well transition toward bigotry and even hatred, embrace Qaedaist worldviews, and become full-fledged, hate-filled ter-rorist operatives. The process by which elements of the amorphous mass of sympathizers/supporters become part of the actual JI organization compels us to begin tentative probes into the inner recesses of the JI in-ductee's mind.

Individual Dimensions of "Knowledge" and Understanding in the World of Terrorists

According to Martha Crenshaw, "it is difficult to understand terrorism without psychological theory, because explaining terrorism must begin with analyzing the intentions of the terrorist actor."[120] At the outset, it must be iterated that there is no single overarching terrorist profile, and even when, as Walter Reich advises, the researcher eschews metatheory construction and focuses specifically on a single terrorist organization such as JI,[121] he remains confronted with constantly shifting patterns of terrorist motivations. Nevertheless, Crenshaw's logic is impeccable; hence, the next two sections of this chapter provide a tentative, nonspe-cialist, preliminary attempt to make sense of why the likes of Mukhlas or Imam Samudra were driven to commit the atrocities they did. One of the key problems faced by counterterrorism analysts everywhere is the lack of access to ready and openly available data on terrorists, as well as con-siderations of operational security even when such access exists. This chapter unfortunately suffers from both limitations. Nevertheless, the information presented here has, as far as possible, been documented and/or cross-checked against other sources.

To begin with, in order to truly understand the JI terrorist, one must understand the psychology of religious behavior. Why do people seek religion? Religion refers to a "system of beliefs in divine or superhuman power, and practices of worship or other rituals directed toward such a power."[122] The major psychological explanation for the attractiveness of religious systems is that of "cognitive need." People have a tendency to organize the environment according to simple cognitive structures. In fact humans, from childhood, seem to possess a need for "cognitive closure"—they desire a definite answer to a particular topic, "as opposed to confusion and ambiguity."[123] There seems to be a universal human desire to reject existential meaninglessness, to find divine explanations for suffering and tragedy, and to seek the promise of a better afterlife; religion thus "meets the need for a meaningful cosmos and meaningful human existence."[124]

This natural human quest for cognitive closure—particularly but not exclusively in non-Western, communitarian societies, which form 70 percent of the world population—has been greatly intensified by the psychosocial dislocations caused by globalization. Globalization has been usefully characterized as "worldwide integration through an ongoing, dynamic process that involves the interplay of free enterprise, democratic principles and human rights, the high-tech exchange of information, and movement of large numbers of people."[125] While it is true that "the juggernaut of free enterprise, democracy, and technology offers the best chance of wealth creation," globalization—the key to "improving the human condition"—has had its downside as well.[126] By privileging "individualistic, impersonal, competitive, privatistic, and mobile" values and attitudes, globalization processes have inadvertently undermined traditional social units such as the family, clan, and voluntary association.[127] More precisely, globalization—which is to many non-Western societies synonymous with Westernization—is destabilizing because it promotes the desacralization of society; encourages religious and moral relativism; places the onus on the individual to determine his "values, career, lifestyle and moral system"; and most disconcertingly, undermines traditional ideas about sexuality and the status of women.[128] Michael Stevens puts it well: "For communitarian societies, keyed to historical continuity, group coherence and security, personal rootedness, and the affirmation of moral righteousness, empowering the individual is equated with rending society asunder." Globalization may thus inadvertently precipitate sociocultural dislocation at the aggregate level, and psychosocial dysfunction at the unit level.[129] Charles Selengut elaborates further, explaining that to "follow the West is to become spiritually and psychologically homeless, without a transcendental anchor to provide security and safety during life's journey."[130]

Various individuals within any society may respond differently to the moral and spiritual complexities inherent within modernity. Personality theorists, building upon the work of Carl Jung, have postulated two basic "sensing" or "perceiving" types of individual: the abstract/intuitive and the concrete/objective. The abstract/intuitive individual tends to be creative in his problem solving; is willing to explore hunches and new ideas; is imaginative and likes change; is problem oriented and subjective. Concrete/objective people, on the other hand, tend to "prefer a concrete way of perceiving the world, are down-to-earth; perhaps simple and possibly simplistic" and strongly "solution-oriented." Ronald Johnson puts it pithily when he suggests that while abstract people see "what could be," concrete people see "what is."[131] Taking this concept to extremes, concrete/objective individuals in non-Western societies undergoing accelerated globalization and Westernization are more likely to experience psychosocial dysfunction. Quite simply, they are psychologically ill equipped to cope with what Jessica Stern calls "a surfeit of choice." For concrete/objective people, too much choice, "especially regarding identity, can be overwhelming and even frightening."[132] This is precisely why religious fundamentalism is so attractive to many. Charismatic fundamentalist leaders "offer their constituencies clear, objective, practical, and absolute directives for their lives and answers for their theological questions."[133] From the perspective of the unsettled concrete/objective individual, relinquishing "one's autonomy in return for absolute ideological security is a powerful motive."[134] In this respect, it is worth noting that many Singapore JI members turned to leaders like (Singapore JI spiritual leader Ibrahim Maidin) because—like true concrete/objective persons—they wished to "free themselves from endless searching as they found it stressful to be critical, evaluative and rational."[135] The fact that the "JI leaders had quoted from holy texts" appeared to have reassured them that "they could not go wrong."[136]

Understanding why absolute ideological security can be so important to concrete/objective individuals requires a brief incursion into the burgeoning new field of psychobiology.[137] Neuroscientists tell us that the seat of human emotions and motivations lies in a primitive area of the brain called the limbic system, comprising *inter alia* the hypothalamus and, importantly, the amygdala. The grape-sized amygdala is linked to the human sensory systems and constantly scans the information flowing through them, looking for signs of "threat or pain, whether physical or mental." Researchers have found that the amygdala plays a role in many emotions, including hate, fear, joy, and love, and "serves as an emotional and behavioral trip wire, capable of automatically triggering a response before we consciously realize what is happening."[138] The amygdala is interconnected with another area of the brain associated with aggression and defence: the hypothalamus. This is a small, bean-sized organ that regulates many of the body's automatic, stereotyped responses to external stimuli. When the amygdala senses danger, the hypothalamus activates the pituitary gland lying just below it; the pituitary releases an emergency hormone into the bloodstream that flows to the adrenal glands, prompting the latter to release stress hormones that galvanize the body for action—be it fight or flight.[139] The limbic system is very important in our analysis of the psychological—or psychobiological—makeup of the JI inductee. Rush W. Dozier, Jr., tells us why:

> Our limbic system has evolved a powerful tendency to blindly interpret any *meaning system* [emphasis added] that we deeply believe in as substantially enhancing our survival and reproduction. Someone who wholeheartedly converts to a particular religion or political ideology, for example, is likely to experience strong primal feelings of joy and well-being coupled with an exciting new sense of purpose. This is true even if the belief system has elements that are bizarre or self-destructive.[140]

Dozier rightly points out that this tendency of the primitive limbic system to identify particular meaning systems as congruent with personal well-being and survival can result in individuals "decoupling" their behavior from "objective criteria of survival and reproduction."[141] This insight sheds some light, for instance, on the inner motivations of the radical Islamist suicide terrorists who perpetrated the September 11 attacks.

This brings us back to the attraction of religious fundamentalism—with its dualistic, black-and-white certitudes—for concrete/objective people. The individual in a rapidly globalizing non-Western sociocultural milieu, who seeks cognitive closure in the midst of moral and spiritual uncertainty, would to a large extent be "limbically" hard-wired to want certainty and closure. He *needs* it. And as suggested above, once he thinks he has found the ideological security he seeks in a particular fundamentalist religious system, he is likely to defend his new beliefs with "great emotional intensity."[142] Any threat to his belief system may even provoke aggression.[143] In this respect scholars like J. Harold Ellens regard fundamentalism less as a system of beliefs than a highly problematic *state of mind*. He feels that fundamentalist mindsets can be found not just within religious systems, but even "political movements, ethical systems, scientific perspectives, and every type of profession in which humans engage."[144] In this regard, one should be wary of the notion that very well-educated people cannot be religious fundamentalists—or ultimately terrorists. Daniel Pipes notes that many Islamists have "advanced education" while a "disproportionate number of terrorists and suicide bombers" possess a "higher education, often in engineering and the sciences."[145] Some JI members are similarly well-educated in technical fields.

Indonesian Agus Dwikarna, who had leadership roles in MMI and DDII and associations with JI, is a civil engineer by training.[146] Malaysian JI operative Shamsul Bahri Hussein studies applied mechanics at Dundee.[147] One should not forget the late Malaysian Dr. Azahari Husin, the top JI bomb-maker who wrote the organization's bomb manual and was involved in the Bali, Jakarta Marriott, and now Jakarta Australian embassy bombings. Husin studied in Adelaide for four years in the 1970s, secured an engineering degree in Malaysia, and later received a PhD in statistical modeling from Reading University in the 1980s. He taught at Universiti Teknologi Malaysia (UTM) before going underground in 2001.[148]

Why do well-educated individuals like Azahari Husin—who have lived and studied to the highest levels in the West—go down the religious extremist path? Moojan Momen argues that the answer lies in the individual's overwhelming desire for "certainty." The concrete/objective/fundamentalist individual tolerates "no ambiguities, no equivocations, no reservations, and no criticism."[149] Ambiguity is "deeply unsatisfactory to the fundamentalist psyche."[150] Momen in fact suggests, perhaps counterintuitively, that "when scientists (especially from the physical sciences) and engineers become religious, they often tend towards fundamentalist religion."[151] This is not without basis. Psychological research, for example, has shown that natural or physical scientists in fact tend to be *more* religious than social scientists (such as sociologists and psychologists). This is because of the so-called "scholarly distance" thesis:

> The reason, in psychological terms, is that the natural sciences apply critical thinking to nature; the human sciences ask critical questions about culture, tradition and beliefs. The mere fact of choosing human society or behavior as the object of study reflects a curiosity about basic social beliefs and conventions and a readiness to reject them. Physical scientists, who are at a greater scholarly distance, may be able to compartmentalize their science and religion more easily.[152]

It is possible that the scholarly distance thesis explains the high proportion of Islamist activists worldwide with backgrounds in the hard sciences and engineering. For example, on university campuses in Iran and Egypt, such activists constitute "25 percent of humanities students, but 60–80% of students in medicine, engineering and science."[153] Islamic scholar Khalid Duran has commented on the "odd" fact that "Islamic fundamentalism" has always had "its strongest appeal among engineers." He observes that in Egypt "they always say the Muslim Brotherhood is really the Engineering Brotherhood."[154] Duran offers his personal explanation for this phenomenon:

> Engineers don't exercise their fantasy and imagination. Everything is precise and mathematical. They don't study what we call 'the humanities.' Conse-

quently, when it comes to issues that involve religion and personal emotion, they tend to see things in very stark terms.[155]

This leads the certainty-seeking Islamist scientist/engineer to engage in what Malise Ruthven calls "monodimensional or literalist readings of scripture," as compared to their "counterparts in the arts and humanities whose training requires them to approach texts multidimensionally, exploring contradictions and ambiguities."[156] Hence Duran, echoing the logic of the scholarly distance hypothesis, believes "having an education in literature or politics or sociology seems to inoculate you against the appeals of fundamentalism."[157] Ultimately, psychologists like J. Harold Ellens consider fundamentalism a form of "psychopathology":

> An essential component of this psychology is a rigid structuralist approach that has an obsessive-compulsive flavor to it. It is the mark of those who have a very limited ability to live with the ambiguity inherent to healthy human life. . . . Fundamentalism is a psychopathology that drives its proponents to the construction of orthodoxies.[158]

Further, critical theorist Stuart Sim, while similarly decrying the "fundamentalist mentality," goes a step further to suggest that not only do fundamentalists seek the "desire for certainty," but they equally seek "the power to enforce that certainty over others."[159] This is what makes the religious fundamentalist, for instance, ultimately a potentially troubling entity: he is not naturally inclined to live and let live in matters of faith. Sim rightly explains that "religious fundamentalism seems to be more to do with power than spiritual matters," and "power is a political rather than a spiritual issue." In essence, the fundamentalist mantra is about "control, control, control."[160] In this respect, political scientist R. Hrair Dekmejian captures aspects of Sim's argument in his description of the "*mutaasib*, or Muslim fundamentalist fanatic," for example, as characterized by "rigid beliefs, intolerance toward unbelievers, preoccupation with power," and a "vision of an evil world."[161] Because such a "close-minded, rigid-thinking dogmatist" is "susceptible to a variety of rigid, and potentially destructive, ideologies"[162] such as Qaedaism, the *potential* for him to participate in violent activities against the hate-object—as the example of Azahari Husin attests—is very real.

Organizational Knowledge and the Dimension of Ingroup Space

The upshot of the preceding discussion is that wider sociocultural pockets of prejudice in Indonesia and the region—especially the particular *usroh* communities linked to Sungkar and Bashir—may throw up a number of individuals whose relatively rigid, dogmatic mindsets may render them vulnerable to Qaedaism. This may compel them to transit from bigots into "limbic," obsessed haters of Westerners. This may in turn prompt some of them to seek entry into the actual JI organization. However, even within a small community of haters, there can be degrees of antipathy. Hence there "will be those who can torture and kill and those who can only passively approve of such actions."[163] For instance, within the Singapore JI cell, not all members were willing to engage in suicide or "martyrdom" operations against U.S. interests.[164] Hence a relatively hate-dominated affective state may help explain why an Islamist from the wider sea of Al-Mukmin alumni, for instance, may decide to join a terrorist outfit like JI; but it does not necessarily explain how that individual can be psychologically prepared to engage in activities designed to *physically obliterate* the hate-object. As many scholars have noted, an additional set of psychic forces, operating within a small group framework, generates the psychological capacity to kill.

To begin with, the element of *frustration* provides the impetus for actual participation in terrorist acts resulting in loss of life. Gaylin explains how frustration is the missing link between objective societal conditions and subjective states of mind:

> Feeling deprived bears no relationship to the actual amount of comfort or goods that a person may possess. One can be surrounded with all the indulgences of the affluent society and still feel deprived. Contrary to this, we can observe people existing in great poverty, where each expenditure must be measured and considered, every nutrient stored and rationed, who still do not feel deprived.[165]

Gaylin argues that "a sense of deprivation thrives on differentials: when others have what we do not." In other words, it is a "relative feeling, more closely associated with entitlement than want."[166] In a similar vein, Kressel argues "the *perception* of injustice is not the same as *actual* injustice."[167] Focusing on "relative deprivation," he notes that individuals are "especially likely to feel frustrated" if they have or receive less than what other people similar to themselves receive.[168] Relative deprivation can be explained systematically with reference to what the French scholar Rene Girard calls *mimetic desire*. Girard suggests that human beings "desire things because others have them."[169] In his view, humans have both the innate capacity to learn their desires from others and the concomitant drive to possess what those others possess. This socially learned desire and the drive to possess the object of that desire together constitute mimetic desire. In short, humans desire "objects"—which may be material, like wealth, or metaphysical, like social status or power—because "their possession by others gives them value in our eyes."[170] The point is that when circumstances arise where socially desired objects are for some reason out of reach of certain individuals or constituencies, mimetic desire may precipitate *frustrations* that may ultimately give rise to conflict.[171]

Mimetic desire presupposes the existence of strong ingroup identity and bias. When one scans the backgrounds of members of the actual JI terrorist organization, one is immediately struck by the fact that many of them had backgrounds in which religion played the dominating role in *identity formation*. This is significant, as psychological research shows that religiosity tends to generate ethnocentric, prejudiced, discriminatory attitudes.[172] In other words, religiosity tends to privilege the ingroup at the expense of the outgroup. Mukhlas, a key operational JI leader, for instance, grew up in Tenggulun village, in Lamongan, East Java, a "very religious region of Indonesia,"[173] and was deeply immersed in an Islamic medium of education throughout. He studied at Al-Mukmin and Universitas Islam Surakarta, and trained as a religious teacher at Payaman in Solokuru in East Java.[174] For his part, the fiery Bali bomb field coordinator Imam Samudra, as noted earlier, came from a family with long-term Persis connections, and attended a "religiously conservative high school" in Serang in Banten province in West Java. Like Mukhlas, he was deeply immersed in an Islamic medium of education, and spent time in Quran reading sessions under DDII auspices, gradually imbibing a deeply anti-Christian worldview.[175] Serang is another "very religious region of Indonesia," where DI had been active.[176]

Afghanistan appears to have played important roles in further narrowing the perspectives of both men. Samudra was in Afghanistan from 1991 to 1993, and received training in the handling of assault rifles and bomb construction in al Qaeda camps,[177] while Mukhlas was there from 1986 to 1989 and claimed to have met Osama bin Laden during the Soviet assault on Joji in 1987. He recalled that he had fought with the mujahideen "from all over the world" against the vociferous Soviet attack.[178] In short, the sum total of the experiences of Mukhlas and Samudra endowed them with a religiously legitimated ethnocentric bigotry that was to ultimately have horrifying consequences. Hence, while Mukhlas had "harbored a virulent hatred of nonbelievers in general, and Westerners in particular since childhood,"[179] Samudra, according to a senior Bali police official, "simply [hated] Americans."[180] Strongly underlying the hatred of both men was *mimetic frustration*. In essence, Qaedaists in Southeast Asia and beyond are merely the most extreme manifestation of the long-running Islamic modernist desire to recapture the power and status that the West has enjoyed for several centuries. It is the "huge contrast between medieval success" and the "more recent tribulations"[181] of Islamic civilization that is the source of frustration for modernists and the corollary sentiment of rage among Qaedaists. In the final analysis, JI's leaders and members want above all else to enhance the *dignity* of their ingroup—that is, Islamic civilization.

There are sound social psychological reasons for this. Individuals define themselves partly by their group membership. Membership of a high-prestige group meets basic psychological needs such as "belongingness, distinctiveness," and "respect."[182] Jerrold Post suggests that many terrorists have deep "affiliative needs" and an "as-yet incomplete sense of individual identity" that generates an intense need to belong. As noted earlier in this discussion, many concrete/objective individuals struggling with the radical choices imposed by modernity would fit into this category. This causes them to defensively "submerge their own identities into the group," so that a kind of "group mind" emerges.[183] What happens is that during intergroup contestation and conflict, group identity becomes more salient than individual identity; concern with ingroup welfare replaces individual concerns; there is a heightened sense of shared grievances; and importantly, ingroups tend to become aggressive behaviorally and engage in outgroup stereotyping.[184] That is, "an attack or affront is personal when directed not only against one's physical self," but against the wider ingroup, or one's "collective self."[185] The salience of the "collective" or "group" self, and by extension what Marilynn Brewer terms "ingroup love," comes out clearly in the case of the Singapore JI members, many of whom suffered from assorted esteem problems and required assimilation into a wider group mind to ameliorate their intrapsychic tensions. Consequently, those inducted into the Singapore JI

> enjoyed a sense of exclusivity and commitment in being in the in-group of a clandestine organization. Secrecy, including secrecy over the true knowledge of jihad, helped create a sense of sharing and empowerment vis-à-vis outsiders. Esoteric JI language or "JI-speak" was used as part of the indoctrination process. Code names, for instance, resulted in a strong sense of "ingroup" superiority, especially since JI members were said to be closer to Allah as they believed in the truth (JI doctrine); even Muslims who did not subscribe to militant jihad were seen as infidels.[186]

The key question, however, is how does "ingroup love" become "outgroup hate"?[187] Precisely because the collective self is so important to the psychic well-being of its members, any serious threat to the former—whether physical or metaphysical, involving power/honor—is likely to generate a "limbic," primal reaction, comprising "hasty generalizations, stereotyping, us-them distinctions, and raw emotions—particularly anger and hate."[188] Hence, if ingroup members, despite their assumed innate moral superiority, perceive that it is the outgroup that enjoys greater power and status resources—and worse, is "holding back" ingroup progress through nefarious means—mimetic frustration culminating in outgroup hatred, possibly murderous hatred, could result. In the specific case of JI, which is heavily shaped cognitively by Qaedaist fantasy war constructs, "ingroup members' perceptions of outgroups and relevant external events" are "distorted, causing them to view the outgroup as an enemy."[189] The intersection between Qaedaist cognitive structures and limbic outgroup hatred can have deadly outcomes. This is illustrated in Imam Samudra's emotionally charged justification for the Bali terrorist atrocity:

> To oppose the barbarity of the U.S. army of the Cross and its allies . . . to take revenge for the pain of . . . weak men, women and babies who died without sin when thousands of tonnes of bombs were dropped in Afghanistan in September 2001 [sic] . . . during Ramadan. . . . To carry out a [sic] my responsibility to wage a global jihad against Jews and Christians throughout the world. . . . As a manifestation of Islamic solidarity between Moslems, not limited by geographic boundaries. To carry out Allah's order in the Book of An-nisa, verses 74–76, which concerns the obligation to defend weak men, weak women, and innocent babies, who are always the targets of the barbarous actions of the American terrorists and their allies. . . . So that the American terrorists and their allies understand that the blood of Moslems is expensive and valuable; and cannot be—is forbidden to be—toyed with and made a target of American terrorists and their allies. So that the [American and allied] terrorists understand how painful it is to lose a [sic] mothers, husbands, children, or other family members, which is what they have so arbitrarily inflicted on Moslems throughout the world. To prove to Allah—the Almighty and most deserving of praise—that we will do whatever we can to defend weak Moslems, and to wage war against the U.S. imperialists and their allies.[190]

According to Olufemi Lawal, a full-blown terrorist "attitude" that expedites the physical destruction of the hate-object, over and above the necessary cognitive structures and affective states, must include the requisite *behavior* involving direct killing.[191] Behavior here would include activity directly related to the actual terrorist operation. This would involve direct physical participation in a terrorist attack, such as shooting, bomb placement and detonation, and of course a suicide attack. *Deliberate ingroup isolation* is thus very important in helping to shape such behavior. Jonathan Drummond argues that deliberately self-isolating communities place huge reliance on "alternative news sources," "home schooling," and "closed religious/ritual systems." These may "pull one away from competing social networks and constructions of reality."[192] In this regard, it is worth noting that in January 2004, Al-Mukmin students were warned not to talk to strangers and were punished if they did.[193] In addition, following the August 2003 J. W. Marriott attack in Jakarta, a radical pamphlet entitled "Marriott Conspiracy Theory"—that blamed "Israeli and U.S. intelligence agents" for the incident—was readily accessible to Al-Mukmin students.[194] The Singapore White Paper notes that JI as an organization deliberately policed its boundaries:

> After their induction into JI, members stayed away from mainstream religious activities and kept to themselves. Keeping together as a closely-knit

group reinforced the ideological purity of the group and kept them loyal to the teachings of their foreign teachers.[195]

Similarly, JI training facilities in Mindanao in the southern Philippines—first Camp Hudaibiyah within the MILF's Abubakar complex, and, since 2001, Camp Jabal Quba on Mount Kararao—have been extremely remote localities. These have not only facilitated extensive training courses in weapons and explosives, but more importantly, they have facilitated ideological programming of new batches of young Indonesians and other Southeast Asians designed to deepen their motivation for *jihad*.[196] The "ingroup," it should be added, does not refer solely to a physical agglomeration of individuals in a particular geographical locality. "Virtual relations can monopolize one's attentions and give rise to cohesive, socially isolated groups populated by geographically dispersed individuals."[197] Mark Juergensmeyer has termed such virtual communities "e-mail ethnicities," where "transnational networks of people are tied together culturally," through the Internet, "despite the diversity of their places of residence and the limitations of national borders."[198] The basic point is that precisely because of its deliberate isolation—virtual and/or physical—from mainstream society, JI is "free to follow abstract and apocalyptic notions of a global war between good and evil."[199]

Ideological induction aside, deliberate ingroup isolation also expedites the amplification and focusing of the mimetic frustrations and humiliation of selected ingroup members at the vast power and status imbalance of the hated outgroup. "Humiliation and envy," Diane Perlman informs us, "go together," and are "exceedingly destructive emotions."[200] She explains:

> Being humiliated is like being filled with poison that has to be expelled in order to regain composure. Humiliation carries a narcissistic wound that contains an implicit demand for rectification, often by taking down the humiliator.[201]

Juergensmeyer adds that what is crucial is the "intimacy with which the humiliation is experienced."[202] Following Perlman's analysis, we may argue that the "intolerable affects" of individuals humiliated by the outgroup are evacuated or "projected" onto the outgroup itself—"the powerful, the envied, the humiliators, the privileged ones."[203] In a very real sense, therefore, when "there seems to be no way out, terrorism is a way of transforming victimhood to mastery."[204] Juergensmeyer calls this dynamic "symbolic empowerment." As Samudra's impassioned justification for the Bali attack suggests, terrorists want to *force* the outgroup to taste—however momentarily—their powerlessness, their despair, their dark "habitus." Terrorists will not permit the powerful outgroup to ignore them.[205] In this regard, psychoanalyst W.R.D. Fairbairn observed that "people would rather be bad than weak."[206] This is not to say, however, that killing comes automatically, even when people feel the overwhelming urge to be bad rather than weak. Social psychologist Albert Bandura has argued that humans in all societies are socialized into accepting socially mandated "self sanctions" that regulate their behavior. Bandura points out that "to slaughter in cold blood innocent women and children in buses, department stores, and in airports" requires "intensive psychological training" in the "moral disengagement" of these self-sanctions. This is the only way to "create the capacity to kill innocent human beings."[207]

According to Bandura, one powerful way to relax self-sanctions is by "cognitively restructuring the moral value of killing, so that the killing can be done free from self-censuring restraints."[208] JI leaders, as we have seen, cognitively reconstrue their attacks on Western targets as part of a fully justified and legitimate defensive *jihad*. Some Singapore JI members, for example, who took part in Muslim-Christian fighting in Ambon in the Maluku archipelago in eastern Indonesia, regarded their activities as justified, as they saw themselves as defenders of fellow Ambonese Muslims from being killed by Christians. The recent attack on the Australian embassy in Jakarta, furthermore, was presented as an attempt to compel the Australian "crusaders" to leave Iraq. A second mechanism for disengaging the inner restraints against killing is what Bandura calls "euphemistic labeling," which "provides a convenient device for masking reprehensible activities or even conferring a respectable status on them."[209] We have seen how JI, like violent Islamist groups elsewhere, has exploited the term *"jihad,"* which has a very respectable pedigree in Islamic history, to justify bomb attacks on civilians. In addition, Sungkar justified criminal activity on the part of his followers by recasting it as *fa'i*, that is, "robbing the infidels or enemies of Islam to secure funds for defending the faith."[210] Third, Bandura argues that "people behave in injurious ways they normally repudiate if a legitimate authority accepts responsibility for the consequences of their conduct."[211] In this respect, several Malaysian and Singaporean JI terrorists have mentioned Osama bin Laden's February 1998 fatwa declaring *jihad* on the Jewish-Crusader alliance as justification for their own terror activities, while it is clear from interrogation reports that JI terrorists took special care to seek spiritual sanction for key operations from JI *amir* Bashir. Finally, Bandura observes that self-sanctions against "cruel conduct can be disengaged or blunted by divesting people of human qualities." In a very important passage, he notes:

> Once dehumanized, the potential victims are no longer viewed as persons with feelings, hopes, and concerns but as subhuman objects. They are portrayed as mindless 'savages', 'gooks' . . . and the like. Subhumans are regarded as insensitive to maltreatment and capable of being influenced only by harsh methods.[212]

In this respect Amrozi, brother of Mukhlas and another convicted Bali bomber, evinced his utter lack of empathy for the humanity of his victims when he shrugged off the suggestion that they had killed Australians instead of Americans by quipping, "Australians, Americans, whatever—they are all white people."[213] If it was bad enough that Amrozi could not see beyond the vacuous abstraction of "white people," Mukhlas himself declared that all Westerners were "dirty animals and insects that need to be wiped out."[214]

This brings us to the final element that marks the transition of the JI hater into the JI killer: in tandem with the moral disengagement mechanisms described above, which can be considered as part of the cognitive underpinnings of the killing mindset, the existing hate obsession of the JI terrorist must be amplified several fold to ensure that he is in a *limbic state*. This is why JI leaders have relied heavily on atrocity propaganda in the form of home-made video CD-ROM discs (VCDs). The Maluku conflict of 1999–2000 in particular provided much raw material for JI leaders, who made VCDs and distributed them across Southeast Asia, from Indonesia to the southern Philippines. These were shown during informal teaching sessions by JI clerics, and the "eager young men in attendance, duly incensed by what they had witnessed, were then briefed on how they could join the jihad."[215] Of particular importance, JI leaders made sure that just before an actual terrorist operation, selected operatives were given the proper "limbic conditioning." One Singaporean JI operative for instance decided to carry out the December 2000 bombing of a Batam church after then-JI operational leader Hambali showed his group a video of Christians killing Muslims in Ambon. Singapore JI leaders routinely employed fiery speeches to elicit an emotional, limbic response from members before requiring them to fill out surveys indicating what kinds of terrorist activities they wished to be involved in. "Having signed their names on the survey, members were not able to alter their decisions later on."[216]

It would seem that the intense ingroup processes of cognitive restructuring and limbic conditioning are also pertinent in the case of suicide bombers. In addition, in the special case of the self-proclaimed *shahid*, an additional element of "entrancement" is probably necessary. According to Don J. Feeney, Jr., entrancement is akin to an altered state of consciousness. In this state the subject, who would normally be an extreme example of an "impressionable" personality seeking absolute ideological security in some leader or ingroup, suspends his critical faculties, loses touch with reality somewhat, and cedes volitional control to some idealized authority figure.[217] For instance, according to one source, Asmar Lanti Sani, the Marriott suicide bomber, was convinced to become a *shahid* (martyr) through his close interactions with JI leader Azahari Husin.[218]

CONCLUSION

Organizational rejuvenation within Jemaah Islamiyah is clearly a complex, multifaceted phenomenon. Drawing on extensive research from many disciplines, this chapter has attempted to illuminate the complex processes by which ordinary young Muslims in Southeast Asia become indoctrinated and well-trained JI terrorists, capable of killing in cold blood. This analysis reveals a variety of ideological, political, social, religious, and psychological aspects of knowledge formation that motivate and facilitate terrorism. While the ideology of Qaedaism is important, it is by no means the only factor influencing the transformation process. Sociocultural pockets of prejudice shaped by history and politics, individual psychologies, and intense ingroup cognitive restructuring and limbic conditioning processes all play their part as well. As the latest JI terrorist outrage in Jakarta illustrates, the threat from this organization has yet to abate despite counterterrorist successes. Significantly, the evidence indicates that losses are being replenished by fresh recruitment. This is important because this means that the JI network is self-regenerating and therefore enduring. This chapter has shown that ultimately, the true root of the JI phenomenon is not poverty but rather the very old one of the mimetic frustrations of the Islamic modernists. Some ideological permutations of Islamic modernism in Southeast Asia have been, like Muhammadiyah today, constructive. Others, like Darul Islam and today's JI, have not. Clearly, while improving law enforcement, military, intelligence, and judicial measures domestically and internationally is important for dealing with the real-time threat of JI, they are powerless to prevent JI from gradually becoming a self-regenerating, existential threat.

What is needed is fresh thinking on a whole range of issues that are not amenable to "hard," military/law enforcement solutions. While programs designed to improve regional state capacities to deal with the real-time threat of terrorism and ameliorate poverty and unemployment should continue to be pursued by regional governments with the assistance of the international community, this chapter suggests that other problems are in need of closer analysis and engagement: the cross-cutting, historically enduring communities of prejudice from which JI terrorists ultimately emerge; ostensibly nonviolent leaders who nonetheless preach polarized, absolutist ideologies that nudge concrete/objective and impressionable individuals along the continuum toward hate obsession and potential terrorist recruitment; certain educational environments that deliberately limit contact with the outside world and appear to construct alternate perceptions of reality; a wider systemic lack of training in critical, creative, multidimensional thinking; and ultimately, the continuing inability of either liberal Muslims or Islamic modernists to design and propagate modern interpretations of the faith that trump the simplistic, us-versus-them radical worldviews in the estimation of the Muslim ground. What is especially important is more systematic control group studies of the Al Mukmin and associated alumni, based perhaps on the model of the West German interior ministry study of the Red Army Faction in the late 1970s, to determine why some alumni proceeded down the JI path.[219] Finally it is not fully appreciated that in an era of globalization, what the U.S. does or does not do in the wider Muslim world can be selectively filtered through Qaedaist ideology and strengthen JI. More than ever, therefore, a greater degree of strategic creativity is required in the war on terror in Southeast Asia.[220]

NOTES

1. Some portions of this discussion have appeared in the following publication: Kumar Ramakrishna, "Indoctrination Processes Within Jemaah Islamiyah," in *The Making of a Terrorist: Recruitment, Training and Root Causes*, ed. James JF Forest (Westport, CT: Praeger, 2005).

2. Singapore Ministry of Home Affairs, *White Paper: The Jemaah Islamiyah Arrests and the Threat of Terrorism* (Singapore: Ministry of Home Affairs, 7 January 2003), 3–4. Hereafter "Singapore WP."

3. Singapore WP, 13.

4. Matthew Moore, "Jakarta Fears JI Has Suicide Brigade," *Age* (Australia), 12 August 2003.

5. "Marriott Blast Suspects Named," *CNN.com*, 19 August 2003, www.cnn.com/2003/WORLD/asiapcf/southeast/08/19/indonesia.arrests.names/ (accessed 11 September 2004).

6. Derwin Pereira, "Jakarta Blast Kills 9, Injures 180," *Straits Times* (Singapore), 10 September 2004. See also Pereira, "Attack Has Imprint of JI's Azahari," *Straits Times* (Singapore), 10 September 2004. Subsequent reports state that eleven people, including the suicide bomber, were killed. See "Militant Jailed for Jakarta Bomb," *BBC News*, 22 September 2005, http://news.bbc.co.uk/2/hi/asia-pacific/4270974.stm (accessed 13 February 2006).

7. Pereira, "Attack Has Imprint of JI's Azahari."

8. Kumar Ramakrishna and See Seng Tan, "Is Southeast Asia a 'Terrorist Haven?'" in *After Bali: The Threat of Terrorism in Southeast Asia*, ed. Kumar Ramakrishna and See Seng Tan (Singapore: World Scientific/Institute of Defence and Strategic Studies, 2003), 1–2.

9. Jerrold M. Post, "Terrorist Psycho-Logic: Terrorist Behavior as a Product of Psychological Forces," in *Origins of Terrorism: Psychologies, Ideologies, Theologies, States of Mind*, ed. by Walter Reich (Washington, DC: Woodrow Wilson Center Press, 1998), 39–40.

10. Azyumardi Azra, "The Megawati Presidency: Challenge of Political Islam," paper delivered at the "Joint Public Forum on Indonesia: The First 100 Days of President Megawati," organized by the Institute of Southeast Asian Studies (Singapore) and the Centre for Strategic and International Studies (Jakarta), 1 November 2001, Singapore.

11. Azyumardi Azra, "Bali and Southeast Asian Islam: Debunking the Myths," in Ramakrishna and Tan, eds., *After Bali*, 46–47.

12. Barry Desker, "Countering Terrorism: Why the 'War on Terror' Is Unending," unpublished paper, September 2004.

13. Peter Symonds, "The Political Origins and Outlook of Jemaah Islamiyah," *World Socialist Website*, Part 2, 13 November 2003, www.wsws.org/articles/2003/nov2003/ji2-n13_prn.shtml (accessed 20 August 2004).

14. Azra, "Bali and Southeast Asian Islam," in Ramakrishna and Tan, eds., *After Bali*, 43.

15. Desker, "Countering Terrorism."

16. Desker, "Countering Terrorism."

17. Azra, "Bali and Southeast Asian Islam," in Ramakrishna and Tan, eds., *After Bali*, 43; Martin van Bruinessen, "'Traditionalist' and 'Islamist' pesantren in contemporary Indonesia,' paper presented at the ISIM workshop on "The Madrasa in Asia," 23–24 May 2004.

18. *Laksamana.Net*, "Rais Wins More Support," 8 June 2004, www.laksamana.net/vnews .cfm?ncat=2&news_id=7123 (accessed 12 Aug 2004)

19. Symonds, "Political Origins."

20. *Laksamana.Net*, "Rais Wins More Support."

21. The Jakarta Charter refers to a draft constitutional preamble that stipulates that Muslim Indonesians are obligated to abide by the strictures of the *shariah* law. Martin van Bruinessen, "Indonesia's Ulama and Politics: Caught Between Legitimizing the Status Quo and Searching for Alternatives," *Prisma—The Indonesian Indicator* (Jakarta), No. 49 (1990): 52–69.

22. *Laksamana.Net*, "Rais Wins More Support."

23. van Bruinessen, "Indonesia's Ulama and Politics."

24. Greg Fealy, "Islamic Radicalism in Indonesia: The Faltering Revival?" *Southeast Asian Affairs 2004* (Singapore: Institute of Southeast Asian Studies, 2004), 111.

25. Bilveer Singh, "The Emergence of the Jemaah Islamiyah Threat in Southeast Asia: External Linkages and Influences," paper presented at a workshop on "International Terrorism in Southeast Asia and Likely Implications for South Asia," organized by the Observer Research Foundation, New Delhi, India, 28–29 April 2004.

26. Fealy, "Islamic Radicalism," 111.

27. Symonds, "Political Origins."

28. Bilveer Singh, "Emergence."

29. Tim Behrend, "Reading Past the Myth: Public Teachings of Abu Bakara Ba'asyir," 19 February 2003, www.arts.auckland.ac.nz/asia/tbehrend/abb-myth.htm (accessed 30 April 2004).

30. Blontank Poer, "Tracking the Roots of Jamaah Islamiyah," *Jakarta Post*, 8 March 2003.

31. Sidney Jones, "Jemaah Islamiyah: A Short Description," *Jurnal Kultur* (Kulture Journal) 3, no. 1 (1 June 2003). Online at www.pbb-iainjakarta.or.id/kultur/?Berita =052403035304&Kategori=16&Edisi=9. Also, see Sidney Jones, "Facing the Enemy Within," *Times Asia* (13 October 2003).

32. Martin van Bruinessen, "The Violent Fringes of Indonesia's Radical Islam," www .let.uu.nl/~martin.vanbruinessen/personal/publications/violent_fringe.htm (accessed 29 July 2004).

33. Poer, "Tracking the Roots."

34. van Bruinessen, "Violent Fringes of Indonesia's Radical Islam."

35. Bilveer Singh, "Emergence."

36. van Bruinessen, "Violent Fringes of Indonesia's Radical Islam."

37. Bilveer Singh, "Emergence."

38. *Tempo*, "Abu Bakar Bashir: The Malaysian Connection," 9 November 2002.

39. *Tempo*, "Abu Bakar Bashir."

40. Barbara D. Metcalf, "Traditionalist Islamic Activism: Deoband, Tablighis, and Talibs." Essay based on the Institute for the Study of Islam in the Modern World (ISIM) Annual Lecture, Leiden University, 23 November 2001.

41. Daniel Pipes, *Militant Islam Reaches America* (New York and London: W. W. Norton, 2003), 8.

42. Pipes, *Militant Islam*, 8.

43. Metcalf, "Traditionalist Islamic Activism."

44. Pipes, *Militant Islam*, 8.

45. Pipes, *Militant Islam*, 8–9.

46. Behrend, "Reading Past the Myth."

47. Poer, "Tracking the Roots."

48. John L. Esposito, *Unholy War: Terror in the Name of Islam* (New York: Oxford, 2002), 56.

49. Azra, "Bali and Southeast Asian Islam," in Ramakrishna and Tan, eds., *After Bali*, 44.

50. Esposito, *Unholy War*, 53.

51. Qutb cited in Esposito, *Unholy War*, 60.

52. This section draws on Behrend, "Reading Past the Myth," and Esposito, *Unholy War*, 52–53.

53. Charles Selengut, *Sacred Fury: Understanding Religious Violence* (Walnut Creek, CA: AltaMira Press, 2003), 80.

54. Marc Sageman, *Understanding Terror Networks* (Philadelphia: University of Pennsylvania Press, 2004), 16.

55. Esposito, *Unholy War*, 62.

56. Mark Juergensmeyer, *Terror in the Mind of God: The Global Rise of Religious Violence*, updated edition, with a new preface (Berkeley and Los Angeles: University of California Press, 2000), 81.

57. Juergensmeyer, *Terror in the Mind of God*, 81.

58. Juergensmeyer, *Terror in the Mind of God*, 81.

59. Sageman, *Understanding Terror Networks*, 16.

60. Van Bruinessen, "Violent Fringes of Indonesia's Radical Islam."

61. Poer, "Tracking the Roots."

62. Sageman, *Understanding Terror Networks*, 17.

63. Azzam cited in Malise Ruthven, *A Fury for God: The Islamist Attack on America* (London and New York: Granta, 2002), 203.

64. Sageman, *Understanding Terror Networks*, 18.

65. Sageman, *Understanding Terror Networks*, 18.

66. Sageman, *Understanding Terror Networks*, 18.

67. Poer, "Tracking the Roots."

68. Behrend, "Reading Past the Myth."

69. Poer, "Tracking the Roots."

70. Poer, "Tracking the Roots."

71. Fealy, "Islamic Radicalism," 112.

72. Bilveer Singh, "Emergence."

73. Fealy, "Islamic Radicalism," 112.

74. "Statement of the Jama'ah al-Islamia in East Asia on Jakarta blast." Translated on 9 September 2004 by the International Centre for Political Violence and Terrorism Research, Institute of Defence and Strategic Studies, Nanyang Technological University, Singapore.

75. Jason Burke in *Foreign Policy*, (May/June) 2004. This discussion will henceforth refer to Global Salafi Jihad ideology as Qaedaism for short.

76. Olufemi A. Lawal, "Social-Psychological Considerations in the Emergence and Growth of Terrorism," in *The Psychology of Terrorism*, vol. 4, *Programs and Practices in Response and Prevention*, ed. Chris E. Stout (London and Westport, CT: Praeger, 2002), 26–27.

77. Lawal, "Social-Psychological Considerations," 27.

78. Lawal, "Social-Psychological Considerations."

79. Lawal, "Social-Psychological Considerations."

80. Lawal, "Social-Psychological Considerations."

81. Lawal, "Social-Psychological Considerations, 29–30.

82. Desker, "Countering Terrorism."

83. Desker, "Countering Terrorism."

84. "Militant Islam in Indonesia," *Sydney Morning Herald*, 25 September 2003.

85. Patricia A. Martinez, "Deconstructing Jihad: Southeast Asian Contexts," in Ramakrishna and Tan, eds., *After Bali*, 73–74.

86. Patricia A. Martinez, "Deconstructing Jihad: Southeast Asian Contexts," in Ramakrishna and Tan, eds., *After Bali*, 73–74.

87. Tim Behrend, "Meeting Abubakar Ba'asyir," 23 December 2002, www.arts .auckland.ac.nz/asia/tbehrend/meet-abb.htm (accessed 2003).

88. *Laksamana.Net*, "Rais wins more support."

89. A point made by Sidney Jones, Indonesia Project Director, International Crisis Group, at the International Seminar on Islamic Militant Movements in Southeast Asia, Jakarta, 22–23 July 2003.

90. Fealy, "Islamic Radicalism," 111–112.

91. Behrend, "Meeting Abubakar Ba'asyir"; Richard C. Paddock, "Terror Network's Academic Outposts," *Los Angeles Times*, 1 April 2003.

92. International Crisis Group (ICG), *Jemaah Islamiyah in Southeast Asia: Damaged But Still Dangerous*, ICG Asia Report No. 63 (Jakarta/Brussels: ICG, 26 August 2003), 26.

93. Wong Chun Wai and Lourdes Charles, "More than 100 Marriages Involve Key JI Members," *Star Online* (Malaysia), 7 September 2004, http://thestar.com.my/news/archives/story.asp?ppath=%5C2004%5C9% (accessed 11 September 2004).

94. *Jemaah Islamiyah in Southeast Asia*, 26–27.

95. Fealy, "Islamic Radicalism," 113.

96. *Jemaah Islamiyah in Southeast Asia*, 26.

97. For a discussion of *"dhimmitude,"* see Robert Spencer, *Onward Muslim Soldiers: How Jihad Still Threatens America and the West* (Washington, DC: Regnery, 2003), 7.

98. Behrend, "Reading Past the Myth."

99. Behrend, "Meeting Abubakar Ba'asyir."

100. Neil J. Kressel, *Mass Hate: The Global Rise of Genocide and Terror*, rev. and updated (New York: Westview, 2002), 211.

101. Kressel, *Mass Hate*.

102. J. Harold Ellens, "The Dynamics of Prejudice," in *The Destructive Power of Religion: Violence in Judaism, Christianity and Islam*, vol. 2, *Religion, Psychology and Violence*, ed. J. Harold Ellens (London and Westport, CT: Praeger, 2004), 96.

103. Willard Gaylin, *Hatred: The Psychological Descent into Violence* (New York: PublicAffairs, 2003), 24.

104. Gaylin, *Hatred*, 26.

105. Gaylin, *Hatred*, 26.

106. Gaylin, *Hatred*, 28.

107. Gaylin, *Hatred*, 28.

108. Cited in Clark McCauley, "Psychological Issues in Understanding Terrorism and the Response to Terrorism," in Stout, ed., *Psychology of Terrorism*, vol. 3, *Theoretical Understandings and Perspectives*, 7.

109. Gaylin, *Hatred*, 26–27.

110. Gaylin, *Hatred*, 27.

111. Anthony Paul, "Enduring the Other's Other," *Straits Times* (Singapore), 4 Dec. 2003.

112. Gaylin, *Hatred*, 245–46.

113. Gaylin, *Hatred*, 244.

114. Zalman Mohamed Yusof and Mohammad Ishak, "Inside a JI School," *New Paper on Sunday* (Singapore), 4 January 2004.

115. Yusof and Ishak, "Inside a JI School."

116. Yusof and Ishak, "Inside a JI School."

117. Yusof and Ishak, "Inside a JI School."

118. Yusof and Ishak, "Inside a JI School."

119. Timothy Mapes, "Indonesian School Gives High Marks to Students Embracing Intolerance," *Asian Wall Street Journal*, 2 September 2003.

120. Martha Crenshaw, "Questions to Be Answered, Research to Be Done, Knowledge to Be Applied," in Reich, ed., *Origins of Terrorism*, 247.

121. Walter Reich, "Understanding Terrorist Behavior: The Limits and Opportunities of Psychological Enquiry," in Reich, ed., *Origins of Terrorism*, 276.

122. Benjamin Beit-Hallahmi and Michael Argyle, *The Psychology of Religious Behavior, Belief and Experience* (London and New York: Routledge, 1997), 6.

123. Beit-Hallahmi and Argyle, *Psychology of Religious Behavior*, 12.

124. Beit-Hallahmi and Argyle, *Psychology of Religious Behavior*, 12.

125. Michael J. Stevens, "The Unanticipated Consequences of Globalization: Contextualizing Terrorism," in Stout, ed., *Psychology of Terrorism*, vol. 3, 37–38.

126. Stevens, "Unanticipated Consequences," 38.

127. Stevens, "Unanticipated Consequences," 39.

128. Selengut, *Sacred Fury*, 157–158.

129. Stevens, "Unanticipated Consequences," 40.

130. Selengut, *Sacred Fury*, 158.

131. Ronald Johnson, "Psychoreligious Roots of Violence: The Search for the Concrete in a World of Abstractions," in Ellens, ed., *Destructive Power of Religion*, vol. 4, *Contemporary Views on Spirituality and Violence*, 200–202.

132. Jessica Stern, *Terror in the Name of God: Why Religious Militants Kill* (New York: HarperCollins, 2003), 69.

133. Johnson, "Psychoreligious Roots," 207.

134. Beit-Hallahmi and Argyle, *Psychology of Religious Behavior*, 115.

135. Singapore WP, 17.

136. Singapore WP, 17.

137. Johnson, "Psychoreligious Roots of Violence," 195; J. Harold Ellens, "Fundamentalism, Orthodoxy, and Violence," in Ellens, ed., *Destructive Power of Religion*, vol. 4, 124.

138. Rush W. Dozier, Jr., *Why We Hate: Understanding, Curbing and Eliminating Hate in Ourselves and Our World* (New York: Contemporary Books, 2002), 6.

139. Dozier, *Why We Hate*, 5–8.

140. Dozier, *Why We Hate*, 11.

141. Dozier, *Why We Hate*, 12.

142. Ted G. Goertzel, "Terrorist Beliefs and Terrorist Lives," in Stout, ed., *Psychology of Terrorism*, vol. 1: *A Public Understanding*, 98.

143. Steve S. Olweean, "Psychological Concepts of the 'Other': Embracing the Compass of the Self," in Stout, ed., *Psychology of Terrorism*, vol. 1, 116.

144. Ellens, "Fundamentalism, Orthodoxy and Violence," 120.

145. Pipes, *Militant Islam*, 56.

146. "Indonesian Linked to Manila, Jakarta Bombings," *Laksamana.Net*, 6 July 2002, www.laksamana.net/vnews.cfm?ncat=22&news_id=3127 (accessed 11 September 2004).

147. Michael Day and David Bamber, "Universities Spy for MI5 on Foreign Students," *news.telegraph.co.uk*, 28 August 2004, www.telegraph.co.uk/news/main.jhtml?xml=/news/2004/03/21/nspy21.xml&sSheet=/news/2004/03/21/ixnewstop.html (accessed 11 September 2004).

148. "Azahari: Professor, Bomb-Maker and Fanatic," *Channelnewsasia.com* (Singapore), 10 September 2004, available at www.channelnewsasia.com/stories/afp_asiapacific/view/105933/1/.html (accessed 10 September 2004); Dan Murphy, "Leaderless, Terror Group Still Potent," *Christian Science Monitor*, 18 August 2003.

149. Moojan Momen, "Fundamentalism and Liberalism: Towards an Understanding of the Dichotomy," *Bahai Studies Review* 2, no. 1 (1992).

150. Momen, "Fundamentalism and Liberalism."

151. Momen, "Fundamentalism and Liberalism."

152. Beit-Hallahmi and Argyle, *Psychology of Religious Behavior*, 181.

153. Beit-Hallahmi and Argyle, *Psychology of Religious Behavior*, 182.

154. See Steven Emerson, *American Jihad: The Terrorists Living Among Us* (New York: The Free Press, 2002), 172.

155. Emerson, *American Jihad*, 173.

156. Ruthven, *Fury for God*, 103.

157. Emerson, *American Jihad*, 173.

158. Ellens, "Fundamentalism, Orthodoxy and Violence," in Ellens, ed., *Destructive Power of Religion*, vol. 4, 120.

159. Stuart Sim, *Fundamentalist World: The New Dark Age of Dogma* (Cambridge: Icon Books, 2004), 29.

160. Sim, *Fundamentalist World*, 100.

161. Cited in Kressel, *Mass Hate*, 199.

162. Kressel, *Mass Hate*, 199, 211.

163. Gaylin, *Hatred*, 26–27.

164. Singapore WP, 16.

165. Gaylin, *Hatred*, 46.

166. Gaylin, *Hatred*, 48.

167. Kressel, *Mass Hate*, 209.

168. Kressel, *Mass Hate*, 209.

169. Mack C. Stirling, "Violent Religion: Rene Girard's Theory of Culture," in Ellens, ed., *Destructive Power of Religion*, vol. 2, 12.

170. Stirling, "Violent Religion," 15.

171. Stirling, "Violent Religion," 17–18.

172. Beit-Hallahmi and Argyle, *Psychology of Religious Behavior*, 243.

173. John Dawson, "The Bali Bombers: What Motivates Death Worship?" *Capitalism Magazine*, 19 October 2003, www.capmag.com/article.asp?ID=3000 (accessed 1 September 2004).

174. Mukhlas Interrogation Report, 13 December 2002.

175. Dan Murphy, "How al Qaeda Lit the Bali Fuse: Part Three," *Christian Science Monitor*, 19 June 2003.

176. Dawson, "Bali Bombers."

177. Murphy, "How al Qaeda Lit the Bali Fuse: Part 3."

178. Mukhlas Interrogation Report.

179. Dawson, "Bali Bombers."

180. Murphy, "How al Qaeda Lit the Bali Fuse: Part 3."

181. Pipes, *Militant Islam*, 5.

182. Stevens, "Unanticipated Consequences," in Stout, ed., *Psychology of Terrorism*, vol. 3, 44.

183. Post, "Terrorist Psycho-Logic," in Reich, ed., *Origins of Terrorism*, 33.

184. Stevens, "Unanticipated Consequences," in Stout, ed., *Psychology of Terrorism*, vol. 3, 45.

185. Jonathan T. Drummond, "From the Northwest Imperative to Global Jihad: Social Psychological Aspects of the Construction of the Enemy, Political Violence and Terror," in Stout, ed., *Psychology of Terrorism*, vol. 1, 60, 75.

186. Singapore WP, 15.

187. Marilynn B. Brewer, "The Psychology of Prejudice: Ingroup Love or Outgroup Hate?" *Journal of Social Issues*, Fall 1999, www.findarticles.com/p/articles/mi_m0341/is_3_55/ai_58549254 (accessed 7 Sep. 2004).

188. Dozier, *Why We Hate*, 45.

189. Stevens, "Unanticipated Consequences," in Stout, ed., *Psychology of Terrorism*, vol. 3, 45.

190. Cited in Ramakrishna and Tan, "Is Southeast Asia a 'Terrorist Haven?'", 26–27.

191. Lawal, "Social-Psychological Considerations," 24.

192. Drummond, "From the Northwest Imperative," 76.

193. Yusof and Ishak, "Inside a JI School."

194. Mapes, "Indonesian School."

195. Singapore WP, 22.

196. See International Crisis Group, *Southern Philippines Backgrounder: Terrorism and the Peace Process* (Singapore/Brussels: International Crisis Group Asia Report No. 80, 13 July 2004), 13–17.

197. Drummond, "From the Northwest Imperative," 76.

198. Juergensmeyer, *Terror in the Mind of God*, 194.

199. Sageman, *Understanding Terror Networks*, 151.

200. Diane Perlman, "Intersubjective Dimensions of Terrorism and its Transcendence," in Stout, ed., *Psychology of Terrorism*, vol. 1, 28.

201. Perlman, "Intersubjective Dimensions," 28.

202. Juergensmeyer, *Terror in the Mind of God*, 195.

203. Perlman, "Intersubjective Dimensions," 30.

204. Perlman, "Intersubjective Dimensions," 32.

205. Juergensmeyer, *Terror in the Mind of God*, 211, 214.

206. Cited in Perlman, "Intersubjective Dimensions," 32.

207. Albert Bandura, "Mechanisms of Moral Disengagement," in Reich, ed., *Origins of Terrorism*, 163.

208. Bandura, "Mechanisms of Moral Disengagement," 164.

209. Bandura, "Mechanisms of Moral Disengagement," 169–170.

210. *Jemaah Islamiyah in Southeast Asia*, 24.

211. Bandura, "Mechanisms of Moral Disengagement," 173.

212. Bandura, "Mechanisms of Moral Disengagement," 180–181.

213. Dawson, "The Bali Bombers."

214. Dawson, "The Bali Bombers."

215. Dan Murphy, "How al Qaeda Lit the Bali Fuse: Part 2," *Christian Science Monitor*, 18 June 2003.

216. Singapore WP, 16.

217. Don J. Feeney, Jr., "Entrancement in Islamic Fundamentalism," in Stout, ed., *Psychology of Terrorism*, vol. 3, 192–201.

218. Communication with Rohan Gunaratna, 30 September 2004.

219. Konrad Kellen, "Ideology and Rebellion," in Reich, ed., *Origins of Terrorism*, 49–50.

220. Kumar Ramakrishna, "U.S. Strategy in Southeast Asia: Counter-Terrorist or Counter-Terrorism?" in Ramakrishna and Tan, eds., *After Bali*, 305–337.

12

Conclusion

James JF Forest

Throughout this volume, authors have explored various dimensions of individual and organizational learning to help us gain an understanding of terrorism, in the hope that this research will contribute to new approaches for combating terrorism. Much of the literature in the field of terrorism and counterterrorism has addressed various dimensions of terrorist motivation and the ways in which terrorist organizations acquire their lethal capabilities. This volume furthers our understanding of these important topics by exploring how terrorist groups apply the principles of organizational learning to improve their ability to motivate new members, equip them with new skills, and become smarter and more lethal terrorists. In doing so, these chapters have revealed the following observations:

- *Knowledge is a critical asset for any terrorist organization.* In a sense, knowledge can be seen as information that becomes useful upon human interpretation. Whether this knowledge is developed from within the organization or acquired by studying other organizations that have developed useful expertise, a terrorist organization must continually obtain, analyze, assimilate, and operationalize certain kinds of knowledge in order to effectively achieve its goals.
- *Successful terrorist organizations are committed to the long-term training and education of their members.* Clearly, the attributes of a learning organization (e.g., fostering the ability to adapt to a changing strategic environment) can be seen among the more sophisticated terrorist organizations like al Qaeda, Hamas, Jemaah Islamiyah, and the FARC. Through the development of doctrines, training manuals, military

exercises, and educational programs (often, but not necessarily, provided at remote training camps), the most violent terrorist organizations work hard to continually improve their lethal capabilities.

• *Successful terrorist organizations learn from the strategies and tactics of other organizations.* They learn by studying each others' training manuals, videos, and other forms of information (particularly via the Internet). They also learn from media accounts of terrorist events (both successes and failures) conducted by other organizations. And, as seen in the examples of Jemaah Islamyiah members training in al Qaeda's Afghanistan camps, or members of the Lebanese Hizballah aiding the Palestinian group Hamas, a global network of information knowledge sharing plays a key role in developing the operational capabilities of learning organizations. Indeed, while the formal means and locations of knowledge sharing are important (for example, training camps), it is the informal knowledge networks among terrorists and their organizations that contribute the most to learning in the terrorist world. In this regard, the insurgency that developed in Iraq—which attracted thousands of foreign fighters who have learned urban terrorist tactics—requires extensive analysis to determine where these fighters go when they eventually leave this region.

• *Terrorist organizations study our counterterrorist strategies and adapt accordingly.* They learn by studying our doctrines, statements, public court records, investigative news stories of counterterrorism successes, and various information resources available on the Internet. As terrorism expert Bruce Hoffman once observed, "success for the terrorist is dependent on their ability to keep one step ahead not only of the authorities but also of counterterrorist technology."[1] The IRA offers a prime example of this adaptation, particularly in how its bomb makers adapted new triggering devices to circumvent the scanners and other technological advances developed by the British Ministry of Defense. Another famous example is the story of bin Laden's satellite phone: In 2001, when it was reported in the news media that the U.S. was tracking bin Laden in Afghanistan by targeting his satellite phone, he gave the phone to someone moving in an opposite direction, thus thwarting our efforts to catch him. And most recently, as described in chapter 4 of this volume, the insurgency in Iraq has become a center of terrorist learning and adaptation. The U.S. military is increasingly concerned about what it calls an "adaptive strategy" that is being combined with "increasingly powerful weapons" to cause more harm to coalition and Iraqi security forces in the region.[2]

• *A variety of social institutions support knowledge transfer in the terrorist world.* While much has been written in recent years about the role of training camps in developing a terrorist group's capabilities, we must also recognize that terrorists can exchange or acquire knowledge in many other ways, from attending a particular madrasa or university to surfing the Internet or simply following the news on CNN or Al Jazeera.

- *Some forms of knowledge are particularly dangerous in the terrorist world.* Advanced knowledge in developing chemical, biological, nuclear, or radiological weapons is, by most accounts, very difficult to acquire. Such knowledge, in the hands of a motivated terrorist organization, would surely lead to catastrophic consequences. How we safeguard such knowledge, without impinging on civil rights, is one of the most complex counterterrorism challenges today.

There are many other observations and implications one could glean from the chapters in this volume. The overall goal in this concluding chapter is simply to reemphasize the centrality of knowledge in the terrorist world, suggest implications for counterterrorism policy and actions, and focus our thinking and research in new directions.

IMPLICATIONS FOR COMBATING TERRORISM IN THE TWENTY-FIRST CENTURY

From the research and perspectives offered in this volume, several implications can be drawn to inform our understanding of the terrorist threat and how the civilized world may respond more effectively to it.

1. We Must Analyze and Understand the Global Dimensions of Knowledge Transfer in the Terrorist World

There is a burgeoning field of research in the study of organizational behavior, which some might call "knowledge traffic analysis."[3] Given the organic and dynamic nature of terrorist organizations, which several chapters in this volume have described as learning organizations, it may be useful to develop conceptual maps of the knowledge traffic that sustains individual and group learning in the terrorist world. Further, our understanding of this knowledge traffic must encompass a truly global, multiorganizational dimension.

The terrorist organizations that the U.S. and its allies are most concerned with, and for good reason, are those that demonstrate the ability to think and act strategically. These are organizations which exhibit a sophisticated understanding of their adversaries, and adapt their tactics in ways that exploit their adversaries' vulnerabilities. The largest terrorist threat faced by the U.S. and its allies today comes in the form of an international Salafist movement, a global community of individuals and groups connected by a common idea of what the world should be, a vision framed by an extremist form of Salafist

Islamic ideology. Additional threats to global security include the support networks that facilitate terrorism; states that facilitate terrorism either willingly or through some type of negligence or incapacity; and regional and local groups that employ similar, deadly tactics to achieve their political or economic goals. Through their actions, these entities contribute to the growth of a global knowledge network in the terrorist world. Thus, we must focus our research and counterterrorism efforts on terrorist groups of all shapes and sizes. This perspective suggests that focusing exclusively or even primarily on one group or movement (like al Qaeda and its affiliates) without addressing others (like LTTE, Hamas, Hizballah, FARC, or other contributors to the global terrorist knowledge network) may not be an effective counterterrorism strategy. This is an international problem, which requires an internationally coordinated response.

2. We Must Strive to Disrupt the Global Transfer of Terrorist Knowledge

Once we have developed an understanding of the characteristics that affect a particular terrorist group's learning abilities, the next step in a comprehensive counterterrorism strategy involves trying to reduce these abilities. A recent study conducted by the RAND Corporation offered a set of "learning-focused strategies for combating terrorism" that inform such efforts.[4] First, the report suggests we must target a terrorist group's learning activities directly, in order to reduce its ability to adapt over time. This could involve actions such as restricting access to the kinds of knowledge it requires to successfully achieve its lethal objectives; identifying and breaking the interconnections among a group's members that facilitate learning; and denying groups the safe havens they require for experimentation, innovation, and training.[5]

The report also recommends that we take action to divert terrorist groups' learning efforts or influence the outcomes of such efforts—in essence, steering the group's learning activities in such a direction as to negatively impact the knowledge it may acquire. An example of this might include replacing Internet-based information on bomb making with incomplete or ineffective recipes.[6] In essence, certain situations may warrant that we intentionally corrupt the quality and integrity of the information that is sought by terrorists. As part of this, we must become smarter in identifying the kinds of information that terrorists can take advantage of. Further, we must find ways to use information (or misinformation) as a weapon for our advantage. Manipulating what the terrorists think they know about our attack plans or capabilities might seem a bit too Machiavellian for some, but when fighting a thinking enemy, any reluctance to use information as a weapon works to the terrorists' benefit, resulting in the loss of innocent life. Overall, the goal of countering terrorism in the knowledge transfer arena should focus on significantly damaging a group's ability to learn and adapt.

This analysis also suggests implications for policies with regard to the incarceration of terrorists. Motivational knowledge can possibly be countered with competing (and hopefully more compelling) messages; little, if anything, can be done to counter operational knowledge, once acquired. The analogy is this: although we can remove or replace your need (or will) to drive a car, we cannot remove or replace your skill to drive. It is particularly instructive to see the increasing number of news reports about how several of the Guantanamo prisoners, once released, returned to the field of battle to cause new casualties among coalition security forces in Afghanistan and Iraq. Keeping prisoners indefinitely at places like Guantanamo Bay may be in our best interests, because we need to restrict these individuals' ability to share knowledge with others in the terrorist world.

In addition to diminishing a terrorist group's internal developmental capabilities, we must also do all we can to prevent one organization from learning and adapting the successful tactics of another group. This would imply restricting the reporting (online and in the media) of terrorist attacks and other events in such a way that the successful tactics are not revealed. However, while offering training manuals and other terrorist resources online could be made a criminal and punishable act, it may be useful for the counterterrorism community to monitor certain websites, and capture information on individuals who download terrorist-related materials. At the very least, our counterterrorism efforts must continue to identify individuals who demonstrate a clear intent to do harm and the willingness to acquire the knowledge to do so, whether they travel to a training camp in Afghanistan to acquire this knowledge or copy bomb-making materials from the Internet.

Our counterterrorism efforts can also be greatly enhanced by identifying the knowledge experts in the terrorist world and constricting their ability to share their knowledge with other would-be terrorists. As the RAND report suggested, focusing on a how a group learns may help analysts identify individuals (from technical specialists to influential strategic thinkers) who play a key role in the learning process.[7] As noted in chapter 4 of this volume, the success of training camps is heavily reliant on experienced trainers. From the Soviet military-trained instructors in the Uzbekistan camps, to the Libyan military's involvement in training Islamic radical (and other) terrorist groups, to the individual participation of William Potter Gale (a U.S. guerrilla strategist during World War II) and Bo Gritz (a former Special Forces commander in Vietnam) in right-wing militia groups in the U.S., there are many examples that indicate the centrality of experts in transferring operational knowledge in the terrorist world. We have yet to agree on what special intelligence or legal measures should be taken toward individuals who are willing to use their operational expertise to develop others' skill to kill. While a good deal of research has focused on understanding what the terrorists are learning before they can operationalize/act on that learning, it is also important to view operational knowledge experts as vital links in nurturing the learning capabilities of any terrorist organization (and thus a critical vulnerability that must be exploited); when learning is lost within an organization, the organization becomes less effective.

3. Different Types of Learning Require Different Counterterrorism Responses

If we view the terrorist threat as one primarily encompassing two forms of knowledge on an individual level—motivational and operational—and recognize the differences in how and where these forms of knowledge are transmitted, we can adapt our responses accordingly. Both types of knowledge are important, but they require different responses. The motivational dimension requires an ambitious effort to combat those who spread messages of hate and violence, and counter these messages with moderate ideas; operational knowledge requires a much different response. Activities to counter the spread of motivational knowledge transfer should include broad, multilingual information and educational campaigns, while activities to combat operational knowledge require better intelligence on where operational learning takes place, a commitment to seek and destroy training camps, information operations (to include tracking and trapping individuals seeking terrorist operational knowledge), the closing of certain websites, and other forceful and covert approaches.

In terms of the global salafi jihadist movement, counterterrorism in the realm of motivational knowledge transfer must involve leaders of Islamic communities, particularly those in which pockets of extremism serve to enable and support jihadist terrorism. In the United Kingdom, for example, Sheikh Omar Bakri Muhammad—the leader of the radical Islamic group al-Muhajiroun—has been allowed to sow discord between Muslims and non-Muslims and distort the image of Islam for many years.[8] Bakri's ties to al Qaeda and other terrorist organizations have historically been in the realm of motivational knowledge, although he has also admitted to providing some operational assistance. For example, in October 2000 Bakri proudly announced that al-Muhajiroun collects funds, recruits militiamen, and "takes care of propaganda requirements in Europe" for Hamas and Palestinian Islamic Jihad. He also stated that "Clinton is a target of the jihad, and American forces are a target of the jihad wherever they are,"[9] and said that he "would like to see Prime Minister Tony Blair dead or deposed and an Islamic flag hanging outside 10 Downing Street."[10]

After September 11, Bakri organized celebrations of al Qaeda's efforts, where he and his supporters referred to the U.S. as "the head of Satan" and described the attacks as "a great achievement by the mujahideen against the evil superpower."[11] At the first anniversary of the September 11 attacks, Bakri and his followers held a conference in London entitled, "A Towering Day in History," where speeches were made on "the positive outcomes of September 11" and the "U.S. conspiracy against Islam and Muslims."[12] In 2003, two of Bakri's students—British citizens Asif Muhammad Hanif and Omar Khan Sharif—were recruited by Hamas to carry out suicide bombings at a Tel Aviv seafront bar. There, Hanif blew himself up, killing three Israelis and wounding a dozen more. The explosives-filled vest worn by Sharif failed to detonate, and the would-be suicide bomber fled the scene. Unfortunately, it was not until after the devastating attack on London's transport system on July 7, 2005, that the British government acted against Bakri and his fellow promoters of Islamist militant violence.

In some cases, new legal instruments are necessary in order to combat the spread of terrorist-related knowledge. For example, in June 1997, the U.S. Congress voted 94–0 to add an amendment to a Department of Defense spending bill to prohibit the distribution of bomb-making instructions in the United States. The penalty for violating this law is a fine of $250,000 and/or a maximum of twenty years imprisonment. Shortly after the London bombings, British authorities announced they were considering new antiterrorism laws that would make it a crime to provide or receive training in the use of explosives. Further, while these laws would punish those responsible for "acts preparatory to terrorism," the proposed legislation would also outlaw "indirect incitement" of terrorism, including praising those who carry out attacks.[13]

Of even greater concern to the counterterrorism community is the fact that some terrorist groups are known to be seeking knowledge in the realm of WMD (weapons of mass destruction). The capacity to cause mass destruction and/or mass casualties, once held almost exclusively by states, is now frequently ascribed to nonstate organizations. Extremist religious groups in particular have demonstrated a willingness and ability to develop weapons of mass destruction capability.[14] According to Gavin Cameron, such groups lack the moderating influence of an external "audience" or "constituency," and to them "violence is perceived to be part of an all-encompassing struggle between good and evil."[15] David Kaplan's study of Aum Shinrikyo supports this view by demonstrating how the group's particular worldview rationalized its plans for mass murder.[16]

As revealed in the February 2001 East Africa bombing trial testimony of Jamal al Fadi—an al Qaeda operative in charge of weapons development in Sudan—uranium was used in "dirty bombs" (weapons that release lethal radioactive material upon detonation) that were tested in 1994 by members of the Sudan-based Islamic National Front.[17] According to a recent Congressional Research Service report, terrorists' ability to produce or obtain WMD may be growing due to looser controls of stockpiles and technology in the former Soviet Union and the dissemination of technology and information.[18] However, as Jonathan Tucker observed in his groundbreaking book, *Toxic Terror*, terrorists are still likely to encounter a variety of difficulties in acquiring, developing, producing, weaponizing, and effectively deploying WMD. He argues that "only a tiny minority of terrorists will seek to inflict indiscriminate casualties" with WMD, and few of them are likely to succeed, predominantly because of the enormous difficulties in developing effective delivery systems. Further, he notes, groups that will try to deploy WMD tend to have certain traits, including apocalyptic ideology, innovation in weapons and tactics, paranoia and grandiosity, charismatic leadership, defensive aggression, and other characteristics.[19] Unfortunately, while there are relatively few groups with all the elements that Tucker identifies, it would take only one, given the right opportunities and circumstances, to cause a catastrophic loss of life.

From this perspective, it becomes clear that monitoring and restricting access to knowledge on how to construct WMD—and their delivery systems—will clearly be an important component in an effective long-term counterterrorism strategy. Most governments are actively cooperating in carefully restricting access to chemical, biological, radiological, and nuclear (CBRN) materials. In part, the world's focus on this issue is due to fears about the fate of unguarded weapons of mass destruction in the former Soviet Union, as well as the activities of now-unemployed weapons scientists. In addition, chemical and biological weapons can in principle be fabricated by groups with relatively modest resources.[20] But it is also important to examine how well we are protecting the knowledge of what to do with these materials. If such materials were to fall into the wrong hands, is there available knowledge that would help these individuals achieve their goals? From this perspective, it is clear that there is no reason to have CBRN weapons-making instructions or component details freely available in a public library or online. This knowledge must be as carefully guarded as the materials used to make the weapons.

In July 2005 the U.S. government requested that the National Academy of Sciences delay publication of a research paper that offered potentially lethal information for terrorists to exploit. The paper assessed the vulnerability of the dairy industry to a bioterrorism attack, and recommended steps to prevent that from happening. However, in a letter to the Academy, Stewart Simonson, assistant secretary of HHS, stated that the paper was a "road map for terrorists." He contended that the paper provided too much detail on potentially vulnerable areas of the milk supply, processing, and distribution systems and argued that its publication "could have very serious health and national security consequences."[21] As this example demonstrates, appreciating the importance of operational knowledge in the terrorist world suggests frightening implications for the academic community and U.S. institutions of higher learning. We have already witnessed the role of flight schools in contributing to an individual's capacity to carry out a terrorist attack. One only hopes that heightened vigilance is now common at such institutions, as well as at truck schools, large ship or tanker pilot programs, and so forth. From civil engineering schools to biochemistry programs, in order to truly understand the terrorist mindset we must develop a clear sense of what sorts of knowledge would be most useful to an ideologically motivated individual seeking to operationalize his or her terrorist intentions. Overall, knowledge is a vital asset in the terrorist world, and the most dangerous knowledge must be protected from those who would use it to cause mass casualties.

4. As Centers of Terrorist Learning Move from the Physical to the Virtual Realms, So Must Our Counterterrorism Efforts

While this may seem a brilliant flash of the obvious to most counterterrorism observers, it warrants repeating here. Clearly, shutting down physical centers (training camps) is important, but it is far from being the only thing we need to do in combating terrorist knowledge transfer. Distance learning is on the rise; centers of learning appear to be decreasing in the physical realm, and increasing in the cyberspace realm. The technical sophistication of today's terrorist organizations and their members should never be underestimated. Many in the terrorist world undoubtedly understand both the benefits and potential hazards of using the Internet to transfer operational knowledge, and are thus often very careful in doing so. Training websites are frequently moved from web server to web server, as changing website addresses can foil even the highly trained investigator's attempt to infiltrate the terrorist network. Coded messages are posted to chat rooms and discussion forums, through which new website addresses for terrorist information are made available. By spreading thousands of propaganda videos and pictures using the latest technology developed in the U.S., the Internet is providing a powerful way of virtually connecting the global community of fighters and creating a shared worldview. According to terrorism expert Jarret Brachman, a Chechen jihadi watching an online video of an Iraqi roadside bombing feels viscerally connected to a universal movement and emboldened to continue in his local fight—as a result, the Internet has allowed jihadis to "see globally and act locally."[22]

Our efforts to combat the global threat of terrorism must obviously address these kinds of activities in cyberspace. However, the U.S. government has shown a remarkable inconsistency in its commitment to online counterterrorism. For example, the U.S. Department of Homeland Security

(DHS) has seen four different cybersecurity chiefs resign within the last three years—a disturbing pattern, at the very least. Most recently, Amit Yoran, a former software executive from Symantec Corp., resigned his position as director of the DHS' National Cyber Security Division (with an $80 million budget and sixty employees) in part because of his lack of authority within the Department.[23] As a result, Congressional leaders have pressed the Bush Administration to elevate this position from a Director (at least three bureaucratic steps below the Secretary) to an Assistant Secretary. Our commitment to counterterrorism must encompass a full recognition of how online centers of learning contribute to the transfer of motivational knowledge as well as operational knowledge in the terrorist world, and one could argue that in addition to greater authority, this also requires more than sixty employees. Counterterrorism experts must locate and shut down online platforms for knowledge exchange in the terrorist world.

There is an important advantage, however, that the Internet provides counterterrorism experts. Because the information can be transmitted electronically to a relatively faceless audience, participant deception becomes easier. Whereas the U.S. has had difficulty infiltrating physical centers of learning such as training camps, electronic centers of learning can be accessed regardless of a participant's physical appearance or true beliefs. Thus, counterterrorism operators are able to see what the terrorists "know" (in terms of what they are teaching new recruits), and thus find ways to counter those strategies and tactics. They can also open and maintain their own websites under the guise of providing training to terrorists, while covertly collecting information on any visitors who come to the site looking for such information (the so-called "honey-pot" approach). Overall, considerable investment in time and effort must be maintained and expanded in order to track the terrorists' use of the Internet as a vehicle for both motivational and operational knowledge transfer.

THE NEED FOR FURTHER RESEARCH

This volume addresses the problem of global terrorism from a central lens of knowledge—specifically, the role that knowledge plays in the terrorist world, and how it is used to maintain a terrorist organization's capacity to carry out its deadly operations. Successful terrorist groups can be considered learning organizations: They capture, store, and analyze knowledge—both from their own history as well as from the experiences of other groups—and by doing so are able to develop the means of achieving their goals with increasing sophistication. Clearly, not just anyone can be a terrorist, nor can someone become a terrorist overnight. Knowledge transfer plays a critical role in transforming the individual into the motivated and capable terrorist. Thus, the more we can learn about how this knowledge is developed, delivered, and received between and among individuals and groups, the more we can devise effective counterterrorism initiatives.

From this perspective, it becomes clear that further research is needed. Specific issues of concern that warrant additional study include:

- How can civilized nations reshape the strategic environment in which terrorist groups operate, in order to significantly deteriorate their capacity for knowledge transfer?
- What are the characteristics of a terrorist organization that enhance or restrict learning?[24]
- How can we restrict the use of the Internet for transferring lethal terrorist knowledge, while maintaining the commitment to open information exchange upon which the Internet was founded?
- How can members of the counterterrorism and international security communities develop formal and informal knowledge networks that are more robust and effective than those of the terrorists?
- How can the media reduce the legitimacy and useful knowledge that terrorist organizations might derive from their news coverage of terrorist events?
- Who are the knowledge experts within a particular terrorist organization?
- What do we need to know about knowledge transfer among terrorists? What don't we know yet, and why don't we know this?

There are many other topics worthy of further exploration. Overall, the study of organizational learning provides a window onto *how* terrorist groups change and adapt, and offers important contributions to planning and operations for combating terrorism.[25] Chapters in this volume have also addressed *where* terrorists learn, and *what* they are learning—topics that warrant additional research as well. Hopefully, the discussions presented throughout this book will encourage new thinking in how we approach the study of terrorism and the practice of counterterrorism. Overall, we must learn to apply the principles of organizational learning to our efforts to combat terrorism—we must gather and analyze useful knowledge, incorporate it into our plans and actions, and grow smarter. And, as suggested throughout this volume, we must do this faster and more effectively than the terrorists do, or risk losing the global struggle against terrorism.

NOTES

The views expressed are those of the author and not of the Department of the Army, the U.S. Military Academy, or any other agency of the U.S. Government.

1. Bruce Hoffman, *Inside Terrorism* (Columbia University Press, 1998), 180.

2. For example, see Matthew Clark, "Adapting to Shifting Sands of Battle in Iraq: U.S. and Iraqi forces adjust to combat changing insurgent tactics," *Christian Science Monitor,* 3 May 2005, online at www.csmonitor.com/2005/0503/dailyUpdate.html; Rowan Scarborough, "Rebels Improve Bomb Schemes in Iraq," *Washington Times,* 25 April 2005, www.washtimes.com/national/20050425-122710-9671r.htm; and "U.S. says Iraqi insurgents are adapting," *ISN Security Watch,* 4 August 2005, www.isn.ch/news/sw/details.cfm?ID=12342.

3. In addition to the organizational behavior literature, there also is a growing discussion about "knowledge traffic" among educators concerned with developing "learning communities." In both areas, a primary concern is the need to transform modes of unidirectional knowledge traffic into multichannel, two-way knowledge traffic. Similar concepts are discussed in several chapters of this volume, but referred to as "knowledge transfer."

4. Brian A. Jackson, *Aptitude for Destruction,* vol. 1, *Organizational Learning in Terrorist Groups and its Implications for Combating Terrorism* (Santa Monica, CA: RAND Corporation, 2005), 51–59.

5. Jackson, *Aptitude for Destruction,* 52.

6. Jackson, *Aptitude for Destruction,* 53.

7. Jackson, *Aptitude for Destruction,* 54

8. Zeyno Baran, "Stop Tolerating Intolerance," *The Counterterrorism Blog,* 8 August 2005, http://counterterror.typepad.com.

9. Aaron Klien, "My Weekend with the Enemy," *Jerusalem Post,* 30 May 2000.

10. Patrick E. Tyler and Don van Natta, Jr., "Militants in Europe Call for Jihad," *New York Times,* 25 April 2004.

11. Thair Shaikh, "London to host Islamic 'celebration' of Sept 11," *Daily Telegraph,* 8 September 2002, www.news.telegraph.co.uk/news/main.jhtml?xml=/news/2002/09/08/nextre08.xml.

12. Shaikh, "London to host Islamic 'celebration' of Sept 11."

13. Michael McDonough, "Britain Intends to Ban Explosives Training," *Associated Press,* 15 July 2005.

14. See Steve Bowman and Helit Barel, *Weapons of Mass Destruction—The Terrorist Threat* (CRS Report for Congress, RS20412) (Washington, DC: Congressional Research Service, 8 December 1999). Available online at www.fas.org/irp/crs/RS20412.pdf.

15. Gavin Cameron, *Nuclear Terrorism: A Threat Assessment for the 21st Century* (New York: St. Martin's, 1999).

16. David Kaplan, "Aum Shinrikyo," in *Toxic Terror: Terror: Assessing Terrorist Use of Chemical and Biological Weapons,* edited by Jonathan B. Tucker (Cambridge, MA: MIT Press, 2000), 207–226. See also Manabu Watanabe, "Religion and Violence in Japan Today: A Chronological and Doctrinal Analysis of Aum Shinrikyo," *Terrorism and Political Violence* 10, no. 4 (Winter 1998), 80–100.

17. Marcia Christoff Kurop, "Al Qaeda's Balkan Links," *Wall Street Journal Europe,* 1 November 2001.

18. See Bowman and Barel, *Weapons of Mass Destruction.*

19. Jonathan B. Tucker, ed., *Toxic Terror: Assessing Terrorist Use of Chemical and Biological Weapons* (Cambridge, MA: MIT Press, 2000).

20. Michael Barkun, "Terrorism and Doomsday," in *The Making of a Terrorist, Recruitment, Training, and Root Causes,* vol. 3, edited by James JF Forest (Westport, CT: Praeger, 2005).

21. See "Scientific Paper on Milk Supply Delayed for Security Reasons," *Associated Press,* 7 June 2005.

22. Jarret Brachman, personal communication with the author, August 20, 2005.

23. Ted Bridis, "U.S. Cybersecurity Chief Resigns," *Associated Press,* 1 October 2004.

24. For an excellent discussion of this topic, see Jackson, *Aptitude for Destruction,* 35–46

25. Jackson, *Aptitude for Destruction,* 27.

Bibliography

Aboul-Enein, Youssef H. "Al-Ikhwan Al-Muslimeen: The Muslim Brotherhood." *Military Review*, July–August 2003, 26–31.

Abu Amr, Ziad. "Hamas: A Historical and Political Background." *Journal of Palestine Studies* 23, no. 4 (1993): 5–15.

Abu-Rabi, Ibrahim M. *Intellectual Origins of Islamic Resurgence in the Modern Arab World.* Albany: State University of New York Press, 1996.

Abuza, Zachary. "Education and Radicalization: Jemaah Islamiyah Recruitment in Southeast Asia." In *The Making of a Terrorist: Recruitment, Training and Root Causes.* Vol. 1, edited by James JF Forest. Westport, CT: Praeger, 2005.

Abuza, Zachary. *Militant Islam in Southeast Asia: Crucible of Terror.* Boulder: Lynne Rienner, 2003.

Aho, James. "Christian Fundamentalism and Militia Movements in the United States." In *The Making of a Terrorist: Recruitment, Training and Root Causes,* vol. 1, ed. James JF Forest. Westport, CT: Praeger Publishers, 2005.

Albright, David, and Corey Hinderstein. "South Africa's Nuclear Weaponization Efforts: Success on a Small-Scale." *ISIS-Working-Paper,* 13 September 2001, www.isis-online.org/publications/terrorism/safrica.pdf.

Alexander, Yonah, and Robert Patter. *Terrorism and the Media: Dilemma for Government, Journalism, and the Public.* New York: Brassey's, 1990.

Anonymous. *Through Our Enemy's Eyes.* Dulles, VA: Brasseys, 2003.

Anti-Defamation League. *Dangerous Convictions: An Introduction to Extremist Activities in Prison.* Washington, DC: ALD, 2002. Available online at www.adl.org/learn/Ext_Terr/dangerous_convictions.pdf.

Argyris, Chris, and Donald Schön. *Organizational Learning: A Theory of Action Perspective.* Reading, MA: Addison-Wesley, 1978.

———. *Organizational Learning II: Theory, Method and Practice.* Reading, MA: Addison-Wesley, 1996.

Armstrong, Karen. *The Battle for God.* New York: Alfred A. Knopf, 2000.

Arquilla, John, and David Ronfeldt. *Networks and Netwars: The Future of Terror, Crime and Militancy.* Santa Monica: RAND, 2001.

Arquilla, John, David F. Ronfeldt, and Michele Zanini. "Networks, Netwar and Information-Age Terrorism." In *Countering the New Terrorism,* edited by Ian O. Lesser, Bruce Hoffman,

John Arquilla, David F. Ronfeldt, Michele Zanini, and Brian Michael Jenkins. Santa Monica: RAND, 1999.

Azra, Azyumardi. "Bali and Southeast Asian Islam: Debunking the Myths." In *After Bali: The Threat of Terrorism in Southeast Asia*, edited by Kumar Ramakrishna and See Seng Tan. Singapore: World Scientific/Institute of Defence and Strategic Studies, 2003.

Azzam, Maha. "Political Islam: Violence and the Wahhabi Connection." In *The Making of a Terrorist: Recruitment, Training and Root Causes*. Vol. 1, edited by James JF Forest. Westport, CT: Praeger, 2005.

Bandura, Albert. "Mechanisms of Moral Disengagement." In *Origins of Terrorism: Psychologies, Ideologies, Theologies, States of Mind*, edited by Walter Reich. Baltimore: Woodrow Wilson Center Press, 1998.

———. "Training for Terrorism through Selective Moral Disengagement." In *The Making of a Terrorist: Recruitment, Training and Root Causes*, Vol. 2, edited by James JF Forest. Westport, CT: Praeger, 2005.

Barkun, Michael. "Terrorism and Doomsday." In *The Making of a Terrorist: Recruitment, Training, and Root Causes*. Vol. 3, edited by James JF Forest. Westport, CT: Praeger, 2005.

Beit-Hallahmi, Benjamin, and Michael Argyle. *The Psychology of Religious Behavior, Belief and Experience*. London and New York: Routledge, 1997.

Bell, J. Bowyer. "The Armed Struggle and Underground Intelligence: An Overview." *Studies in Conflict and Terrorism* 17 (1994): 115–150.

———. *The IRA, 1968–2000: Analysis of a Secret Army*. London: Frank Cass, 2000.

Bergen, Peter L. *Holy War, Inc.: Inside the Secret World of Osama bin Laden*. New York: Free Press, 2001.

Black, Antony. *The History of Islamic Political Thought*. New York: Routledge, 2001.

Blanke, Debra J., and Gina M. Wekke. "Distance Education." In *Higher Education in the United States*, edited by James J. F. Forest and Kevin Kinser. Santa Barbara, CA: ABC-CLIO Press, 2002.

Bok, Sissela. *Mayhem: Violence as Public Entertainment*. Reading, MA: Addison-Wesley, 1998.

Boucek, Christopher. "Libyan State-Sponsored Terrorism: An Historical Perspective." *Terrorism Monitor* 3, no. 6 (March 24, 2005).

Bowman, Steve, and Helit Barel. *Weapons of Mass Destruction—The Terrorist Threat* (CRS Report for Congress, RS20412). Washington, DC: Congressional Research Service, 8 December 1999. Available online at www.fas.org/irp/crs/RS20412.pdf.

Brachman, Jarret. "Jihad Doctrine and Radical Islam." In *The Making of a Terrorist: Recruitment, Training, and Root Causes*. Vol. 1, edited by James J. F. Forest. Westport, CT: Praeger, 2005.

Brownfeld, A. "Bin Ladin's activities exposed in New York trial." *Jane's Terrorism & Security Monitor*, 14 March 2001, http://newsite.janes.com/security/ international_security/news/ jtsm/jtsm010314_1_n.shtml.

Bukharin, Oleg. "Problems of Nuclear Terrorism." *The Monitor: Nonproliferation, Demilitarization and Arms Control* (Spring 1997), 8–10.

Bukharin, Oleg. "Upgrading Security at Nuclear Power Plants in the Newly Independent States." *The Nonproliferation Review* (Winter 1997).

Bunker, Robert, ed. *Non-State Threats and Future Wars*. London: Frank Cass Publishers, 2002.

Bunn, Matthew. "The Next Wave: Urgently Needed New Steps to Control Warheads and Fissile Material." Washington, DC: Carnegie Endowment for International Peace and Harvard Project on Managing the Atom, April 2000. Available online at http://ksgnotes1 .harvard.edu/BCSIA/Library.nsf/pubs/Nextwave.

Cameron, Gavin. *Nuclear Terrorism: A Threat Assessment for the 21st Century*. New York: St. Martin's Press, 1999.

Carley, Kathleen. "Organizational Learning and Personnel Turnover." *Organization Science* 3 (1992): 20–46.

Collins, Eamon, with Mick McGovern. *Killing Rage*. London: Granta Books, 1997.

Combs, Cindy C. *Terrorism in the Twenty-First Century*. Upper Saddle River, NJ: Prentice-Hall, Inc., 2002.

Combs, Cindy C., Elizabeth A. Combs, and Lydia Marsh. "Christian Militia Training: Arming the 'Troops' with Scripture, the Law and a Good Gun." In *The Making of a Terrorist: Recruitment, Training, and Root Causes*. Vol. 2, edited by James JF Forest. Westport, CT: Praeger, 2005.

Cragin, Kim, and Bruce Hoffman. *Arms Trafficking and Colombia*. Santa Monica: RAND National Defense Research Institute, 2003.

Crenshaw, Martha. "Questions to Be Answered, Research to Be Done, Knowledge to Be Applied." In *Origins of Terrorism: Psychologies, Ideologies, Theologies, States of Mind*, edited by Walter Reich. Baltimore: Woodrow Wilson Center Press, 1998.

———. "The Logic of Terrorism: Terrorist Behavior as a Product of Strategic Choice." In *Origins of Terrorism: Psychologies, Ideologies, Theologies, States of Mind*, edited by Walter Reich. Baltimore: Woodrow Wilson Center Press, 1998.

Cyert, Richard M., and James G. March. *A Behavioral Theory of the Firm*. Englewood Cliffs, NJ: Prentice Hall, 1963.

Daft, Richard L., and Robert H. Lengal. "Organizational Information Requirements: Media Richness and Structural Design." *Management Science* 32 (1986): 554–571.

Darby, John. *Northern Ireland: The Background to the Conflict*. Belfast, Northern Ireland: Appletree Press, 1983.

Deikman, Arthur J. "The Psychological Power of Charismatic Leaders in Cults and Terrorist Organizations." In *The Making of a Terrorist: Recruitment, Training and Root Causes*. Vol. 2, edited by James JF Forest. Westport, CT: Praeger, 2005.

della Porta, Donatella. *Social Movements, Political Violence and the State: A Comparative Analysis of Italy and Germany*. London: Cambridge University Press, 1995.

Dobson, Christopher, and Ronald Payne. *The Terrorists, Their Weapons, Leaders and Tactics*. New York: Facts on File Publications, 1982.

Dodgson, Mark. "Organizational Learning: A Review of Some Literature." *Organizational Studies* 14 (1993): 375–394.

Dolnik, Adam. "Die and Let Die: Exploring the Links between Suicide Terrorism and Terrorist Use of Chemical, Biological, Radiological, and Nuclear Weapons." *Studies in Conflict and Terrorism* 26, no. 1 (January–February 2003): 17–35.

Dolnik, Adam. "Learning to Die: Suicide Terrorism in the 21st Century." In *The Making of a Terrorist: Recruitment, Training and Root Causes*. Vol. 2, edited by James JF Forest. Westport, CT: Praeger, 2005.

Dozier, Rush W., Jr. *Why We Hate: Understanding, Curbing and Eliminating Hate in Ourselves and Our World*. New York: Contemporary Books, 2002.

Drummond, Jonathan T. "From the Northwest Imperative to Global Jihad: Social Psychological Aspects of the Construction of the Enemy, Political Violence and Terror." In *Psychology of Terrorism*. Vol. 1, *A Public Understanding*, edited by Chris E. Stout. London and Westport, CT: Praeger, 2002.

Easterby-Smith, Mark, Mary Crossan, and Davide Nicolini. "Organizational Learning: Debates Past, Present and Future." *Journal of Management Studies* 37, no. 6 (2000): 783–796.

Echandía, Camilo. *El Conflicto Armado y las Manifestaciones de la Violencia en las Regiones de Colombia*. Bogotá: Presidencia de la República–Oficina del Alto Comisionado para la Paz, 1999.

Ellens, J. Harold. "Fundamentalism, Orthodoxy, and Violence." In *The Destructive Power of Religion: Violence in Judaism, Christianity and Islam*. Vol. 4, *Contemporary Views on Spirituality and Violence*, edited by J. Harold Ellens. London and Westport, CT: Praeger, 2004.

———. "The Dynamics of Prejudice." In *The Destructive Power of Religion: Violence in Judaism, Christianity and Islam*. Vol. 2, *Religion, Psychology and Violence*, edited by J. Harold Ellens. London and Westport, CT: Praeger, 2004.

Elliott, Marianne. *The Catholics of Ulster: A History.* New York: Basic Books, 2002.

Emerson, Steven. *American Jihad: The Terrorists Living Among Us.* New York: The Free Press, 2002.

Enders, Walter, and Todd Sandler. "The Effectiveness of Antiterrorism Policies: A Vector-Autoregression-Intervention Analysis." *American Political Science Review,* vol. 87, no. 4 (December 1993): 829–844.

Esposito, John L. "Overview: The Significance of Religion for Global Order." In *Religion and Global Order,* edited by John L. Esposito and Michael Watson, 17–37. Cardiff: University of Wales Press, 2000.

———. *Unholy War: Terror in the Name of Islam.* New York: Oxford University Press, 2002.

Esposito, John L., and Michael Watson, eds. *Religion and Global Order.* Cardiff: University of Wales Press, 2000.

Fealy, Greg. "Islamic Radicalism in Indonesia: The Faltering Revival?" *Southeast Asian Affairs 2004.* Singapore: Institute of Southeast Asian Studies, 2004.

Feeney, Don J., Jr. "Entrancement in Islamic Fundamentalism." In *Psychology of Terrorism.* Vol. 3, *Theoretical Understandings and Perspectives,* edited by Chris E. Stout. London and Westport, CT: Praeger, 2002.

Ferguson, Charles, Tahseen Kazi, and Judith Perera. "Commercial Radioactive Sources: Surveying the Security Risks." Occasional Paper No. 11. Monterey: Center for Nonproliferation Studies, 2003.

Ferro, Juan Guillermo, and Graciela Uribe. *El Orden de la Guerra. Las FARC-EP: Entre la Organización y la Política.* Bogotá: Centro Editorial Javeriano, 2002.

Finn, John E. "Media Coverage of Political Terrorism and the First Amendment: Reconciling the Public's Right to Know with Public Order." In *Violence and Terrorism: 98/99.* Guilford, CT: Dushkin/McGraw-Hill, 1990.

Fiol, C. Marlene, and Marjorie A. Lyles. "Organizational Learning." *Academy of Management Review* 10 (1985): 803–813.

Fischer, Thomas. "La constante guerra civil en Colombia." In *Sociedades en guerra civil. Conflictos violentos de Europa y Latin America,* edited by Peter Waldman and Fernando Reinares, 255–276. Barcelona: Paidos, 1999.

Flynn, Kevin, and Gary Gerhardt, *The Silent Brotherhood: Inside America's Racist Underground.* New York: Free Press, 1989.

Forest, James JF. "Teaching and Learning in Higher Education." In *The International Handbook of Higher Education,* edited by James Forest and Philip Altbach. Dordrecht, Netherlands: Springer, 2006.

Forest, James JF. "Teaching Terrorism: Dimensions of Information and Technology." In *The Making of a Terrorist: Recruitment, Training and Root Causes.* Vol. 2, edited by James JF Forest. Westport, CT: Praeger, 2005.

Forest, James JF. "Terrorist Training Centers around the World: A Brief Review." In *The Making of a Terrorist: Recruitment, Training and Root Causes.* Vol. 2, edited by James JF Forest. Westport, CT: Praeger, 2005.

Gaess, Roger. "Interviews from Gaza: What Hamas Wants." *Middle East Policy* 9, no. 4 (2002): 102–121.

Galanter, Marc. *Cults: Faith, Healing and Coercion,* 2nd ed. New York: Oxford University Press, 1999.

Galanter, Marc, and James JF Forest. "Cults, Charismatic Groups and Social Systems: Understanding the Behavior of Terrorist Recruits." In *The Making of a Terrorist: Recruitment, Training and Root Causes.* Vol. 2, edited by James JF Forest. Westport, CT: Praeger, 2005.

Ganor, Boaz. "Libya and Terrorism." *Survey of Arab Affairs—A Periodic Supplement to Jerusalem Letter/Viewpoints* 28 (1 June 1992). Available online at www.ict.org.il/articles/article3.htm.

Garfinkel, Simson L. "Leaderless resistance today." *First Monday* 8, no. 3 (2003), http://firstmonday.org/issues/issue8_3/garfinkel/index.html.

Garratt, Robert. *The Learning Organization.* London: Fontana: Collins, 1987.

Garvin, David A. "Building a Learning Organization." *Harvard Business Review* 71 (July–August 1993): 78–91.

Gaylin, Willard. *Hatred: The Psychological Descent into Violence.* New York: PublicAffairs, 2003.

Goertzel, Ted G. "Terrorist Beliefs and Terrorist Lives." In *Psychology of Terrorism.* Vol. 1, *A Public Understanding,* edited by Chris E. Stout. London and Westport, CT: Praeger, 2002.

Gruen, Madeleine. "Innovative Recruitment and Indoctrination Tactics by Extremists: Video Games, Hip Hop, and the World Wide Web." In *The Making of a Terrorist: Recruitment, Training and Root Causes.* Vol. 1, edited by James JF Forest. Westport, CT: Praeger, 2005.

Gunaratna, Rohan. *Inside Al Qaeda.* New York: Columbia University Press, 2002.

———. *Sri Lanka's Ethnic Crisis and National Security.* Colombo: South Asian Network on Conflict Research, 1998.

Gunaratna, Rohan, and Arabinda Acharya. "The Al Qaeda Training Camps of Afghanistan and Beyond." In *The Making of a Terrorist: Recruitment, Training and Root Causes.* Vol. 2, edited by James JF Forest. Westport, CT: Praeger, 2005.

Hamas. "The Charter of Allah: The Platform of the Islamic Resistance Movement Hamas." In *The 1988–1989 Annual on Terrorism,* edited by Y. Alexander and H. Foxman. Dordrecht, Netherlands: Kluwer Academic Publishers, 1990.

Hedberg, Brian. "How Organizations Learn and Unlearn." In *Handbook of Organizational Design,* edited by Paul C. Nyström and William H. Starbuck. Oxford: Oxford University Press, 1981.

Heehs, Peter. *The Bomb in Bengal: The Rise of Revolutionary Terrorism in India, 1900–1910.* Oxford University Press, 1996.

Heyman, Edward, and Edward Mickolus. "Observations on Why Violence Spreads." *International Studies Quarterly* 24, no. 2 (June 1980): 299–305

———. "Imitation by Terrorists: Quantitative Approaches to the Study of Diffusion Patterns in Transnational Terrorism." In *Behavioral and Quantitative Perspectives on Terrorism,* edited by Yonah Alexander and John M. Gleason, 175–228. New York: Pergamon Press, 1981.

Hickey, Neil. *The Struggle Against Terrorism.* New York: The H. W. Wilson Company, 1977.

Hoffman, Bruce. *Inside Terrorism.* New York: Columbia University Press, 1998.

———. "Terrorism Trends and Prospects." In *Countering the New Terrorism,* edited by Ian O. Lesser, Bruce Hoffman, John Arquilla, David F. Ronfeldt, Michele Zanini, and Brian Michael Jenkins. Santa Monica: RAND Corporation, 1999.

———. "Plan of Attack." *Atlantic Monthly,* June 2004, www.theatlantic.com/issues/2004/07/hoffman.htm.

Hroub, Khaled. *Hamas: Political Thought and Practice.* Washington, DC: Institute for Palestine Studies, 2000.

Huber, George P. "Organizational Learning: The Contributing Process and the Literatures." *Organizational Science* 2 (1991): 88–115.

Hudson, Rex A. *Who Becomes a Terrorist and Why: The 1999 Government Report on Profiling Terrorists.* Guilford, CT: The Lyons Press, 2001.

International Crisis Group (ICG). *Al-Qaeda in Southeast Asia: The Case of the Ngruki Network.* Brussels: ICG, 2002.

———. *Dealing with Hamas.* Brussels: ICG, 2003.

———. *Jemaah Islamiyah in Southeast Asia: Damaged But Still Dangerous.* Jakarta/Brussels: ICG, 2003.

International Crisis Group. *Southern Philippines Backgrounder: Terrorism and the Peace Process.* Singapore/Brussels: ICG, 2004.

Jaber, Hala. *Hezbollah, Born with a Vengeance.* New York: Columbia University Press, 1997.

Jackson, Brian A. "Technology Acquisition by Terrorist Groups: Threat Assessment Informed by Lessons from Private Sector Technology Adoption." *Studies in Conflict and Terrorism* 24 (2001): 183–213.

——. "Provisional Irish Republican Army." In *Aptitude for Destruction.* Vol. 2, *Case Studies of Organizational Learning in Five Terrorist Groups,* edited by Brian Jackson, John C. Baker et al. Santa Monica: RAND, 2005.

——. "Training for Urban Resistance: The Case of the Provisional Irish Republican Army." In *The Making of a Terrorist: Recruitment, Training and Root Causes.* Vol. 2, edited by James JF Forest. Westport, CT: Praeger, 2005.

——. *Aptitude for Destruction, Volume 1: Organizational Learning in Terrorist Groups and its Implications for Combating Terrorism.* Santa Monica, CA: RAND, 2005.

Jarbawi, Ali, and Roger Heacock. "The Deportations and the Palestinian-Israeli Negotiations." *Journal of Palestine Studies* 26, no. 3 (1993): 32–45.

Jenkins, Brian. "High Technology Terrorism and Surrogate War: The Impact of New Technology on Low-Level Violence." In *Contemporary Terrorism: Selected Readings,* edited by John D. Elliott and Leslie K. Gibson. Gaithersburg, MD: International Association of Chiefs of Police, 1978.

Jerusalem Media and Communications Center (JMCC). *Israeli Military Orders in the Occupied Palestinian West Bank: 1967–1992,* 2nd ed. Jerusalem: JMCC, 1995.

Johnson, Ronald. "Psychoreligious Roots of Violence: The Search for the Concrete in a World of Abstractions." In *The Destructive Power of Religion: Violence in Judaism, Christianity and Islam.* Vol. 4, *Contemporary Views on Spirituality and Violence,* edited by J. Harold Ellens. London and Westport, CT: Praeger, 2004.

Jones, Kevin K. "Competing to Learn in Japan." *McKinsey Quarterly* 1 (1992): 45–57.

Joshi, Manoj. "On the Razor's Edge: The Liberation Tigers of Tamil Eelam." *Studies in Conflict and Terrorism* 19, no. 1 (January–March, 1996): 19–42.

Juergensmeyer, Mark. *Terror in the Mind of God: The Global Rise of Religious Violence.* Berkeley and Los Angeles: University of California Press, 2000.

Kaplan, David E., and Andrew Marshall. *The Cult at the End of the World.* New York: Crown Publishers, 1996.

Kaplan, David. "Aum Shinrikyo." In *Toxic Terror: Assessing Terrorist Use of Chemical and Biological Weapons,* edited by Jonathan B. Tucker. Cambridge, MA: MIT Press, 2000.

Karmon, Ely. "Islamic Terrorist Activities in Turkey in the 1990s." *Terrorism and Political Violence* 10, no. 4 (Winter 1998): 101–121.

Kellen, Konrad. "Ideology and Rebellion: Terrorism in Western Germany." In *Origins of Terrorism: Psychologies, Ideologies, Theologies, States of Mind,* edited by Walter Reich, 43–58. Baltimore: Woodrow Wilson Center Press, 1998.

Khan, Khwaja Geedar. "Peshawar: The Obdurant Bastion of Soviet-Era Mujahideen." *Terrorism Monitor* 2, no. 17 (9 September 2004).

Kidder, Rushworth. "Manipulation of the Media." In *Violence and Terrorism 98/99.* Guilford, CT: Dushkin/McGraw Hill, 1998.

Kim, Daniel H. "The Link Between Individual and Organizational Learning." *Sloan Management Review* 35, no. 1 (1993): 37–50.

Kohlmann, Evan. "The Bosnian Mujahideen: Origins, Training and Implications." In *The Making of a Terrorist: Recruitment, Training and Root Causes.* Vol. 2, edited by James JF Forest. Westport, CT: Praeger, 2005.

Kressel, Neil J. *Mass Hate: The Global Rise of Genocide and Terror.* New York: Westview, 2002.

Lawal, Olufemi A. "Social-Psychological Considerations in the Emergence and Growth of Terrorism." In *The Psychology of Terrorism.* Vol. 4, *Programs and Practices in Response and Prevention),* edited by Chris E. Stout. London and Westport, CT: Praeger, 2002.

Levitt, Barbara, and James G. March. "Organizational Learning." *Annual Review of Sociology,* 14, no. 324 (1988).

Levitt, Matthew A. "Hamas Social Welfare: In the Service of Terror." In *The Making of a Terrorist: Recruitment, Training and Root Causes,* edited by James JF Forest. Westport, CT: Praeger, 2005.

Levy, J. S. "Learning and Foreign Policy: Sweeping a Conceptual Minefield." *International Organization* 48, no. 2 (Spring 1994): 292.

Lifton, Robert J. *The Future of Immortality.* New York: Basic Books, 1987.

———. *Thought Reform: The Psychology of Totalism.* Chapel Hill: University of North Carolina Press, 1989.

Lind, William S., Keith Nightengale, John F. Schmitt, Joseph W. Sutton, and Gary I. Wilson. "The Changing Face of War: Into the Fourth Generation." *Marine Corps Gazette* (October 1989): 22–26.

Lipshitz, Raanan, Micha Popper, and Victor J. Friedman. "A Multifacet Model of Organizational Learning." *Journal of Applied Behavioral Science* 38, no. 1 (2002).

Locke, Gerhardt. *Aufbau und Funktionsweise von Kernspaltungswaffen, Bericht INT 25.* Euskirchen, 1982.

March, James G., and Johan P. Olsen. "The Uncertainty of the Past: Organizational Learning Under Ambiguity." *European Journal of Policy Review* 3, no. 2 (1975): 147–171.

Marks, Thomas. *Colombian Army Adaptation to FARC Insurgency.* Carlisle, PA: Strategic Studies Institute, U.S. Army War College, 2002.

Martinez, Patricia A. "Deconstructing Jihad: Southeast Asian Contexts." In *After Bali: The Threat of Terrorism in Southeast Asia,* edited by Kumar Ramakrishna and See Seng Tan. Singapore: World Scientific/Institute of Defence and Strategic Studies, 2003.

McCauley, Clark. "Psychological Issues in Understanding Terrorism and the Response to Terrorism." In *Psychology of Terrorism.* Vol. 3, *Theoretical Understandings and Perspectives,* edited by Chris E. Stout. London and Westport, CT: Praeger, 2002.

McCloud, Kimberly, and Matthew Osborne. "WMD Terrorism and Usama Bin Laden." *CNS Report,* 14 March 2001, http://cns.miis.edu/pubs/reports/binladen.htm.

McDermott, Jeremy. "Financing Insurgents in Colombia." *Jane's Intelligence Review* 15, no. 2 (2003): 16–19.

McGill, Michael E., and John W. Slocum, Jr. "Unlearning the Organization." *Organization Dynamics* 22 (1993): 67–79.

Merrari, Ariel. "The Readiness to Kill and Die: Suicidal Terrorism in the Middle East." In *Origins of Terrorism: Psychologies, Ideologies, Theologies, State of Mind,* edited by Walter Reich. Baltimore: Woodrow Wilson International Center Press, 1998.

Mishal, Shaul, and Avraham Sela. *The Palestinian Hamas.* New York: Columbia University Press, 2000.

Mitchell, Robert. *The Society of Muslim Brothers.* London: Oxford University Press, 1969.

Momen, Moojan. "Fundamentalism and Liberalism: Towards an Understanding of the Dichotomy." *Bahai Studies Review* 2, no. 1 (1992).

Nacos, Brigitte. "The Role of the Media." In *The Making of a Terrorist: Recruitment, Training and Root Causes.* Vol. 1, edited by James JF Forest. Westport, CT: Praeger, 2005.

Nacos, Brigitte L. "Mediated Terrorism: Teaching Terror through Propaganda and Publicity." In *The Making of a Terrorist: Recruitment, Training and Root Causes.* Vol. 2, edited by James JF Forest. Westport, CT: Praeger, 2005.

———. "Communication and Recruitment of Terrorists." In *The Making of a Terrorist: Recruitment, Training and Root Causes.* Vol. 1, edited by James JF Forest. Westport, CT: Praeger, 2005.

Nakhleh, Khalil. *Indigenous Organizations in Palestine: Towards a Purposeful Societal Development.* Jerusalem: Arab Thought Forum, 1991.

National Academy of Sciences, Commission on Physical Sciences, Mathematics, and Applications. *Containing the Threat from Illegal Bombings: An Integrated National Strategy for Marking, Tagging, Rendering Inert, and Licensing Explosives and Their Precursors.* Washington, DC: National Academies Press, 1998. Available online at http://books.nap.edu/books/0309061261/html.

National Commission on Terrorist Attacks Upon the United States. *Final Report of the National Commission on Terrorist Attacks Upon the United States (The 9/11 Commission*

Report). Washington, DC: U.S. Government Printing Office, 2004. Available online at www.gpoaccess.gov/911.

O'Neill, Bard E. *Insurgency and Terrorism: Inside Modern Revolutionary Warfare*. Washington, DC: Potomac Books, 2001.

Olcott, Martha Brill, and Bakhtiyar Babajanov. "Teaching New Terrorist Recruits: A Review of Training Manuals from the Uzbekistan Mujahideen." In *The Making of a Terrorist: Recruitment, Training and Root Causes*. Vol. 2, edited by James JF Forest. Westport, CT: Praeger, 2005.

Olcott, Martha Brill, and Bakhtiyar Babajanov. "The Terrorist Notebooks." *Foreign Policy* (March–April 2003): 30–40.

Olweean, Steve S. "Psychological Concepts of the 'Other': Embracing the Compass of the Self." In *Psychology of Terrorism*. Vol. 1, *A Public Understanding*, edited by Chris E. Stout. London and Westport, CT: Praeger, 2002.

Ortiz, Román D. "El Estado colombiano frente a las FARC: Buscando respuestas a una nueva amenaza insurgente." In *Terrorismo y Seguridad*, edited by Reinaldo Botero, et al. Bogotá: Planeta-Semana, 2003.

———. "Insurgent Strategies in the Post–Cold War: The Case of the Revolutionary Armed Forces of Columbia." *Studies in Conflict and Terrorism* 25 (2002): 127–143.

Ortiz, Roman David. "The Human Factor in Insurgency: Recruitment and Training in the Revolutionary Armed Forces of Colombia (FARC)." In *The Making of a Terrorist: Recruitment, Training and Root Causes*. Vol. 2, edited by James JF Forest. Westport, CT: Praeger, 2005.

Pape, Robert A. "The Strategic Logic of Suicide Terrorism." *American Political Science Review* 97, no. 3 (August 2003): 343–361.

Parachini, John V. "The Making of Aum Shinrikyo's Chemical Weapons Program." In *The Making of a Terrorist: Recruitment, Training and Root Causes*. Vol. 2, edited by James JF Forest. Westport, CT: Praeger, 2005.

Paz, Reuven. *Tangled Web: International Islamist Networking*. Washington, DC: The Washington Institute for Near East Policy, 2002.

———. "Sawt al-Jihad: New Indoctrination of Qa'idat al-Jihad." *Occasional Papers Published by PRISM*, volume 1, no. 8 (2003). Available online at www.e-prism.org.

Perl, Ralph F. *Terrorism, the Media, and the 21st Century*. Washington, DC: Congressional Research Service, 1998.

Perlman, Diane. "Intersubjective Dimensions of Terrorism and Its Transcendence." In *Psychology of Terrorism*. Vol. 1: *A Public Understanding*, edited by Chris E. Stout. London and Westport, CT: Praeger, 2002.

Pipes, Daniel. *Militant Islam Reaches America*. New York and London: W. W. Norton, 2003.

Pizarro, Eduardo. *Insurgencia sin Revolución. La Guerrilla en Colombia en una Perspectiva Comparada*. Bogotá: Tercer Mundo Editores-IEPRI, 1996.

———. *Las FARC 1949–1966. De la Autodefensa de Masas a la Combinación de Todas las Formas de Lucha*. Bogotá: Tercer Mundo Editores-IEPRI, 1992.

———. *Una democracia asediada. Balance y Perspectivas del Conflicto Armado en Colombia*. Bogotá: Norma, 2004.

Podolny, Joel, and Karen Page. "Network Forms of Organization." *Annual Review of Sociology* 24 (1998): 57–76.

Post, Jerrold M. "Terrorist Psycho-logic: Terrorist Behavior as a Product of Psychological Forces." In *Origins of Terrorism: Psychologies, Ideologies, Theologies, States of Mind*, edited by Walter Reich. Baltimore: Woodrow Wilson Center Press, 1998.

———. "When Hatred Is Bred in the Bone: The Socio-Cultural Underpinnings of Terrorist Psychology." In *The Making of a Terrorist: Recruitment, Training and Root Causes*. Vol. 2, edited by James JF Forest. Westport, CT: Praeger, 2005.

President's Foreign Intelligence Advisory Board. *Science at its Best, Security at its Worst: A Report on Security Problems at the Department of Energy* (the Rudman Report). Washington, DC: President's Foreign Intelligence Advisory Board, June 1999. Available online at www.fas.org/sgp/library/pfiab.

Rabasa, Angel, and Peter Chalk. *Colombian Labyrinth. The synergy of drugs and insurgency and its implications for regional stability.* Santa Monica: RAND, 2001.

Ramakrishna, Kumar. "Indoctrination Processes Within Jemaah Islamiyah." In *The Making of a Terrorist: Recruitment, Training and Root Causes.* Vol. 2, edited by James JF Forest. Westport, CT: Praeger, 2005.

———. "U.S. Strategy in Southeast Asia: Counter-Terrorist or Counter-Terrorism?" In *After Bali: The Threat of Terrorism in Southeast Asia,* edited by Kumar Ramakrishna and See Seng Tan. Singapore: World Scientific/Institute of Defence and Strategic Studies, 2003.

Ramakrishna, Kumar, and See Seng Tan. "Is Southeast Asia a 'Terrorist Haven?'" In *After Bali: The Threat of Terrorism in Southeast Asia,* edited by Kumar Ramakrishna and See Seng Tan. Singapore: World Scientific/Institute of Defence and Strategic Studies, 2003.

Ramati, Yohanan. "Islamic Fundamentalism Gaining." *Midstream* 39, no. 2 (1993).

Rangel, Alfredo. "Las FARC-EP: una mirada actual." In *Reconocer la guerra para construir la paz,* edited by Malcolm Deas and María Victoria Llorente. Bogota: Cerec-Uniandes-Norma, 1999.

———. "Parasites and Predators: Guerrillas and the Insurrection Economy of Colombia." *Journal of International Affairs* 53, no. 2 (2000): 577–601.

Ranstorp, Magnus. "The Hizballah Training Camps of Lebanon." In *The Making of a Terrorist: Recruitment, Training and Root Causes.* Vol. 2, edited by James JF Forest. Westport, CT: Praeger, 2005.

Rapoport, David C. "Fear and Trembling: Terrorism in Three Religious Traditions." *The American Political Science Review* 78, no. 3 (September 1984): 658–677.

———. "Sacred Terror: A Contemporary Example from Islam." In *Origins of Terrorism: Psychologies, Ideologies, Theologies, States of Mind,* edited by Walter Reich. Baltimore: Woodrow Wilson Center Press, 1998.

Rashid, Ahmad. *Jihad: The Rise of Militant Islam in Central Asia.* New Haven: Yale University Press, 2002.

Raymond, Gregory A. "The Evolving Strategies of Political Terrorism." In *The New Global Terrorism: Characteristics, Causes, Controls,* edited by Charles W. Kegley. Upper Saddle River, NJ: Prentice Hall, 2003.

Reich, Walter. "Understanding Terrorist Behavior: The Limits and Opportunities of Psychological Enquiry." In *Origins of Terrorism: Psychologies, Ideologies, Theologies, States of Mind,* edited by Walter Reich. Baltimore: Woodrow Wilson Center Press, 1998.

Ressa, Maria. *The Seeds of Terror: An Eyewitness Account of Al Qaeda's Newest Center of Operations in Southeast Asia.* New York: Free Press, 2003.

Romme, Georges, and R. Dillen. "Mapping the Landscape of Organizational Learning." *European Management Journal* 15, no. 1 (1997): 68–78.

Roux-Dufort, Christophe, and Emmanuel Metais. "Building Core Competencies in Crisis Management through Organizational Learning: The Case of the French Nuclear Power Producer." *Technological Forecasting and Social Change* (1999), 113–127.

Russell, Charles A., Leon J. Banker, Jr., and Bowman H. Miller. "Out-Inventing the Terrorist." In *Terrorism: Theory and Practice,* edited by Yonah Alexander, David Carlton, and Paul Wilkinson. Boulder, CO: Westview, 1979.

Ruthven, Malise. *A Fury for God: The Islamist Attack on America.* London and New York: Granta, 2002.

Sageman, Marc. *Understanding Terror Networks.* Philadelphia: University of Pennsylvania Press, 2004.

Schaper, Annette. "Nuclear Smuggling in Europe: Real Dangers and Enigmatic Deceptions." In *Illegal Nuclear Traffic: Risks, Safeguards, and Countermeasures: Proceedings of the International Forum, Science for Peace Series.* Vol. 4, edited by Vladimir Kouzminov and Maurizio Martellini. Venice: UNESCO, 1998.

———. "The Case for Universal Full Scope Safeguards on Nuclear Material." *The Nonproliferation Review* 5, no. 2 (Winter 1998): 69–80.

———. "Looking for a Demarcation between Nuclear Transparency and Nuclear Secrecy." PRIF Reports No 68. Peace Research Institute Frankfurt, 2004. Available online at www.hsfk.de/publication_detail.php?publicationid=2467&language=en.

Schmid, Alex P., and J. de Graff. _Violence as Communication: Insurgent Terrorism and the Western News Media_. Beverly Hills, CA: Sage Publications, 1982.

Schmid, Alex P., and Albert J. Jongman. _Political Terrorism_. Amsterdam: North-Holland Publishing, 1988.

Schweiger, David M., Tugrul Atamer, and Roland Calori. "Transnational project teams and networks: making the multinational organization more effective." _Journal of World Business_ 38 (2003): 127–140.

Seale, Patrick. _Abu Nidal: A Gun for Hire_. New York: Random House, 1992.

Selengut, Charles. _Sacred Fury: Understanding Religious Violence_. Walnut Creek, CA: AltaMira Press, 2003.

Senge, Peter. _The Fifth Discipline: The Art and Practice of the Learning Organization_. New York: Doubleday, 1990.

Serber, Robert. _The Los Alamos Prime—The First Lectures on How To Build an Atomic Bomb_. Berkeley: University of California Press, 1982.

Shrivastava, Paul. "A Typology of Organizational Learning Systems." _Journal of Management Studies_ 20 (1983): 7–28.

Sim, Stuart. _Fundamentalist World: The New Dark Age of Dogma_. Cambridge: Icon Books, 2004.

Simon, Herbert A. "Bounded Rationality and Organizational Learning." _Organization Science_ 2 (1991): 125–133.

Singer, Peter W. "Pakistan's Madrassahs: Ensuring a System of Education, not Jihad." Analysis Paper #14. Washington, DC: Brookings Institution, 2001.

Smith, David E. "The Training of Terrorist Organizations." CSC Report, 1995. Available online at www.globalsecurity.org/military/report/1995/SDE.htm.

Smith, Paul J. "Transnational Terrorism and the al Qaeda Model: Confronting New Realities." _Parameters_ (Summer 2002): 33–46.

Soo Hoo, Kevin J., Seymour E. Goodman, and Lawrence T. Greenberg. "Information Technology and the Terrorist Threat." _Survival_ 39, no. 3 (1997): 135–155.

Spencer, David. "A Lesson for Colombia." _Jane's Intelligence Review_ 9, no. 10 (1997): 474–477.

Spencer, Robert. _Onward Muslim Soldiers: How Jihad Still Threatens America and the West_. Washington, DC: Regnery, 2003.

Sprinzak, Ehud. "The Psychopolitical Formation of Extreme Left Terrorism in a Democracy: The Case of the Weathermen." In _Origins of Terrorism: Psychologies, Ideologies, Theologies, States of Mind_, edited by Walter Reich. Baltimore: Woodrow Wilson Center Press, 1998.

Stahelski, Anthony. "Terrorists Are Made, Not Born: Creating Terrorists Using Social Psychological Conditioning." _Journal of Homeland Security_, March 2004, www.homelandsecurity.org/journal/Articles/stahelski.html.

Stern, Jessica. _The Ultimate Terrorists_. Cambridge, MA: Harvard University Press, 1999.

———. "The Protean Enemy." _Foreign Affairs_ 82, no. 4 (July–August 2003).

———. _Terror in the Name of God: Why Religious Militants Kill_. New York: Ecco, 2003.

Stevens, Michael J. "The Unanticipated Consequences of Globalization: Contextualizing Terrorism." In _Psychology of Terrorism_. Vol. 3, _Theoretical Understandings and Perspectives)_, edited by Chris E. Stout. London and Westport, CT: Praeger, 2002.

Stirling, Mack C. "Violent Religion: Rene Girard's Theory of Culture." In _The Destructive Power of Religion: Violence in Judaism, Christianity and Islam_. Vol. 2, _Religion, Psychology and Violence)_, edited by J. Harold Ellens. London and Westport, CT: Praeger, 2004.

Taylor, Bron. "Religion, Violence and Radical Environmentalism: From Earth First! to the Unabomber to the Earth Liberation Front." _Terrorism and Political Violence_ 10, no. 4 (1998): 1–42.

Taraki, Lisa. "The Islamic Resistance Movement in the Palestinian Uprising." _Middle East Report_, 1989.

Thomas, Timothy L. "Al Qaeda and the Internet: The Danger of 'Cyberplanning.'" *Parameters* (Spring 2003): 112–123.

Tucker, David. *Skirmishes at the Edge of Empire: The United States and International Terrorism.* Westport, CT: Praeger, 1997.

Tucker, Jonathan B., ed. *Toxic Terror: Assessing Terrorist Use of Chemical and Biological Weapons.* Cambridge, MA: MIT Press, 2000.

Tzfati, Yariv, and Gabriel Weimann. "WWW.Terrorism.com: Terror on the Internet." *Studies in Conflict and Terrorism* 25, no. 5 (2002): 317–332.

Tzu, Sun. *The Art of War.* New York: Dover Publications, 2002.

Ulph, Stephen. "The Voice of the Caucasus—A New Jihadi Magazine." *Terrorism Focus* 2, no. 8 (28 April 2005).

———. "Syrian website calls for experienced mujahideen, as Aleppo becomes key point of departure for Iraq." *Terrorism Focus* 2, no. 13 (13 July 2005).

Department of Energy. *Plutonium: The First 50 Years. United States plutonium production, acquisition, and utilization from 1944 to 1994.* Washington, DC: Department of Energy, February 1996.

Van Bruinessen, Martin. "Indonesia's Ulama and Politics: Caught Between Legitimizing the Status Quo and Searching for Alternatives." *Prisma—The Indonesian Indicator* (Jakarta), no. 49 (1990): 52–69.

Van Tuyle, Gregory J., Tiffany L. Strub, Harold A. O'Brien, Caroline F. V. Mason, and Steven J. Gitomer. "Reducing RDD Concerns Related to Large Radiological Source Applications." LA-UR-03-6664. Los Alamos, September 2003.

Verton, Dan. *Black Ice: The Invisible Threat of Cyber-Terrorism.* New York: McGraw-Hill Osborne Media, 2003.

von Baeckmann, Adolf, Garry Dillon, and Demetrius Perricos. "Nuclear Verification in South Africa." *IAEA Bulletin* 37, no. 1 (March 1995).

Waller, J. Michael. "Prisons as Terrorist Breeding Grounds." In *The Making of a Terrorist: Recruitment, Training and Root Causes.* Vol. 1, edited by James JF Forest. Westport, CT: Praeger, 2005.

Ward, Adam. "The IRA's Foreign Links: Externalising Its Expertise?" *IISS Strategic Comments* 9, no. 5 (2003).

Wardlaw, Grant. *State Response to International Terrorism: Some Cautionary Comments.* Symposium on International Terrorism. Washington, DC: Defense Intelligence Agency, 1985.

Watanabe, Manabu. "Religion and Violence in Japan Today: A Chronological and Doctrinal Analysis of Aum Shinrikyo." *Terrorism and Political Violence* 10, no. 4 (Winter 1998): 80–100.

Weaver, Mary Anne. "A Land of Madrassahs." *APF Report* 20, Alicia Patterson Foundation, 2002. Available online at www.aliciapatterson.org/APF2002/Weaver.

Weimann, Gabriel. 2004. *WWW.Terrorism.Net: How Modern Terrorism Uses the Internet.* USIP Special Report 116. Washington, DC: U.S. Institute of Peace, 2004.

———. *Cyberterrorism: How Real Is the Threat?* USIP Special Report. Washington, DC: United States Institute of Peace, 2004.

Weimann, Gabriel, and Conrad Winn. *The Theater of Terror.* New York: Longman Publications, 1994.

Weinberg, Leonard. "Political and Revolutionary Ideologies." In *The Making of a Terrorist: Recruitment, Training and Root Causes.* Vol. 1, edited by James JF Forest. Westport, CT: Praeger, 2005.

White Paper: The Jemmah Islamiyah Arrests and the Threat of Terrorism. Singapore: Ministry of Home Affairs, 7 January 2003.

Willoughby, Case. "Learning Organizations." In *Higher Education in the United States: An Encyclopedia,* edited by James J.F. Forest and Kevin Kinser. Santa Barbara, CA: ABC-CLIO, 2002.

Zanini, Michele, and Sean J. A. Edwards. "The Networking of Terror in the Information Age." In *Networks and Netwars,* edited by John Arquilla and David Ronfeldt. Santa Monica: RAND, 2001.

Zorpette, Glenn, and Steve Miller. "Unconventional Nuclear Weapons." *IEEE Spectrum Online,* November 2001, www.spectrum.ieee.org/WEBONLY/publicfeature/nov01/nterr.html.

Index

285

About the Contributors

Cindy C. Combs is a Professor in the Department of Political Science, University of North Carolina at Charlotte, where she teaches courses on security policy, terrorism, political violence, and international law. Dr. Combs is author of the bestseller *Terrorism in the Twenty-First Century* (4th edition, 2005) and coauthor of the *Encyclopedia of Terrorism* (2002). She also directs the university's Model United Nations program. She earned her Ph.D. in political science from George Washington University and master's and bachelor's degrees from Appalachian State University.

R. Kim Cragin is an Associate International Policy Analyst at RAND. Her research focuses on terrorism-related issues, including arms trafficking by the FARC in Latin America, suicide bombings, anti-U.S. extremism, the relationship between terrorism and development, terrorist groups' operational requirements, and border security. She has also provided research support to the Advisory Panel to Assess Response Capabilities for Weapons of Mass Destruction Terrorism (Gilmore Commission) and manages the RAND-MIPT Terrorism Incident Database. Before coming to RAND in 2000, Kim attended the Sanford Institute of Public Policy at Duke University in North Carolina, where she was awarded the Boren Fellowship by the National Security Education Program (funded by Congress) to study Hamas and Israeli right-wing extremism. Kim holds an M.P.P. (Masters in Public Policy) from Duke University, where she wrote her thesis on U.S. counternarcotics policy with regards to Plan Colombia and the FARC.

Rohan Gunaratna is Director of the Institute of Defence and Strategic Studies (IDSS), Nanyang Technological University, Singapore. He is author of the bestseller *Inside Al Qaeda: Global Network of Terror* (2003). His previous positions include research fellow at the Centre for the Study of Terrorism and Political Violence, University of St. Andrews, Scotland, and honorary fellow at the International Policy Institute for Counter-Terrorism in Israel. He was principal investigator of the United Nations' Terrorism Prevention Branch, and he has served as a consultant on terrorism to several governments and corporations. He has also been a visiting scholar at the University of Illinois, the University of Maryland, and the University of Notre Dame, and has lectured widely in Latin America, the Middle East, and Asia on terrorism and countermeasures. He is the author of several books on armed conflict. His current research interests include terrorist organizations; terrorist operational and support networks; maritime terrorist tactics, technologies, and techniques; suicide terrorism; and terrorism in the Asian Pacific.

Brian A. Jackson is an Associate Physical Scientist in RAND's Science and Technology Policy Institute. He holds a Master's Degree in Science, Technology, and Public Policy from the George Washington University's Elliott School of International Affairs and a Ph.D. in Bio-Inorganic Chemistry from the California Institute of Technology. Current and recent research activities include an ongoing project on personal protective technology for emergency responders for the National Personal Protective Technology Laboratory at NIOSH (National Institute for Occupational Safety and Health), preparation of a post-9/11 lessons-learned report on protecting emergency workers at terrorist incident sites, work on national R&D priorities for information infrastructure protection, analysis of federal R&D activities relevant to counterterrorism and weapons of mass destruction, study of biometric technologies, a study on technology acquisition by law enforcement organizations, and an examination of the adoption of new technologies by terrorist groups.

Michael Kenney is Assistant Professor of Public Policy at the School of Public Affairs, Pennsylvania State University, Harrisburg. He received his Ph.D. in Political Science from the University of Florida in May 2002. In 2004 Dr. Kenney was a postdoctoral scholar in Organizational Learning for Homeland Security with Stanford University. Previously, he has held research fellowships with the Center for International Security and Cooperation at Stanford and the Center for International Studies at the University of Southern California. Dr. Kenney's research interests include the Colombian drug trade, counternarcotics law enforcement, terrorism, intelligence, and organization theory. His published work has appeared in

Survival, the *International Journal of Intelligence and Counterintelligence*, *Transnational Organized Crime*, and the *Wall Street Journal*. His forthcoming book, *From Pablo to Osama: Trafficking and Terrorist Networks, Government Bureaucracies, and Competitive Adaptation*, will be published in 2006.

Román D. Ortiz is Professor and Researcher at the Department of Political Science, School of Social Sciences at Los Andes University (Bogotá), where he focuses on the analysis of political violence and terrorist phenomena in Latin America. He has previously taught and researched these topics at Spanish academic institutions such as the General Gutiérrez Mellado Institute and the Ortega y Gasset Institute. Included in his most recent publications is the paper "President Alvaro Uribe´s Counterinsurgency Strategy: Formula for Victory or Recipe for a Crisis?" published by the Elcano Institute in Madrid. He has a degree in political science.

Kumar Ramakrishna is Assistant Professor and Head (of Studies) at the Institute of Defence and Strategic Studies (IDSS), Nanyang Technological University, Singapore. His current research interests include British propaganda in the Malayan Emergency; propaganda theory and practice; history of strategic thought; and counterterrorism. His book *Emergency Propaganda: The Winning of Malayan Hearts and Minds*, 1948–1958, was published in February 2002. He has also coedited two books, *The New Terrorism: Anatomy, Trends and Counter-Strategies* (2003), and *After Bali: The Threat of Terrorism in Southeast Asia* (2004).

Annette Schaper is a Senior Research Fellow at the Peace Research Institute, Frankfurt (Germany). Dr. Schaper has a Ph.D. in experimental physics. Her main focus of work is nuclear arms control and its technical aspects, including the test ban, verification of nuclear disarmament, fissile materials disposition, and nonproliferation problems. Her latest project explores the nuclear transparency and secrecy of the nuclear weapon–possessing states. Schaper has published numerous articles and reports on these subjects. She is also a member of the Board of Directors of the Bulletin of Atomic Scientists.

Horacio R. Trujillo is an international security and economics analyst who has worked with various national and multilateral institutions, including the U.S. Congress, the World Bank, and the United Nations. Most recently, at the RAND Corporation, his research focused on the intersection of the fields of international development and security. In addition to his work on the organizational dynamics of terrorist groups, he is currently working on the development of tools for evaluating the long-range cost effectiveness of complex counterterrorism strategies.

Gabriel Weimann is a Full Professor of Communication at the Department of Communication at Haifa University, Israel. His research interests include the study of media effects, political campaigns, persuasion and influence, media and public opinion, and modern terrorism and the mass media. He has published six books, including *Terror on the Internet: The New Arena, the New Challenges* (2006), *Communicating Unreality* (2000), *The Influentials: People Who Influence People* (1995), and *The Theater of Terror* (1994). His work has also appeared in academic journals such as the *American Sociological Review,* the *Journal of Communication, Public Opinion Quarterly, Communication Research,* and the *Journal of Broadcasting and Electronic Media.* He has received numerous grants and awards from international foundations, including the Fulbright Foundation, the Canadian-Israel Foundation, the Alexander von Humboldt-Stiftung, the German National Research Foundation, the Sasakawa Foundation, and the United States Institute of Peace.

ABOUT THE EDITOR

James JF Forest is director of terrorism studies at the U.S. Military Academy, where he teaches courses in the Department of Social Sciences and directs several projects for the Combating Terrorism Center. Recent publications include *The Making of a Terrorist: Recruitment, Training and Root Causes* (3 volumes, 2005), *Homeland Security and Terrorism* (2005, with Russell Howard and Joanne Moore), and *Terrorism and Oil in the New Gulf* (2006, with Matt Sousa). His research has also appeared in the *Cambridge Review of International Affairs,* the *Journal of Political Science Education,* and *Democracy and Security.* Dr. Forest has been an invited speaker at numerous conferences and workshops on terrorism and counterterrorism. He received his graduate degrees from Stanford University and Boston College, and undergraduate degrees from Georgetown University and De Anza College.